W9-CTI-767

The Handbook of Career Advising

The Handbook of
Career Advising

Kenneth F. Hughey, Dorothy Burton Nelson,
Joanne K. Damminger, Betsy McCalla-Wriggins,
and Associates

Foreword by Charlie Nutt

JOSSEY-BASS
A Wiley Imprint
www.josseybass.com

Published by Jossey-Bass
A Wiley Imprint
989 Market Street, San Francisco, CA 94103-1741—www.josseybass.com

Jossey-Bass books and products are available through most bookstores. To contact Jossey-Bass directly call our Customer Care Department within the U.S. at 800-956-7739, outside the U.S. at 317-572-3986, or fax 317-572-4002.

Jossey-Bass also publishes its books in a variety of electronic formats. Some content that appears in print may not be available in electronic books.

Library of Congress Cataloging-in-Publication Data
    The handbook of career advising/Kenneth F. Hughey . . . [et al.]; foreword by Charlie Nutt.
       p. cm.
    Includes bibliographical references and index.
    ISBN 978-0-470-37368-2 (cloth)
       1. Counseling in higher education—United States.   2. Vocational guidance—United States.   3. Career development—United States.   4. College students—Employment—United States.   I. Hughey, Kenneth F.
    LB2343.H2727 2009
    378.1'9425—dc22

2009019776

Printed in the United States of America

FIRST EDITION

HB Printing   10 9 8 7 6 5 4 3 2 1

The Jossey-Bass
Higher and Adult Education Series

CONTENTS

TABLES, FIGURES, AND EXHIBITS

Figures

Exhibits

FOREWORD

Charlie Nutt

As our student bodies grow more diverse and the number of options for majors and careers increases dramatically, assisting students in colleges and university with their career exploration and planning is a major element in ensuring the highest quality educational experiences. As executive director of the National Academic Advising Association (NACADA), I am so pleased that you have recognized this major issue and have chosen this book, *The Handbook of Career Advising*, as a resource to assist you in making career advising an integral part of academic advising. The editors and authors have developed a resource that not only provides the theory and foundations of career advising but also provides hands-on strategies and applications you can utilize on your campus. The text promises to be a key resource for us all.

NACADA is pleased to again have partnered with Jossey-Bass to publish this text as we have with the second edition of *Academic Advising: A Comprehensive Handbook*. NACADA, with nearly 11,000 members internationally, is the leader within the global education community for the theory, delivery, application, and advancement of all issues surrounding academic advising that enhance student learning and development. For 30 years, NACADA has been recognized for providing quality programming, publications, and networking opportunities that support the work of all university staff and faculty who create the academic advising experiences, including career advising experiences, that support student learning and success.

As you read, you will gain the most from this text by using the following questions as a guide:

- What are key concepts and theories related to career advising that will enhance my advising?
- How can knowledge of the changing workplace be used to enhance my advising?
- What have I learned that will assist me in working with students who are undecided about their major or career?

- What have I learned that will assist me in working with decided students who are exploring or changing their majors or career choices?
- What are considerations in addressing diversity in my career advising?
- How can I use the strategies and skills I learned to more effectively integrate career and academic advising to best meet the needs of all students on my campus?
- What have I learned that triggers my own thoughts for research and publications within the field?

My goal in providing these leading questions is for you to utilize this text as a working resource that will help you in multiple ways and multiple times to enhance not only your own work with students but the work of your institution and the lives of your students.

PREFACE

Career advising is an increasingly important activity for academic advisors. Advisors are uniquely positioned to make career advising an integral part of academic advising and to facilitate and support students' career and academic development. *The Handbook of Career Advising* addresses topics that will enhance academic advisors' knowledge and competence in career advising of students.

On behalf of the editors, I would like to thank the chapter authors for their contributions to the *Handbook*. Their involvement and commitment were essential to the success of this endeavor. In addition, strengths of the presentation are the areas of expertise of the authors, career development or academic advising, which led to the focus on career advising as integral to academic advising. The following is an overview of the chapters:

Chapter One—Judith K. Hughey and I discuss foundations of career advising, including background and relevant topics related to career advising, career advising as integral to academic advising, and a rationale for career advising.

Chapter Two—Rich Feller and Brian O'Bruba describe the changing workplace, competencies needed for student success, and changing assumptions related to career development, as well as implications and insights for advisors and students.

Chapter Three—Eileen Mahoney discusses the career advising competencies that support and facilitate students' academic and career planning.

Chapter Four—Spencer G. Niles and Brian Hutchison focus on theories of career development that can be used to inform and enhance career advising. The application of these theories and related constructs provides a foundation for facilitating students' career development.

Chapter Five—Heidi Koring and Beverly C. Reid elucidate use of theories of student development to inform career advising.

Chapter Six—Aaron H. Carlstrom, Marilyn S. Kaff, and Karen R. Low address career advising and diversity. They present characteristics, relevant issues, and implications of diversity in career advising.

Chapter Seven—Darrin L. Carr and Susan A. Epstein discuss career information and resources intended to facilitate career advising and help students make informed decisions.

Chapter Eight—Joanne K. Damminger offers a framework for the career advising process and a step-by-step process for academic advisors to help students make academic and career decisions.

Chapter Nine—Dorothy Burton Nelson and Betsy McCalla-Wriggins describe integrated career and academic programs that provide various activities and interventions to enhance students' career and academic planning and to prepare them for the future.

Chapter Ten—Catherine A. Buyarski addresses students who are undecided and implications for career advising. She also presents career advising activities and programs to address the needs of these students.

Chapter Eleven—Peggy Jordan and Terri Blevins delineate characteristics of specific student groups, along with implications for career advising of the students.

Chapter Twelve—Rich Robbins addresses evaluation and assessment practices and issues focused on career advising.

Chapter Thirteen—Betsy McCalla-Wriggins and co-editors conclude the *Handbook* by presenting and discussing challenges, opportunities, and recommendations regarding career advising.

In addition, the Appendixes include narratives of exemplary practices of integrated career and academic advising centers focused on helping students with academic and career planning. These narratives describe centers in which career advising is integral to academic advising and where professionals effectively address the academic and career advising needs of students.

On behalf of the editors, I would like to acknowledge and thank the members of the Content Review Panel for their contributions to the publication of the *Handbook*. Their reviews of the chapter outlines and chapters provided excellent feedback. The Content Review Panel included the following professionals: Katie Beres, Colleen Doherty, Karen Evans, Brian Glankler, Patricia Griffin, Mark Lee, Tina Loudon, Jim Peacock, Joan Pederson, David Spight, and George Steele. In addition, we thank Katie Beres and Jim Peacock, who assisted the editors in selecting the exemplary practices to be included in the *Handbook*.

The support and assistance of the NACADA staff was so very important and helpful in this project. In particular, Marsha Miller's consultation, guidance, expertise, and patience facilitated and supported the entire process. In addition, thanks to Charlie Nutt for his support and encouragement throughout the project and to Bobbie Flaherty for her support and work with Jossey-Bass on behalf of the *Handbook*.

Finally, I would like to thank Dorothy Burton Nelson, Joanne Damminger, and Betsy McCalla-Wriggins for their commitment, dedication, and contributions to the *Handbook of Career Advising*. It was a pleasure to work as a team on this project subsequent to our initial meeting at the 2005 NACADA conference.

My hope is that the content of the *Handbook of Career Advising* adds value to the career advising of academic advisors. As a result, the academic and career planning and development of students will be enhanced. Best wishes in this important work with students!

Kenneth F. Hughey
Manhattan, Kansas

THE AUTHORS

Terri Blevins is currently the director of student and career development at the University of Colorado Denver School of Medicine. She has been an active member of NACADA since 1999, serving as South Central Region 7 chair in 2005–2007, and is currently serving on the national Finance Committee and the 2009 annual Conference Committee. Blevins received her master's degree from the University of Iowa in Counseling and Postsecondary Student Development. At the University of Iowa she worked with student athletes on career and personal development, and taught undergraduate classes on choosing a major and career development. For several years after that, she worked as a therapist and counselor for various state agencies and schools. In 1999, she returned to the college campus, serving as the academic advisor to Arts and Sciences students at Oklahoma State University-Tulsa, where all students are transfer students and many are nontraditional adult students. She was instrumental in developing articulation agreements with local community colleges, and she designed an orientation class specifically for transfer students. She then moved to Oklahoma State University College of Medicine, creating and implementing a four-year career development program for medical students.

Catherine A. Buyarski is the assistant dean and executive director of academic and career planning in University College at Indiana University-Purdue University Indianapolis (IUPUI). In this role she oversees academic advising, career counseling, career services, student employment, and several scholarship programs for students from at-risk backgrounds. Previous to this position, she served as director of advising at IUPUI and director of student academic services at the University of North Dakota. With experience in residence life, new student orientation, enrollment management, retention, and parent programs, Buyarski's career has focused primarily on the needs of first-year students as well as issues of collegiate access and success. She holds a bachelor of business administration degree from the University of Wisconsin-Whitewater, a master's degree in counseling and student personnel administration from Oklahoma State University, and a doctorate in educational policy and administration from the University of Minnesota-Twin Cities. She also serves as an adjunct assistant professor in the Indiana University School of Education and is a graduate of the Harvard University Management Development Program.

Aaron H. Carlstrom is an assistant professor in the Department of Special Education, Counseling, and Student Affairs at Kansas State University, where he is a faculty member in the graduate program in academic advising. He received his doctorate in counseling psychology from the University of Wisconsin-Milwaukee. He also worked as a psychologist at K-State's Counseling Services, a community services worker, and as a child care counselor. His published works include journal articles and book chapters, and he has presented at both national and international conferences. His research and professional interests include diversity in advising and counseling; career and academic development interventions with high school and college students; and the interaction of mental health and career and academic issues.

Darrin L. Carr serves as the program director for career advising, counseling, and programming at the Career Center at Florida State University (FSU) in Tallahassee, Florida. His current initiative is to enhance student intake and advising services via a performance support system based in the Cognitive Information Processing approach to career development. A recent graduate of the combined doctoral program in counseling psychology and school psychology at FSU, Carr completed his predoctoral internship requirement at the Kansas State University Counseling Center. Prior to this, he worked on projects for the FSU Center for the Study of Technology in Counseling and Career Development, obtained a master's in instructional systems technology, and served six years at the Indiana Career and Postsecondary Advancement Center (ICPAC) at Indiana University-Bloomington. At ICPAC, Darrin worked with the state department of workforce development to design and deploy one of the first Internet-based career information delivery systems. He also trained hundreds of secondary educators on the effective use of the Internet in student career planning and developed print-based, career development products used throughout Indiana schools and homes. He is a member of the American Counseling Association, American Psychological Association, and the Association of Computer-Based Systems for Career Information.

Joanne K. Damminger is the director of the Student Transition and Leadership Programs at Rowan University in Glassboro, New Jersey. Her work focuses on designing first-year and sophomore-year experiences to increase student satisfaction, academic success, intentional learning, social adjustment, and retention. She directs freshman and transfer orientations and the sophomore-year experience program, and coordinates a first-year learning community for undeclared students. Damminger taught in the Masters for Counseling in Educational Settings Program for eight years before currently teaching in the doctoral program in educational leadership. Damminger presents nationally and regionally on topics related to first-year experiences, creating living/learning communities, helping students to become intentional learners, second-year experiences, leadership, and job searching. Some of her current NACADA service activities include chair of the Finance Committee and co-chair of the 2010 Region 2 Conference Committee. She was named to the Rowan University Wall of Fame for her contributions to academic advising and received the Rowan University D.W.S. Hoffner Award for Outstanding Administrator and the Outstanding Greek Advisor Award in 2007. Damminger earned her doctorate in educational leadership, an M.A. in student personnel services, and a B.A in elementary education from Rowan University.

Susan A. Epstein was the Florida State University Career Center's librarian from 1994 to 2009, providing access to the quality information people need for career decision making. While at the Career Center, she has created user guides and workshops for researching employers and job searching on the Internet; systematized the processing, cataloging, and filing of print, multimedia, and online resources in the Career Center Library; and documented best practices for career resource library managers. Her writings include the National Career Development Association monograph series publication (with Janet Lenz) *Developing and Managing Career Resources* (2008) and a chapter on career resource library development and management issues (with Kirsten Kinsley) in *Career Counseling and Services: A Cognitive Information Processing Approach* (2004). Epstein has also presented concurrent sessions on developing and managing career resources at several professional conferences. She earned a bachelor of arts in Spanish and a bachelor of science in family and community development from the University of Maryland, College Park, and a master's in library and information science from the Florida State University. Epstein is an active member of the Special Libraries Association, the Career Resource Managers Association, and the North Florida Library Association.

Rich Feller is professor of counseling and career development and University Distinguished Teaching Scholar at Colorado State University. Recent contributions include coeditor of *A Counselor's Guide to Career Assessment Instruments*, coauthor of the Harrington-O'Shea *Career Decision Making System* print and Internet versions, and co-author of the DVD *Making the Most of Your Abilities*.

Judith K. Hughey, a National Certified Counselor, is an associate professor at Kansas State University in the Department of Special Education, Counseling, and Student Affairs. She earned an Ed.D. at the University of Missouri-Columbia, and a master's degree and bachelor's degree from Southeast Missouri State University. Hughey's teaching responsibilities include teaching graduate courses in counselor education and supervision and undergraduate educational psychology. Hughey is the coordinator of the master's program for school counseling. She also serves as the chair of the College of Education Faculty Assembly and Executive Committee, is a member of the University Faculty Senate, and serves on numerous university and college committees. Hughey has also served as a project director or associate director on multiple grants and has served as assistant managing editor for the *Journal of Vocational Special Needs* and assistant to the editor for *Professional School Counseling*.

Kenneth F. Hughey is professor and chair of the Department of Special Education, Counseling, and Student Affairs at Kansas State University (KSU) and teaches the career development course in the online graduate certificate and master's degree programs in academic advising offered by KSU. He served as Associate Director of Counseling for High Skills (1992–1998), a DeWitt Wallace–Reader's Digest Fund project designed to assist counselors in addressing the career development of students planning to attend community colleges, technical institutions, and proprietary institutions. Prior to coming to K-State in 1990, Hughey had experience in career guidance and counseling, including working with college students and adults in transition. Hughey has published articles on career development in professional journals, such as *Professional School Counseling* and the *Journal of Career Development* and has presented at numerous conferences, including NACADA conferences. He is also the former editor of *Professional School Counseling* and currently serves on the editorial board of the *Journal of Career Development*. He served on the editorial boards of the *Journal of Counseling & Development*, *Professional School Counseling*, and *Counseling and Values*.

Brian Hutchison is assistant professor in the Division of Counseling and Family Therapy at the University Missouri–Saint Louis. He has authored and coauthored several book chapters, articles, and other materials on career theory and development and presented on these topics at numerous conferences and invited workshops. Hutchison has worked as a college career and school counselor. He is the past-president of the Pennsylvania Career Development Association as well as an active member of the National Career Development Association through its National Leadership Academy. Hutchison's research focuses on the impact of social class on counseling relationships, career development, and career planning behaviors. He has taught career and multicultural classes in a variety of settings for high school, undergraduate, and graduate students.

Peggy Jordan is the director of the Center for Learning and Teaching and Professor of Psychology at Oklahoma City Community College. She was awarded the National Academic Advising Association's (NACADA's) 2007 Outstanding

Advising Award in the Faculty Advising category and the 2008 Service to Commission Award from the Two-Year Colleges Commission. She previously served as NACADA's Two-Year Colleges Commission Chair. Jordan coauthored a chapter, "Theoretical Foundations of Academic Advising" in the second edition of *Academic Advising: A Comprehensive Handbook* (2008) and was coeditor for the NACADA monograph on "Advising Special Student Populations" (2007). She has written for other NACADA monographs and for the NACADA Journal. Jordan served as a faculty member for NACADA's Faculty Seminar and Summer Institute and presented numerous workshops for NACADA regional and national conferences. Jordan earned her Ph.D. in counseling psychology from Oklahoma State University. For the first twenty years of her professional career, she worked in various state agencies and a private practice. After years of teaching clients coping skills and strategies to enhance motivation and feelings of worth, she returned to the college campus, with a strong belief that teaching and advising students offers them the greatest opportunities for empowerment.

Marilyn S. Kaff is associate professor in the Department of Special Education, Counseling, and Student Affairs. She has a B.A. from Washburn University in Topeka, Kansas; an M.S in special education from Kansas State University in Manhattan, Kansas; an Ed.S. in school psychology from Emporia State University, Emporia, Kansas; and her Ph.D. from the University of Kansas in special education. She has pursued advanced training in autism spectrum disorders. In the course of her career, she has served in a variety of capacities including paraprofessional, classroom teacher, special education teacher, inclusion facilitator, behavioral consultant, school psychologist, college professor, and most important of all, parent. Her research interests include the impact of public policies on K–16 educators and students. Currently she is working on an oral history of the field of emotional and behavioral disorders. She also conducts research on effective educational interventions for students with significant disabilities. In addition, she provides consultation services to students with autism spectrum disorders who are planning on attending college.

Heidi Koring has been director of academic advising at Lynchburg College since 1984. During this time she has published and presented widely in the fields of advising as teaching, advisor training and development, faculty advising, freshman advising, mentoring, and peer advising at regional and national NACADA conferences, Freshman Year Experience conferences, and in advising and freshman year experience publications. She is coeditor of the NACADA monograph *Peer Advising: Intentional Connections to Support Student Learning.* She has been an active NACADA member, serving as chair of the Advisor Training and Development Commission, for which she received a Service to Commission Award (2005), as cochair of the Peer Advising and Mentoring Interest Group, and as a member of various national task forces. In additional to consulting, presenting, and publishing on topics related to advising and student success, she has published and presented on ceremonial communication and public commemoration. She is coauthor of two books, *Remembering Overlord* (2002) and *Pomp and Circumstance* (2003).

Karen R. Low is the assistant director of Student Life at Kansas State University, where she is also finishing her doctoral degree in Counselor Education and Supervision. Before accepting the Student Life position, Low was assistant director of Adult Student Services at K-State. Low moved to Kansas from Montana, where she was assistant professor and director of the Master of Science in Counseling program at the University of Great Falls. In addition to program administration and teaching at the undergraduate and graduate levels, student advising and mentoring have been central to her mission of helping students succeed. A nontraditional, first-generation college student herself, Low earned her bachelor's degree in human services and master's degree in professional counseling while her children were also in school. Her professional interests include student judicial affairs, nontraditional and multicultural student services, and program assessment.

Eileen Mahoney is the director of University Advising and the Gateway Student Success Center at Northern Arizona University. She was first introduced to academic advising through an assistantship at the University Advising Center during her first year of graduate studies at Northern Arizona University. In her second year, she had an assistantship in Career Services and became convinced that the two services should be combined. Over 20 years later, after working as a career counselor, academic advisor, and administrator, she has the opportunity to lead the integration of career and academic advising services at Northern Arizona University. She remains interested in adult career development and conducted her doctoral research on the impact of chance and locus of control on career development.

Betsy McCalla-Wriggins is director emeritus of the Career and Academic Planning Center at Rowan University. This center provides academic and career advising for undeclared and change of major students as well as career advising for all students and alumni. This center was one of the first fully integrated units in the nation and has served as a model for integrating these two critical functions. She currently writes, presents, and consults in this area. She coauthored the chapter "Integrated Career and Academic Advising Programs" in the *The Handbook of Career Advising* and wrote the chapter "Integrating Academic Advising and Career and Life Planning" in *Academic Advising: A Comprehensive Handbook*. She coedited the FYE/NACADA monograph "Academic Advising: New Insights for Teaching and Learning in the First Year." McCalla-Wriggins served as president of the National Academic Advising Association from 2001 to 2003. She led the association through a total restructuring and initiated a number of new services. Since that time, membership in the association has almost doubled. Prior to being in higher education, she worked for Butterick Fashion Marketing Company in Boston, Dallas, and New York in the marketing, customer service, and training areas.

She holds a B.S. and M.S. from the University of Tennessee in Knoxville, Tennessee.

Dorothy Burton Nelson, a Nationally Certified Counselor, earned her Ph.D. in Human Resources Education from Louisiana State University, with an emphasis on career advising in postsecondary institutions. Nelson has worked in the field of career development for the past 20 years and began at Southeastern Louisiana University teaching an entry-level career planning course. After recognizing the career needs of upper classification students, she developed a follow-up course focused on the dynamics of the job search. Dorothy became a member of NACADA in 1991 and with the guidance of NACADA professionals she developed and directed a career and academic planning (CAP) center. The CAP Center targeted exploring students from all majors and specifically served the undecided student population. Currently, Nelson directs a freshman success center at Southeastern Louisiana University, the Center for Student Excellence. Nelson maintains professional involvement with all levels of NACADA. She has served as a faculty member at the NACADA Summer Institute, as a NACADA consultant, as president of the Louisiana Academic Advising Association, and as a member of the NACADA regional Steering Committee. She is an active member of the American Counseling Association and the National Career Development Association.

Spencer G. Niles is professor and department head for Counselor Education, Counseling Psychology, and Rehabilitation Services at Penn State. He is the recipient of the National Career Development Association's Eminent Career Award, a NCDA Fellow, an American Counseling Association Fellow, ACA's David Brooks Distinguished Mentor Award, the ACA Extended Research Award, and the University of British Columbia Noted Scholar Award. Within NCDA, Niles has served in roles such as president, governing council representative, North Atlantic Region trustee, trustee-at-large, editor of *The Career Development Quarterly*, chair of the Public Policy and Career Development Council, cochair, Long Range Planning Committee, and Research Awards Committee. Niles is on the editorial board for the *International Journal for Educational and Vocational Guidance* and the *International Journal for the Advancement of Counseling*. He is the editor of the *Journal of Counseling & Development* and has authored or coauthored approximately 95 publications and delivered over 90 presentations on career development theory and practice. He is an honorary member of the Japanese Career Development Association, the Italian Association for Educational and Vocational Guidance, and the Ohio Career Development Association.

Brian O'Bruba is the associate director for Career Counseling Services with The Career Center at Colorado State University, where he is helping students in career transition, as well as career education and job readiness. His experience spans over 13 years in a variety of higher education settings.

Prior appointments were at the Ohio State University (senior career counselor) and Peirce College (director of Academic Advising) in Philadelphia.

Beverly C. Reid is director, Career Development, at Lynchburg College. Beverly has spent 24 years working on college and university campuses in Virginia and Ohio, with 20 of those years in career development. After graduating from James Madison University with a bachelor's degree in psychology, Bev went immediately into a master's program in counseling, also at JMU. She first worked full-time in student affairs at the University of Virginia, then William and Mary, eventually starting to work in career development at Virginia Wesleyan College. After relocating to Ohio in 1993 and working in career development at Wittenberg University, Reid moved back to Virginia in 2000 to work at Lynchburg College. She is currently the director of Career Development at Lynchburg College and living with her husband and their three daughters on the family farm.

Rich Robbins is associate dean of Arts and Sciences at Bucknell University. He holds a Ph.D. in social psychology from the University of Nevada, Reno, and initially served as a behavioral sciences faculty member, followed by a move into higher education administration and adjunct teaching. He has developed advising programs at two institutions and headed advising programs at four institutions, receiving national awards and research grants as well as several campus advising awards. His service to NACADA includes chair of the Research Committee, member of the Council, Board of Directors, and *NACADA Journal* Editorial Board, faculty and chair of the Summer Institute Advisory Board, and faculty for both the Administrators' Institute and Assessment Institute. He is currently a member of the NACADA Consultants and Speakers Service and will become coeditor of the *NACADA Journal* in 2009. Rich has over 100 professional presentations and numerous book reviews and articles, including editor for the 2004 NACADA monograph *Giving Advice to Students: A Road Map for College Professionals*, and coauthor of the 2005 NACADA CD *Guide to Assessment in Academic Advising*. Rich is also a manuscript reviewer for the *Journal of College Student Retention* and a reviewer for textbooks in psychology.

The Handbook of Career Advising

CHAPTER ONE

Foundations of Career Advising

Kenneth F. Hughey, Judith K. Hughey

Academic advisors have an important role in supporting and facilitating students' career and academic planning and development. They are well positioned to contribute to students' making courageous choices (Feller & Whichard, 2005), both academic and career choices. Through career advising, academic advisors empower students to prepare for a changing, evolving future and workplace. Gordon (1992) stated, "Career advising is an important part of academic advising because of students' concern about their work life after college" (p. 71). As a result of effective career advising, students make career and academic decisions, set goals, develop plans to meet the goals, and implement the plans. Facilitating students' career development through career advising has never been more important, challenging, and exciting.

According to Gordon (2006), "All students need career advising, even those who enter college already decided on an academic major" (p. 5). Students are at different places with respect to their career development and have unique needs. Carroll McCollum (1998) stated, "The overall challenge to the advisor is to meet the advisees' developmental needs whether they are emotional, academic, or career oriented" (p. 15). Through the process of integrating career and academic advising, the opportunity is provided to contribute to meeting students' needs, enhancing students' learning, and preparing students for the future.

The challenge for the profession is to respond to and address the career advising needs of students and make this work an integral part of academic advising. It is an opportunity to contribute to students' personal and professional development. Although there are varying views on academic advisors' role in career advising, it is an important role for academic advisors. For some, making career advising a priority and an integral part of academic advising requires a paradigm shift. O'Banion (1994) stated, "For real change to occur in educational institutions—change that will expand and increase

1

opportunities for students to broaden and deepen their learning—systemic change is required" (p. 119). Promoting change to make career advising an essential part of academic advising and academic advising programs will add value to students' learning, development, and future.

The purpose of this chapter is to present a foundation for *The Handbook of Career Advising*. To accomplish this, the following topics are addressed: historical highlights related to career advising; *career* and *career development* as important ideas for career advising; career advising and the career advising process; comparison and contrast of career advising and career counseling; and a rationale for career advising and making it an integral part of academic advising. The chapter will conclude with a discussion of advisors' perceived needs with respect to career advising.

HISTORICAL HIGHLIGHTS OF THE EVOLUTION OF CAREER ADVISING

From a historical perspective, career advising evolved from academic advising. In addition, the history of vocational guidance and career counseling has contributed to the evolution of career advising. In a sense, the evolution of the perspectives of academic advising and vocational guidance/career counseling are similar. Both perspectives contribute to career advising as an important part of academic advising. Gordon (2006) stated, "Academic advising today is recognized as a critical service; the need for academic and career advising is reflected in a complex, ever-changing world" (p. 4).

Gordon and Habley (Gordon, Habley, & Associates, 2000) stated, "Academic advising has a long and fascinating history" (p. 1). The history and foundations of academic advising have been addressed by several authors (e.g., Ender, Winston, & Miller, 1984; Frost, 2000; Gordon, 1992). Frost (2000) described the history of academic advising with three themes—pre-advising higher education, advising defined and unexamined, and advising defined and examined. Gordon (1992) noted that the history of higher education and academic advising are intertwined.

Several significant events influenced the profession of academic advising. In the early 1970s Crookston (1972) and O'Banion (1972) discussed advising more broadly from a developmental perspective. Gordon (1992) noted that in the 1970s the importance of advising was supported and that in the 1990s "a more developmental perspective is used to assist students in decisions relating to academic and life goals" (p. 17). With respect to the profession, the establishment of the National Academic Advising Association (NACADA) in 1979 and the publication of the first issue of the *NACADA Journal* in 1981 were significant events (Beatty, 1991).

Drawing from the history of career counseling and development, there are significant historical events that provided a foundation for career advising. Parsons (1908), the father of vocational guidance, wrote *Choosing a Vocation* in which he stated the following about the factors involved in making a career decision:

> In the wise choice of a vocation there are three broad factors: (1) a clear under-standing of yourself, your aptitudes, abilities, interests, ambitions, resources, limitations, and their causes; (2) a knowledge of the requirements and condi-tions of success, advantages and disadvantages, compensation, opportunities, and prospects in different lines of work; (3) true reasoning on the relations of these two conditions. (p. 5)

Parsons further noted these three factors were needed by all students.

Miller and Hawley McWhirter (2006) presented a history of the field of career counseling. They presented themes or stages related to events occur-ring in the field and country, including testing and measurement (1920s), the Great Depression (1930s), World War II and theoretical influences (1940s and 1950s), and the space race (beginning in 1958). Throughout the history of the field, various pieces of legislation were passed (e.g., National Defense Education Act, Americans with Disabilities Act); theories evolved (e.g., Holland, Super); assessments, computerized systems, and resources were developed; and the economy and programs (e.g., government) influenced the career field. Similar to the history of academic advising, an association was estab-lished and a journal published. The National Vocational Guidance Association was established in 1913 and in 1984 was renamed the National Career Development Association (Miller & Hawley McWhirter, 2006). The profes-sion's publication evolved from the *National Vocational Guidance Bulletin* through several iterations to *The Career Development Quarterly* in 1984.

Career advising evolved and represents an important responsibility for aca-demic advisors. The writing and work related to career advising seems to follow from developmental advising (Ender et al., 1984; Gordon, 1992; Mash, 1978; O'Banion, 1972; Walsh, 1979). Gordon (1984, 1992, 1995, 2006, 2007a, 2007b) made and continues to make significant contributions to career advising and its application by professional academic advisors. In addition to Gordon (1992, 2006), others have addressed the integration of career and academic advising (e.g., Habley, 1984; McCalla-Wriggins, 2000). Career and academic advising are so integrally related that discussing one area frequently involves or relates to the other area. As Gordon (2006) stated, "Perhaps some day the term *career advising* will disappear when it becomes so ingrained in the academic advising process that its separate designation is no longer necessary" (p. 12).

CAREER AND CAREER DEVELOPMENT

Career and *career development* are relevant concepts for career advising. Having an understanding of the concepts and applying them effectively can be important in facilitating students' career planning. Sears (1982) defined *career* as "The totality of work one does in his/her lifetime" (p. 139). Niles and Harris-Bowlsbey (2005) advocated "viewing *career* as a lifestyle concept"

(p. 12), which is consistent with Super's (1976) perspective. One's career involves much more than one's occupation or profession; it involves multiple roles (e.g., student, parent, worker) in which one is involved over the course of a lifetime. For students, the focus of their careers during postsecondary school is likely to be academics, including majors and other activities; however, there are additional roles, some of which are more important than others. Viewing career more broadly leads one to consider the various factors involved in living that influence careers.

According to Herr, Cramer, and Niles (2004), "careers are unique to each person and created by what one chooses or does not choose. They are dynamic and unfold throughout life" (p. 42). Students' careers are "unfolding and evolving every day" (Gysbers, Heppner, & Johnston, 2003, p. 16), and "Careers exist only as people pursue them; they are person-centered" (Super, 1976, p. 20). Academic advisors have a critical role in helping students develop and pursue their careers.

Career development, as a concept, is essential for career advising. Sears (1982) defined *career development* as "The total constellation of psychological, sociological, educational, physical, economic, and chance factors that combine to shape the career of any given individual over the life span" (p. 139). Niles and Harris-Bowlsbey (2005) described *career development* as "the lifelong psychological and behavioral processes as well as contextual influences shaping one's career over the life span" (p. 12).

Career development is a lifelong, complex process that is influenced by a variety of factors. Being aware of and responding to relevant factors influencing students' career choices is essential for academic advisors. Academic advisors with relevant knowledge and expertise can facilitate career development through career advising activities (e.g., individual advising, group advising, career courses).

ACADEMIC ADVISING AND ITS RELATIONSHIP TO CAREER ADVISING

Career advising and academic advising are viewed as being closely related and often both areas of advising are addressed concurrently with students. As Habley (1984) stated, "The career- and life-planning process is inextricably woven into the function of academic advising" (p. 171). The extent to which an integrated approach to career and academic advising is operationalized is likely to depend on a variety of factors, including advisors' knowledge and competencies (e.g., student development theory, career development theory), advisors' view of career advising as part of their roles and responsibilities (Gordon, 2006), other student affairs staff's view of career advising as the responsibility of advisors, institutional or organizational philosophy of academic advising and the role of advisors, limited numbers of advisors and limited time to work with students, and limited support for making the transition to this perspective.

Definitions of advising from the developmental perspective support career advising by academic advisors. According to O'Banion (1972), "The purpose of academic advising is to help the student choose a program of study which will serve him in the development of his potential" (p. 62). Further, he stated, "The process of academic advising includes the following dimensions: (1) exploration of life goals, (2) exploration of vocational goals, (3) program choice, (4) course choice, and (5) scheduling courses" (p. 62). Crookston (1972) noted that developmental advising was "concerned not only with a specific personal or vocational decision but also with facilitating the student's rational processes, environmental and interpersonal interactions, behavioral awareness, and problem-solving, decision-making, and evaluation skills" (p. 12). In addition, Ender et al. (1984) defined developmental academic advising "as a systematic process based on a close student-advisor relationship intended to aid students in achieving educational, career, and personal goals through the utilization of the full range of institutional and community resources" (p. 19). According to Ender et al. (1984), "Advising is goal related. The goals should be established and owned by the student and should encompass academic, career, and personal development areas" (p. 20). Ender and Wilkie (2000) further noted that advising focused on themes of "academic competence, personal involvement, and developing or validating a life purpose" (p. 119). To address the outcomes noted requires that academic advisors work from an integrated perspective and collaborate with campus student affairs professionals to facilitate students' development, including career development.

Similarly, Creamer and Creamer (1994) described developmental advising as "the use of interactive teaching, counseling, and administrative strategies to assist students to achieve specific learning, developmental, career, and life goals" (p. 19). The use of teaching is consistent with the learning-centered approach to academic advising (Lowenstein, 2005). Lowenstein (2005) stated the following:

> Every time the student needs to make a choice (of majors, of tracks within a major, of individual courses), the advisor has a teachable moment, and the excellent advisor seeks to help the student decide, in the context of his or her emerging understanding, the direction and goals as well as the logic of his or her education as a whole. (p. 70)

The learning-centered approach facilitates career and academic advising and contributes to student learning relative to academic, career, and personal goals.

NACADA's (2005) discussion of academic advising presents and supports an integrated perspective of academic and career advising. As such, the relationship of career advising and academic advising is established for the benefit of students and their development. As stated in the document titled the *Concept of Academic Advising*, "Academic advising, based in the teaching and learning mission of higher education, is a series of intentional interactions with a curriculum, a pedagogy, and a set of student learning outcomes" (NACADA, 2006). As an integral part of the educational process, "academic advising fosters individual potential" (NACADA, 2005). Through interactions with students, advisors gain insights to enable them to help students develop academic and career goals, and develop as successful learners (NACADA, 2005). Further, "Advisors encourage self-reliance and support students as they strive to make informed and responsible decisions, set realistic goals, and develop lifelong learning and self-management skills" (NACADA, 2005).

The emphasis on *career* in the definitions and descriptions of academic advising supports academic advisors' providing career advising and career advising being an important part of academic advising. Career advising will be discussed as a unique process; however, ideally, we believe making this an integral part of academic advising has the potential to maximize benefits to students and contribute to students' development as educated individuals and professionals prepared for the future. For students, career and academic advising are closely related (Gordon, 1992) and it is difficult to differentiate between the two.

CAREER ADVISING: INTEGRAL TO ACADEMIC ADVISING

Gordon's (2006) very good work and contributions to career advising are significant, noteworthy, and serve as the foundation for defining career advising. Career advising is a dynamic, interactive process that "helps students understand how their personal interests, abilities, and values might predict success in the academic and career fields they are considering and how to form their academic and career goals accordingly" (Gordon, 2006, p. 12). It is a process aimed at helping students effectively use information about themselves (e.g., interests, abilities, values, strengths) and the options available (e.g., majors, occupations, internships). Through the process, students integrate this information to set goals, make academic and career decisions, and develop plans to make meaning of their goals and decisions. Career advising can help students learn the skills needed for career decision making. In addition, career advising can add value to students' academic and career development and more effectively prepare them for the future. It is a process in which students must take personal responsibility and advisors have a critical role in facilitating the process.

Habley (1984) presented 11 tasks related to the career and life-planning process. The tasks identified are as follows: become aware of individual values, abilities, and interests; clarify life goals based on self-awareness; explore relationships between life and career goals; explore the world of work; clarify career goals; explore educational combinations leading to life and career goals; select the educational combination; explore elective courses; sequence and select courses; schedule courses; and evaluate experiences for confirmation or redirection. At each of these tasks, advisors may work with the student or, if appropriate, refer the student to other student affairs professionals. This process provides a framework for the integration of academic and career issues and might be used or adapted to fit individual and institutional needs.

More recently, Gordon (2006) presented the 3-I Process (i.e., inquire, inform, integrate) that provides a framework to make career advising an integral part to academic advising. Following are descriptions of the phases of the process:

> The *inquire* phase "involves identifying students' academic and career concerns, clarifying their needs, and making appropriate responses that help them move to the information-collecting phase" (p. 47).

> The *inform* phase involves "the acquisition and effective use of educational and career information" (p. 63).

> During the *integrate* phase "advisors and students determine what additional assistance is needed to help students organize and make meaningful connections between the information sources they have collected" (p. 79).

For effective career advising, advisors use and apply the competencies needed for effective academic advising (e.g., listening, questioning, challenging, goal-setting). Light (2001) described effective advisors as those who asked questions and challenged students to consider the relationship between academics and their lives. In addition, effective career advising requires additional knowledge and competencies. Examples include knowledge and competencies with respect to students' career development, career development theories and relevant constructs, student development theories, recognition of career-related problems that require referral, career information and resources, career decision-making models, and career needs and issues related to special populations. Career advising knowledge and competencies can be developed and enhanced through formal education programs (e.g., graduate degrees or certificates) or professional development programs.

With the relevant knowledge and competencies, academic advisors can make career advising a natural part of their work with students. In addition, other campus professionals can provide career advising to students (e.g., faculty advisors, career advisors, career counselors, student affairs professionals). Various academic advising approaches can be used to address the career advising needs of students. As noted earlier, developmental advising, as an approach, can be applied to address career advising issues. Also, the prescriptive approach can address career-related issues. Further, career advising can be addressed through intrusive advising (Varney, 2007), appreciative advising (Bloom & Archer Martin, 2002; Habley & Bloom, 2007), and strengths-based advising (Schreiner & Anderson, 2005). Goals of career advising, as applied through various approaches, are to enhance students' academic and career development and planning and effectively prepare them for the future. In the process, the intent is to contribute to individuals' personal and professional development.

Career advising, whether completed with individuals, with groups of students, or by teaching a class, is intended to address student learning outcomes. Career advising is a dynamic teaching and learning process intended to contribute to students' development. According to Council for the Advancement of Standards (CAS, 2005), academic advising programs "must identify relevant and desirable student learning and development outcomes and provide programs and services that encourage the achievement of those outcomes" (p. 1). Related to facilitating students' career development and planning, CAS (2005) noted the following as desirable learning outcomes: intellectual growth, personal and educational goals, realistic self-appraisal, clarified values, career choices, effective communication, and leadership development. The following are provided as examples of achievement of learning outcomes of career choices:

- Describes career choice and choices of academic major and minor based on interests, values, skills, and abilities
- Documents knowledge, skills, and accomplishments resulting from formal education, work experience, community service, and volunteer experiences
- Makes the connections between classroom and out-of-classroom learning
- Identifies the purpose and role of career services in the development and attainment of academic and career goals (CAS, 2005, p. 2)

Under the personal and educational goals learning outcome, examples of achievement include, "Sets, articulates, and pursues individual goals," (p. 2) and, "Uses personal and educational goals to guide decisions" (p. 2). Further, an example of the realistic self-appraisal learning outcome is, "Evaluates personal and academic skills, abilities, and interests and uses this appraisal to establish appropriate educational plans" (p. 2). As part of the clarified values learning outcome, an example of achievement provided is, "Identifies personal, work, and lifestyle values and explains how they influence decision-making in regard to course selection, course load, and major and minor selections" (p. 2). Addressing career advising learning outcomes is an important part of the role of academic advisors and facilitates students' learning and development.

Herr et al. (2004) conceptualized the career development needs of postsecondary students consistent with the CAS (2005) student learning outcomes. These needs included selection of an educational major, self-assessment, understanding of the world of work and its relationship to academics, decision-making, and assistance with preparation for and access to work. As part of the process, students develop meaningful academic and career goals that are often interrelated. Also, students develop meaningful academic and career plans to meet their goals.

Career advising is an essential function needed to facilitate and support students' development and planning. From an institutional perspective, Habley and Bloom (2007) presented imperatives for advising programs to be effective. These apply to career advising as an important part of academic advising programs. The imperatives include the following: advising is more than giving information; advising is a process; advising involves a student-centered relationship; advising is teaching and learning; advising is central to the mission of the institution; and advising is the central student support service and builds networks with other services. Viewing career advising in this way has the potential to have a significant impact on students' future and their preparation for life as contributing citizens and professionals.

CAREER ADVISING VERSUS CAREER COUNSELING

Understanding career advising and career counseling, the overlapping aspects of the two, and the distinct features of the processes is essential. Being clear about the potential areas of similarities and differences can help establish appropriate boundaries. On college campuses there are likely to be academic advisors who perform counseling, including career counseling, along with academic advising and career advising. Also, there may be counselors who provide advising. There is considerable overlap in the roles and responsibilities due, in part, "to an institutional lack of agreement about the responsibilities associated with either position" (Kuhn, Gordon, & Webber, 2006, p. 25). Clearly, as stated by Gordon (2006), "Academic advisors are not expected to be career counselors but to assist students in gathering and processing the information needed to engage in realistic academically related career planning" (p. 8).

Niles and Harris-Bowlsbey (2005) stated, "Career counseling involves a formal relationship in which a professional counselor assists a client, or group of clients, to cope more effectively with career concerns (e.g., making a career choice, coping with career transitions, coping with job-related stress, or job search)" (p. 13). In addition, Herr et al. (2004) defined career counseling as "a dynamic and collaborative relationship, focused on identifying and acting on the counselee's goals, in which the counselor employs a repertoire of diverse techniques or processes, to help bring about self-understanding, understanding of the career concerns involved and behavioral options available, as well as informed decision making in the counselee, who has the responsibility for his or her own actions" (p. 42). Career advising, however, is typically viewed as being less psychologically intense (Gordon, 2006) and less problem focused than career counseling. In addition, career advising could be viewed more with a developmental focus with respect to facilitating students' academic and career planning.

There are similarities with some professional competencies used by academic advisors and career counselors. Examples include communication competencies, relationship-building competencies, knowledge of career decision making, knowledge of career resources, and knowledge of technology. In addition, Kuhn et al. (2006) presented issues academic advisors and counselors typically address. The areas of overlap, issues that could be addressed by advisors or counselors, included the following related to career planning: mid-life career change, decision-making, academic goals, personal goals, and career goals. There is overlap in terms of activities of counselors and advisors as both "help students set goals so they can improve their personal functioning, identify barriers that may impact successful accomplishment of their goals, develop strategies to accomplish these goals, and assess whether or not the strategies are successful" (Kuhn et al., 2006, p. 26).

Kuhn et al. (2006) described an advising-counseling continuum that presents informational advising at one end and counseling at the other end. Next to informational advising on the continuum is explanatory advising followed by developmental advising; mentoring is the next level followed by counseling. The first three levels are for all advisors but mentoring is most frequently associated with faculty advisors.

Whereas Kuhn et al. (2006) presented a continuum related to advising and counseling, Ender and Winston (1982) presented a continuum of student concerns that can serve as a guide for advisors and help differentiate between academic and career advising and career counseling. Winston (1989) adapted and added to the continuum of student concerns. On one end of the continuum were concerns of a developmental nature. For a concern determined to be developmental, the advisor can implement appropriate strategies (e.g., setting goals, exploring academic and career options). At the other end of the continuum of student concerns are the remedial, problem-focused issues that require the expertise of a counselor, psychologist, or career counselor.

With respect to career advising and career counseling, academic advisors recognize the key issues involved in student concerns, assess the nature of the concerns (e.g., developmental or problematic), and determine the process that would be most effective in addressing the concerns (i.e., career advising or career counseling). Being knowledgeable of the issues requiring referral and making referrals are essential for advisors and benefit students.

A RATIONALE FOR CAREER ADVISING

Career advising as an integral part of academic advising is the focus of this book. Academic advisors are in a key position to facilitate and assist students in their career decision making and planning. The purpose of this section is to provide a rationale for academic advisors providing career advising. The extent to which this occurs will probably vary and depend on the individual advisor, programs, centers, and institutions. Regardless, career advising as a professional function is an important responsibility that must be addressed.

The complexity of the choices and factors involved in decision making support the need for career advising. Bullock, Reardon, and Lenz (2007) described students making academic and career decisions feeling "as though they were trying to solve a riddle" (p. 193). There is a vast amount of information on career options, and advisors are in a key position to help students turn data into information to inform academic and career decision making (Niles & Harris-Bowlsbey, 2005). Also, a variety of factors affect choices and decision making (e.g., family, peers, economy); helping students consider these as they make academic and career decisions is essential.

Another issue that provides support for career advising is the changing economy and workplaces. Being aware of these issues and the extent to which they influence students can be important for advisors. The changing assumptions relative to the workplace and career development (Feller, 2003; Hughey & Hughey, 2006) are relevant for advisors, and consideration of these can enhance students' planning, decision making, and preparation for the future. Clearly, the economy is knowledge-based, information-oriented, and technology-driven. Habley (1984) stated, "it becomes critical for institutions to develop programs for assisting students in coping with a life and a career in which change and technological growth are the only inevitabilities" (p. 150). Now there are likely to be other inevitabilities and change will continue. Therefore, the competencies needed to be successful in the workplace and future are changing (e.g., independent and critical thinking, problem solving). Advisors working collaboratively with faculty can help students become engaged in learning experiences, both in and out of the classroom, focused on the changing workplace and the competencies needed.

High school students' aspirations and preparation for college work are factors that support the need for career advising for students as they enter postsecondary education. Gray and Herr (2006) stated, "Today, most youth aspire to baccalaureate education" (p. 62). They also reported that many more students expected to be working in professional occupations as compared to technical occupations (59% versus 6%). Also, Gray and Herr (2006) noted, based on their review of data, "that, at best, about half of high school students graduate even semi-prepared to do college-level academics" (p. 62). McCarthy and Kuh (2006) reported that even though 80% of high school students indicated they planned to attend postsecondary institutions, many did not engage in the academic activities that prepared them for this. Bettinger and Long (2005) noted that annually thousands of high school graduates are not prepared for the academic rigors of college. Misguided aspirations and underpreparedness for college work potentially have an impact on both career and academic advising.

Many students need help with their academic and career planning, and advisors have a key role in this process. Noel-Levitz (2007), in a survey of first-year college students' attitudes, reported that 65.7% of students surveyed responded affirmatively to "I would like some help selecting an educational plan that will prepare me to get a good job" (p. 6). Habley (2006) noted that 5% of students expect to seek career guidance while 25% do so. Herr et al. (2004) noted that career-related problems are experienced by at least 50% of students.

Students who are undecided often need career advising; some need career counseling. Gordon (1984, 1995, 2007a) described students who were undecided as an "academic and career advising challenge." One challenge for professionals, including academic advisors, is to assist students in determining academic and career goals and developing plans to meet the goals. In a survey of first-year college freshmen, Noel-Levitz (2007) reported the following: 61.1% reported having made an occupational decision and were developing plans; 24.8% of the students reported becoming very confused when trying to choose an occupation; and 20.6% reported being very confused about the occupation to pursue. Habley (2006) noted that 8% of students expected to be undecided but 20% experienced being undecided. Gordon (2007a) stated, "Undecided students are such a heterogeneous group and the administrative variations on campuses are so different that it is difficult to comprehend generally the enormity and complexity of trying to identify and advise them" (pp. ix–x). With appropriate education and institutional support, academic advisors are ideally situated to respond to students who are undecided about their majors or career goals.

Similarly, students who change majors (Gordon & Steele, 1992; Steele & McDonald, 2000), some of whom are likely undecided, are a group who could benefit from career advising. Gordon (2007a) noted that students who change majors make up approximately 75% of college students. Based on data reported by Habley (2006), 65 to 85% of students changed majors whereas only 14% of students expected to do so. Students change majors for a variety of reasons—some decide to change, some are undecided and go from one major to another, some may be denied admission to specific colleges or programs, some choose unrealistic options. In addition, Gordon (2007a) cited research that being unsuccessful in determining majors or the inability to develop career goals may lead to attrition.

Retention of students is a key issue on campuses, and academic advising, including career advising, has the potential to affect student retention. In a Web-based survey of two-year, nonprofit, degree-granting institutions, Noel-Levitz (2007) reported that, based on institutional report, advising was an effective retention strategy. Tinto (2004) stated, "Effective advising is an essential part of successful retention programs" (p. 8). In addition, Hull-Blanks, Robinson Kurpius, Befort, Sollenberger, Foley Nicpon, and Huser (2005) cited studies that supported having defined career goals was related to retention. Based on the results of their study, Hull-Blanks et al. (2005) stated, "job-related career goals were the ones found to relate to persistence decisions" (p. 24). Also, they stated, "Clearly, having an identified goal that is dependent on successful completion of an education facilitates decisions to remain in school" (p. 24). Career advising can support students in the development and implementation of academic and career goals and plans.

The numbers and diversity of postsecondary students and their career and academic needs support the need for effective career advising of students. According to Snyder (2007), there were 13.8 million undergraduates in 1990 and 17.5 million in 2005. Of the 2005 enrollment, 11 million were enrolled in four-year institutions and 6.5 million were enrolled in two-year institutions. In 1980 minorities comprised 16.1% of the students and in 2005 it was 30.9%. Between 2005 and 2016, undergraduate enrollment is projected to increase by 16% for undergraduate students, from 15 million to 17.4 million (Hussar & Bailey, 2007). In addition, the proportion of students who are minorities is increasing; from 15% in 1976 to 30% in 2004. Also, 11% of undergraduate students reported having a disability in 2003–04 (Horn & Griffith, 2006). Responding to the career and academic needs of all students is important, and considering their unique needs is essential.

The need for career advising is clear; the challenge is to implement programs and services to enhance students' academic and career planning and development. Doing so will facilitate and support students' preparation to be contributing citizens and professionals.

ADVISORS' PERCEPTIONS AND NEEDS RELATED TO CAREER ADVISING

To assess academic advisors' perceptions of career advising and professional needs related to career advising, an online survey of academic advisors who were members of NACADA was conducted in early 2007. Respondents had approximately one month to respond to the survey. The survey was completed by 2161 of a total of 5672 (response rate = 38%) advisors who were sent the survey. Of the survey respondents, 1997 indicated their role was academic advisor/counselor, faculty advisor, or advising administrator. Approximately 80% of the respondents indicated their institutions were public and almost 58% reported the highest degrees offered by their institutions were professional degrees (e.g., Ph.D., M.D., J.D.). The respondents reported working with undecided students (33.7%), students in a specific major (59.1%), students within a special population (e.g., student athletes, students with disabilities, 15.5%), and students changing majors (10.9%).

As part of the online survey, respondents reported their level of agreement (choices ranged from strongly disagreed to strongly agreed) with statements related to career advising. Approximately 74% of the respondents agreed (including agreed and strongly agreed) that helping students make career decisions was an important part of their roles as academic advisors. Also, just over 90% agreed that students' self-assessment was important for effective academic advising. Approximately 85% agreed that career information was very important for effective advising. Seventy-seven percent of the respondents indicated they knew how to incorporate career advising into academic advising sessions; just over 37% agreed that they regularly used career theory in advising students.

On a second part of the online survey, respondents responded affirmatively or negatively to the phrase "I would like to know more about . . ." that addressed career-related topics. More than 80% of the respondents, as shown in Table 1.1, reported that they would like to know more about how to motivate students with respect to career and academic planning, how to ask better questions to facilitate advising with students, the changing workplace and implications for students, and how to recognize and respond to career issues in advising with students. In addition, more than 70% of respondents reported wanting to know more about how to effectively help students make career decisions, how to integrate career and academic advising, career information and resources (including the Internet and career software) and their use with students, career development theory and how to apply it in advising

Table 1.1. Percentage of Academic Advisors Indicating Need to Know More About Career Topics

Career Topic	Percent
How to motivate students with respect to career and academic planning	88.7
How to ask better questions to facilitate advising with students	84.9
The changing workplace and implications for students	83.9
How to recognize and respond to career issues in my advising with students	81.3
How to effectively help students make career decisions	79.0
How to integrate career and academic advising	78.0
Career information and resources (including Internet and software) and their use with students	75.2
Career development theory and how to apply it in my advising of students	74.2
How to help specific groups of students (e.g., students with disabilities, student athletes, honor students, nontraditional students, GLBT students)	74.0
How to work with exploratory/undecided students	68.3
How to use computerized career guidance systems (e.g., DISCOVER) to enhance advising with students	59.7

Note: $n = 2161$.

students, and how to help specific groups of students (e.g., students with disabilities, student athletes, honor students, nontraditional students, GLBT students) enhance their career and academic choices.

Based on the results of this online survey of academic advisors who are NACADA members, there are career topics about which respondents would like to learn more to enhance their academic and career advising of students. Providing learning experiences (e.g., courses, professional development sessions) and applying the learning to advising would be likely to lead to a more integrated approach to academic and career advising. Further, this will lead to enhanced career advising of students.

CLOSING THOUGHTS

"For many college students, making good academic and career decisions can be a daunting task—one that is full of riddles—and it can be challenging for those academic advisors and career counselors who seek to help them" (Bullock et al., 2007, p. 211). In addition, Gore and Metz (2008) stated, "By providing career advising interventions that draw on theory, are developmentally and contextually appropriate, make use of evidence-based techniques, and promote the acquisition or development of academic and workplace success skills, attitudes, and behaviors, advisors are promoting the long-term academic and career success of their students" (p.113). Postsecondary students need career advising as they move through their academic programs and prepare for their careers and lives. Career advising as an integral part of academic advising is increasingly important and essential for students and has the potential to add significant value to students' education and career. Further, career advising can enhance the work of academic advisors as they assist students with their academic and career planning.

Through career advising, academic advisors contribute to students' career and academic development. In addition, with an integrated approach to academic and career advising, advisors contribute to students' development and decision making by nurturing passion, identifying potential, and honoring courage (Feller, 2005). Through career advising as an integral part of academic advising, advisors contribute to students' development as people and professionals.

References

Beatty, J. D. (1991). The National Academic Advising Association: A brief narrative history. *NACADA Journal, 11*(1), 5–25.

Bettinger, E. P., & Long, B. T. (2005). *Addressing the needs of under-prepared students in higher education: Does college remediation work?* (NBER Working Paper No. 11325). Cambridge, MA: National Bureau of Economic Research.

Bloom, J. L., & Archer Martin, N. (2002). Incorporating appreciate inquiry into academic advising. *The Mentor: An Academic Advising Journal, 4*(3). Retrieved on October 29, 2007, from http://www.psu.edu/dus/mentor/020829jb.htm

Bullock, E. E., Reardon, R. C., & Lenz, J. G. (2007). Planning good academic and career decisions. In G. L. Kramer & Associates, *Fostering student success in the campus community* (pp. 193–213). San Francisco: Jossey-Bass.

Carroll McCollum, V. J. (1998). Career advising: A developmental approach. *NACADA Journal, 18*(1), 15–19.

Council for the Advancement of Standards. (2005). *Academic advising program: CAS standards and guidelines.* Retrieved February 6, 2008, from http://www.nacada. ksu.edu/Clearinghouse/Research_Related/CASStandardsForAdvising.pdf

Creamer, D. G., & Creamer, E. G. (1994). Practicing developmental advising: Theoretical contexts and functional applications. *NACADA Journal, 14*(2), 17–24.

Crookston, B. B. (1972). A developmental view of academic advising as teaching. *Journal of College Student Personnel, 13*, 12–17.

Ender, S. C., & Wilkie, C. J. (2000). Advising students with special needs. In V. N. Gordon, W. R. Habley, & Associates, *Handbook of academic advising* (pp. 118–143). San Francisco: Jossey-Bass.

Ender, S. C., & Winston, R. B., Jr. (1982). Training allied professional academic advisors. In R. B. Winston, Jr., S. C. Ender, & T. K. Miller (Eds.), *Developmental approaches to academic advising* (pp. 85–103). San Francisco: Jossey-Bass.

Ender, S. C., Winston, R. B., Jr., & Miller, T. K. (1984). Academic advising reconsidered. In R. B. Winston, T. K. Miller, S. C. Ender, T. J. Grites, & Associates, *Developmental academic advising* (pp. 3–34). San Francisco: Jossey-Bass.

Feller, R. W. (2003). Aligning school counseling, the changing workplace, and career development assumptions. *Professional School Counseling, 6*, 262–271.

Feller, R. (2005, October). *Post-secondary success planning.* Webinar presented by the American School Counselor Association. Alexandria, VA.

Feller, R., & Whichard, J. (2005). *Knowledge nomads and the nervously employed: Workplace change & courageous choices.* Austin, TX: PRO-ED.

Frost, S. H. (2000). Historical and philosophical foundations of academic advising. In V. N. Gordon, W. R. Habley, and Associates, *Academic advising: A comprehensive handbook* (pp. 3–17). San Francisco: Jossey-Bass.

Gordon, V. N. (1984). *The undecided college student: An academic and career advising challenge.* Springfield, IL: Charles C. Thomas.

Gordon, V. N. (1992). *The handbook of academic advising.* Westport, CT: Greenwood Press.

Gordon, V. N. (1995). The undecided college student: An academic and career advising challenge (2nd ed.). Springfield, IL: Thomas.

Gordon, V. N. (2006). *Career advising: An academic advisor's guide.* San Francisco: Jossey-Bass.

Gordon, V. N. (2007a). The undecided college student: An academic and career advising challenge (3rd ed.). Springfield, IL: Thomas.

Gordon, V. N. (2007b). Undecided students: A special population. In L. Huff & P. Jordan (Eds.), *Advising special student populations* (pp. 187–222). Manhattan, KS: NACADA.

Gordon, V. N., Habley, W. R., & Associates. (2000). *Academic advising: A comprehensive handbook.* San Francisco: Jossey-Bass.

Gordon, V. N., & Steele, G. E. (1992). Advising major-changers: Students in transition. *NACADA Journal, 12*(1), 22–27.

Gore, P. A., Jr., & Metz, A. J. (2008). Foundations: Advising for career and life planning. In V. N. Gordon, W. R. Habley, & T. J. Grites (Eds.), *Academic advising: A comprehensive handbook* (2nd ed.). San Francisco: Jossey-Bass.

Gray, K. C., & Herr, E. L. (2006). *Other ways to win: Creating alternatives for high school graduates* (3rd ed.). Thousand Oaks, CA: Corwin Press.

Gysbers, N. C., Heppner, M. J., & Johnston, J. A. (2003). *Career counseling: Process, issues, and techniques* (2nd ed.). Boston: Allyn and Bacon.

Habley, W. R. (1984). Integrating academic advising and career planning. In R. B. Winston, T. K. Miller, S. C. Ender, T. J. Grites, & Associates, *Developmental academic advising* (pp. 147–172). San Francisco: Jossey-Bass.

Habley, W. (2006, October). *Look who's coming to college.* Paper presented at the NACADA 31st Annual Conference on Academic Advising, Baltimore, MD.

Habley, W. R., & Bloom, J. L. (2007). Giving advice that makes a difference. In G. L. Kramer & Associates, *Fostering student success in the campus community* (pp. 171–192). San Francisco: Jossey-Bass.

Herr, E. L., Cramer, S. H., & Niles, S. G. (2004). *Career guidance and counseling through the lifespan: Systematic approaches* (6th ed.). Boston: Allyn and Bacon.

Horn, L., & Griffith, J. (2006). *Profile of undergraduates in the U.S. postsecondary institutions: 2003–04* (NCES 2006–184). Washington, DC: U.S. Department of Education, National Center for Education Statistics, Institute for Education Sciences.

Hughey, J. K., & Hughey, K. F. (2006). The changing workplace: Implications for academic and career advising. *Academic Advising Today, 29*(3). Retrieved from http://www.nacada.ksu.edu/AAT/NW29_3.htm

Hull-Blanks, E., Robinson Kurpius, S. E., Befort, C., Sollenberger, S., Foley Nicpon, M., & Huser, L. (2005). Career goals and retention-related factors among college freshmen. *Journal of Career Development, 32,* 16–30.

Hussar, W. J., & Bailey, T. M. (2007). *Projections of education statistics to 2016* (NCES 2008–060). Washington, DC: U.S. Department of Education, National Center for Education Statistics, Institute of Education Sciences.

Kuhn, T., Gordon, V. N., & Webber, J. (2006). The advising and counseling continuum: Triggers for referral. *NACADA Journal, 26*(1), 24–31.

Light, R. J. (2001). *Making the most of college.* Cambridge, MA: Harvard University Press.

Lowenstein, M. (2005). If advising is teaching, what do advisors teach? *NACADA Journal, 25*(2), 65–73.

Mash, D. J. (1978). Academic advising: Too often taken for granted. *The College Board Review, 107,* 32–36.

McCalla-Wriggins, B. (2000). Integrating academic advising and career and life planning. In V. N. Gordon, W. R. Habley, & Associates, *Handbook of academic advising* (pp. 162–176). San Francisco: Jossey-Bass.

McCarthy, M., & Kuh, G. D. (2006). Are students ready for college? What student engagement data say; how realistic are high school students' educational aspirations? *Phi Delta Kappan, 87,* 664–669.

Miller, D. S., & Hawley McWhirter, E. (2006). The history of career counseling: From Frank Parsons to twenty-first-century challenges. In D. Capuzzi & M. D. Stauffer (Eds.), *Career counseling: Foundations, perspectives, and applications* (pp. 3–39). Boston: Pearson Allyn and Bacon.

National Academic Advising Association. (2005). *NACADA statement of core values of academic advising.* Retrieved February 4, 2008, from the NACADA Clearinghouse of Academic Resources Web site: http://www.nacada.ksu.edu/Clearninghouse/AdvisingIssues/Core-Values.htm

National Academic Advising Association. (2006). *NACADA concept of academic advising.* Retrieved February 4, 2008, from http://www.nacada.ksu.edu/Clearninghouse/AdvisingIssues/Concept-Advising.htm

Niles, S. G., & Harris-Bowlsbey, J. (2005). *Career development interventions for the 21st century* (2nd ed.). Upper Saddle River, NJ: Pearson Merrill Prentice Hall.

Noel-Levitz, Inc. (2007). *2007 National freshman attitudes report.* Coralville, IA: Author.

O'Banion, T. (1972). An academic advising model. *Junior College Journal, 42*(6), 62–69.

O'Banion, T. (1994). Retrospect and prospect. *NACADA Journal, 14*(2), 117–119.

Parsons, F. (1908). *Choosing a vocation.* Boston: Houghton Mifflin.

Schreiner, L., & Anderson, E. (2005). Strengths-based advising: A new lens for higher education. *NACADA Journal, 25*(2), 20–29.

Sears, S. (1982). A definition of career guidance terms: A National Vocational Guidance Association perspective. *The Vocational Guidance Quarterly, 31,* 137–143.

Snyder, T. D. (2007). *Mini-digest of education statistics 2006.* Washington, DC: U.S. Department of Education, National Center for Education Statistics, Institute of Education Sciences.

Steele, G. E., & McDonald, M. L. (2000). Advising students in transition. In V. N. Gordon, W. R. Habley, & Associates, *Academic advising: A comprehensive handbook* (pp. 144–161). San Francisco: Jossey-Bass.

Super, D. E. (1976). *Career education and the meanings of work.* Washington, DC: U.S. Department of Health, Education, and Welfare.

Tinto, V. (2004). *Student retention and graduation: Facing the truth, living with the consequences.* Washington, DC: Pell Institute for the Study of Opportunity in Higher Education.

Varney, J. (2007). Intrusive advising. *Academic Advising Today, 30*(3). Retrieved on October 5, 2007, from http://www.nacada.ksu.edu/AAT/NW30_3.htm#10

Walsh, E. M. (1979). Revitalizing academic advisement. *Personnel and Guidance Journal, 57,* 446–449.

Winston, R. B., Jr. (1989). Counseling and advising. In U. Delworth, G. R. Hanson, & Associates, *Student services: A handbook for the profession* (pp. 31–400). San Francisco: Jossey-Bass.

CHAPTER TWO

The Evolving Workplace

Integrating Academic and Career Advising

Rich Feller, Brian O'Bruba

To those who promote and support quality academic advising, the challenge of providing career advising has never been greater as "Our entire economy is in danger" (Bush, 2008), and Palley (2008) reported "the growth paradigm that has driven our economy for the past generation is exhausted" (p. B10). Integrating career advising with academic advising is timely because the "commitment to student access must now be matched with a commitment to student success" (National Commission on Community Colleges, 2008, p. 7). With society facing unprecedented economic restructuring, students confront workplace transformation whereby most jobs can be completed, outsourced, and created anyplace in the world. And 85 to 90 million adults (about half of the workforce) do not have the skills to function well in the global economy or to earn family-sustainable wages according to the National Commission on Adult Literacy (2008).

In addition, alone among advanced industrial countries, American 25–35-year-olds are not as well educated as their parents even though a disruptive technology called "student centric-learning" in which students progress at their own pace, guided by computer programs tailored to their learning levels and personal learning strengths, "has started to displace big chunks of schooling" (Christensen, Johnson, & Horn, 2008, p. 3). With employers expecting "talent on demand" (Cappelli, 2008) yet unable to forecast their business or talent needs, the significance of academic and career advising and the development of professional and faculty advisors deserves attention.

Sophisticated technologies, globalization, and electronic trading have dramatically affected learning, work, and success expectations. The speed of change challenges the ability to stay apace, and a growing "risk shift" (Hacker, 2006) produced by "the Ownership Society" creates uncertainty and insecurity.

Innovation and creativity cumulatively produce change faster than higher education and students can often adapt. Complexity, information overload, and infinite choices demand focus, reflection, and student resilience. Greater personal responsibility is required of students aiming to be a positive force in enriching people, communities, and the environment, as suggested by Sanders (2008). Such aspirations offer hope to students, employees, and employers committed to remaining relevant. Meeting aspirations requires greater commitments from advisors responsible for guiding students to meet desired educational and occupational expectations that maximize students' strengths and inspire commitments to efforts larger than themselves. As Mellow (2008) stated:

> With the advent of what has been termed the *Knowledge Era*, or the *Innovation Economy*, a college education is more important than ever before. We are all keenly aware that people in this economy must be highly educated to be both productively employed and to participate meaningfully in their communities. But this is also the bad news, because it means that in order for us to be of service to the people of our country, higher education has to do a better job. Colleges and universities must learn to not only effectively educate every student who enters our institutions, but we must recruit and succeed with a significantly larger swath of the adult population in America. (p. 3)

Fortunately, academic advising empowers students to navigate their college experience to achieve learner outcomes and develop leadership competencies that enhance critical thinking and attributes of success necessary for citizens in a world appropriately described as *Hot, Flat, and Crowded* (Friedman, 2008). Advisors need to think critically as well about "how advising can serve the students who inhabit our campuses and prepare them for a world that is changing dramatically" (Gordon, 2000, p. 381). Advising is influenced by information and assumptions held about future workplace demands and the need to prepare students for turbulent and insecure times. Determining the workplace competencies and leadership development skills needed for success is addressed each time students enter an advising office. With the importance of developing career management competencies, and the call for closing the "innovation gap" (Estrin, 2008) within an "innovation nation" (Kao, 2007), advisor effectiveness is tied to awareness of workplace change, career and academic assumptions, and the ability to navigate a global workplace.

To enhance professional and faculty advisors' work in career and academic planning, this chapter suggests characteristics of the evolving workplace and the attributes needed for student success. With the goal of providing students with a process to identify their parachute's color (Bolles, 2009) within a future demanding a "whole new mind" (Pink, 2005), insights and approaches are offered to provide career advising as integral to academic advising.

CAREER ADVISING FOR A "WHOLE NEW MIND"

Academic advising has been described as "an educational activity that depends on valid explanations of complex student behaviors and institutional conditions to assist college students in making and executing educational and life plans" (Creamer, 2000, p. 18). Further, Creamer (2000) noted that "the purpose of academic advising is student learning and personal development" (p. 19). As a result, career advising and planning is an integral part of the advising process performed by various individuals, including faculty and staff expert in curriculum, pedagogy, and learning outcomes. "While navigating educational requirements and career decision making grows in complexity, assumptions about career development and the changing workplace need to be re-evaluated" (Feller, 2003, p. 262).

Career advising is a dynamic, interactive process that "helps students understand how their personal interests, abilities, and values might predict success in the academic and career fields they are considering and how to form their academic and career goals accordingly" (Gordon, 2006, p. 12). It is a process aimed at helping students effectively use information about themselves (e.g., interests, abilities, values, strengths) and the options available (e.g., majors, occupations, internships). Through the process, students integrate this information to set goals, make academic and career decisions, and develop plans.

The changing workplace has implications for advisors working with students to prepare for future transitions as well. Herman, Oliva, and Gioia (2003) noted that "We are trapped in an era of escalating change" (p. 3), and the rate of change continues to increase. "Change is the 'new status quo'" (Feller, 1991, p. 14), and "Advisors can no longer rely on advising habits that reflect the status quo" (Gordon, 2000, p. 390). In the process of advising and planning, students are responsible for their learning and managing their own career (Feller, 2003). According to Krieshok (2003), it is important to help "citizens become more adaptive in today's marketplace" (p. 7). In the process of making decisions, information about the changing workplace, skills, and success attributes are directly related to the quality of advising one receives. It follows, as noted by Gordon (2000), that "Advising that offers career information and actively supports career planning can and should play a more important role in the future" (p. 388). The need for students to become motivated lifelong learners who "focus on monitoring and interpreting change" (Feller, 2003, p. iii) has become a survival skill.

Advising learners to plan for satisfying careers by finding the perfect job is naïve and short sighted, especially when students are experientially impoverished and need accelerated career exploration. Integrated academic and career advising demands intentional interactions. These efforts would synthesize and contextualize educational experiences with learner aspirations, abilities, and lives that extend beyond the classroom. Suggesting that the workplace be understood through Pink's (2005) lens offers students a new way to conceptualize how they need to integrate their academic and career plans. Pink argues that the workplace is dramatically shaped by three factors: (a) automation taking place in "rule-based jobs"; (b) Asia's ability to provide an expanded workforce; and (c) abundance within the world creating more demanding and discriminating consumers. In response, he urges all workers to find within themselves answers to the following three questions: (a) Can someone overseas do it cheaper than you can? (b) Can a computer do it faster than you? and (c) Is what you're selling in demand in an age of abundance?

Workplace turbulence, pervasive life style choices, and questions about, "What kind of person do I want to be?"; "What am I doing with my life?"; and "Am I living the way that I want to live?" demand considerable reflection. They are best facilitated with advisors committed to constantly scanning the employment and learning environment, valuing the implications of changing career opportunities, and believing that it is more important to help students find a cause rather than settle for a career.

WORKING IN AMERICA: PROMISES BROKEN AND EXCEPTIONAL GAINS

It can be said that how one sees the show has much to do with where one sits in the theater. The same is true of the 2001–2007 business and employment cycle analyzed by Mishel, Bernstein, and Shierholtz (2008), in which they identified five dominant and emerging themes: strong growth in productivity; weak growth of jobs; stagnant or falling real household income for families; increasingly unequal distribution of the benefits of economic growth; and increased income immobility produced by the previous factors. Those at the very top 10% of the income ladder reaped 90% of all the growth from 1986–2006. For the top 1%, income more than tripled while the bottom half of the top 10% income grew 32%.

Much of the upheaval contributing to such bifurcated income distribution can be attributed to what O'Toole and Lawler (2006) identified as low-cost operators, global competitor corporations, and high-involvement companies. To keep goods and services prices as low as possible, managers of *low-cost companies* developed a business model focused on continuously reducing all operation costs. *Global competitor corporations* are agile, global "wave-riders" that move products, services and capital, jobs, operations, and people quickly and frequently across time zones and continents. Egalitarian workplace organizations with few class distinctions between managers and workers, called *high-involvement companies,* offer employees challenging and enriched jobs, a say in managing their own tasks, and a commitment to low turnover and few layoffs. O'Toole and Lawler reported on how these three kinds of organizations were managed and the consequences they created for American workers, the nation's economy, and society. Their analysis suggested the following themes essential to understanding workplace change and gaining insight to employment opportunities:

1. Insufficient creation of new "good jobs"
2. Increased choice and risk for workers
3. Increased influence of competitive and economic drivers
4. Increased tension between work and family life

5. Mismatch between skills and business needs

6. Increased social stratification based largely on educational attainment

7. Changing nature of careers

8. Reduction in community and commitment

9. Shortcomings of the health care system

10. The boomer demographic imperative

11. Unrealized opportunities to make more efficient use of human capital (pp. 14–18)

Incorporating the nature of such changes at the local level and understanding globalization's impact on careers can shape an advisor's ability to provide sound career advising.

GLOBALIZED CAREERS

Globalization means many things and can have an impact on college graduates' careers much more than they anticipate. Increasingly, globalization is debated in terms of "zero sum" whereby one person loses a job and one gains one, or "the expanding pie" notion whereby if one person gains, then prices, profits, and jobs expand however unequally. Regardless, experts agree that globalization is a reality that touches all careers. Sirkin, Hemerling, and Bhattacharya (2008) described how rapidly developing economies such as those of India and China have changed global business from a "one-way street" benefiting Western multinationals to a two-way competition in which blending the best of the East with the best of the West is the winning formula.

Most significantly to advising, globalization continually influences curriculum design, internships and field experiences, study and travel abroad options, and career opportunities. Conscientious career advising helps students evaluate their opportunity costs as they consider these options. Insight into the relationship among globalization, success attributes, and career opportunities is a highly valued competency of academic advisors.

Globalization reduces the time, location, and shelf life of all competitive advantages and career assets necessitating that "countries and workers need to find new ways to round off the edges of globalization and to ensure national economic vitality and social cohesion" (Stern, 2006, p. 24). Table 2.1 presents four examples useful in understanding globalization in practical terms: capital mobility, direct foreign investments, instant communication, and technology diffusion (Feller & Whichard, 2005).

Generally, economic globalization refers to free trade, free capital flows, the diffusion and transfer of technology among producing and consuming nations, international financial mechanisms, and financial trade regulations. As a result, national economies have become integrated through trade, direct

Table 2.1. Globalization Examples

Capital Mobility	Money moves around the globe 24/7. Excess capital navigates the globe 24/7, allowing investors to get the best possible interest rates and venture capital to connect with innovative added-value ideas regardless of the next boom or bust location.
Direct Foreign Investments	Because stock markets are accessible internationally, one never really knows who owns what company. Companies are bought and sold frequently, and with their branch offices across multiple countries in multiple towns, in multiple time zones, it is often difficult to determine in which country a company resides.
Instant Communication	Through access to the World Wide Web, electronic communication can be in "real time." Auctioned off to the highest bidders, satellites traveling around the globe report international events as they happen. Just as Desert Storm was broadcast live through CNN, any citizen with access to electronic communication experienced the "thrill of victory and the agony of defeat" at the same time as Olympic athletes. If something is discovered at Colorado State University today, it can be introduced in Beijing tonight.
Technology Diffusion	Technology can go anywhere that a literate user can take it. If one is technophobic, technologically illiterate, or unaware of the latest technological advance, one faces an uncompromising "digital divide."

foreign investment (by corporations and multinationals), short-term capital flows, international flows of workers and humanity, as well as technology (Thurow, 1999).

For many students and advisors, globalized careers initially translated into sending manufacturing and low-skilled jobs to low-wage countries, with the expectation that college completion ensured the acquisition of obtaining a secure high-wage and high-skill career. It is increasingly understood that almost any work completed at any skill level can be completed outside the U.S. workplace, often at a lower wage. Most recently, globalization has been described as an issue of power and rank in the global conversation. Zakaria's (2008) central thesis is that although the United States still has many unique assets, "the rise of the rest," including China, India, Brazil, and even small non-state actors, is creating a world in which many other countries are slowly moving up to America's level of economic strength. Zakaria suggests that America's research universities, free markets, and diversity of human talent compensated for low savings rates, an absence of a health care system, or any strategic plan to improve competitiveness. With the best of the rest of the world's employees running fast, working hard, saving well, and thinking long term, the "nervously employed" (Feller & Whichard, 2005) U.S. worker faces a unique and eroded position in the world marketplace.

Rothkopf (2008) argues that the influence of nation-states waned, leaving the system of addressing global employment ineffective. Thus, a power void created room for a new global elite, or what Feller and Whichard (2005) call "knowledge nomads," ably suited and agile enough to succeed on the global stage and often influencing global outcomes more than designated leaders and elected governments. Global elites include business, finance, and technology titans; media masters; and creators and communicators of value-added ideas who are skilled in reaching mass markets.

Risk abounds within globalized careers. Risk is natural when considering the magnitude of the implied changes such careers bring to the workplace. Cultural beliefs and values are in question, economic vitality and security are moving targets, few accepted international regulations exist, and new technology proliferates overnight. In combination, these changes seem daunting to students and most advisors. Yet navigating the globalized workplace demands engaging in careers that require risk to initiate "the innovation, incentives and imagination that carry the world forward" (Yergin & Stanislaw, 2002, p. 417).

CONVERTING RISK AND INSECURITY TO SATISFACTION

Exposing relationships among opportunities, risk, and satisfaction is a valued way to explain advising outcomes regardless of campus size, location, or type. Opportunities abound for students able to learn, understand, evaluate, and access them. Weighing the risks and trade-offs of decisions is required to consciously integrate academic and career advising that leads to satisfaction.

High-quality advising is driven by advisors who understand the context of choices and can ably explain relationships among factors that create learning and work opportunities. Figure 2.1 illustrates key elements and interactions that shape how learning and work relationships are changing.

Global economic integration and competition (Box 1 in Figure 2.1); technical innovation, satellite, and broadband transmission (Box 2); and demographic shifts (Box 3) are the primary driving forces in the evolving workplace (Feller, 1997; Feller & Whichard, 2005). The implications are significant and create a need for a more flexible, integrated, and efficient "learning system" (note Box 14) that services more diverse learners in a wider variety of settings.

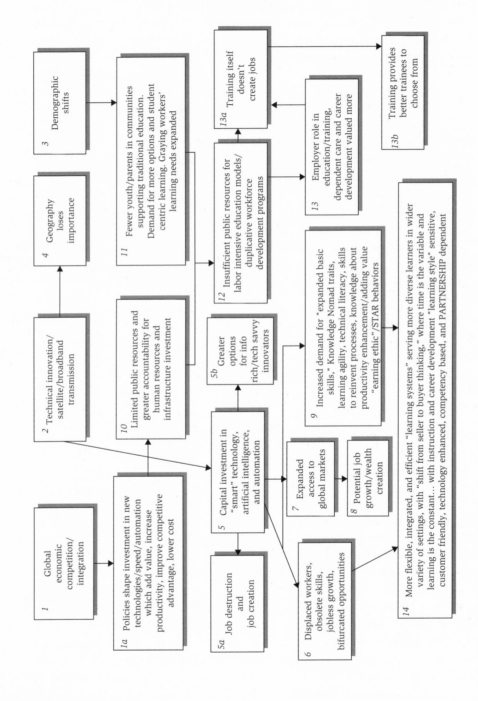

Figure 2.1 The Evolving Workplace: Implications Chart.

Learners now want programs accessible in real-time and distant formats. Instruction (including instruction to facilitate career development) must become increasingly learning-style sensitive, customer friendly, technologically enhanced, competency based, and partnership dependent.

As implied in Figure 2.1, when the workplace changes so must curriculum design, instructional delivery, and instructional styles. Consider the following implications of the evolving workplace and learning realities:

1. The best jobs are filled by those who can manipulate symbols, scan and comprehend reading material quickly, and write (communicate) persuasively and technically; are part science, technology, engineering, and math (STEM) expert and part marketing specialist; are technically savvy; are those who see challenges as problems to be solved; and have convincing intrapersonal and interpersonal skills that can attract, motivate, and inspire followers.

2. Opportunities to learn are everywhere. The obstacles of time and place no longer exist, as learners can access educational opportunities any time and any place in multiple formats.

3. Professors can no longer "own" content, nor compete with technology's appealing dissemination of information.

4. Technological dissemination means that instruction is becoming more student-centric, encourages cooperative learning, stimulates (ironically) student–teacher interaction, and helps students take greater responsibility for learning.

5. Since information drives the workplace, the timeliness of workers' information affects their ability to add value. Accessing, evaluating, and disseminating information via the Internet provides unlimited "learning on demand" opportunities.

6. Flexible, efficient, readily accessible, and customer-friendly learning opportunities are typically becoming competency based and partnership dependent.

As programs are influenced by feedback from professional and faculty advisors, staff are challenged to help students understand uncertain times to prepare for postgraduation employment and career transitions. A defining task for advisors is to align an advisee's occupational and educational goals with the required level of education (e.g., course, certificate, associate's or bachelor's degree). A more difficult task is the evaluation of the relationship among present motivation, internal and external resources, and a student's sense of urgency and time frame. Indebtedness, the relationship of program strength and placement, and student capacity to persevere must be rigorously assessed. Conversations lacking critical thinking about the "how and why of education proposition" (Figure 2.2) prove costly to advisees.

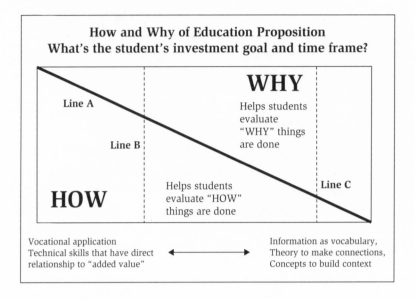

Figure 2.2 The How and Why Education Proposition.

The How and Why Education Proposition

This schema of the How and Why Education Proposition suggests how the varied types and purposes of education relate to different outcomes. As students understand this proposition, the trade-offs among programs can be articulated and evaluated. Especially when CNNMoney.com (Wang, 2008) asks, "Is College Still Worth the Price?" and reports that "Costs are soaring twice as fast as inflation, even as salaries for graduates are falling. Is it time to examine the old belief that college is worth whatever you can pay?"

The "how" within learning tends to focus on vocational goals, technical skills, and direct application to "added value." This kind of education helps students evaluate "how things are done." (Note the area below Line A.) The "why" of learning illustrated above Line A helps students evaluate "why" things are done. The "why" tends to focus on the vocabulary and language of material being taught, theories, and connections of concepts that build content and structure to convert information to knowledge.

For illustrative purposes, Line B notes a program constructed with a larger proportion of a "how" than a "why" orientation. These courses, programs, or majors typically are shorter in length or lean toward more "hands-on" or experiential learning. Line C suggests courses, programs, or majors with a larger proportion of "why" and small degree of "how" that are typically longer in length, described as more passive and professor led, and content- and information-rich forms of learning. As students evaluate their goals, time frames, and learning options by using this schema, they are better prepared to make decisions about level of personal and financial commitment to courses, certificates, or degree programs.

Advising plays a significant role in supporting a rigorous and relevant education when curriculum choices, in and out of class activities, and faculty encouragement and feedback reinforce student goals. Gordon (2008) stated:

Research has shown that students understand and retain knowledge best when they have applied it in a practical and relevant setting. An instructor who relies on lecturing does not provide students with maximum learning opportunities. According to the International Center for Leadership in Education (n.d.), relevance is critical if we want to get students to rigor. Relevance can create the conditions and motivation needed for students to make a personal investment in rigorous work for optimal learning. Students are more likely to invest more of themselves, work harder, and learn better when the topic is connected to something that they already know and in which they have interest. (p. 322)

Rigor and Relevance Framework

The Rigor and Relevance Framework (Figure 2.3) developed by the International Center for Leadership in Education (n.d.) is a tool developed to examine curriculum, instruction, and assessment. It is based on two dimensions of higher standards and student achievement.

First, there is the Knowledge Taxonomy, a continuum based on the six levels of Bloom's Taxonomy (Bloom, Engelhart, Furst, Hill, & Krathwohl, 1956), which describes the increasingly complex ways in which people think. The low end involves acquiring knowledge and being able to recall or locate that knowledge. The high end labels the more complex ways in which individuals use knowledge, such as taking several pieces of knowledge and combining them in both logical and creative ways.

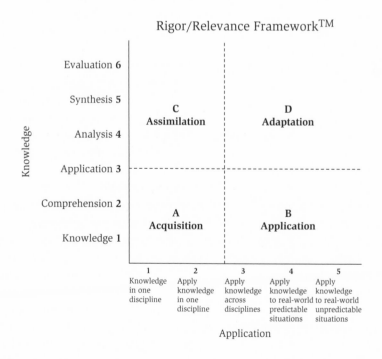

Figure 2.3 Rigor and Relevance Framework.

Source: ©International Center for Leadership in Education, www.leadered.com

The second continuum, known as Application, is one of action. Its five levels describe putting knowledge to use. While the low end is knowledge acquired for its own sake, the high end signifies use of that knowledge to solve complex real-world problems and to create unique projects, designs, and other works for use in real-world situations. The Rigor/Relevance Framework has four quadrants. Each is labeled with a term that characterizes the learning or student performance at that level. The following presents descriptions of each quadrant:

- Quadrant A—Acquisition: Students gather and store bits of knowledge and information and are primarily expected to remember or understand this knowledge.

- Quadrant B—Application: Students use acquired knowledge to solve problems, design solutions, and complete work. The highest level of application is to apply knowledge to new and unpredictable situations.

- Quadrant C—Assimilation: Students extend and refine their acquired knowledge to be able to use that knowledge automatically and routinely to analyze and solve problems and create solutions.

- Quadrant D—Adaptation: Students have the competence to think in complex ways and to apply their knowledge and skills. Even when confronted with perplexing unknowns, students are able to use extensive knowledge and skill to create solutions and take action that further develops their skills and knowledge.

The How and Why of Education Proposition and the Rigor and Relevance Framework provide useful insights as advisors attend to workplace insecurities and educational investment risks that influence student decision making. Integrating these two viewpoints with Feller and Whichard's (2005) career observations can provide support and insights to career advising. They noted the following:

1. Job security as previous generations knew it is a thing of the past.
2. The bar has been raised for achieving livable wages in all industries.
3. All work is best understood as "problems to be solved."
4. Excellence comes from using one's strengths (which are *not* field specific but applicable in any work, role, or activity).
5. What and when one studies is more important than where one goes to school.
6. "Knowledge nomads" are increasing in numbers, and can be found worldwide, responding to the highest bidder for skill sets and competing against world wages.
7. Paternalistic company loyalty decreases as profits are determined more and more by a worker's ability to translate the timeliness and currency of what they know into added value.

8. How one enhances, or adds value to an organization is how one's contributions and benefits are judged and rewarded.

9. Employee loyalty is increasingly tied to organizational climate, the opportunity to learn new skills, and a sense of engagement.

10. Job security decreases as the availability of lower cost worldwide labor becomes accessible.

11. Gainful, fulfilling employment means demonstrating behaviors that propel workers from average to STAR producers, and demonstrating learning agility on a daily basis.

12. The "psychology of earning" ethic (in which one needs to earn one's work relationship) is challenging the "entitlement ethic" (in which one feels entitled to future options because of past performance) in work relationships.

13. Accepting that change is normal and never ending requires gaining the emotional skills to manage continuous transitions.

14. Defining oneself as more than a job title is necessary to hold a healthy identity.

15. Understand the paradox of relinquishing security to gain freedom.

16. Recognize the trade-offs tied to both "workaholism" and balance.

17. Seeing oneself as consultant or "free agent" in charge of one's own careers is a healthy and empowering work identity.

As advisors advocate for curriculum innovation and schemas that explain the types and purposes of education and promote rigor and relevance, students can reframe program options in ways that convert risk to satisfaction. Challenging beliefs and assumptions about academic advising complements the advisor's role as a "futurist" with special expertise and insights about the evolving workplace.

CAREER AND ACADEMIC ADVISING: EXAMINING BELIEFS AND ASSUMPTIONS

Changing employer needs, although dynamic and unscientifically forecast, require a higher level of worker readiness. Consequently, assumptions about career and academic development need periodic assessment. As with any major social, economic, or educational shift, professional advisors and faculty are expected to tailor their skills to suit the times. Shifting assumptions have an impact on how advising is provided and received. Building on Feller and Whichard's (2005) work, Table 2.2 compares traditional assumptions to what are seen as emerging assumptions pivotal to career advising.

Challenging assumptions offers advisors ways to reframe how they conduct their work. Such efforts can lead to more effective ways of fostering

Table 2.2. Comparison of Traditional to Emerging Advising Assumptions

Dimension	Traditional Assumptions	Emerging Assumptions
Advising	Advising sessions focus on pointing students toward particular course options.	Advising sessions discuss courses and integrating learning outcomes to career plans.
Career advising	Major emphasis is on labor market information.	Emphasis on skills, attitudes, EQ, character, and the power of students' future sense.
Educational contexts	Instructional design and delivery do not matter; "teach to the middle" and all students will progress. *Seat time* is constant and learning is the variable.	Students do not learn in the same way, time frame, or with the same physical and emotional structures. Honor differences so that *learning* is constant and time the variable.
Pedagogy	Students commit bits of knowledge to memory in isolation from practical application; academics are important in and of themselves.	Effective teaching/learning motivates students to connect knowledge content with the context of application, developing and utilizing the "thinking brain"; problem-solving and decision-making skills are promoted.
Classroom learning	Success in learning across the curriculum illustrates mastery and real-world skills and work experience distracts from academic rigor.	Opportunities to gain real-world skills and experience complement the academic curriculum. Experience in the form of internships, externships, or other field experiences provide "real world" feedback. Internships reveal the nuance and atmosphere of particular disciplines and provide field specific networks and evaluation.
Exploration in college	College is not meant for exploring, and career maturity means having a designated major.	College is a great place to explore majors because of its high volume of majors to choose and sample.

Undergraduate mentorship	Many undergraduate students rely on advisors to provide guidance in knowledge needed as they progress through their studies and into a career. Advisors may have little to no recent industry experience or insight to employer needs.	Advisors need to connect advisees to university resources to transition to the global workplace. At least one person should continually monitor individual journeys, possible pathways, and professional development.
Career decision making	Anchoring is reinforced by the classic question asked by many college students to a career advisor, "What can I do with a major in…?" Anchoring, the affinity to rely greatly, or "anchor," on one piece of information when making decisions, creates dependency rather than shared relationship with academic major. Students believe that if they make a decision about what to study, it sets up career success after graduating.	Planned happenstance requires individuals to curiously explore new learning opportunities, to persist despite setbacks, to meet changing attitudes and circumstances with flexibility, to optimistically view opportunities as possible, and to risk being proactive in the face of uncertain outcomes. This helps individuals develop skills to recognize, create, and use chance or unexpected events.
Accessing career information	Learn about careers independently; the key to success is for students to learn to write their own ticket; they need to make it on their own.	Access allies and become an ally; people progress as much by whom they know, and who knows them, as on what they know.
Use of electives	Use electives to deepen knowledge in major area of study.	Elective courses are important for skill development and building knowledge. International/global studies, technology, public speaking, business communication, and foreign languages are highly recommended.
Education to work transitions	Education-to-work transition is the bridge that connects classroom to employers.	Education-to-work transition is strengthened through academic learner outcomes and career development competencies in college and follows nonlinear events which connect classrooms to employment and workplace induction.

(Continued)

Table 2.2. (*Continued*)

Job skills acquisition	Learn while in the classroom, then one's career will be assured; postsecondary degrees are fundamental to success.	Learning is lifelong and everywhere; acquire informal and formal learning. More than half of all jobs require short to moderate training.
Importance of GPA and academic major	Employers hire based on GPA and specific academic major.	Employers hire based on a candidate's strengths, skills sets, and passion for product line, industry, or sector. (Note: Increased numbers of employers are willing to train the "right" candidate rather than exclusive major recruiting.)
Interviewing process	Trait-factor approach and matching for "fit" process.	Behavioral interviewing is standard. Global culture and diversity, leadership, communication skills, organizational management, project management, and ethical competencies need to be documented.
New hire factors	Academic training supersedes all other factors.	Documented leadership and "soft skills" are growing in importance.
Job longevity	Secure jobs do exist; find companies where this has proven true and stick with them and rewards will follow.	Security comes from the ability to anticipate, make, and manage changes; change is the only constant.

students' career and academic development. The list of emerging assumptions encapsulates

1. What is known about pedagogy from the science of cognition
2. The importance of education's role in developing "social capital" and character development through what some have called "apprenticeships to adulthood" and "apprenticeships in democracy"
3. The emergent worker skills needed for success in the changing workplace
4. The need for hope when deciding career goals in uncertain times
5. The value of beginning advising activities early in the educational experience
6. The redefinition of education-to-work as a process rather than an event
7. A new vision for advising programs
8. A new way to redirect career exploration and transition

Those advocating career preparation at the expense of preparation for life roles and social capital are urged to consider the emerging roles of citizen engagement in sustainable and peaceful communities. Those convinced that the market-driven global economy enhanced by technology and entrepreneurship is the only way to prosperity, democracy, and security are encouraged to consider the vision of a civil society or a society committed to "the values of community, faith, responsibility, civic virtue, neighborliness, stewardship, and mutual concern for each other" (Yankelovich, 1999, p. 202). Further, higher education institutions of all types and levels have a role in helping students develop the character needed to resist ploys leading to corporate scandals and political corruption that undermine institutional trust, ethical workplaces, and community building. Academic and career plans need to include academic and technical skills and lessons in democracy (Goodlad, 2002), activities to promote developmental assets (Search Institute, 1997), and opportunities to become self-reliant career managers (Jarvis, 2003).

Taking a global view of career advising and the emerging assumptions driving it is necessary and invigorates advisor professional development. A key professional development competency for advisors and faculty is to challenge the notion that career planning is a logical and linear activity. "Planned happenstance," as Mitchell, Levin, and Krumboltz (1999) argued, includes both an attitude that students gain and actions they take. This view can help advisees create opportunities by taking action on curiosity and chance events.

PLANNED HAPPENSTANCE TO INTENTIONAL CONNECTIONS

If academic and career development does not always follow a logical and linear sequence, then the conventional decision theory of matching major to a career field needs to be reconsidered. Changing one's mind is an essential skill in the future (Gelatt, 1989). "Planned happenstance" requires students to exercise curiosity to explore new learning opportunities, to persist despite setbacks, to meet changing attitudes and circumstances with flexibility, to optimistically view new opportunities as possible and attainable, and to take risks by being proactive in the face of uncertain outcomes (Mitchell et al., 1999). Planned happenstance theory advocates that people be active in initiating contacts with people and in learning from a wide variety of sources throughout their lives. As the case study below illustrates, embracing happenstance opens doors not seen as open.

Case Study of Maria

Maria is a 21-year old Hispanic American female who met with her advisor three times since enrolling at a medium-sized state university. She entered majoring in geology because she did well in science and cared deeply about the development of the West. When large unengaged classes failed to capture her attention, and as her grades declined, she switched to "undeclared." After holding retail jobs this past summer, she floundered into her junior year, planning to finish college but with no plans after that. She likes to write and has thoughts about working as a journalist or a researcher. Little satisfaction with her advising session just before the holiday was reflected in resistance to complete an interest assessment and discomfort with the pressure to select an academic major. She was startled when a faculty member asked, "Do you think it is worth staying in school considering the debt you are taking on?"

Over semester break Maria stayed with her roommate's family in Colorado. During the visit her family showed Maria how they have a greener, more efficient home after a recent renovation according to ecological principles. Maria began to ask questions of the family about sustainability. They recommended a couple of Web sites and magazines to explore. Having competed some reading and research, Maria came across a course on sustainable landscaping, which is part of a bachelor of science in sustainability. Not content with only studying the interaction of environmental, economic, and social systems, Maria joined a student organization called "For a Greener Future," and recently led an initiative on community composting. She entered her most recent advising session with a newfound excitement about college and was eager to discuss the trade-offs of pursuing majors related to sustainability.

Today's students want and seek more from an advising experience than planning schedules. Advisor-advisee relationships need to engage students in discussions and reflection of current career issues—especially as they relate to coursework, family, intercultural experience, and research or creative work interests. Advisors need to encourage students "to think more about causes and less about careers" as they craft their career identity.

The phenomenally successful and first "manga" business book for the American market (Pink, 2008) provides testimony to the value of engaging students in new and creative ways. Pink advises students that no matter what their career path looks like, they should follow six promising career tips: (a) there is no plan . . . do things because you think they are valuable; (b) think strengths not weaknesses; (c) it's not about you . . . it's about adding value; (d) persistence trumps talent; (5) make excellent mistakes; and (e) leave an imprint.

Making connections between in and out-of-class experiences is a developmental task frequently undervalued. According to Amundson's (2006) "crisis of imagination," dynamic advising reinvigorates the imagination by creating new possibilities and structures by encouraging the use of multiple perspectives.

Rather than focusing on linear and "either-or" thinking about college majors, there is the acceptance of ambivalence, intuition, and flexibility and the recognition that in many instances problems need to be approached from a "both-and" perspective (Amundson, 2006). The power of integrating career and academic advising rests in helping students make connections among their experiences (planned and unplanned) in ways that encourage reflection on what students learned and how they grew through each experience. As insight to deeper motivations grow, students connect to their passions and find direction to the problems they care most about solving in their worklife.

Working on solving problems related to student interests connects them to like-minded peers, faculty mentors, potential internship opportunities, graduate fellowships, and the hidden job market. As advisors encourage students to see all learning experiences as laboratories to learn skills and promote work as problems to be solved, the advisor-advisee relationship grows richer. Highly engaged advising relationships offer the potential for students to identify, develop, and apply skills and success attributes noted in Table 2.3.

Table 2.3. Skill Development and Application from Advisor-Advisee Relationship

Skill	Examples of Application of Skill
Decision making	Choosing or changing a major; selection of courses, minors, and extracurricular activities.
Working through difficult situations	Completing challenging classes, not withdrawing from a course at the first sign of trouble, seeking tutoring or mentoring, resolving conflicts with other students on project teams, and being an advocate for themselves.
Accountability	Project management, timeliness of completed work, class attendance, and follow-though.
Engaging in lifelong learning	Learning for learning's sake, planning for graduate study, research skills, and learning across a lifespan. The ability to learn on one's own is a desirable employment skill of the future.
Building working relationships	Especially with faculty (managers) and other students (coworkers) within a large and ever-changing environment (university, organization, or company).
Performing with integrity	Doing what you say you will; developing a reputation for honesty and consistency.
Navigating beyond barriers and boundaries	Taking courses outside of a specific major, studying abroad, joining a student or professional organization, and even working part-time while in school.

SKILL SHORTAGES AND SUCCESS ATTRIBUTES

Zogbe (2008) suggests that the American Dream is itself in transition and rapidly being redefined by four meta-movements: living within limits as consumers and citizens; embracing diversity of views and ways of life; looking inward to find spiritual comfort; and demanding authenticity from the media, leaders, and leading institutions. Defining success is no easy task. It is both personally value driven and highly contextual.

Whereas Erickson (2008) offers a different lens about Gen Xers' happiness at work, Handel (2005) argues that it is unclear how much of the skills-mismatch problem is a shortage of cognitive skills rather than an expression of employer dissatisfaction with effort levels of work-related attitudes. Handel questions whether any such problem extends beyond a transitory stage of young adults or some fraction of disadvantaged minorities. He alleges:

> [F]irm conclusions about the alleged skills mismatch are hampered by three problems: difficulties in ascertaining the job-relevant skills workers possess, an even more striking scarcity of information on the skills their jobs require, and problems relating the two kinds of evidence to one another. (p. 77)

As interest in the "creative class" grows, Florida (2002) suggests that organizations place greater importance on attracting talent who possess capabilities such as big-picture thinking and the ability to bring together disparate ideas to create new products and services. Casner-Lotto and Barrington's research (cited in Schramm, 2007) lists the top 10 knowledge and skills expected to increase in importance over the next five years (see Table 2.4).

Table 2.4. Top 10 Knowledge and Skills Expected to Increase in Importance over the Next Five Years

Rank	Basic Knowledge and Applied Skills
1	Critical thinking, problem solving
2	Information technology application
3	Teamwork, collaboration
4	Creativity, innovation
5	Diversity
6	Leadership
7	Oral communications
8	Professionalism, work ethic
9	Ethics, social responsibility
10	Written communications

With a different perspective, the National Academies of Science (2007), noted the rapid erosion in U.S. competitiveness in science and technology—and thus in the United States as a global economic leader. The National Academies cautioned that the U.S. position as a global leader may be abruptly lost without a greatly expanded commitment to achieving success in advanced education in science, technology, math, and engineering:

> In the 21st century, scientific and technological innovations have become increasingly important as we face the benefits and challenges of both globalization and a knowledge-based economy. To succeed in this new information-based and highly technological society, all students need to develop their capabilities in science, technology, engineering, and mathematics (STEM) to levels much beyond what was considered acceptable in the past. (p. 1)

Friedman (2005) argues that not enough young people in America's schools are now being educated or inspired about interest in advanced math, science, and engineering. "The education in American junior high schools, in particular, seems to be a black hole that is sapping the interest of young people, particularly young women, when it comes to the sciences" (p. 351).

However daunting a student's advising needs appear as he or she tries to ascertain the skills sets needed in the workplace, the advisor can be a student's best promoter by synthesizing student potential with market need. Such a responsibility requires expertise in scanning the best literature and engaging with employers from a wide range of industries and corporate cultures to identify success expectations. Exhibit 2.1 presents Feller and Whichard's (2005) assessment of "success attributes" needed at an employment and personal level regardless of specific technical skills. They propose the term "knowledge nomad" for a person who is

> in heightened demand, able to add value with intuition and agility anywhere and at any time. Their ability to maximize technology and negotiate databases surpasses the influences of time and geography as they produce and deliver on-demand excellence. And, as their name implies, these "Nomads" are increasingly loyal to their ideas, skill sets, and learning opportunities rather than to their temporary employer or company. (p. xvi)

To encourage discussion of these "success attributes," we offer 10 career advising questions for advisors to use in any session (Exhibit 2.2). We believe they effectively integrate career concepts within academic advising.

DEVELOPING ADVISING ACTION PLANS

Advisors naturally assume responsibility for building an alliance intent on identifying and developing student competencies needed for academic and career satisfaction and adjustment. Commitment to maximizing advisees' strengths, articulating concrete goals, and building action plans captures how

Exhibit 2.1. Success Attributes of Knowledge Nomads.

See self as project-based "free agent" rather than lifetime employee

Display high learning agility (perform well under first-time conditions)

Avoid routine and repetitive tasks and processes (which make one at-risk)

Comfortable with ambiguity (creating the new and different)

Seek intellectual stimulation to remain energetic and enthusiastic

Seen as a lifelong learner (use 27 learning strategies and habits of Lominger.com)

Scan media (papers, journals, Web sites, blogs) widely and efficiently

Neutralize negativity (reframe discounting language, situations, attitudes, and blame)

Use stress reduction methods (refuse to personalize failure and rejection)

Easily mobile (can geographically relocate, travel with grace)

Highly agile (readily adapt to new situations, local cultures, and languages)

Seek adventure and new experiments to gain insights and opportunities

Entrepreneurial in attitude and actions

Offer ideas as value-added propositions

See problems as growth opportunities

Think strategically (see system implications)

Quickly evaluate the quality of data

Accurately identify the core issues in a conflict

Welcome variety and diversity

Believe excellence is achieved by identifying and maximizing strengths

Believe greatness comes from disciplined thought and action

Continually apply needs analysis to move from current to "better"

Identify all gaps (or weakness) as development issues

Highly technically literate (can negotiate databases, creatively use multimedia tools)

Organized and comfortable with backward planning

Inspire others to experiment, consider options, and accept responsibility

Technically and functionally out-perform peers

Identify and form expert networks

Challenge traditional methods, systems, and thinking (ask, Why not?)

Do the "right" thing (make courageous choices considering impact on self and others)

Team player (lead and follow according to need)

Emotionally engaged without being overwhelmed

Focus energy to be action oriented and empathic

Identify options when blocked, challenged, or rebuffed

Seek authentic and assertive relationships (seek clarity of intent)

Understand STP (service/trade/profession) and special, specialized, anchored, and adaptable career options

Understand personal income–happiness and time–money relationships

Seek big picture

Seek significance as well as success

Seek to be the best for the world rather than the best in the world

Hold an attitude that craves improvement

advisors add value. Knowledge about systems that support the development of advising action plans is another key advisor competency.

Emerging advising assumptions challenge traditional beliefs about the competencies needed for navigating a career. Spawned by business leaders, attention to competencies has helped employees prepare for greater career satisfaction and improved performance, as well as interviews. Research notes that "to sustain superior performance, emotional competence matters—twice as much as IQ and technical skills combined" (Kivland & Nass, 2002–2003, p. 136). Dubois and Rothwell (2000) suggest that competencies are more enduring than jobs and are inherent to individuals rather than residing in the work employers do.

Exhibit 2.2. Ten Career Advising Questions for Any Session.

How can I help you . . .

1. discover what motivates you… what gets the best out of you?
2. become curious and innovative (entrepreneurial thoughts/ideas)?
3. get the people skills needed to work in teams (cooperate, inspire)?
4. get the oral skills you need to persuade or change another's attitude or opinion?
5. embrace technology (productivity)?
6. gain higher math and science competencies without "saying uncle"?
7. practice business writing (regardless of field, the more responsibility gained the more persuading others in writing and using documentation is valued)?
8. see education is a means to develop competencies not an end in itself (lifelong learning)?
9. read, travel, and experiment with new environments to see beyond present boundaries?
10. see that polished effort looks a lot like ability?

Strengths-based programs represent a recent development in career advising. Arguing that discovering and capitalizing on one's strengths increases the potential for excellent performance, as well as success in work and satisfaction in life. The StrengthsFinder, an online adult assessment within the *Now Discover Your Strengths* (Buckingham & Clifton, 2001), and its counterpart *StrengthsQuest: Discover and Develop Your Strengths in Academics, Career and Beyond* (Clifton & Anderson, 2002), helps identify 5 of 34 student strength themes. This feedback helps uncover dormant or neglected talents and serves as a foundation for goal setting and planning. In addition, Savickas (2003) offers a career adaptability framework to assess development delays and distortions in building human strengths and then offers interventions to build strengths needed to cope with newly encountered situations.

Lombardo and Eichinger (2002b) identified 67 competencies, falling into six factors or categories: strategic skills, operating skills, courage, energy and drive, organizational positioning skills, and personal and interpersonal skills. Their work (Lombardo & Eichinger, 2002a) provides a common language for assessing and developing individual competencies and strengths. It identifies 10 performance dimensions and 19 career inhibitors and stoppers, while proposing competencies in positive and straightforward language.

Students experience tension any time a gap exists between a vision of what they want and their current reality. Feedback about a mistake, failing at something important, or seeing a need to learn are examples of instances where gaps and consequent tension surface. Handled prudently, this tension can be used to motivate students to master competencies at higher levels of effectiveness. However, where and when it occurs is pivotal. Lombardo and Eichinger (2002a) stated, "The odds are that [tension leading to subsequent] development will be about 70% from on-the-job experience, working on tasks and problems; about 20% from feedback or working around good and bad examples . . . ; and 10% from courses and reading" (p. v). Moreover, they argue that feedback, even when informed, is not adequate by itself for advisee development.

Because tensions most often occur in situations in which advisors are not present, providing as many coping techniques and tools for skill mastery as possible that students can use outside of sessions allows them to maximize development opportunities. Lombardo and Eichinger (2002b) provided 10 "remedies" for overcoming skill weaknesses for each of the 67 competencies, 10 performance dimensions, and 19 career stallers and stoppers that advisors can process with students. Although it is understood that no student would be expected (or need) to be good at all 67 competencies at any one point, the need for all competencies tends to come into play over a career as positions, functions, and levels of responsibility change.

Such systems offer tremendous resources for advisors who are helping students enhance strengths, develop "middle skills" into strengths, remedy weaknesses, work on untested areas, or compensate for overused strengths. The secret of success seems to reside in continuously learning to do what one does not know how to do. This should be the basic tenet of any advising development plan.

Regardless of the student, good advising traits and strong working alliances (Bordin, 1979) are fundamental for successful advising outcomes. Bordin suggests three essential requirements to facilitate goal creation: (a) agreement between the student and the advisor on the outcomes expected, (b) agreement on the tasks involved to achieve the outcomes, and (c) commitment between the student and advisor on the importance of the outcomes and tasks to both of them.

Developing advising plans, like the progression of a career, is seldom a sequential, linear process. Students start and stop; reframe; and try out new thoughts, feelings, and behaviors as they explore feedback and options. One approach to help students articulate concrete goals is Figler's "1–2–3 career counseling" system. This approach (Figler & Bolles, 2007) submits three questions to be woven together throughout the entire advising process: (a) What do you want to do? (b) What is stopping you from doing it? and (c) What are you doing about it?

Understanding student career development, particularly age and stage, gender, and diversity issues, helps advisors negotiate the context within which goals are articulated. A useful acronym to guide goal selection, while keeping context in mind, is SMART. SMART proposes that goals should be kept *specific, measurable, achievable, realistic*, and *time* bound. Creating goals within the SMART framework assists the advisor in integrating the student's unique contextual issues into a manageable plan.

Helping students look inward, outward, and forward helps move them toward developing action plans. One strategy often employed is encouraging students to find "allies of support" to help keep them focused on completing tasks within the action plan. At times, the action phase will need to be modified and perhaps expanded. Advisors should be ready for such eventualities, preparing students for the necessary flexibility while recognizing their need for closure. Providing homework assignments, Web sites, and additional resources can keep students continuously engaged between sessions. Renewing student commitments, following time lines, focusing on the ultimate outcomes, and concretely measuring progress are all effective strategies for ensuring success throughout action planning.

SUMMARY

Being mediocre or without passion is not a good place to be in the evolving workplace. In a world with walls, when the United States dominated the world economy and yearly wage gains transferred to the middle class in line with productivity increases, "mediocrity could still earn you a decent living" (Friedman, 2005, p. 279). We have argued that the economy, the workplace, and the attributes of success have changed to such a degree that innovation and creativity within higher education and specifically advising must change to respond to meet new needs.

Advising is a great asset to any world-class higher education system. In challenging and transformative times, the importance of access to and value of sound career advising increases as educational consumerism grows among students and funding sources. Each year, bright and eager students enter campuses holding dreams, hopes, and future promise. For many, access and opportunity are highly probable due to pre-college familial resources, established social networks, and perseverance. But for an increasing majority of students, the relationship among higher education achievement, success, and career management is a matter of economic life and death.

As the increasingly competitive global workplace receives more college graduates, those receiving academic and career advising can better utilize their strengths and find greater opportunity to succeed and find satisfaction. As a result, the need to integrate academic and career advising has become indispensible. Demographic, economic, and skill-shortage trends demand that professional and faculty advisors shape curriculum, pedagogy, and learner outcomes if students are to demonstrate "responsibility at work" (Gardner, 2008) and have hope about "saving the world at work" (Sanders, 2008). In doing so, academic advisors will prosper as worthy activists advocating for the social opportunity, mobility, and responsibility required in a democratic society.

References

Amundson, N. (2006). Challenges for career interventions in changing contexts. *International Journal for Educational and Vocational Guidance, 6*, 3–14.

Bloom, B. S., Engelhart, M. D., Furst, E. J., Hill, W. H., & Krathwohl, D. R. (1956). *Taxonomy of educational objectives: Handbook I: Cognitive domain.* New York: David McKay.

Bolles, R. (2009). *What color is your parachute.* Berkeley, CA: Ten Speed Press.

Bordin, E. S. (1979). The generalizability of the working alliance. *Psychotherapy: Theory, Research and Practice, 16*, 252–260.

Buckingham, M., & Clifton, D. O. (2001). *Now, discover your strengths.* New York: Free Press.

Bush, G.W. (2008). *Bush: Bailout plan necessary to deal with crisis.* Retrieved September 25, 2008, from http://www.cnn.com/2008/POLITICS/09/24/bush.bailout/

Cappelli, P. (2008). *Talent on demand: Managing talent in an age of uncertainty.* Boston: Harvard University Press.

Christensen, C., Johnson, C., & Horn, M. (2008). *Disrupting class: How disruptive innovation will change the way the world learns.* Columbus, OH: McGraw Hill.

Clifton, D.O., & Anderson, E. (2002). *StrengthsQuest: Discover and develop your strengths in academics, career, and beyond.* Washington, DC: The Gallup Organization.

Creamer, D. G. (2000). Use of theory in academic advising. In V. N. Gordon, W. R. Habley, & Associates, *Academic advising: A comprehensive handbook* (pp. 18–34). San Francisco: Jossey-Bass.

Dubois, D., & Rothwell, W. (2000). *The competency toolkit.* Amherst, MA: Human Resource Development Press.

Erickson, T. (2008). *10 reasons Gen Xers are unhappy at work.* Retrieved May 15, 2008, from http://www.businessweek.com/managing/content/may2008/ca20080515_250308.htm

Estrin, J. (2008). *Closing the innovation gap: Reigniting the spark of creativity in a global economy.* Columbus, OH: McGraw-Hill.

Feller, R. (1991). Employment and career development in a world of change: What is ahead for the next twenty-five years? *Journal of Employment Counseling, 28,* 13–20.

Feller, R. (1997). Redefining "career" during the work revolution. In R. W. Feller & G. Walz (Eds.), *Career transitions in turbulent times: Exploring work, learning and careers* (pp. 143–154). Greensboro, NC: ERIC/CASS.

Feller, R. (2003). Connecting school counseling to the current reality. *Professional School Counseling, 6*(4), ii–v.

Feller, R., & Whichard, J. (2005). *Knowledge nomads and the nervously employed: Workplace change & courageous career choices.* Austin, TX: Pro-ed.

Figler, H., & Bolles, R. (2007). *The career counselor's handbook.* Berkeley, CA: Ten Speed Press.

Florida, R. (2002). *The rise of the creative class: And how it's transforming work, leisure, community and everyday life.* New York: Perseus Books Group.

Friedman, T. (2005). *The world is flat.* New York: Picador.

Friedman, T. (2008). *Hot, flat, and crowed.* New York: Farrah, Straus and Giroux.

Gardner, H. (2008). *Responsibility at work: How leading professionals act (or don't act) responsibly.* San Francisco: Jossey-Bass.

Gelatt, H. (1989) Positive uncertainty: A new decision-making framework for counseling. *Journal of Counseling Psychology, 33,* 252–256.

Goodlad, J. (2002). Kudzu, rabbits, and school reform. *Phi Delta Kappan, 84*(1), 16–23.

Gordon, H. (2008). *The history and growth of career and technical education in America.* Long Grove, IL: Waveland Press.

Gordon, V. N. (2000). Meeting the needs of tomorrow's learners and tomorrow's workplace. In V. N. Gordon, W. R. Habley, & Associates, *Academic advising: A comprehensive handbook* (pp. 381–392). San Francisco: Jossey-Bass.

Gordon, V. N. (2006). *Career advising: An academic advisor's guide.* San Francisco: Jossey-Bass.

Hacker, J. (2006). *The great risk shift: The assault on American jobs, families, health care and retirement and how you can fight back.* New York: Oxford University Press.

Handel, M. (2005). *Worker skills and job requirements: Is there a mismatch?* Washington, DC: Economic Policy Institute.

Herman, R., Olivo, T., & Gioia, J. (2003). *Impending crisis: Too many jobs, too few people.* Winchester, VA: Oakhill Press.

International Center for Leadership in Education. (n.d.). *Rigor and relevance for all students: Rigor/relevance framework.* Retrieved July 22, 2008, from http://www.leadered.com/rigor.html

Jarvis, P. (2003, January). *Career management paradigm shift.* Paper presented at the National Consultations on Career Development annual convention, Ottawa, Canada.

Kao, J. (2007). *Innovation nation: How America is losing its innovation edge, why it matters, and what we can do to get it back.* New York: Free Press.

Kivland, C., & Nass, L. (2002–2003). Applying the use of emotional intelligence competencies: A business case report. *Career Planning and Adult Development Journal, 18*(4),136–160.

Krieshok, T. S. (2003, April). *The postmodern virtues of being an undecided major.* Paper presented at the 50th Anniversary Celebration of Counseling Psychology Accreditation at the University of Missouri, Columbia, MO.

Lombardo, M., & Eichinger, R. W. (2002a). *The career architect development planner.* Minneapolis, MN: Lominger.

Lombardo, M. W., & Eichinger, R. W. (2002b). *The leadership machine: Architecture to developing leaders for any future.* Minneapolis, MN: Lominger.

Mellow, G. (2008). *Each and all: Creating a sustainable American higher education system.* Retrieved September 16, 2008, from www.laguardia.edu/atwell

Mitchell, K. E., Levin, A. S., & Krumboltz, J. D. (1999). Planned happenstance: Constructing unexpected career opportunities. *Journal of Counseling & Development, 77,* 115–124.

Mishel, L., Bernstein, J., & Shierholtz, H. (2008). *The state of working America 2008–09.* Retrieved October 16, 2008, from http://www.stateofworkingamerica.org/

National Commission on Adult Literacy. (2008). *Reach higher, AMERICA: Overcoming crisis in the U.S. workforce.* New York: Author.

National Commission on Community Colleges. (2008). *Winning the skills race and strengthening America's middle class: An action agenda for community colleges.* New York: The College Board.

National Academies of Science. (2007). *Rising above the gathering storm.* Report from the Committee on Prospering in the Global economy of the 21st Century. Washington, DC: National Academies Press.

O'Toole, J., & Lawler, E. (2006). *The new American workplace.* New York: Palgrav Macmillan.

Palley, T. (2008, April 11). America's exhausted growth paradigm. *The Chronicle of Higher Education.* Retrieved on October 31, 2008, from http://chronicle.com/weekly/v54/i31/31b01001.htm

Pink, D. (2005). *A whole new mind: Moving from the information age to the conceptual age.* New York: Riverhead.

Pink, D. (2008). *The adventure of Johnny Bunko: The last career guide you'll ever need.* New York: Riverhead.

Rothkopf, D. (2008). *Superclass: The global elite and the world they are making.* New York: Farrar, Straus and Giroux.

Savickas, M. (2003). Toward a taxonomy of human strengths: Career counseling's contribution to positive psychology. In W. B. Walsh (Ed.), *Counseling psychology and optimal human functioning* (pp. 229–249). Mahwah, NJ: Erlbaum.

Sanders, T. (2008). *Saving the world at work: What companies and individuals can do to go beyond making a profit to making a difference.* New York: Random House.

Schramm, J. (2007). Workplace visions: Exploring the future of work. *Society of Human Resource Management, 1,* 1–8.

Search Institute. (1997). *The asset approach: Giving kids what they need to succeed.* Minneapolis, MN: Author.

Sirkin, H., Hemerling, J., & Bhattacharya, A. (2008). *Globality: Competing with everyone from everywhere for everything.* New York: Business Plus.

Stern, A. (2006). *A country that works.* New York: Free Press.

Thurow, L. (1999). *Building wealth: The new rules for individuals, companies, and nations in an knowledge-based economy.* New York: Harper Collins.

Wang, P. (2008). *Is college still worth the price?* Retrieved August 22, 2008, from http://money.cnn.com/2008/08/20/pf/college/college_price.moneymag/index.htm?postversion = 2008082214

Yankelovich, D. (1999). *That magic of dialogue.* New York: Touchstone.

Yergin, D., & Stanislaw, J. (2002). *The commanding heights: The battle for the world economy.* New York: Touchstone.

Zakaria, F. (2008). *The post-American world.* New Work: Norton.

Zogbe, J. (2008). *The way we'll be.* New York: Random House.

CHAPTER THREE

Career Advising Competencies

Eileen Mahoney

Academic advising has undergone a significant evolution over the past 20 years as a result of the changing needs and demographics of college students, increased institutional emphasis on persistence and gradua-tion, and the dynamic nature of the world of work (Cuseo, 2003; Gordon, 2006; Laird, Chen, & Kuh, 2008). The content of advising sessions evolved from a focus on academic progression to the inclusion of student develop-mental needs with an increasing emphasis on the relationship of academic endeavors to career opportunities. Gone are the days of advising that pri-marily required a college catalog, a course schedule, registration forms, and a departmental stamp. Today advising requires an extensive skill set and a wide array of informational resources. Advisors must be professionally nimble to weave the practical dissemination of information into the relational pro-cesses of assessment, exploration, and empowerment. This is especially true of career advising that requires a robust and diverse set of competencies.

This chapter focuses on the knowledge and competencies required for effective career advising. As context for that discussion, the chapter provides information on the changes in higher education and how they fueled the trend toward integrating career and academic advising. The foci of the chap-ter are the conceptual, informational, relational, and personal competencies required to engage in career advising with students. The conceptual compe-tencies are grounded in the theories associated with student development and career development, and the expectations and standards of the advising pro-fession (Habley, 1995; Nutt, 2003). Informational competencies are primarily knowledge based and examine the areas of institutional knowledge, technical skills, student assessment, occupational information, and employment skills (Habley, 1995; Nutt, 2003). Relational competencies address the importance of building rapport, conducting effective interviews, and influencing student development and behavior (Habley, 1995; Nutt, 2003). Personal competencies are the bedrock skills required to effectively function in the changing global work environment (McClellan, 2007b). These competencies provide a basis for career advising as an integral part of academic advising.

THE GROWING INTEREST IN CAREER PREPARATION

Every year, the Higher Education Research Institute (HERI) administers the Cooperative Institutional Research Program (CIRP) survey of first-year students. The data are part of a national longitudinal study sponsored by the American Council on Education to assess the characteristics of incoming freshmen (http://www.gseis.ucla.edu/heri/cirpoverview.php). The CIRP has been administered to over 400,000 entering students at 700 two-year colleges and four-year colleges and universities. One part of the survey is designed to examine students' motives for attending college. Over the past few years, a clear trend has developed in student responses when asked to rate their reasons for going to college. The following have consistently ranked as "very important" to first-year students over the past three years:

1. To be able to make more money
2. To learn about the things of interest
3. To be able to get a better job
4. To gain a general education and appreciation of ideas
5. To get training for a specific career
6. To prepare for graduate or professional school

Four of the six reasons for going to college relate to professional preparation and earning power, thus indicating that current college students perceive a strong link between education and career.

Although students are seeing education as a stepping stone to a successful career, they are also considering multiple education options and do more "shopping around" than students of previous generations. Institutions are faced with growing demands from students, parents, and legislators for accountability related to graduation rates and student success (Titus, 2006). This has led to increased interest in identifying variables that influence retention. Two factors that emerged as having an impact on student retention are academic advising and career development. When students' academic experiences are directly connected to their long-term career and life goals, their education is more meaningful and they are more likely to stay in school (Cuseo, 2003; Feldman, 2005; Kuh, Kinzie, Buckley, Bridges, & Hayek, 2007).

Connecting academic experiences with long-term career goals is not an easy process. The erratic global economy is creating unprecedented changes and challenges, making it hard to predict future employment prospects. According to Gordon (2006), "students today are entering a workplace that is unlike any other in . . . history. Globalization, downsizing, reengineering, and changing organizational structures have left the old workplace unrecognizable" (p. viii). These circumstances underscore the importance of teaching students to base decisions on a solid understanding of self and to adopt an attitude of flexibility when planning for the future.

These circumstances require students to plan with a long-term perspective the kinds of lives they want to live and people they want to be. They need to be encouraged to take advantage of the opportunities available in college to develop a foundation for continued growth and achievement throughout their lives. Encouraging them in this way leads to a thoughtful decision-making process. It supports exploration and evaluation prior to making a commitment and at the same time recognizes that the future will require new decisions and adjustments to their plans. Begley and Johnson (2001) describe this as "living an examined life," and make the case that advisors need to promote the value of reflection and lifelong growth when advising students.

INTEGRATION OF CAREER AND ACADEMIC ADVISING

Advising professionals seem to be embracing the goals of developing student potential and encouraging lives of purpose; however, advisors' responsibilities still involve sharing the nuts and bolts required to navigate a complex system of policies, processes, and curriculum requirements. Some of what makes advising challenging is that it requires the rote delivery of old information to new students while reserving time and space for meaningful interactions.

This chapter is presented from the perspective that career advising requires competencies associated with both prescriptive and developmental advising. Prescriptive interactions traditionally treat advising as a relationship between expert and novice (Crookston, 1972) with an emphasis on the dissemination of information to facilitate and expedite students' progress toward degree completion (Jeschke, Johnson, & Williams, 2001). Developmental advising is a holistic approach to student interactions that encourages self-awareness, independence, and intentional decision-making (Frost & Brown-Wheeler, 2003). The relationship between advisor and advisee is one of shared responsibility that results in learning and growth for both the advisor and the student (Crookston, 1972). Advisors encourage students' exploration of values, interests, and abilities to increase their understanding of themselves and their potential. This exploration and understanding is then linked to decision making and goal setting.

Career advising has traditionally been viewed as distinctly different from career counseling and employment services (Gordon, 2003, 2006). There is another paradigm emerging, however, in which career advising is more expansive and advisors may bring career assessment, job search strategies, and employment relations into their work with students. The competencies presented in this chapter can apply to both paradigms. In organizations where there has not been full integration of academic advising and career assistance, advisors will be making referrals rather than providing full service to the students.

CAREER ADVISING COMPETENCIES

Advisors that have evolved with the profession must now possess an impressive assortment of competencies to engage in career advising. A review of the Council for the Advancement of Standards in Higher Education (CAS, 2006) reveals three broad categories of advising competencies:

1. " . . . an understanding of student development, student learning, career development . . .

2. " . . . a comprehensive knowledge of the institutions program, academic requirements, policies and procedures . . .

3. " . . . an interest and effectiveness in working with and assisting students . . . " (p. 32)

   The knowledge and competencies required for advisors to address varied concerns and assist students at all levels of development can be daunting to new professionals. To mitigate this, advisor training programs often categorize advisor proficiencies into the following three content areas related to the CAS categories: conceptual, informational, and relational (Habley, 1995; Nutt, 2003). Another important content area for advising is personal competencies (McClellan, 2007b). These four content categories (conceptual, informational, relational, and personal) will be used to provide a structure for organizing and presenting career advising competencies.

CONCEPTUAL COMPETENCIES

Conceptual competencies provide a contextual framework for career advising activities. They offer the big picture point of view for advisors about why they do what they do. They provide an understanding of what advising is and the impact it can have on students. Conceptual competencies are also the starting place for developing a common culture for advising. Advisors should develop a working knowledge of the conceptual areas to inform their career advising.

Academic Advising Principles

At a basic level, advisors should understand that advising is not just a job but a profession. The National Academic Advising Association (NACADA) has made significant contributions to the profession by nurturing a cohesive organization that demonstrates pride in the work its members perform. Advisors need to be familiar with the defining principles of the profession.

The mission of advising. The NACADA Web site (http://www.nacada.ksu .edu) is an excellent resource for a national perspective on the mission of advising. Advisors need to be familiar with their institutional and departmental perspectives. The advising mission of an institution or department provides insight into the level of career expertise an advisor will be expected to perform. It will determine whether an advisor assists students with career exploration processes and employment strategies or refers them to other offices for those services.

Professional standards. The CAS (2006) Professional Standards for Higher Education is a good resource for standards for advising. For those advisors working in environments where career and academic advising are fully integrated, CAS also provides standards for career services.

Core values of academic advising. NACADA (2004) provides a statement of the values guiding the work of advising professionals. The Statement of Core Values delineates advisor responsibilities and establishes guidelines for advisor interactions with students and colleagues.

Student Development Theory

Being familiar with student identity development theories increases effectiveness because the theories can be used to explain and predict student needs, as well as influence student behavior. This information can then be used to develop programs or interventions (Evans, Forney, & Guido-DiBrito, 1998). There are a variety of student development theories, some of which are associated with specific populations, particular life stages, or distinct issues. The depth and breadth of developmental theory is vast; however, here are some examples of theories that offer pertinent information for career advising interactions.

Identity development. Chickering and Reisser (1993) presented a model of college student development that focuses on seven vectors of identity development that can be influenced by the campus environment. This theory provides a good overview of how college students develop intellectually, emotionally, socially, and ethically, and can provide advisors with greater understanding of the concerns that might manifest as students mature.

Intellectual development. Perry (1981) provides a theory of intellectual development that examines how traditional-age college students perceive the world and determine truth and meaning. His theory offers suggestions for creating learning situations that foster students' growth toward the next stage of their development. Perry's theory is valuable in providing insight in how students may move through the career decision-making process and how their expectations of advisors' role can change.

Transition theory. Schlossberg (1981) was one of the first theorists to concentrate on transition. Her theory examined how people experience transition and the factors that influence movement from being preoccupied with the transition to integrating the transition into their lives and moving forward in a positive way (Schlossberg, Lynch, & Chickering, 1989). Transition theory can increase advisor effectiveness with students experiencing life changes (e.g., incoming freshmen or graduating students who will be getting a professional job).

Career Development Theory

As noted previously, first-year college students report one of the main reasons for attending college is that they perceive a relationship between college experiences and career opportunities. This trend means that students desire and expect career planning assistance from academic advisors. Career development theories can provide advisors with the theoretical background to engage in career discussions and help facilitate students' career development.

Personality type, person-environment fit. Holland (1997) developed a career theory that is widely used and the bedrock for many career assessment instruments. It is an elegantly simple approach for categorizing personalities and work environments by using six different types (Realistic, Investigative, Artistic, Social, Enterprising, Conventional). Holland's theory can be easily understood and readily applied by advisors.

Cognitive information processing. Sampson, Reardon, Peterson, and Lenz (2004) developed a cognitive model of career decision making. Their approach does a good job of demystifying the career decision-making process. It offers a decision-making model (CASVE cycle) intended to enhance students' career decision-making and problem solving and "increase the likelihood of making effective career choices" (p. 25).

Values-based career decision making. Brown (1995) contributed a unique approach to career planning that emphasizes the role values play in career selection. Clarifying values can offer students "aha" moments when they are able to see that some of their struggles are the result of holding two seemingly incompatible values as equally important. It also can be instrumental in helping students separate their values from those of significant others in their lives.

Social learning and planned happenstance. Krumboltz (1983) developed a career decision-making approach based on social learning. He proposed that people develop a set of personal rules and beliefs as a result of learning that occurs in response to environmental influences and unexpected life events. Career decision making can be enhanced by clarifying personal rules and beliefs and understanding their effect on choices students make. Krumboltz and colleagues' later work focused on the idea of "planned happenstance" and the positive impact unexpected events can have on careers (Krumboltz & Levin, 2004; Mitchell, Levin, & Krumboltz, 1999). Often when assisting students with academic and career decisions, advisors ignore the reality that plans are frequently derailed by unexpected events. Planned happenstance offers strategies for creating and taking advantage of unexpected events and learning to embrace change for the new alternatives it offers.

Advising Competencies in Action: Student Development Theory

Expanding perspective through the mastery of conceptual competencies strengthens advisors' interactions with students. It can also have a positive impact on job satisfaction and professional confidence. The vignette of Darelle provides an example of a positive shift in perspective for one advisor after learning about student intellectual development.

Darelle has been hired to work in an office that advises first-year students—the majority of whom are 17- and 18-year-olds who have not yet declared a major. Darelle's own experience as an undergraduate was nontraditional. She did not start college directly after high school but worked for a few years and gained a sense of direction. She feels some frustration in her role as an academic advisor because she finds it hard to relate to many of her students.

Darelle's students typically come in the day before preregistration begins and say they need classes for next semester. When she asks them what classes they are considering, they say, "I don't know. What do you think I should take?" At this juncture, she asks questions about their interests or possible career goals. They often respond with a shoulder shrug and the question, "Can't you give me one of those tests that will just tell me what I should do?" She refers them to an online career decision-making program. When they come back with the results, she asks them what they think and they often respond with a comment such as, "Well. I don't know. It didn't really help that much. What do you think I should do?" She starts to think the students are lazy and apathetic and wonders whether she is in the wrong field.

One day in a staff training session, she is introduced to Perry's Theory of Intellectual and Ethical Development. She learns that first-year students often come in with a dualistic view of the world—thinking there are right and wrong decisions, being very afraid of being wrong, and looking to authority figures to tell them what the right decision is. She learns about the other stages of development typical for traditional-age college students and how she can facilitate growth and progression through the other stages. This knowledge changes Darelle's views about her students and improves the quality of her interactions. With the context of Perry's theory, she recognizes that students' hesitancy about making decisions is a normal indicator of their development and she is motivated to help them learn to be become more independent and confident decision makers.

INFORMATIONAL COMPETENCIES

Informational competencies and the knowledge associated with them are the pragmatic foundation for much of the work advisors perform. Advisors who provide career advising can be described as "knowledge workers" because they are required to learn, apply, and share vast amounts of knowledge crucial to student success (Freitag, 2008). Grasping informational competencies can seem a monumental task because of the breadth and depth of knowledge that advisors apply. Some informational skills are very concrete (e.g., institutional policies and technological proficiency); these are often the initial focus of advisor training programs because they can be learned and applied relatively quickly. Other areas of knowledge related to student assessment, occupational information, and employment information are more complex and may take longer to acquire.

Institutionally Specific Knowledge

There is a great quantity of detailed information specific to institutional policies and procedures. Much of this information may seem dull as it does not typically open interesting discussions, lead to helpful insight, or generate enthusiasm among students. However, it is vitally important in teaching students to navigate institutions, progress toward graduation, and prepare for employment.

Degree requirements and curriculum options. It is important to remember that curriculum requirements are related to learning outcomes. These outcomes are usually connected to job-specific knowledge or to transferable skills that have been identified as necessary to function effectively in diverse work settings, or to both. Advisors should be familiar with the goals of academic requirements so they can teach students to draw connections between academics and career preparation.

Dates and deadlines. Students need to learn to keep important dates on their radar because much of their academic success relies on meeting deadlines. Advisors are often good about reminding students of enrollment dates and drop deadlines, but it is equally important to share information specifically related to career advising (e.g., dates of career and job fairs and deadlines for on-campus interview registration).

Technological Competencies

Advisors need to be comfortable in using technology to obtain information and to communicate. The typical 17- or 18-year-old college students were born into the world of technology in which advisors have been slowly evolving. Thus, the majority of students are more advanced in digital communication than most professionals in higher education (Prensky, 2005). Students are moving steadily forward in expanding their use of technology as a way to stay connected to what is important to them. Advisors need to know how to effectively use technology to disseminate information and to engage students. The options for digital communication are vast, but at minimum, advisors should have the basic technological aptitudes and use related resources.

Student information systems. Most institutions use electronic data systems for student records and enrollment processes. Advisors need to be able to use these systems and show students how to use them to access course schedules, college catalogs, degree progress reports, and enrollment processes.

Online information. The information available on the Internet is infinite. Advisors need to bookmark local Web pages for campus services to which they make frequent referrals. They also need to know how to use search engines to access occupational information.

Digital communication. Traditional-age college students are very comfortable communicating via technology, and prefer using instant communication methods such as Instant Messenger (IM) and text messaging to e-mail or phone (Prensky, 2005). Social networking sites (e.g., Facebook) are also popular among students and are used as means of sharing information and forming relationships (Traxler, 2007). Students use e-mail but report that they do not use it frequently and consider it a more formal method of communication used for interacting with faculty and staff (Carnevale, 2006). At a minimum, advisors need to be able to use e-mail to communicate with advisees, but with the trend clearly moving toward the use of electronic environments (e.g., IM, Facebook, blogs, and Twitters), advisors would be well served to become comfortable in those venues as well (Carter, 2007; Lipschultz & Musser, 2007; Nutt, 2008).

Student Assessment

An important aspect of career advising is helping students identify their values, interests, and abilities. There are multiple ways to engage students in the self-assessment process, but the underlying goal is to identify themes in the ways students view themselves and interact with their environments. By examining their interests, the abilities they have demonstrated, and the values they hold important, students develop a set of criteria with which to evaluate potential careers.

Personality and interest inventories. Some of the most frequently used self-assessment inventories for career decision making are the Strong Interest Inventory, Holland's Self-Directed Search, and the Myers-Briggs Type Indicator (MBTI). There are also proprietary online programs such as SIGI III by Valpar and DISCOVER by ACT that are in use at institutions. Advisors need to be fully trained before using any of these instruments or products. The Strong Interest Inventory and the MBTI require some background in master's level coursework related to testing and assessment.

Self-assessment activities. There are numerous activities in career decision-making books and articles that can be used to engage students in self-assessment. Some advisors believe that the "low tech" self-assessment techniques are more meaningful to students than professional inventories because they require students to reflect on their lives and draw their own conclusions rather than looking to an external source for answers.

Advising Competencies in Action: Student Assessment

A commonly used assessment exercise involves asking students to reflect on previous accomplishments as a way to clarify their values, interests, and abilities.

The vignette of Jose provides an example of how an advisor used this method to help a student expand her career options.

Jose is meeting with Monica, a sophomore student who came to school with the goal of getting an accounting degree. She is half-way through her second attempt of an accounting class and reports that she is afraid she might have a D at midterm. Her grades in her other business classes are low Cs—a stark contrast to her 4.0 GPA in high school. When Jose asks Monica why she chose accounting, she tells him that she has always been good in math and a high school teacher said she would be a natural in accounting. Monica also says that she has an aunt who is an accountant and she makes "good money." Jose asks Monica whether there are other areas of study or careers that have been of interest to her. Monica says no—she always thought accounting was the right field until she discovered she hated her business classes, but she does not know what else she might do.

Jose suggests to Monica that she try something a little different—take on the task of investigator to discover whether there are some options she might be overlooking because she decided so early in high school that she wanted to be an accountant. He gives her the following homework assignment: "Write down 10 accomplishments or moments of great satisfaction from your past. The accomplishments or satisfying moments must be personally rewarding. They can be very small, private, and come from any point of your life—even childhood. The only criteria are that the accomplishments required effort and action from you and that they were memorably satisfying. After you finish your list, choose two or three of the events and write a detailed account of all you can remember related to that accomplishment."

Jose tells Monica that at their next appointment he is going to interview her and get as much information as he can about the events. He wants to hear every detail so that he can try to determine her interests, skills, and the things she considers important in life. Monica agrees to the assignment.

At their next appointment, Monica shares a description of a surprise party she held for her parent's twenty-fifth wedding anniversary. She arranged with friends of the family to use their house for the party, solicited their assistance in inviting her parents out on the evening of the event, sent invitations, prepared a budget, made decorations, ordered food, and managed parking and transportation so her parents would not see any cars. She says it was a great success, her parents were shocked, and they had a wonderful time.

Jose compliments her on the accomplishment and reflects the joy she exhibits in her narrative and then tells her he is going into an investigative mode and will ask many questions. He tells her he may be jotting down some notes about her answers so that he can remember any important points he wants to make. He then proceeds to ask a series questions to solicit details about the skills Monica used in planning the event such as: "How did you come up with the idea? How did you persuade people to help you? How did you figure out how much it would cost? What were the biggest challenges and how did you overcome them?" He also asks questions of her feelings related to the accomplishment as a way to identify possible value and interests. For example, "What made you think it was important to have this event? What is your favorite part of this story? What did you enjoy most?"

After Jose has finished an extensive list of questions, he tells Monica he will take a few minutes to summarize the feedback he wants to give her about what he thinks he learned about her. Before he shares his observations, he asks that she not respond to the ideas he shares until he has finished sharing all of it. He tells her he wants her to really listen to his comments and think about them. Jose then shares what he thinks he learned about her. After he finishes, Monica seems pleased with the observations and expresses some surprise that she has not realized some of this until now. She is eager to go on to another accomplishment.

After they go through the process a second time, Jose suggests that Monica examine the other accomplishments on her list in the detailed questioning manner he has modeled. He wants to see what else she can uncover about her values, interests, and skills. She agrees to do this and they schedule another meeting.

At their next session, Monica reports that she realizes she likes organizing and planning, is creative, and likes entertaining people and anticipating their needs. She says that she was telling a friend about this process and her friend said there was a hospitality major in business that offered a class on event planning. Monica says that another friend told her about someone who works on campus in student events and activities and would probably be willing to talk to Monica about his job. She is excited about doing some further investigating and seems well on her way to identifying new options.

Occupational Information

Students need to learn how to access occupational information to make informed decisions about how well career options match their personal profiles. This is not something they intuitively know how to do, so advisors must be able to demonstrate how to gather information from a variety of sources and use it in the decision-making process. Advisors should not strive to become a font of career information but rather develop the ability to find career information and teach that skill to students they advise (Figler & Bolles, 1999). There are numerous venues that advisors can use to bring occupational information into advising sessions.

Written resources. There are books and Web resources that are easily accessible. The *Occupational Outlook Handbook* published by the Department of Labor is a staple in career advising and available free online (http://www .bls.gov/oco/home.htm). *O*NET* (http://online.onetcenter.org/) is another free resource from the Department of Labor that has a wealth of information. A quick search on the Internet reveals other resources such as Web sites of professional organizations. Advisors should be able to show students how they can retrieve information so that students will be able to do research independently.

Informational interviewing. There is great value in having a real-life view of what a given occupation might be like. Students can gain insight from informational interviews with people in the jobs they are considering as well as by participating in job shadowing experiences, internships, part-time work, or volunteer activities (Figler, 1999). Advisors should familiarize themselves with the basic premise of informational interviewing and other methods of obtaining career information from professionals to coach students on how to connect with people and gather details.

Employment Knowledge

Advisors can enrich their interactions with students by providing them access to employment information. The ultimate goal of integrating career and academic advising is for students to be satisfactorily and successfully employed after completing their education. As a result, students and advisors need to know how to access employment opportunities.

Job postings. Many institutions have online listings, bulletin boards, or notebooks with local job openings. There are also numerous national job search engines available online, some of which are specific to professions. When possible, advisors should help students locate job vacancy listings on their campuses and demonstrate how to use the Internet to find job postings.

On-campus interviews and job fairs. Some institutions have regional and national recruiters visit campus to interview graduating seniors and students seeking internships. Advisors need to alert students to any opportunities available on their campuses.

Hidden job market strategies. Advisors understand that the majority of successful job searches require tapping into the hidden job market; that is, jobs that are not posted anywhere but are filled through word of mouth, networking, and people being in the right place at the right time. Students need to be prepared to tap into that market by having a good résumé, understanding how to effectively leverage relationships, knowing how to make a positive impression, and being able to articulate their skills to a potential employer. Advisors need to be competent in helping students successfully infiltrate the hidden job market. Advisors working in organizations that have fully integrated career services and advising services will need to be competent in résumé writing, interview practices, networking, and job search coaching. Advisors working in offices that do not include the employment aspects of career advising will need to know how to make appropriate referrals for employment assistance.

Advising Competencies in Action: Occupational Information and Employment Knowledge

Career advising can occur with students of all majors at any stage of their academic progression. The vignette of Lily provides an example that demonstrates how competencies related to occupational and employment information allowed an advisor to help a student change his outlook about work possibilities after graduation.

When Lily meets with Landon to select classes for the final semester of his under-graduate degree, she asks him what he wants to do with his business major. Landon admits he has no idea and is probably going to do seasonal work in his hometown after he graduates. He tells Lily he has never been engaged with his major but he selected it because he thought it would lead to a secure future. Lily notes his attitude of resignation and asks about his other interests outside of school. Landon tells her that he is very interested in graphic novels and comics. She asks more questions to better understand what it is about graphic comics that he finds appealing and eventually they discover he likes that the genre has a reputation for discovering new talent and publishing "underground, undiscovered" authors and artists. Landon tells Lily that he particularly likes one independent magazine that showcases these artists. He says he would love to work for that magazine.

Lily suggests that Landon contact the publisher of that magazine to express his interest in the area and to conduct an informational interview with someone at the magazine. She shows him a Web site explaining what informational interviewing is and offers to help him develop a strategy for identifying and contacting several other magazines of the same type.

To prepare for informational interviews, she suggests he use the Internet as a resource to gain some background about employment in the publishing field. Together they look at *O*NET* for "magazine publishing" and review qualifications, education, and other relevant information. In the course of their conversation, Landon mentions he is an avid blogger, so Lily asks if there might be blogs related to graphic novelists, graphic comics, or independent publishing. Landon is enthusiastic about the idea and says he could explore it.

Landon mentions that he is planning to go to a comic book convention over the summer and Lily chooses the opportunity to talk about networking and how it can lead to jobs in the "hidden job market." She asks him if he has a résumé. He replies that he does not and tells Lily that he has never really conducted a job search.

Landon appears energized about the idea of learning more about the field of graphic literature and publishing but Lily knows that too much information can be overwhelming. She also recognizes that they got off track in selecting classes for his final semester. She reflects this to him and asks how he would like to proceed. He is uncertain so she suggests that they meet briefly later in the week to finalize his classes for next semester. She tells him she will e-mail the key points of their con-versation and suggests that they schedule a follow-up meeting to talk in more detail about the different ideas that emerged. Landon leaves Lily's office with more energy than he came in with and seems motivated about further discussions related to his postgraduation employment plans.

RELATIONAL COMPETENCIES

Interpersonal and communication competencies are the primary focus of rela-tional content. Good advising requires the ability to establish relationships that promote a climate of mutual respect. If an advisor fails to develop relational abilities, the advising relationship is vulnerable to ineffectiveness. Even if interactions are brief and of a practical nature, good relational competencies will leave the student feeling confident with the information received and comfortable about returning if further assistance is required.

Building Rapport

Establishing rapport is an important first step in building relationships with students. According to Mottarella, Fritzsche, and Cerabino (2004), "an advisor needs to give specific care to establish a relationship with the advisee and convey warmth and support in this relationship" (p. 57). How that is accomplished will vary from advisor to advisor and student to student, but there are some specific skills that can facilitate developing rapport.

Appreciating the individual. It is important for advisors to see the student—not the "appointment type." It is easy to categorize students based on their presenting concerns and have a mental agenda ready when that "undecided student," "academically suspended student," or "student athlete" walks through the door. The mental agendas can be helpful in organizing thoughts; however, they need to be flexible and allow the individuality of each student to ultimately determine the course of the conversation.

Presence. In a busy time of year, an advisor can see one student after another without a break. It is valuable to take a deep breath between students and create mental and emotional space for the next student. Bloom (2002, ¶4) stated, "each student that walks through our doors deserves our full attention and passionate interest." Three seconds of eye contact and a genuine smile can help establish a comfortable environment and convey interest in a student's concern.

Compassion. Glaser (2005) describes compassion as a "practice of unconditional presence" that results in "not only *seeing* ourselves and others but *feeling* ourselves and others" (p. 12). Unconditional positive regard and empathy are other terms used for this ability to experience another person's perspective without negative judgment, and it is considered the core characteristic of effective helping relationships (Egan, 2002). Suspending judgment and trying to see a situation from a student's perspective combined with a desire to help is the foundation for building rapport.

Interviewing

An important competency in building relationships is getting information that can provide a full picture about a given situation without making a student feel defensive. Effective interviewing is also instrumental in helping students identify their strengths and abilities and reach their full potential (Bloom, 2002). When done well, interviewing feels like an invitation to talk, which can increase student trust as it conveys an advisor's interest and sincerity (Figler & Bolles, 1999).

Effective questioning. Castor (2005) notes that well-crafted questions can be crucial in developing appropriate responses to student needs. Advisors need to ask open-ended questions that will elicit more than a yes/no response and encourage a rich range of responses (Figler & Bolles, 1999). The case of Jose presented previously demonstrates the value of open-ended questions in the assessment process. "What did you enjoy most?" is a more valuable question than "Did you enjoy it?" When asking open-ended questions, it is valuable to fully listen and acknowledge a student's response before asking another question in order to avoid an impression of interrogation (Bloom, 2002).

Verification. In order to address student concerns, advisors need to verify that they have heard what students are saying. After students have shared a considerable amount of information, advisors can repeat, summarize, or clarify what they have heard in order to reassure the students they were listening. Verification requires identifying and reflecting the emotional quality of a student's message as well as the content (Figler & Bolles, 1999).

Active listening. Nonverbal messages can also make students feel heard. Eye contact, body posture (e.g., leaning forward), and occasionally making appropriate "listening noises" (e.g., "uhuh," "hmm," or "oh") can send a message of interest and investment in what a student is saying. Advisors also need to develop the ability to notice nonverbal behaviors of students; facial expressions, posture, voice tone, and inflections can provide additional information related to what is being said (Egan, 2002).

Identification of attributes. An important goal of effective interviewing techniques is to help students discover their positive attributes such as strengths, abilities, skills, passions, and values that influence their career aspirations (Bloom, 2002; Figler & Bolles, 1999). This requires advisors to ask insightful questions and listen carefully as students describe current and previous experiences. The vignettes of Jose and Lily provide examples of how powerful this can be for generating new ideas and options.

Influencing Development

Advisors are in a situation that affords great opportunity to positively influence student growth and development (McClellan, 2007a). Brown (2004) determined that relationships with individuals such as advisors, faculty, and career counselors play a significant role in students' post-college career plans. Advisors need to enter interactions with integrity and intention to positively influence student development and decision making.

Modeling. Advisors are recognized as important role models for students, especially in relation to ethical behavior (Landon, 2007). Modeling is also central in helping students develop professional behaviors in how they present themselves, the language they use, and how they develop rapport. Advisors can also use role modeling as a way to demonstrate appropriate interview behaviors.

Coaching. In describing the role career counselors can play in students' lives, Iittman-Ovadia (2008) indicated that they "enhance [students'] self-worth and self-efficacy; support [their] desires to take on new challenges and acquire new skills; affirm their abilities to deal with challenges; and encourage their personal growth" (p. 435). These are important elements in coaching students to explore options, make decisions, and establish goals.

Challenging. Advisors may have to confront behaviors or give difficult feedback to students. They may need to have a frank discussion about the disparity between major or career aspirations and student abilities. They may also be faced with giving students feedback about appearance or behaviors that interfere with the ability to make a positive first impression. This information will not be well received if the advisor has not established rapport and gained students' trust.

Creative imagining. Figler and Bolles (1999) use "creative imagining" to describe the process of helping students to envision career options. Bloom (2002) identifies this as the process of "dreaming" about possible lives and careers. As demonstrated the vignettes of Jose and Lily, students can get "stuck" in beliefs about their futures and need an objective person to help them expand their thinking.

PERSONAL COMPETENCIES

Personal competencies encompass a broad range of characteristics and abilities that are developed through educational and work experience and transfer across disciplines and careers. These competencies are typically what organizations look for when hiring advisors and, when present, allow individuals to excel.

In 2007, the National Leadership Council for Liberal Education and America's Promise (LEAP) published a report on the competencies required in the new century. The report summarizes the challenges facing the modern workforce and presents the skills employers are seeking to meet those challenges. According to the report, "To succeed in a chaotic environment, [employees] will need to be intellectually resilient, cross-culturally and scientifically literate, ethically anchored, fully prepared for a future of continuous and cross-disciplinary learning" (p. 15). The report also identifies the competencies essential for the global environment of the twenty-first century. Several of the competencies seem to be especially critical for advisors.

Inquiry and analysis. Career advising requires the ability to appropriately seek information from resources and people and to isolate it into its essential elements. Asking the big questions and analyzing responses are more valuable than having ready answers.

Critical and creative thinking. Advisors need to generate ideas and seek creative ways to combine multiple interests into satisfying vocational and avocational activities. They need to critically analyze student strengths and characteristics and help students brainstorm options.

Written and oral communication. There are numerous occasions when advisors must demonstrate good writing skills in communicating with students.

Oral communication extends beyond the one-to-one relationship, and advisors need to be prepared to present to groups of students.

Quantitative literacy. Assessment is a crucial part of advising programs, and advisors should be able to understand basic statistical analysis in order to interpret data and effectively use it to inform their interactions with students.

Teamwork and problem solving. Helping students explore career options and prepare for employment opportunities requires that advisors work collaboratively with students, colleagues, and employers. Unique circumstances and situations regularly arise that require the ability to problem solve—often with input and influence from others.

Intercultural knowledge and competence. Whether working with students, talking to employers, or collaborating with colleagues, advisors will encounter numerous situations requiring the ability to work effectively with people different from themselves. Advisors need to develop an understanding of cultural differences and an appreciation for diversity.

SUMMARY

The conceptual, informational, relational, and personal competencies presented are only a starting place. Each organization will determine whether advisors require additional or different competencies to meet the career advising needs of students within their particular institution. Career advising must be responsive to the changing needs of students. As the global marketplace continues to influence employment opportunities and preparation, the career needs of students will continue to evolve; these competencies will change in response. Though difficult, it is essential for advisors to monitor the latest developments and to maintain an evolving skill set in order to effectively prepare students for the future.

Despite the challenges, career advising is uniquely rewarding and an integral part of academic advising. Watching students discover their passions, develop their potential, and pursue lives of purpose leaves one with a sense of hope about the future. A colleague recently commented that "career advisor" is not a very descriptive job title and suggested that "developer of human potential" would be more accurate. The suggested title applies equally well to academic advisors providing career and academic advising. Put that way, it is difficult to imagine a more engaging or gratifying profession than advising.

References

Begley, P. T., & Johnson, J. (2001). Academic advising and living the examined life: Making the case for a values perspective. *NACADA Journal, 21*(1&2), 8–14.

Bloom, J. L. (2002, August 29). Incorporating appreciative inquiry into academic advising. *The Mentor: An Academic Advising Journal, 4*(3). Retrieved December 20, 2008, from http://www.psu.edu/dus/mentor

Brown, D. (1995). A values-based model for facilitating career transitions. *The Career Development Quarterly, 44,* 4–11.

Brown, S. C. (2004). Where this path may lead: Understanding career decision-making for postcollege life. *Journal of College Student Development, 45,* 375–390.

Carnevale, D. (2006, October 6). E-mail is for old people. *The Chronicle of Higher Education, 5*(7), p. A27.

Carter, J. (2007). *Utilizing technology in academic advising.* Retrieved December 2, 2008, from NACADA Clearinghouse of Academic Advising Resources Web site: http://www.nacada.ksu.edu/Clearinghouse/AdvisingIssues/Technology.htm#tech

Castor, D. T. (2005). Challenges for two-year college advisors. *Academic Advising Today, 28*(2). Retrieved December 20, 2008, from http://www.nacada.ksu.edu/AAT/NW28_2.htm

Chickering, A. W., & Reisser, L. (1993). *Education and identity* (2nd ed.). San Francisco: Jossey-Bass.

Council for the Advancement of Standards in Higher Education. (2006). *CAS professional standards for higher education* (6th ed.). Washington, DC: Author.

Crookston, B. B. (1972). A developmental view of academic advising as teaching. *Journal of College Student Personnel, 13*(1), 13–17.

Cuseo, J. (2003). *Academic advisement and student retention: Empirical connections and systemic interventions.* Retrieved May 6, 2008, from NACADA Clearinghouse of Academic Advising Resources Web site: http://www.nacada.ksu.edu/Clearinghouse/advisingIssues/retain.htm

Egan, G. (2002). *The skilled helper.* Pacific Grove, CA: Brooks/Cole.

Evans, N. J., Forney, D. S., & Guido-DiBrito, F. (1998). *Student development in college: Theory, research, and practice.* San Francisco: Jossey-Bass.

Feldman, R. S. (2005). *Improving the first year of college: Research and practice.* Mahwah, NJ: Lawrence Erlbaum Associates.

Figler, H. (1999). *The complete job search handbook: Everything you need to know to get the job your really want.* New York: Henry Holt.

Figler, H., & Bolles, R. N. (1999). *The career counselor's handbook.* Berkeley, CA: Ten Speed Press.

Freitag, D. (2008). *Are academic advisors knowledge workers? Yes!* Retrieved December 2, 2008, from NACADA Clearinghouse of Academic Advising Resources Web site: http://www.nacada.ksu.edu/AAT/NW31_3.htm

Frost, S. H., & Brown-Wheeler, K. E. (2003). Evaluation and examination: Philosophical and cultural foundations for faculty advising. In G. L. Kramer (Ed.), *Faculty advising examined* (pp. 223–244). Bolton, MA: Anker.

Glaser, A. (2005). *A call to compassion.* Berwick, ME: Nicolas-Hays.

Gordon, V. (2003). Advisor training and the future. In C. Nutt, K. Davis, H. Koring, A. Mills-Novoa, E. Clow, M. A. Miller, B. Albers, & V. Gordon, *Advisor training: Exemplary practices in the development of advisor skills* (Monograph No. 9, pp. 115–119). Manhattan, KS: National Academic Advising Association.

Gordon, V. N. (2006). *Career advising: An academic advisor's guide.* San Francisco: Jossey-Bass.

Habley, W. (1995). Advisor training in the context of a teaching enhancement center. In R. E. Glennen & F. N. Vowell (Eds.), *Academic advising as a comprehensive campus process* (Monograph No. 2, pp 75–79). Manhattan, KS: National Academic Advising Association.

Holland, J. L. (1997). *Making vocational choices: A theory of vocational personalities and work environments* (3rd ed.). Odessa, FL: PAR.

Iittman-Ovadia, H. (2008). The effect of client attachment style and counselor functioning on career exploration. *Journal of Vocational Behavior, 73*, 434–439.

Jeschke, M. P., Johnson, K. E., & Williams, J. R. (2001). A comparison of intrusive and prescriptive advising of psychology majors at an urban comprehensive university. *NACADA Journal, 21*(1&2), 8–14.

Krumboltz, J. D. (1983). *Private rules in career decision making.* Columbus, OH: The National Center for Research in Vocational Education.

Krumboltz, J. D., & Levin, A. S. (2004). *Luck is no accident.* Atascadero, CA: Impact.

Kuh, G., Kinzie, J., Buckley, J., Bridges, B., & Hayek, J. (2007). *Piecing together the student success puzzle: Research, propositions, and recommendations.* ASHE Higher Education Report, 32(5). Washington, DC: Jossey-Bass.

Laird, T. F. N., Chen, D., & Kuh, G. D. (2008). Classroom practices at institutions with higher-than-expected persistence rates: What student engagement data tell us. *New Directions for Teaching & Learning, 115*, 85–99.

Landon, P. A. (2007). *Advising ethics and decisions.* Retrieved December 12, 2008, from NACADA Clearinghouse of Academic Advising Resources Web site http://www.nacada.ksu.edu/Clearinghouse/AdvisingIssues/Advising-Ethics.htm

Lipschultz, W., & Musser, T. (2007). *Instant messaging: Powerful flexibility and presence.* Retrieved December 2, 2008, from the NACADA Clearinghouse of Academic Advising Resources Web site: http://www.nacada.ksu.edu/Clearinghouse/AdvisingIssues/Instant-Messaging.htm

McClellan, J. L. (2007a). The advisor as servant: The theoretical and philosophical relevance of servant leadership to academic advising. *NACADA Journal, 27*(2), 41–48.

McClellan, J. L. (2007b). *Content components for advisor training: Revisited.* Retrieved May 10, 2008, from NACADA Clearinghouse of Academic Advising Resources Web site: http://www.nacada.ksu.edu/Clearinghouse/AdvisingIssues/Training-Revisited.htm

Mitchell, K. E., Levin, A. S., & Krumboltz, J. D. (1999). Planned happenstance: Constructing unexpected career opportunities. *Journal of Counseling & Development, 77*, 115–124.

Mottarella, K. E., Fritzsche, B. A., & Cerabino, K. C. (2004). What do students want in advising? A policy capturing study. *NACADA Journal, 24*(1&2), 48–61.

NACADA. (2004). *NACADA statement of core values of academic advising.* Retrieved December 2, 2008, from the NACADA Clearinghouse of Academic Advising Resources Web site: http://www.nacada.ksu.edu/Clearinghouse/AdvisingIssues/Core-Values.htm

National Leadership Council for Liberal Education & America's Promise. (2007). *College learning for the new global century.* Washington, DC: Association of American Colleges and Universities.

Nutt, C. L. (2003). Creating advisor-training and development programs. In *Advisor training: Exemplary practices in the development of advisor skills* (Monograph No. 9, pp. 9–16). Manhattan, KS: National Academic Advising Association.

Nutt, C. L. (2008, November 25). To infinity and beyond. Charlie's Blog. Retrieved December 2, 2008, from http://www.nacada.ksu.edu/web/index.php/Blogs/Charlie-s-Blog/academic-advising-to-infinity-and-beyond.html

Perry, W. G., Jr. (1981). Cognitive and ethical growth: The making of meaning. In A. W. Chickering & Associates, *The modern American college* (pp. 76–116). San Francisco: Jossey-Bass.

Prensky, M. (2005). Listen to the natives. *Educational Leadership, 63*, 8–13.

Sampson, J. P. Jr., Reardon, R. C., Peterson, G. W., & Lenz, J. G. (2004). *Career counseling & services: A cognitive information processing approach.* Belmont, CA: Brooks/Cole.

Schlossberg, N. K. (1981). A model for analyzing human adaption to transition. *The Counseling Psychologist, 9*, 2–18.

Schlossberg, N. K., Lynch, A. Q., & Chickering, A. W. (1989). *Improving higher education environments for adults: Responsive programs and services from entry to departure.* San Francisco: Jossey-Bass.

Titus, M. A. (2006). No college student left behind: The influence of financial aspects of a state's higher education policy on college completion. *The Review of Higher Education, 29*, 293–317.

Traxler, J. (2007). Advising without walls: An introduction to Facebook as an advising tool. *Academic Advising Today, 30*(1). Retrieved December 2, 2008, from http://www.nacada.ksu.edu/AAT/NW30_1.htm#10

CHAPTER FOUR

Theories of Career Development to Inform Advising

Spencer G. Niles, Brian Hutchison

Maria is a 19-year-old Latina, first-generation university student in her second year of study at a large predominantly White suburban state university in the mid-Atlantic region of the United States. She is "normal" in intelligence but reports that she dislikes school. She is undecided about her major except for the fact that she is not interested in "anything related to math or science." Her current grade point average is a 2.2 on a 4.0 scale. She shares that she routinely hands in her class assignments late, if at all. Maria is not involved in any university-related activities but does work 20 hours per week at the fast food restaurant across the street from her residence hall. She associates with a group of students who also have little involvement in university-related activities and tend to not take studying that seriously. Some of her friends have been in trouble with the police for drug-related activities. It is your impression, however, that these friendships are superficial. Maria is respectful but shows little enthusiasm for meeting with her advisor. Her parents have called asking you to help her find a choice of major about which she can be enthusiastic.

Academic advisors help students like Maria construct educational plans that lead to occupational options. Thus, academic and career advising connect to career counseling and career development. Because academic decisions are educationally related career decisions, possessing knowledge pertaining to how careers develop provides academic advisors with important resources for performing their work. Career development theories differ in perspective. Some theories emphasize the *process* of career development and others emphasize the *content* of career decision making. No single theory provides all the information that academic advisors need to assist students.

Understanding multiple theories helps advisors provide comprehensive career advising to their students.

Unfortunately, many career theorists fall short relative to providing practical advice to academic advisors. Our goal in this chapter, therefore, is to describe a limited number of career development theories in ways that offer advisors a useful framework for integrating career theory into their work. Essentially, we focus on describing the two most venerable career theories—those developed by Donald Super (1969, 1990), whose theory emphasizes the process of career development, and John Holland (1973, 1985, 1992, 1997), whose theory emphasizes the content of career decision making. We also describe social cognitive career theory (Lent, Brown, & Hackett, 1996), the cognitive information processing approach to career interventions (Sampson, Peterson, Lenz, & Reardon, 1992), and the social learning theory of career decision making (Mitchell & Krumboltz, 1996). The latter represent several recent career theories that address cognitive dimensions of career development. Cognitive theories of career development tend to address both the career development process and the content of career decision making. We encourage readers to stay mindful of the fact that the question of "Which theory is better?" is specious because the theories complement each other in addressing various facets of career behavior. We hope that this brief discussion of several career theories will be useful in itself while also stimulating readers to learn more about these and other career theories. Finally, we use the case study of Maria to help readers translate theory to practice.

SUPER'S LIFE-SPAN, LIFE-SPACE CAREER THEORY

Donald Super's theory highlights the complex and multifaceted nature of career development. His theory also offers a useful framework for understanding how careers develop across the life span. Such understanding helps academic advisors working with both traditionally aged and nontraditional-age students.

Super's theory is arguably the leading developmental approach describing how careers unfold while proposing developmentally appropriate career interventions (Super, 1990; Super, Savickas, & Super, 1996). The life span, life-space theory evolved over a 40-year period as Super and his colleagues worked to elaborate and refine the various aspects of the theory (Super et al., 1996). Although Super's theory is primarily developmental in nature, he labeled it a "differential-developmental-social-phenomenological career theory" (Super, 1969). This label communicates Super's efforts to synthesize and extend extant developmental and career theories. Super understood that describing a process as complex as career development requires synthesizing the work of scholars from various disciplines (e.g., psychology and sociology).

Rather than developing a unified theory, however, Super developed his theory segmentally. In fact, in one sense "there is no 'Super's theory'; there is just the assemblage of theories that Super sought to synthesize. In another sense, the synthesis is a theory" (Super, 1990, p. 199). The result is really a "segmental theory" describing three key aspects of career development: (a) life span, (b) life space, and (c) self-concept.

Super's life span, life-space theory builds upon 14 assumptions. Of these, the assumptions listed below are most relevant for advisors who make career advising an integral part of academic advising. Note that after the initial introduction of each assumption, we clarify the relevance of the assumption for academic advisors.

1. "People differ in their abilities and personalities, needs, values, interests, traits, and self-concepts" (Super, 1990, p. 206).

   Advising relevance: Each person is unique and should be advised as such. The questions become: "What is this student's unique constellation of abilities, values, interests, and needs?" and "What are the academic implications of these characteristics?"

2. "People are qualified, by virtue of these characteristics, each for a number of occupations" (Super, 1990, p. 206).

   Advising relevance: It is unlikely that there is one perfect major for any student. Rather, each student is suited for several possible majors.

3. "Vocational preferences and competencies, the situations in which people live and work, and, hence, their self-concepts change with time and experience" (Super, 1990, p. 206).

   Advising relevance: The relevance of this assumption is largely conceptual. Specifically, this assumption highlights the fact that career development is part of human development. As students acquire more life experience, they will change in both subtle and significant ways. The adaptive response to such changes is to consider whether they have implications for one's educational and career planning. Helping students understand the importance of being open to such considerations provides an important lesson for career self-management.

4. "Success in coping with the demands of the environment and of the organism in that context at any given life career stage depends on the readiness of the individual to cope with these demands" (Super, 1990, p. 207).

   Advising relevance: Many decision points are arbitrary. There is, for example, no genetic or biological reason that students should be ready to make an academic decision in their second year of university study. The educational system expects this of students, but being ready to make such a decision requires students to have engaged in the necessary academic and self-exploration that leads to being able to make an informed choice. Some students have engaged in such behaviors; others have not. It would be developmentally inappropriate to ignore this fact. When students have not yet engaged in the behaviors that are necessary, then they must first learn more about themselves and educational options before choosing a course of study. Informational interviews, self-assessment activities, and enrolling in courses for exploratory purposes represent some of the behavioral possibilities that offer increased self-understanding.

5. "The process of career development is essentially that of developing and implementing occupational self-concepts. It is a synthesizing and compromising process in which the self-concept is a product of the interaction of inherited aptitudes, physical makeup, opportunity to observe and play various roles, and evaluations of the extent to which the results of role playing meets with the approval of superiors and fellows (interactive learning)" (Super, 1990, p. 207).

   Advising relevance: Academic advisors realize that there are times when a student articulates a preference for an academic major but, in reality, the student is not ready to make such a decision. Students need to be able to articulate clear reasons for considering a particular academic major. What informed their choice? How much do they know about the major? How well do their interests, abilities, and values mesh with a potential choice? If students cannot respond to such questions readily, they probably need to engage in additional self-exploration and reality testing before confirming a potential choice. The natural tendency is to move quickly to declaring a choice, often without the necessary foundation for choosing.

6. "The degree of satisfaction people attain from work is proportional to the degree to which they have been able to implement their self-concepts" (Super, 1990, p. 208).

   Advising relevance: Students must feel that their choices represent who they understand themselves to be and who they wish to become. If this is not the case, there is a strong possibility that students will not be satisfied with their choices. When this occurs, motivation and performance are often inadequate.

7. "Work and occupation provide a focus for personality organization for most men and women, although for some persons this focus is peripheral, incidental, or even nonexistent. Then other foci, such as leisure activities and homemaking, may be central. (Social traditions, such as sex-role stereotyping and modeling, racial and ethnic biases, and the opportunity structure, as well as individual differences, are important determinants of preferences for such roles as worker, student, leisurite, homemaker, and citizen.)" (Super, 1990, p. 208).

   Advising relevance: Educational and occupational decisions are but two dimensions of a person's career. The term *career* today is conceptualized as a lifestyle concept. It encompasses the total life structure. One's work role interacts with the other life roles one plays. Life is not lived in compartmentalized silos. An educational and work decision must fit into a person's total life structure or it will not be a satisfying choice. Many times, students fail to consider this basic fact of life. Academic advisors must encourage students to consider how they hope to structure the basic roles of living into a life and how the student envisions a particular educational choice fitting within their desired life structure.

The assumptions incorporate statements from diverse theoretical perspectives (e.g., trait-and-factor, developmental, social learning, and psychodynamic), thus supporting Super's (1984) contention that his theory is more than a developmental one. Super's assumptions also introduced some relatively novel concepts into the career development literature. Specifically, Super expanded career development concepts by encouraging the field to consider the notion that there is intraoccupational variability among workers, that multiple life-role development is important to consider in career development, and that self-concepts evolve over time, making choice and adjustment a continuous process. Super's assumptions provided the impetus for shifting the paradigm within the field from one that focuses on "vocation" to one that focuses on "career"; from one that focuses exclusively on the content of career choice to one that highlights the process of career development over the life span.

Life Span

Careers develop within the context of psychosocial development and societal expectations and against the backdrop of the occupational opportunity structure. Early in life, career development is relatively homogeneous and age related. Most young people are enrolled in educational institutions that require them to make decisions at specific grade levels (e.g., students in eighth grade must select a curriculum of study for high school, students leaving high school must make choices about what they will do when their secondary-school experience ends, students enrolled in higher education are expected to choose an academic major). Career development beyond secondary school becomes much less uniform. "Career adaptability" is used when referring to a person's career decision making readiness. Career adaptability reflects the fact that "as people cope with their changing work and working conditions, they make an impact on their environments and their environments make an impact on them" (Niles, Anderson, & Goodnough, 1998, p. 273). Just as the self-concept evolves over time through a continuous process of choice and adjustment, educational and work environments also change over time and require continually choosing and adjusting. Complacency becomes the enemy of effective career self-management. In this sense, career adaptability parallels Piaget's (1967) model of adaptation based on the two processes of assimilation and accommodation. Career adaptability also supports the view that adults are "responsible agents acting within dynamic environmental settings" and striving to find ways to effectively manage their career development (Super & Knasel, 1981, p. 199).

Super (1990) conceptualized career as "the life course of a person encountering a series of developmental tasks and attempting to handle them in such a way as to become the kind of person he or she wants to become" (pp. 225–226). Super identified the series of developmental tasks typically encountered and related these tasks to stages and substages of career development. The stages of career development in their typical sequence are growth (childhood), exploration (adolescence), establishment (early adulthood), maintenance (middle adulthood), and disengagement (late adulthood). Of these, growth, exploration, and establishment have the most relevance for academic advising.

Growth. People are confronted with the career development tasks of developing self-clarity and a basic understanding of the world of work. Growth tasks are first encountered in childhood. Children progress through the substages of fantasy, interest, and capacity. They progress through these substages by using their innate sense of curiosity, first to engage in occupational fantasies and then through exploring their environment (e.g., home, school, parental and peer relationships). Their curiosity leads them to acquire information about work and about their own interests and capacities. When things go well, children begin to develop a sense of mastery and control over their environment and in their ability to make decisions. Moving through the growth stage, children begin to realize the importance of planning for the future and that their behavior in the present influences their future lives. Moreover, they are increasingly able to use what they have learned about themselves and work to explore the viability of various educational and occupational opportunities.

Many university students have not yet realized the importance of systematic planning regarding their educational and career plans. They have not demonstrated sustained curiosity that connects their career fantasies, interests, and capacities to their educational plans, which, in turn, are linked to possible future selves. Thus, they possess rather basic levels of understanding regarding self-characteristics, educational options, and occupational environments. Others may have attempted to declare an academic major without sufficient engagement in the processes required for self- and occupational understanding. Indeed, it is a common tendency to lack tolerance for the ambiguity associated with being unsure about one's educational and occupational plans. Academic advisors must, therefore, assess the degree to which each student with whom they work has engaged in activities leading to self-understanding and understanding pertaining to academic and occupational options. Inquiring as to what a student has done to learn about himself or herself, educational options, and occupational options is a relevant first step for making such an assessment.

For students who have engaged in few activities to learn about themselves, it makes sense to begin with whatever interests them and what they enjoy doing. Fostering a sense of sustained curiosity about themselves and then using this curiosity to lead them into specific learning activities that inform their understanding of themselves, academic options, and occupational possibilities provides the growth experiences needed for more focused educational and career exploration.

Exploration. Within the career development domain, future planning involves addressing the tasks of crystallizing and specifying occupational preferences. Once a preference is specified, individuals turn to implementing an occupational choice. Collectively, these represent exploration tasks.

Crystallizing an occupational preference requires that people clarify the type of work they would enjoy. The process of crystallization builds upon the occupational and self-information acquired during the growth activities. Using this information, people focus on acquiring more in-depth educational and occupational information to explore the degree to which specific occupations may allow for self-concept implementation. Thus, accurate self-understanding is essential for identifying appropriate educational and occupational preferences.

The process of specifying educational and occupational preferences requires the ability to make decisions by choosing from among the academic majors and related occupations being considered. The process of implementing varies depending on the choice specified. Some choices require further information gathering to learn more about training and educational requirements. Other choices provide the opportunity for direct entry into an occupation. Regardless of the choice, implementing requires taking action toward getting started in one's chosen academic major or occupational field.

Establishment. The career development tasks associated with establishment are stabilizing, consolidating, and advancing. Stabilizing begins immediately after entering a major or an occupation as one evaluates whether the preference one has implemented provides adequate opportunity for self-concept expression. Specifically, one must assess the environmental culture and determine whether one possesses the skills and interests necessary for succeeding in the academic major or occupation one has entered.

As one becomes more stabilized in the implemented choice, one turns attention away from questioning whether the choice was a good one and begins focusing on becoming a dependable producer and developing a positive reputation in the academic major or occupation (i.e., consolidating). At any time in this process, however, one may decide that the educational or occupational choice made is no longer a good one. If this occurs, recycling to exploration occurs so that a more appropriate choice can be crystallized, specified, and implemented.

Maintenance. During maintenance people encounter the career development tasks of holding, updating, and innovating. Relative to work, many workers are confronted with the choice of either keeping up with the advancements in their field to maintain or improve their level of performance or opting for changing occupational fields. In the latter instance, workers must recycle through exploration- and establishment-stage tasks. Sometimes, returning adult students fit into this category. In the former (i.e., holding), workers turn their attention to updating their skills and applying new skills in innovative ways within their current occupations (e.g., when one pursues graduate training in one's chosen field). Workers who decide to stay in their current occupations but not to update their skills often become poor performers and stagnate in their work (i.e., they become "stuck" at the holding task). In these instances, career interventions addressing career renewal are required. Workers who update and innovate often become excellent mentors to less experienced workers. One of the facts related to rapid changes within work is that updating and innovating are continuous requirements.

Disengagement. At some point, often as physical capacities begin to decline, interest in work activities begins to wane. Workers become more concerned with planning for retirement living. Thus, the disengagement stage involves the career development tasks of deceleration, retirement planning, and retirement living. As workers begin decelerating from their work activities, they begin to become concerned about their lifestyle and activities in retirement. Often these concerns contain physical, spiritual, and financial considerations.

Refining Super's Stage Theory

Although career development stage theory originally represented a rather linear version of career development, Super (1990) readily acknowledged that recycling through career stages and tasks occurs with frequency throughout one's life, thereby suggesting a process that *could* be linear in nature but in all likelihood will not be for most people. We suggest a further refining of stage theory. Specifically, we make two recommendations regarding use of Super's stage theory in career counseling and academic advising. First, we suggest that career and advising professionals understand that people can be concerned with multiple career development tasks and multiple stages simultaneously. Second, we recommend that career and advising professionals conceptualize stages in a fashion that is similar to the notion of "status."

Regarding the former recommendation, it is not hard to imagine, for example, that a person can be concerned both about deciding what she or he will do next in their career (i.e., exploration) while also being concerned about whether they will have the resources to survive financially in retirement (i.e., disengagement). Such a person is likely to explore more narrowly than another person who may only be concerned with exploration stage tasks. We think that understanding the constellation of career concerns a student experiences at any point in time provides important information regarding the support and resources the student will find useful. Viewing the student's constellation of career concerns from the perspective of status moves away from linear notions of career stage theory and helps reinforce the point that career tasks present themselves to persons in ways that are not always restricted by chronological age. Thus, Super's stages and tasks provide important information regarding the potential array of career concerns, or societal expectations, that a person may be attempting to cope with at any point in his or her life. Understanding the life-span segment of Super's theory in this way will foster a greater understanding of a person's career development experience.

Academic advisors can use Super's life-span model to develop a clear sense of their students' career development status related to educational planning.

Remembering that students cannot appropriately implement and advance in their educational planning without adequate exploration provides a useful guideline for identifying the types of advising interventions that may be most useful at any particular time.

Life Space

While workers are busy earning a living, they are also busy living a life (Super et al., 1996). The "simultaneous combination of life roles we play constitutes the lifestyle; their sequential combination structures the life space and constitutes the life cycle. The total structure is the career pattern" (Super, 1980, p. 288). Life roles interact so that the same job holds different meaning for two individuals who live in different situations.

The salience people attach to the constellation of life roles they play defines what Super referred to as the life structure. The life-space segment of Super's theory acknowledges that people differ in the degree of importance they attach to work. Unfortunately, many people link work with self-worth in such a way that devalues the various life roles that have so much to contribute to their sense of self-esteem and self-efficacy (not to mention to society). Many models of career advising and career counseling have disregarded the effects of life–role interactions and that effective participation in multiple life roles allows for maximal opportunities for expression of values. Because students must live out their educational decisions within a greater life context, treating educational planning as though it is disconnected from life planning is shortsighted and limits its effectiveness.

Super (1980) noted that people tend to play nine major roles throughout their lives. In approximate chronological order these roles are (a) son or daughter, (b) student, (c) leisurite, (d) citizen, (e) worker, (f) spouse (or partner), (g) homemaker, (h) parent, and (i) pensioner. The individual's career comprises the total constellation of life roles engaged in over the course of a lifetime (Super, 1980). Life roles are generally played out in specific theaters. These theaters are (a) the home, (b) the school, (c) the workplace, and (d) the community.

Effective life-role participation is very difficult to achieve (Perrone, Webb, & Jackson, 2007). Conflicting life-role demands make effective life-role participation feel like a "moving target." At times, priority must be given to specific life roles. Sometimes deciding which role takes priority is relatively easy (e.g., giving priority to one's job when there are low demands from one's children) and sometimes not (e.g., when the demands from work, school, and family are concurrently high). At times, life roles typically played in one theater spill over into another theater and create conflict. For example, when work spills over from the workplace to the home, the roles of worker, partner, and parent become enmeshed and insufficient attention is paid to each role. Thus, life roles interact in ways that can be extensive or minimal, supportive, supplementary, compensatory, or neutral. Life is best when the life roles played nurture each other and offer opportunities to express one's values.

Life is stressful when the life roles are at odds with each other and provide little opportunity for people to express their values.

Although the role of an academic advisor clearly emphasizes academic planning, teaching students about the importance of placing their plans in a greater life context is important. Exploring students' thoughts regarding how they envision integrating their occupational options within their desired life structure fosters a comprehensive planning process that acknowledges life the way people live it. Helping students consider how they will structure the basic roles of living into a life that they find satisfying represents a comprehensive and holistic approach to academic and career advising.

Self-Concept

Super (1963) defined self-concept as a "picture of the self in some role, situation, or position, performing some set of functions, or in some web of relationships" (p. 18). Self-concepts contain both objective and subjective elements (Super, 1961). Objectively, people develop self-understanding by comparing themselves with others (e.g., "I am like accountants in that I am good with numbers" or "I am in the 35th percentile on mechanical ability"). Subjectively, people develop understanding through focusing on their uniqueness emerging out of the life stories they construct. People's life stories represent their efforts at constructing meaning from their life experiences. There is relative homogeneity in a person's objective career experience (e.g., almost everyone reading this book is focused on the work of academic advising). There is tremendous heterogeneity in people's subjective career experience (e.g., everyone reading this book has a unique history of personal experience that led them to the desire to provide effective career advising). People use their objective and subjective understanding to identify appropriate career goals. Such understanding guides people as they make choices about the degree and the nature of their life-role participation. Because self-concepts continue to develop over time, the need to make choices and the process of adjusting to the choices implemented represent lifelong tasks.

Applying Super's Theory

Maria (presented at the beginning of the chapter) is confronting the career development tasks of crystallizing and specifying educational and occupational preferences. Not surprising, her parents are focused on implementing a choice, but it is likely that Maria is not developmentally ready to implement. To cope effectively with the exploration-stage tasks, Maria will need to acquire much more self-information (e.g., values, interests, and abilities) and information about the world of work. She may also need to learn about the career decision making process (i.e., how good career decisions are made). Then she will need assistance in translating the information she acquires into an academic and career plan. That is, she must be able to make concrete connections between the information she acquires and her future career. It is hoped that in the process of developing a career plan, Maria will also be able to make connections between her academic activities and her future, thereby becoming a more motivated student. As Maria crystallizes her occupational self-concept, she will need to reality test her tentative choices. Activities such as role playing, participating in school clubs, job shadowing, information interviewing, and volunteering will be useful to her in increasing her self-, educational, and career awareness.

To help Maria develop her life space understanding Maria can be encouraged to consider questions such as: How do you spend your time during a typical week? How important are the different roles of life to you? What do you like about participating in each of the life roles you play? What life roles do you think will be important to you in the future? What do you hope to accomplish in each of the life roles that will be important to you in the future? What life roles do members of your family play? What do your family members expect you to accomplish in each of the life roles? What helpful (and not so helpful) lessons have you learned about playing each life role? Questions such as these would be important to discuss with Maria to help her consider what life roles will be important to her in the future and what she can do in the present to begin preparing for those life roles. Asking students to describe how they spend their time in the course of a typical week and then to consider the values reflected in their weekly activities is also a useful strategy for inviting students to consider life-structure issues.

To help Maria further clarify her self-concept, she might find it helpful to completed interest and value inventories or card sorts. These assessment results can then be used to guide further exploration. Some occupations might be appropriate for Maria's interests and abilities, but they may not provide sufficient opportunities for values expression. For students like Maria who are attempting to crystallize educational and occupational preferences, values inventories or values card sorts may be especially helpful supplements to results from measures of interests and abilities.

Using Super's theory in academic and career advising represents a comprehensive approach to educational and career planning. It also provides academic advisors with opportunities to educate students regarding the career development process and how their educational choices fit into that process. Supplementing information from Super's theory with a theory focused on career decision making content represents a useful blend of theoretical perspectives.

JOHN HOLLAND'S THEORY OF TYPES AND PERSON–ENVIRONMENT INTERACTIONS

Holland's (1973, 1985, 1992, 1997) theory belongs to a long tradition of theoretical perspectives that seek to describe individual differences in personality types (e.g., Murray, 1938; Spranger, 1928). It is also a theory that focuses on the content of career decision making. Holland's theory has been described as structural-interactive because it links personality characteristics with occupational environments and also organizes massive data about people and jobs. The theory is based on four basic assumptions:

1. In our culture, most persons can be categorized as one of six types: realistic, investigative, artistic, social, enterprising, or conventional.

2. There are six kinds of environments: realistic, investigative, artistic, social, enterprising, and conventional.

3. People search for environments that will let them exercise their skills and abilities, express their attitudes and values, and take on agreeable problems and roles.

4. A person's behavior is determined by an interaction between personality and the characteristics of the environment. (Holland, 1973, pp. 2–4)

Holland (1992) contends that, to a large degree, career interests are an expression of the individual's personality. As Spokane (1996) elaborated, "Interests, however, are complex measures that reflect personality as well as preferences, values, self-efficacy and so on. Types, then, are complex theoretical groupings based upon personality and interests" (p. 40). Personality traits are identified by preferences for leisure activities, school subjects, avocational interests, and work. To varying degrees, each individual resembles one of six basic personality types. The more one resembles any particular personality type, the more likely it is that the person will manifest the behaviors and traits associated with that type. Following is a discussion of each of the six personality types defined by Holland (1973, pp. 14–18; 1994b, pp. 2–3):

The Realistic Type

The realistic (R) personality type prefers activities that entail the explicit, ordered, or systematic manipulation of objects, tools, machines, and animals and has an aversion to educational or therapeutic activities. The realistic person has mechanical abilities but may lack social skills. Realistic types prefer jobs such as automobile mechanic, aircraft controller, surveyor, farmer, or electrician.

The Investigative Type

The investigative (I) personality type prefers activities that entail the observational, symbolic, systematic, and creative investigation of physical, biological, and cultural phenomena in order to understand and control such phenomena. Investigative types have an aversion to persuasive, social, and repetitive activities. These tendencies lead to an acquisition of scientific and mathematical competencies and to a deficit in leadership ability. Investigative types prefer jobs such as biologist, chemist, physicist, anthropologist, geologist, or medical technologist.

The Artistic Type

The artistic (A) personality type prefers ambiguous, free, unsystematized activities that entail the manipulation of physical, verbal, or human materials to create art forms or products. Artistic persons have an aversion to explicit systematic and ordered activities. These tendencies lead to an acquisition of artistic competencies in language, art, music, drama, and writing and to a deficit in clerical- or business-system competencies. Artistic types like jobs such as composer, musician, stage director, writer, interior decorator, or actor or actress.

The Social Type

The social (S) personality type prefers activities that entail the manipulation of others to inform, train, develop, cure, or enlighten. Such persons have an aversion to explicit, ordered, and systematic activities involving materials, tools, or machines. These tendencies lead to an acquisition of human relations competencies such as interpersonal and educational competencies and to a deficit in mechanical and scientific ability. Social types like jobs such as teacher, religious worker, counselor, clinical psychologist, psychiatric caseworker, or speech therapist.

The Enterprising Type

The enterprising (E) personality type prefers activities that entail the manipulation of others to attain organizational or economic gain. They have an aversion to observational, symbolic, and systematic activities. These tendencies lead to an acquisition of leadership, interpersonal, and persuasive competencies and to a deficit in scientific ability. Enterprising types like jobs such as salesperson, manager, business executive, television producer, sports promoter, or buyer.

The Conventional Type

The conventional (C) personality type prefers activities that entail the explicit, ordered, and systematic manipulation of data, such as keeping records, filing materials, reproducing materials, organizing written and numerical data according to a prescribed plan, and operating computers to attain organizational or economic goals. Conventional types have an aversion to ambiguous, free, exploratory, or unsystematized activities. These tendencies lead to an acquisition of clerical, computational, and business system competencies and to a deficit in artistic competencies. Conventional types like jobs such as bookkeeper, stenographer, financial analyst, banker, cost estimator, or tax expert.

Holland (1973, 1985, 1996, 1997) used the same six types to describe occupational environments. For example, the realistic environment requires the explicit, ordered, or systematic manipulation of objects, tools, machines, and animals. It encourages people to view themselves as having mechanical ability. It rewards people for displaying conventional values and encourages them to see the world in simple, tangible, and traditional terms.

The investigative environment requires the symbolic, systematic, and creative investigation of physical, biological, or cultural phenomena. It encourages scientific competencies and achievements and seeing the world in complex and unconventional ways. It rewards people for displaying scientific values.

The artistic environment requires participation in ambiguous, free, and unsystematized activities to create art forms or products. It encourages people to view themselves as having artistic abilities and to see themselves as expressive, nonconforming, independent, and intuitive. It rewards people for the display of artistic values.

The social environment requires participation in activities that inform, educate, develop, cure, or enlighten others. It requires people to see themselves as liking to help others, being understanding of others, and seeing the world in flexible ways. It rewards people for the display of social values.

The enterprising environment requires participation in activities that involve the manipulation of others to attain organizational and self-interest goals. It requires people to view themselves as assertive, popular, self-confident, sociable, and as possessing leadership and speaking ability. It encourages people to view the world in terms of power and status and in stereotyped and simple terms. It rewards people for displaying enterprising goals and values.

The conventional environment requires participation in activities that involve the explicit, ordered, or systematic manipulation of data, such as record keeping, filing materials, and organizing written and numerical data according to a prescribed plan. It requires people to view themselves as conforming, orderly, nonartistic, and as having clerical competencies. It rewards people for viewing the world in stereotyped and conventional ways.

Congruence

The key construct in Holland's (1973, 1985, 1996, 1997) theory, and the one that has the most relevance for academic advisors, is that of congruence. Congruence describes the degree of fit between an individual's personality type and current or prospective work environment. A person is in a congruent work environment when the person's personality type matches the occupational environment (e.g., a social type working as a counselor). Conversely, incongruence occurs when individuals are in environments that do not match their personality type (e.g., a social type working as an auto mechanic). Individuals tend to be more satisfied and perform better in environments that match (or are congruent with) their personality types. Thus, congruence is based on the assumption that "birds of a feather flock together" and that "different types require different environments" (Holland, 1973, p. 4). Also, environments are characterized by the people who occupy them. A primary goal of career and academic advising is helping students identify and connect with congruent academic environments.

Differentiation

To describe people and their work environments, Holland (1973, 1985, 1996) focuses on the three Holland types the person or environment most closely resembles. However, some people and environments are more clearly defined, or differentiated, than others. For example, a person may more predominantly resemble one Holland type and have little resemblance to other types (a high level of differentiation), or a single type may dominate an environment. Other persons or environments may resemble multiple types equally and, therefore, be relatively undifferentiated or poorly defined. Holland referred to the degree of distinctness among types representing a person's personality profile as "differentiation." Because people who are undifferentiated can have difficulty making career decisions, career interventions are often directed toward helping students achieve greater differentiation among Holland types.

Consistency

The degree of relatedness within types is referred to as "consistency." Holland uses a hexagonal model to represent the degree to which the types are related to each other. Specifically, he places them in the following order: R, I, A, S, E, C. Types located next to each other on the hexagon (e.g., realistic and investigative) have more in common than types that are farther apart (e.g., realistic and social). Higher degrees of consistency within personality types suggest more integration or harmony regarding traits, interests, values, and perceptions than lower degrees of consistency. Holland assumes that consistent persons are more predictable in their behavior and more likely to be higher achievers in their careers than persons who are not consistent. It is important for students with low consistency (e.g., a realistic-social personality type) to be aware of the fact that it may be difficult for them to find an occupational environment that will allow them to express the diverse aspects of their personality. In such cases it is often necessary for students to identify avocational activities that provide opportunities for expressing a personality type(s) that is not expressed in work. For example, a realistic-social personality type working as a social worker may choose to spend her leisure time in woodworking activities.

Identity

"*Identity* is an indicator of the degree of clarity of the picture of one's goals, interests, and talents" (Spokane, 1996, p. 46). Many students present for academic advising with a diffuse identity. Although there are various ways to assess a student's degree of clarity relative to his identity, querying a student regarding what his goals, interests, and talents are provides an obvious step in identity assessment. Clear (e.g., "I like mathematics and science") and reasonable (e.g., "my grades so far in my math and science courses have been all As and Bs") responses provide an indication that the student has achieved a reasonable level of vocational identity. When a student is unable to provide clear (e.g., "I'm really unsure about what I like and what I'm good at") and reasonable (e.g., "I like math but the best I have done thus far in my math courses is a grade of D") responses, it is important to help the student understand her Holland types, the degree of consistency represented among those types, and the degree of differentiation within her primary Holland types. This will help to increase the student's vocational identity. Vocational identity is essential for effective academic and career decision making.

Applying Holland's Theory

Congruence, differentiation, consistency, and identity are the key theoretical constructs used to link Holland's theory to practice. Assessment instruments developed by Holland and his associates are typically used to measure these constructs and the results from these measures provide the stimuli for discussing academic and career plans.

For example, the Self-Directed Search (SDS; Holland, 1994a) is used to translate individuals' self-estimates of interests and competencies into Holland types. The SDS consists of an assessment booklet (used to identify the individual's Holland type), *The Occupations Finder* (two versions are available; each contain a listing of 1334 occupations classified according to either three-letter Holland codes or presented in alphabetical order), and an interpretive guide entitled *You and Your Career*. The latter provides individuals with additional information, activities, and readings related to using Holland's theory in career decision making.

The SDS provides a useful starting point and straightforward approach for focusing Maria's career exploration and information gathering. First, Maria can use the assessment booklet to identify her three-letter summary code. (Because researchers have found a high error rate in summary code calculations [e.g., Miller, 1997], it is important that academic advisors take precautions to minimize such errors.) Then Maria and her academic advisor can review her summary code to explore how her abilities and interests relate to the characteristics of the types comprised in her summary code. There are myriad directions this discussion could follow, depending upon Maria's levels of consistency, congruence, and differentiation, as well as her three-letter summary code.

When incorporating Holland's theory in career advising, for example, it is especially important to discuss with the student his or her summary code when the code lacks consistency. A student with a code of RSA, for example, may have difficulty finding majors and occupations that resemble this code exactly (e.g., few jobs require workers to have strong mechanical abilities and strong social skills). Students who do not understand this fact can experience a sort of "pendulum shifting" in their career choices. That is, a person may opt for a realistic, or R, major or occupation and find that it is satisfactory for a while in that it offers the opportunity for engaging in R tasks and rewards R competencies. Over time, however, the person may begin noticing the absence of social, or S, opportunities in his or her R work or major. The absence of S opportunities may lead to a growing sense that the R environment needs to be replaced with an S environment. If this change occurs, it may provide satisfaction initially, but over time the person may experience that the environment as involving too many S tasks and not enough R and the pendulum may shift back toward desiring an R occupation.

Helping the student who is low in consistency become aware of the possible "pendulum shifting" that can occur in career-related decision making is important because if a congruent environment is not possible, appropriate avocational activities may provide the solution (rather than an ongoing shifting from one Holland environment to another). It is important for academic advisors to understand that achieving consistency is not a goal of career advising; rather, consistency is a construct that helps students understand who they are and then use this understanding to make effective career decisions.

Students with codes that lack differentiation (determined by comparing either the student's highest score minus the lowest score among the six types or by examining the numerical difference among the student's three-letter code) often experience a lack of focus in their career direction for a number of reasons. Persons may lack differentiation because (a) they lack exposure to activities across Holland environments, (b) they have difficulty in decision making, (c) they have multipotentiality, or (d) they are depressed.

Students lacking in exposure to Holland environments (e.g., young people with little or no work experience, homemakers returning to higher education after an extended departure) may need help increasing their self-understanding related to interests, abilities, and values. In such instances, academic advisors or career counselors may use activities such as values inventories, values card sorts, or skills checklists to foster student understanding of these career decision making variables.

With a general understanding of the Holland typology and a specific understanding of their own Holland summary codes, students are ready to examine *The Occupations Finder* (as noted previously, this is part of the SDS assessment) to locate occupations that resemble their summary codes. Each student focuses on occupations resembling all combinations of his or her summary code. Students then identify specific occupations within these categories that are of interest to them and can discuss the academic major(s) that seem appropriate for the desired career direction.

Next, advisors can encourage students to take some sort of action (e.g., information interviewing, reading about occupational requirements, job shadowing) to increase their understanding of majors or occupations of interest. Students can then discuss with their academic advisors the information they acquire from these activities and narrow their list of educational options. In these discussions, advisors encourage students to take additional steps (e.g., volunteering, taking courses related to a particular occupation) toward implementing tentative educational plans. In discussing the information the student obtains, the advisor and the student also review how each specific option provides opportunities for expressing the types comprising the student's summary code.

The strength of Holland's theory is that it provides a useful structure that organizes a tremendous amount of information that can be readily applied to the career advising process. It offers a vocabulary that helps advisors guide student exploration. The theory offers a structure for students to understand themselves and the degree to which they connect to different educational and occupational environments. Moreover, Holland's theory can be effectively supplemented with one that incorporates the cognitive dimensions of career development and decision making.

SOCIAL COGNITIVE CAREER THEORY

Social cognitive career theory (SCCT, Lent & Brown, 1996, 2002; Lent, Brown, & Hackett, 2002) incorporates the triadic reciprocal model, developed as part of social cognitive theory by Bandura (1986), to describe the complex relationship among self-efficacy beliefs, outcome expectations, and personal goals in the career decision making process. This cognitive career theory is particularly useful when working with college-age students in addressing two relevant areas of career concern: performance attainment and persistence at overcoming obstacles. In addition, Lent (2005) views SCCT as a complementary model to both trait-factor and developmental theories.

To incorporate SCCT into your advising practice, it is important to understand the three factors of the triadic reciprocal model. Self-efficacy beliefs are "people's judgments of their capabilities to organize and execute courses of action required to attain designated types of performances" (Bandura, 1986, p. 391). These beliefs, or self-judgments, are shaped both positively and negatively within four domains: (a) personal performance accomplishments, (b) vicarious learning, (c) social persuasion, and (d) physiological states and reactions (Bandura, 1986). In the case of personal performance accomplishments, successful accomplishment in any of these domains results in a more positive self-efficacy belief in that particular domain, whereas failures lead to more negative domain-specific self-efficacy beliefs.

Self-efficacy beliefs play an essential role in both the academic and career decision making process. One tends to move either toward or away from tasks and occupations depending upon one's belief in developing the capabilities required for success. Self-efficacy beliefs provide answers to "Can I do it?" questions. In the advisor's office, these questions may include the following: Can I lead this class group? Can I pass this calculus exam? Can I be successful in the engineering major? Can I be successful in business after graduation?

Outcome expectations are behavior specific belief expectations that are developed in the context of extrinsic reinforcement (i.e., tangible rewards), self-directed consequences (i.e., pride of accomplishment), or outcomes resulting from the activity itself (being "in the zone") (Lent et al., 1996, p. 381). In other words, these describe what a person expects to happen if he or she takes action. Although outcome expectations have less influence on behavior than self-efficacy beliefs, they still play an important role in the academic and career decision making process. In the advisor's office, these expectations may manifest themselves through questions such as these: Do I have a chance of getting the scholarship if I apply? Will I get a job after graduation if I don't obtain an internship? What job opportunities will be available to me if I pursue graduate school?

Personal goals relate to a person's determination to obtain a particular outcome by engaging in activities designed to achieve that outcome over time (Bandura, 1986). Goals help organize and determine one's academic and career-oriented behaviors over long periods. In the advising process, personal goals may be found in statements such as the following: I will get a second part-time job to stay in school. I will stay in this chemistry course because it is required to get into medical school.

The interaction of these three factors informs a student's beliefs about his or her ability to play a central role in his or her own academic and career decision making process. This interaction is seen as interlocking and bidirectional in that all three factors affect the other two. SCCT can be a powerful orientation from which to work with college age students in an advising environment.

Applying Social Cognitive Career Theory

As stated in the introduction to this theory, SCCT is particularly useful in addressing both performance attainment and persistence at overcoming obstacles. Personal ability, self-efficacy, outcome expectations, and personal goals dynamically interact to influence performance. According to Lent and Brown (1996), "Higher self-efficacy and anticipated positive outcomes promote higher goals, which help to mobilize and sustain performance behavior" (p. 318). Intervention is suggested when inaccurate self-efficacy beliefs or outcome expectations cause the student to prematurely foreclose on occupational options due to barriers that are perceived as insurmountable. In this case the advisor may explore the self-efficacy beliefs and experiences that led to potentially premature foreclosure while identifying and appropriately challenging any inaccuracies. "The basic processes for facilitating interest exploration are, therefore, fairly straightforward and include assessing discrepancies between self-efficacy and demonstrated skill and between outcome expectations and occupational information" (Brown & Lent, 1996, p. 357).

A card sort exercise is one suggested approach to interest exploration. Occupations (or majors) are sorted into three categories: (a) those one would choose, (b) those one would not choose, and (c) those one would question. The focus of the intervention is then on the last two categories. The student is asked which occupations she might choose if she had the skills (self-efficacy beliefs) and which she might choose because she thinks the occupation offers her something she values (outcome expectations). The student is also asked which majors or occupations she definitely would not choose. The list of occupations or majors determined from the first two card-sort categories is then examined for accuracy in terms of self-efficacy and outcome expectations (Lent & Brown, 1996).

Lent (2005) recommends adapting a decision balance sheet procedure (Janis & Mann, 1977) when working with students who are overcoming obstacles to career development. One approach to this would be to ask students to list their preferred career or major options along with the negative consequences they can imagine occurring if they pursue each specific option. Each negative consequence is explored by asking students to consider (a) the probability of encountering that obstacle and (b) strategies for preventing or managing those they are most likely to encounter.

Several interventions are available to advisors to help students modify their self-efficacy beliefs. When students have sufficient ability but low self-efficacy beliefs due to factors such as sex-role stereotyping and racism, advisors can encourage relevant vicarious learning experiences such as successful role models. These students can also be encouraged to gather ability-related data to counteract these inaccurate beliefs from friends, family, and teachers. The goal is to help students experience and examine success experiences to strengthen their weak self-efficacy beliefs.

In the case of Maria, the academic advisor may develop several hypotheses within the context of the triadic reciprocal model. The advisor might think about the formation of Maria's self-efficacy beliefs: How have her past performance accomplishments affected her academic performance? How have her past performance accomplishments affected her foreclosure on majors in math and the sciences? The advisor may consider the impact that social persuasion has on her engagement with the university and choice of peer group. Further reflection may lead an advisor to realize that Maria seems to lack clear personal goals. This would have an impact on Maria's decisions regarding her educational path and choice of major. The absence of personal goals may make career decisions feel overwhelming to Maria and could explain her undecided status and poor grade-point average.

Maria's academic advisor has several options. The advisor may begin to guide Maria's major exploration by using the card sort exercise to examine her self-efficacy beliefs for accuracy. If, for example, the advisor finds that Maria does not believe that someone from her background can ever get into medical school, she can connect Maria to successful alumni from a similar cultural background or ask Maria to test these beliefs by interviewing people she admires from her home town. Once Maria begins to dispel these negative self-efficacy beliefs and begins to experience success, the advisor may use the balance sheet procedure to explore the obstacles to her academically preparing for and applying to medical school.

Cognitive theories of career development address an important dimension of the career decision making process (i.e., factors that influence how people think about themselves and their world). Often, it is one's cognitions, especially one's sense of self-efficacy, that determine whether one is willing and motivated to select an educational or career path.

THE COGNITIVE INFORMATION PROCESSING APPROACH

The cognitive information processing (CIP) approach to career counseling (Peterson, Lumsden, Sampson, Reardon, & Lenz, 2002; Peterson, Sampson, Reardon, & Lenz, 1996; Sampson, Reardon, Peterson, & Lenz, 2004) stems from the three-factor Parsonian model of career decision making (i.e., develop self-understanding and occupational knowledge to arrive at a career choice) but also includes current knowledge about cognitive information processing. The CIP approach is useful for academic advisors in that it provides an additional layer to understanding the process of career decision making (meta-cognitions). Many academic advisors also appreciate the utility of using the established sequential models discussed below as tools to guide students through the process of making career decisions.

Four assumptions provide the theoretical foundation of the CIP approach. First, there is an interaction between cognitive and affective processes that occurs during any career decision. Second, available cognitive operations and knowledge determine an individual's capacity for solving career problems.

Third, knowledge structures and, therefore, career development are always evolving. Finally, the aim of career counseling is to enhance the client's information processing skill set (Peterson et al., 2002). The cognitive processes described by this approach occur in four career decision making domains: (a) self-knowledge, (b) occupational knowledge, (c) decision making skills, and (d) metacognitions. The fourth domain, metacognitions, adds to the traditional foundation of most career theories by incorporating self-talk, self-awareness, and the monitoring and control of cognitions. These four domains are often presented as a pyramid with self-knowledge and occupational knowledge acting as the base, decision making skills as the middle, and metacognitions as the apex (Sampson et al., 1992).

The CASVE (communication, analysis, synthesis, valuing, execution) cycle provides a sequential model through which one can understand the CIP approach to incorporating information-processing skills to career decision making. The CASVE cycle begins with the recognition of a gap between the student's ideal career state and current career circumstances. This gap is often realized because of external or internal stimuli. The interpretation of the cues occurs during the first or *communication* stage of the CASVE model. Once a gap is identified, the student must *analyze* what is needed to resolve the problem and how to attain the resources (e.g., career inventory, informational interview) necessary for resolution. *Synthesis* includes elaborating upon solutions to career problems to develop an extensive list of alternatives before crystallizing the options that best fit the student's needs (e.g. abilities, interests, or values). The information gathered in the first three stages allows the student to prioritize the alternatives through a process called *valuing*. Finally, the student is prepared for the *execution* phase of the CASVE model, which includes developing a plan of action to apply the optimal solutions to the student's problem (Peterson et al., 1996).

There is one final dimension of the CIP approach called the executive processing domain. This domain controls the storage and retrieval of information (Peterson, Sampson, & Reardon, 1991). The executive processing domain represents the additive component of CIP to the traditional Parsonian three-factor model. Metacognitive skills include self-talk, self-awareness, and control. Self-talk can be either positive or negative. Positive self-talk is needed for effective career decision making; negative self-talk leads to career indecision. Self-awareness allows the student to monitor and control factors, both internal and external, that have an impact on career decision making so that information can be deciphered in a context that results in the best solutions to career problems. The executive processing domain operates as a form of quality control as a student progresses through the steps of the CASVE model (Peterson et al., 1991).

Applying Cognitive Information Processing

The CIP approach provides several avenues an academic advisor can use to guide his or her career advising practice. The pyramid model is an excellent framework for guiding career interventions. Each of the four domains may represent an element of the student's development to be addressed with an intervention designed specifically for that domain. For example, self-knowledge deficits may require formal or informal values assessments, occupational knowledge deficits may be addressed with informational interviews or internships, the CASVE model can be taught to encourage effective decision making, and negative self-talk may best be addressed through a referral to career counseling (Peterson et al., 1991).

Peterson et al. (1991) provide a seven-step outline for delivering career interventions that may be used to plan individual, group, and classroom interventions.

1. Conduct an initial interview to help understand the nature and context of the student's career problems. During this meeting the advisor will establish an effective working relationship and introduce the student to the pyramid and CASVE model in the context of using them to clarify the student's concerns. The advisor will use the models to identify the student's skill level in each domain as well as dysfunctional metacognitions (Sampson et al., 1992).

2. Make a preliminary assessment of the student's career decision making readiness. The Career Thoughts Inventory (CTI; Sampson, Peterson, Lenz, Reardon, & Saunders, 1996) is an assessment that can be used to assess career readiness. This inventory is designed to identify dysfunctional thoughts that will need to be addressed through interventions before effective decision making can occur. For assessments, it is important to note the specialized education, skills, and qualifications needed for their use.

3. Collaborate with the student to identify the gaps between the student's current and ideal situations.

4. With the student, identify the achievable goals that will close the gaps found in step three.

5. Collaborate with the student to develop an individual learning plan to serve as a guide to the activities the student will need to perform to attain the goals outlined in step four. This plan will be a tool used in future steps to hold the student accountable and monitor progress toward goal attainment.

6. The student executes the individual learning plan. The advisor may provide needed support and challenge during implementation of the learning plan.

7. Finally, with the student discuss and review student progress toward goals, enumerate the learned skills, and project use of these skills toward potential future career problems.

Incorporating these seven steps and the pyramid and CASVE models into advising practice provides a useful framework for helping students make important career decisions while learning cognitive skills that will benefit them when addressing career problems in the future.

In the case of Maria, the seven-step process outlined above will facilitate progress toward making important career decisions about college. During the initial session, the advisor might expand upon the information presented in the case study at the beginning of this chapter by focusing on questions such as these: How has Maria made important decisions in the past? What does Maria's self-talk communicate? How does Maria respond to the concepts of the pyramid and CASVE model? An important clue is Maria's dislike of school. What metacognitions surround this negative outlook? What metacognitions or influences have kept her in school thus far? All of this information will be important as the advisor collaborates with Maria in the remaining steps of the process.

Steps two and three will be instrumental in determining the direction of the advisor's work with Maria. What dysfunctional thoughts are identified via the CTI or other preliminary assessments? The results of the preliminary assessment will be discussed to help identify the gaps between her current and ideal situations. Does she wish to be in college? If yes, what would college ideally look like? Can she picture a typical class or day she might experience if she were to like her major choice? What does she look like in this picture (e.g., inside or outside, hands-on or theoretical)? What aspects of her life encourage positive self-talk? Does this information provide any insight? The aim of this discussion is to identify problems and potential solutions (step four). In career advising there will be situations that call for referral to a career counselor to address students' problems and issues.

The first four steps of the process could lead many ways. The possibility exists that step five will include the exploration of temporarily or permanently leaving school. But if Maria decides to solve the career problem by choosing a major, the individual learning plan might include learning about the world of work (the relationship between majors and occupations) and her decision making skills (CASVE model). Judging from the case description, the advisor might need to work on modifying some dysfunctional self-talk surrounding her dislike of school. Once goals and a plan have been determined, the academic advisor will switch roles to that of a supportive advisor who monitors progress and holds Maria accountable for the plan she developed. The time involved in step six is largely determined by Maria and her progress toward making decisions to solve her career problem. Once goals have been reached, the process is summarized and analyzed so that the skills learned may be reinforced and applied to future career decisions. In the end, the advisor will have helped guide Maria through a difficult period in her career development while also teaching her skills that will empower her to make future decisions that resolve developmental problems.

SOCIAL LEARNING THEORY OF CAREER DECISION MAKING

Krumboltz and his colleagues developed the "social learning theory of career decision making" (SLTCDM, Krumboltz, 1979; Mitchell & Krumboltz, 1996). This theory is based on the application of Bandura's (1977) social learning theory to career decision making. Bandura's theory emphasizes the influence of reinforcement theory, cognitive information processing, and classical behaviorism on human behavior. Social learning theory "assumes that people's personalities and behavioral repertoires can be explained most usefully on the basis of their unique learning experiences while still acknowledging the role played by innate and developmental processes" (Mitchell & Krumboltz, 1996, p. 234). Social learning theory also assumes that "humans are intelligent, problem-solving individuals who strive at all times to understand the reinforcement that surrounds them and who in turn control their environments to suit their own purposes and needs" (Mitchell & Krumboltz, 1996, p. 236).

Krumboltz and his colleagues drew upon these theoretical assumptions in developing SLTCDM. Specifically, in SLTCDM they identify four factors that influence career decision making:

1. *Genetic endowment and special abilities.* Genetic endowments are inherited qualities, such as sex, race, and physical appearance. Special abilities such as intelligence, athletic ability, and musical and artistic talents result from the interaction of genetic factors and exposure to selected environmental events.

2. *Environmental conditions and events.* Factors in this category are generally outside one's control and can involve a wide variety of cultural, social, political, historical, and economic forces.

3. *Instrumental and associative learning experiences.* Instrumental learning experiences involve antecedents, behaviors, and consequences. Associative learning experiences occur when a neutral stimulus is paired with a positive or negative stimulus or consequences.

4. *Task approach skills.* These include the individual's work habits, mental set, emotional responses, cognitive processes, and problem-solving skills.

These four factors influence one's beliefs about oneself (e.g., what one is good at, what one's interests are, what one values) and one's beliefs about the world (e.g., "hard work always pays off," "all academic advisors value altruism over economic rewards"). Beliefs can be facilitative or problematic in career decision making. Although the interactions of these four factors influence people differently, there are generally four ways in which they can influence career decision making:

1. *Self-observation generalizations.* These are overt or covert statements evaluating one's actual or vicarious performance or self-assessments of one's interests and values (Mitchell & Krumboltz, 1996). Learning experiences lead people to draw conclusions about themselves. People compare their performance with the performance of others and to their own performance expectations. They then use these comparisons to draw conclusions about their performance capabilities. Conclusions about interests and values also result from learning experiences. In SLTCDM, interests link learning experiences with specific actions. Self-observations about values are, in essence,

statements about the desirability of specific outcomes, behaviors, or events (Mitchell & Krumboltz, 1996). For example, the statement, "It is important that my academic major provides ample time for me to be with my family," is a values-related self-observation generalization about desirable outcomes resulting from previous learning experiences.

2. *Worldview generalizations.* These are generalizations about the nature and functioning of the world (e.g., "It's not what you know, it's who you know," "Once you choose an academic major, you cannot change your mind") that are formed from learning experiences. The accuracy of worldview generalizations is dependent on the learning experiences shaping such generalizations.

3. *Task approach skills.* Mitchell and Krumboltz (1996) defined these outcomes as "cognitive and performance abilities and emotional predispositions for coping with the environment, interpreting it in relation to self-observation generalizations, and making covert and overt predictions about future events" (p. 246). As noted previously, task approach skills both influence career decision making and are outcomes of learning experiences that shape individuals' career development. Task approach skills critical to career development are those involved in decision making, problem solving, goal setting, information gathering, and values clarifying.

4. *Actions.* Learning experiences lead individuals to take actions related to their educational and career planning. These actions can include implementing a choice of major, entering an internship, applying to graduate school, changing jobs, or taking other overt steps to make progress in one's educational and career planning.

Applying SLTCDM

According to Krumboltz (1996), making career decisions is a learned skill. Advisors therefore have an important role in teaching career decision making skills. Through career advising, students can be helped to learn these skills individually or in groups (e.g., career courses). In addition, advisors can contribute to creating learning opportunities and to helping students identify learning experiences that will be helpful in making career decisions. As a part of career advising, advisors can encourage and support students as they take advantage of learning opportunities to facilitate their career development.

Consistent with the goal of student learning, Mitchell, Levin, and Krumboltz (1999) recommend helping students learn to create and take advantage of chance events in their career: "Chance plays an important role in everyone's career. . . . Unplanned events can become opportunities for learning" (p. 115). The following are skills recommended for recognizing, creating, and using unplanned events:

1. Curiosity: exploring new learning opportunities

2. Persistence: exerting effort despite setbacks

3. Flexibility: changing attitudes and circumstances

4. Optimism: viewing new opportunities as possible and attainable

5. Risk taking: taking action in the face of uncertain outcomes (Mitchell et al., 1999, p. 118)

Consider Maria's situation from the perspective of SLTCDM. As a 19-year-old Latina first-generation university student in her second year of study at a large, predominantly White suburban state university in the mid-Atlantic region of the United States, she possesses "normal" intelligence but it appears that she has not been exposed to positive learning experiences related to her academic activities (she notes that she dislikes school). She is undecided about her major except that she is not interested in "anything related to math or science." One imagines that she has had negative learning experiences related to those academic subjects. Her current grade point average is a 2.2 on a 4.0 scale. She is not failing academically but clearly there is room for improvement. Her lack of interest, plus association with others who seem similarly unenthusiastic toward school, does not seem to be fostering much academic motivation and she has had only marginal success. She shares that she routinely hands in her class assignments late, if at all. Maria is not involved in any university-related activities. So, although her genetic endowments suggest that she should be able to be more successful academically, the current environmental conditions, as well as her past and current learning experiences, seem to result in her concluding that school is not all that interesting and important to her. Her academic advisor might consider constructing positive learning experiences for Maria. Identifying school activities that she might find enjoyable, connecting her with a mentor, and engaging her in academic tutoring would all be strategies linked to creating instrumental and associative learning experiences for her. Challenging some of her potentially less than useful self-observation generalizations and worldview generalizations would also be valuable.

Cognitive theories of career development address an important dimension of the career decision making process (i.e., factors that influence how people think about themselves and the world). Often, it is the person's cognitions, especially one's sense of self-efficacy, that determine whether one is willing and motivated to select an educational or career path.

SUMMARY

Academic advising represents a crucial activity in the career development of students. Effective advising can help students construct educational and career plans that foster educational and career success. Because academic choices are educationally based career choices, understanding career development theory helps academic advisors offer developmentally appropriate career advising to their students. Helping students develop self-understanding regarding their interests, values, abilities, and personality types and how these important self-characteristics relate to educational and occupational environments furnishes

the foundation for effective decision making. Moreover, when advisors understand how the social learning process guides educational planning and career
behavior, they are better equipped to positively influence the academic success
their advisees experience. We encourage readers to use the brief descriptions of
a limited number of career theories provided in this chapter as a springboard
to learning more about career development theory and its use in making career
advising an integral part of academic advising.

References

Bandura, A. (1977). *Social learning theory.* Upper Saddle River, NJ: Prentice Hall.

Bandura, A. (1986). *Social foundations of thought and action: A social-cognitive theory.*
Upper Saddle River, NJ: Prentice Hall.

Brown, S. D., & Lent, R. W. (1996). A social cognitive framework for career choice
counseling. *The Career Development Quarterly, 44,* 354–366.

Holland, J. L. (1973). *Making vocational choices: A theory of careers.* Upper Saddle
River, NJ: Prentice Hall.

Holland, J. L. (1985). *Making vocational choices: A theory of vocational personalities
and work environments* (2nd ed.). Upper Saddle River, NJ: Prentice Hall.

Holland, J. L. (1992). *Making vocational choices* (2nd ed.). Odessa, FL: Psychological
Assessment Resources.

Holland, J. L. (1994a). *Self-Directed Search* (Form R, 4th ed.). Odessa, FL:
Psychological Assessment Resources.

Holland, J. L. (1994b). Separate but unequal is better. In M. L. Savickas & R. W. Lent
(Eds.), *Convergence in career development theories: Implications for science and
practice* (pp. 45–51). Palo Alto, CA: CPP Books.

Holland, J. L. (1996). Integrating career theory and practice: The current situation
and some potential remedies. In M. L. Savickas & W. B. Walsh (Eds.), *Handbook of
career counseling theory and practice* (pp. 1–12). Palo Alto, CA: Davies-Black.

Holland, J. L. (1997). *Making vocational choices: A theory of vocational personalities
and work environments* (3rd ed.). Odessa, FL: Psychological Assessment Resources.

Janis, I. L., & Mann, L. (1977). *Decision making: A psychological analysis of conflict,
choice, and commitment.* New York: Free Press.

Krumboltz, J. D. (1979). A social learning theory of career decision making. In A. M.
Mitchell, G. B. Jones, & J. D. Krumboltz (Eds.), *Social learning and career decision
making* (pp. 19–49). Cranston, RI: Carrole Press.

Krumboltz, J. D. (1996). A learning theory of career counseling. In M. L. Savickas &
W. B. Walsh (Eds.), *Handbook of career counseling theory and practice* (pp. 55–80).
Palo Alto, CA: Davies-Black.

Lent, R. W. (2005). A social cognitive view of career development and counseling. In
S. D. Brown, & R. W. Lent (Eds.), *Career development and counseling: Putting
theory and research to work* (pp. 101–127). New York: Wiley.

Lent, R. W., & Brown, S. D. (1996). Social cognitive approach to career development:
An overview. *The Career Development Quarterly, 44,* 310–321.

Lent, R. W., & Brown, S. D. (2002). Social cognitive career theory and adult career development. In S. G. Niles (Ed.), *Adult career development: Concepts, models, and practices* (3rd ed., pp. 77–98). Tulsa, OK: National Career Development Association.

Lent, R. W., Brown, S. D., & Hackett, G. (1996). Career development from a social cognitive perspective. In D. Brown, L. Brooks, & Associates (Eds.), *Career choice and development* (3rd ed., pp. 373–416). San Francisco: Jossey-Bass.

Lent, R. W., Brown, S. D., & Hackett, G. (2002). Social cognitive career theory. In D. Brown & Associates (Eds.), *Career choice and development* (4th ed., pp. 255–311). San Francisco: Jossey-Bass.

Miller, M. J. (1997). Error rates on two forms on the Self-Directed Search and satisfaction with results. *Journal of Employment Counseling, 34,* 98–103.

Mitchell, L. K., & Krumboltz, J. D. (1996). Krumboltz's theory of career choice and counseling. In D. Brown, L. Brooks, & Associates (Eds.), *Career choice development* (3rd ed., pp. 233–280). San Francisco: Jossey-Bass.

Mitchell, L. K., Levin, A. S., & Krumboltz, J. D. (1999). Planned happenstance: Constructing unexpected career opportunities. *Journal of Counseling & Development, 77,* 115–124.

Murray, H. (1938). *Explorations in personality.* New York: Oxford University Press.

Niles, S. G., Anderson, W. P., & Goodnough, G. (1998). Exploration to foster career development. *The Career Development Quarterly, 46,* 262–275.

Perrone, K. M., Webb, L. K., & Jackson, Z. V. (2007). Relationships between parental attachment, work and family roles, and life satisfaction. *The Career Development Quarterly, 55,* 237–248.

Peterson, G. W., Lumsden, J. A., Sampson, J. P., Jr., Reardon, R. C., & Lenz, J. G. (2002). Using a cognitive information processing approach in career counseling with adults. In S. G. Niles (Ed.), *Adult career development: Concepts, models, and practices* (3rd ed., pp. 99–120). Tulsa, OK: National Career Development Association.

Peterson, G. W., Sampson, J. P., Jr., & Reardon, R. C. (1991). *Career development and services: A cognitive approach.* Pacific Grove, CA: Brooks/Cole.

Peterson, G. W., Sampson, J. P., Jr., Reardon, R. C., & Lenz, J. G. (1996). A cognitive information processing approach. In D. Brown, L. Brooks, & Associates (Eds.), *Career choice and development* (3rd ed., pp. 423–476). San Francisco: Jossey-Bass.

Piaget, J. (1967). *Biology and knowledge.* Chicago: Chicago University Press.

Sampson, J. P., Jr., Peterson, G. W., Lenz, J. G., & Reardon, R. C. (1992). A cognitive approach to career services: Translating concepts into practice. *The Career Development Quarterly, 41,* 67–74.

Sampson, J. P., Jr., Peterson, G. W., Lenz, J. G., Reardon, R. C., & Saunders, D. E. (1996). *The Career Thoughts Inventory.* Odessa, FL: Psychological Assessment Resources.

Sampson, J. P. Jr., Reardon, R. C., Peterson, G. W., & Lenz, J. G. (2004). *Career counseling and services: A cognitive information processing approach.* Pacific Grove, CA: Brooks/Cole.

Spokane, A. R. (1996). Holland's theory. In D. Brown, L. Brooks, & Associates (Eds.), *Career choice and development* (3rd ed., pp. 33–74). San Francisco: Jossey-Bass.

Spranger, E. (1928). *Types of men: The psychology and ethics of personality* (Paul J. W. Pigors, Trans.). Halle, Germany: Max Niemeyer Verlag.

Super, D. E. (1961). The self-concept in vocational development. *Journal of Vocational and Educational Guidance, 8*, 13–29.

Super, D. E. (1963). Self-concepts in vocational development. In D. E. Super, R. Starishevsky, N. Matlin, & J. P. Jordaan (Eds.), *Career development: Self-concept theory* (pp. 17–32). New York: College Entrance Examination Board.

Super, D. E. (1969). Vocational development theory: Persons, positions, processes. *The Counseling Psychologist, 1*, 2–9.

Super, D. E. (1980). A life span, life-space approach to career development. *Journal of Vocational Behavior, 16*, 282–298.

Super, D. E. (1984). Career and life development. In D. Brown, L. Brooks, & Associates (Eds.), *Career choice and development* (pp. 192–234). San Francisco: Jossey-Bass.

Super, D. E. (1990). A life span, life-space approach to career development. In D. Brown, L. Brooks, & Associates (Eds.), *Career choice and development: Applying contemporary theories to practice* (2nd ed., pp. 197–261). San Francisco: Jossey-Bass.

Super, D. E., & Knasel, E. G. (1981). Career development in adulthood: Some theoretical problems and a possible solution. *British Journal of Guidance and Counseling, 9*, 194–201.

Super, D. E., Savickas, M. L., & Super, C. (1996). A life-span, life-space approach to career development. In D. Brown, L. Brooks, & Associates (Eds.), *Career choice and development* (3rd ed., pp. 121–128). San Francisco: Jossey-Bass.

CHAPTER FIVE

Using Student Development Theory to Inform Career Advising

Heidi Koring, Beverly C. Reid

College creates change. Whether entering postsecondary institutions directly after high school or later, students find that higher education profoundly affects all aspects of their lives, including their career development. Some students enter college without a clear career path; others adjust their heading several times. Advisors need more than knowledge of career opportunities and a variety of advising approaches to work successfully with students facing decisions about majors and careers. They must understand the students and the developmental changes those students experience. Advisors need a working knowledge of student development theory.

In this chapter, we introduce advisors to student development concepts and discuss major student development theories; those that relate to major and career exploration and decision making are highlighted. We emphasize the work of Perry (1968) and Chickering (1969), who formed the foundation for later theories, models, and approaches that have been helpful in understanding student decision making, engagement, and collaborations in career advising. After explaining each theory, we present approaches and interventions along with specific programs and practices that can be applied to career advising programs. Finally, we bring together the concepts that student development theory provides to guide advisors as they support students in the career development process.

FOUNDATIONS OF STUDENT DEVELOPMENT THEORY AND CAREER ADVISING

In *Childhood and Society* Erikson (1950) introduced developmental psychology by proposing that the human life span can be characterized in stages.

He suggested that the individual faces a specific challenge or conflict that must be overcome before reaching the next developmental stage. He incorporated concepts of human psychosocial development of people from infancy to old age. He also considered an individual's role within the world of work, as well as within interpersonal relationships and society, as crucial to identity development. He posited that adolescents must grapple with identity and role confusion as they enter adult society. Thus, from Erikson's perspective, career choice is a central development task and the traditional college years (late adolescence and early adulthood) constitute the key period in which individuals concentrate on career decisions as an integral part of identity development.

Student affairs practitioners in higher education quickly realized that the developmental approach added value to the curricular and cocurricular education of college students. As a result, they adopted a developmental approach to higher education soon after the dissemination of Erikson's (1950) theory.

The turbulent era of the 1960s ushered changes and challenges into higher education that were addressed by using developmental theory. As they scrambled to respond to chaotic student-initiated changes, college and university administrators sought to distinguish indiscriminate change from purposeful student development and find ways to encourage the latter.

To address the issues created by a new generation of college students, Sanford (1966) expressed the belief that institutions of higher education should embrace a clear, student-centered conception of student development goals. He viewed student development as "planned action" (p. ix) that the institution should use to lead to "the maximum development of the individual, bringing forth as much of his potential as possible, and setting in motion a process, that will continue throughout his lifetime" (pp. 41–42). Therefore, from the earliest adoption of developmental theory, colleges and universities accepted the responsibility of purposeful intervention to encourage student development, not only through the college years, but beyond.

Even a cursory examination of developmental theory in higher education holds lessons for career advising. Erikson (1950) saw career choice and identity development as inextricably intertwined. Sanford (1966) emphasized the importance of purposeful action that encourages student development. As part of the advising process, and not solely in response to student inquiries, the advisor should plan strategic interventions, such as those based on the foundational theories of Perry (1968) and Chickering (1969) that focus on career development within the context of identity development.

COGNITIVE DEVELOPMENT AND CAREER ADVISING

The means by which students cognitively process information affect the ways they use information to make career decisions. Cognitive development of college students was first studied by Perry (1968) as he attempted to understand how they transformed during their undergraduate years. He expected to find that personality differences would account for varying developmental pathways. Instead he discovered that college students engage in a consistent developmental journey that he called "an intellectual Pilgrim's Progress" (Perry, 1968, p. 3). He proposed that undergraduates experience four stages of cognitive and ethical development that affect them both in and out of the classroom: dualism, multiplicity, relativism, and commitment.

Students experiencing dualism see the world in black and white. They crave certainty, assume that authorities have the correct answers, and believe that learning is simply a matter of consuming authoritative information. Dualistic students believe that experts have the responsibility of sharing correct answers and students have the responsibility for mastering the knowledge.

As students advance into the multiplicity stage, they appreciate the many plausible answers to a question or a problem. If the right answer is undetermined, they believe that all options are equally valid. They may question why solutions posed by authorities, such as professors and advisors, are considered to be more important than student opinion.

As students enter the relativism stage, they begin to understand that opinions must be supported by facts. Knowledge becomes qualitative, and students realize that some viewpoints are more defensible than others.

Finally, in the commitment phase, students hold to a position by integrating the knowledge they have learned with their own experiences. They face issues of personal responsibility and understand that commitment is not a static event but evolves over a lifetime.

The metamorphosis of preference specifically characterizes the 21st century workforce. According to Hall (2004), a modern individual's core values, not those of the hiring organization, drive career choice and commitment, and as these personal values evolve, decisions about opportunities are transformed. For example, due to increased maturity and additional responsibilities, college seniors may alter their career aspirations.

Several researchers applied Perry's (1968) scheme directly to career development. Knefelkamp and Slepitzka (1976) applied Perry's ideas to describe cognitive complexity as related to career decision making. Jones and Newman (1993) described how Perry's theory can be used to discover diversity among students deciding on careers. For advisors, perhaps the most important application of Perry's theory is in creating appropriate interventions for students undertaking career exploration and decision making.

According to Perry's (1968) theory, typical first-year students assume that only one career choice will yield desired outcomes and that advisors should prescribe this correct choice. Advisors who understand the dynamics of dualism can help the student move onto the next development phase. In general, they redirect students who think that a chosen major will narrow career options to a single, correct choice. Specifically, they should speak explicitly about career exploration rather than encourage early choice of major or career, and they should recommend activities that foster career exploration (e.g., finding major or career Web sites or interviewing college graduates about the career decision-making process).

Because undecided students at the dualist stage crave certainty, they may bristle at the designation "undecided" and select a major to avoid the label they believe stigmatizes them. Advisors can assure students that indecision is a natural stage in the career development process. They may also suggest that institutional stakeholders re-title "undecided" to "exploratory" or "open option." In addition, they can gather resources in a single place to provide the structure and authority dualist students find helpful and informative. For example, Indiana University offers a Web page (http://www.indiana.edu/ ~ college/ado/exploratory.shtml) as does Florida International through the University Undecided Student E-Newsletter (http://undergrad.fiu.edu/advising/undecided/index.htm) that target multiple resources to undecided students.

Students who have reached the stage of multiplicity understand that more than one major or career may be viable options, but they may be unwilling to commit to a single choice and, in fact, may be reluctant to make an original major or career selection. Understanding the multiplistic stage of student development can mitigate advisor frustration with students who are unable to commit to a choice. While encouraging exploration, advisors may want to remind students that an initial commitment is not a lifetime decision. Advisors can indicate that individuals will be likely to make multiple career changes during their working lives. To move multiplistic students toward relativism, advisors should encourage reflection on their career exploration by querying them about the links they have found between careers and identity. Examples of such questions include the following: Which of the careers you explored will best allow you to realize your hopes and values? Which of the careers you explored is most compatible with the life you hope to lead after you graduate?

Students in the relativism stage are ready to evaluate options and narrow choices. They need detailed information about specific careers (e.g., working conditions, national and regional earnings, job outlooks, and education requirements), and they are often willing to seek internships or shadowing opportunities. To help students reach the commitment phase, advisors can teach students how to evaluate information. Laughlin and Creamer (2007) noted, "Simply exposing students to divergent views and sources of knowledge without supporting true engagement with those views may not be the most effective way to foster development" (p. 50). Advisors should follow up with students who have explored the alternatives and encourage them to reflect on their experiences and evaluate the information gathered.

Commitment is the final stage of Perry's (1968) scheme, but it evolves throughout a lifetime. With the support of advisors, advisees integrate information received from others with personal knowledge and experience. Advisees accept responsibility for the commitment and understand it to be an ongoing activity that will change with circumstances and with continuing personal development. At the end of the career search, advisors can ask questions that encourage advisees to consider the decision-making process. An example is, "What information or experience was most important as you made your career decision?" Advisors should support advisees' decisions, acknowledge the difficulty of the commitment, and help them celebrate the journey they made.

By understanding Perry's (1968) scheme, advisors can assess the stages of students' cognitive development with respect to career decision making. They will also appreciate that career decision making is dynamic and will change as students develop cognitively. As a result, advisors are aware of advisees' specific needs at different stages of cognitive development and can target interventions for each stage.

THE SOCIAL CONTEXT FOR CAREER ADVISING

In addition to understanding the role of cognitive development, advisors should realize that a broad context of social and cultural issues informs career development. Chickering's (1969) theory places student development in a broad, multifaceted context. By understanding Chickering's theory, advisors appreciate the many factors that contribute to student development, including aspects of career choice, and consider these issues in career advising interventions.

In the study, *Education and Identity*, published in 1969 and revised with Reisser in 1993, Chickering examined the emotional, ethical, interpersonal, and vocational development of college students. In his 1969 work, he postulated that seven vectors of development are responsible for the identity formation of young adults. Although presented as a list, the vectors do not necessarily constitute a rigid or linear path for students. Although his research shows that the earlier factors tend to precede the later factors in developmental sequence, Chickering chose the term "vectors" rather than "stages" to avoid the implication of lockstep progression, noting that "the direction may be expressed by a spiral or by steps rather than by a straight line" (p. 8). Chickering and Reisser (1993, pp. 43–52) presented these vectors as follows:

1. Developing competence includes intellectual and interpersonal aptitudes in addition to physical and manual skills.

2. Managing emotions describes the ability to recognize, accept, express, and control emotions.

3. Moving through autonomy toward interdependence involves self-direction, the ability to solve problems, and the acceptance of social interconnectedness.

4. Developing mature interpersonal relationships describes the process of respecting and appreciating diversity, as well as developing the capacity for healthy relationships.

5. Establishing identity includes a sense of comfort with one's appearance, heritage, role, and lifestyle, resulting in self-acceptance and self-esteem.

6. Developing purpose requires personal and interpersonal commitments as well as commitment to vocational choices.

7. Developing integrity involves commitment to a value system that balances the needs of self and others as well as affirming one's own core values while respecting others' values and beliefs.

To maximize student development in these seven vectors, Chickering and Reisser (1993) proposed the following three basic principles to guide practice:

1. Integration of work and learning, including collaborative relationships among the educational institution, the business community, and the wider community, will enhance the experience for students.

2. Recognition and respect for difference, as demonstrated by institution-wide respect for individual diversity, is engendered by the acknowledgment that different approaches and interventions may be needed for students with different backgrounds, lifestyles, and ethnic heritage.

3. Acknowledgment of cyclical learning and development allows for multiple points of developmental intervention by various agents who use unique approaches throughout students' academic career.

Students' major and vocational choices are always intertwined with multiple developmental tasks. When supporting students in the career advising process, advisors can apply Chickering's (1969) theory by asking probing questions that acquaint them with the advisee in relationship to all seven vectors, not solely with regard to developing purpose, which most closely relates to career choice. For instance, advisors may ask students the role of family and close friends in their decisions about careers. They may ask students how their lifestyle choices affect career decisions. In addition, they may encourage students to write a mission statement that combines a description of personal purpose and values with career objectives.

Foubert, Nixon, Sisson, and Barnes (2005) found that freshmen and seniors are most concerned with Chickering's (1969) sixth vector, but that the career development process continues throughout the undergraduate years. Therefore, advising interventions directed toward career choice should take place during each year and an intensive focus should be placed on the first and the final year.

Some colleges and universities provide opportunities for students to explore career and major choices within the curriculum. Modules for career and major exploration are embedded within a credit-bearing freshman orientation or seminar. Stark (2002) recommended a semester-long orientation course for undecided freshmen that would allow them time to focus on all the issues relating to major and career exploration. To provide course-based career support for students throughout their college careers, Lynchburg College offers two career-development courses for students, one targeted toward freshmen and sophomores, the other targeted toward juniors and seniors.

Using Chickering's (1969) work, advisors understand that students make decisions, including those regarding careers, within a broad context of (sometimes competing) developmental tasks. Therefore, advisors should help students discover how relationships, values, and sense of purpose are integral to their career choice.

STUDENT DEVELOPMENTAL PATHWAYS AND CAREER ADVISING

At first glance, Perry's (1968) scheme appears to present a well-defined developmental route to decidedness; however, like *Pilgrim's Progress*, the allegory to which Perry compared it, the path is circuitous. Students may experience dead ends, impenetrable forests, and other unexpected obstacles. Perry's interviews with students indicate that developmental stages are not static and that a student can simultaneously operate in multiple phases when responding to experiences. Likewise warning against the expectation of linear development progression, Chickering and Reisser (1993) noted that student development is usually cyclical in nature. With a theory that extends the work of Erikson (1950), Marcia (2002) further explained how events can foster or impede the development of students in career exploration and decision-making processes and how advisors can support students during these arduous tasks.

Marcia (2002) elaborated upon Erikson's (1950) theory to show how individuals progress through the stages of identity formation. Two sets of contrasting factors contribute to identity formation: crisis and commitment. When events or information challenge one's perspectives, values, or belief systems, the individual faces a crisis. Some individuals use challenges to their identity to make a commitment to a new viewpoint or a recommitment to original perspectives, values, or belief systems. The interplay between crisis and commitment affects a person's equilibrium, which can be grounded on an actual or a false sense of resolution. While equilibrium gives an individual a sense of being in control and comfortable with his or her situation, disequilibrium refers to a person's sense of struggle. Disequilibrium can be the result of a purposeful search for a new equilibrium or a flailing attempt to deal with crisis. According to Marcia (2002, pp. 11–13), the following four stages may result from the dichotomies of identity formation:

1. Crisis leading to commitment results in identity formation. As a result of struggle and reflection, the individual makes a mature commitment to new ways of thinking, values, or beliefs or recommits to original perspectives with increased maturity.

2. Commitment without crisis results in foreclosure. The individual has made commitments based on external belief systems and without reflection. The commitments tend to be rigid, dogmatic, or conformist.

3. Crisis without commitment results in moratorium. The individual is in a state of struggle and searching.

4. Lack of commitment or of crisis results in diffusion. The individual avoids commitment or reflection and may show signs of aimless drifting.

Marcia (2002) observed that individuals cycle through these stages as part of the developmental process.

According to Marcia (2002), crises provide the impetus that propels individuals through developmental stages. For instance, a student at the dualistic stage may experience disequilibrating events or information, such as the discovery that more than one major will lead to a preferred career goal, which causes uncertainty of the initial major declaration. By forcing the person to question his or her perspectives, such challenges can lead to a new level of functioning at the multiplistic position or can lead to moratorium and continued struggle. By applying Marcia's developmental theory, advisors can create a careful balance of challenge and support, as recommended by Sanford (1966), to help students purposefully develop their career exploration and decision-making processes. Without challenge, student inertia leads to diffusion; without support, students succumb to disorganization or moratorium. While Marcia cautioned that individuals may regress to earlier modes, he noted that it is "regression with a purpose" (p. 15) and a temporary setback in the cycle that ultimately leads to the next developmental stage.

In their article about undecided students, Slowinski and Hammock (2003) remarked that undecided students may be in a cyclical process; they will make a decision and then return to undecidedness due to a variety of factors (e.g., doubt, lack of information, peer influence, fear, and parental pressure). All students in the exploring phase must be assessed as individuals, which is a process that probably cannot be completed in one 30-minute appointment with an advisor.

Advisors may be frustrated when their advisees appear to have regressed with regard to the career decision-making process. However, an advisor knowledgeable of the works of Marcia (2002) and Sanford (1966) understands the student may have chosen to rethink a decision or reexamine issues once thought resolved. The advisor may suggest a reflection on the events that caused the change of direction so that the disequilibrating events (or information) that have affected the major or career commitment process can be addressed. The advisor should assure the student that setbacks are a normal part of career exploration and decision processes.

In fact, rather than being surprised or frustrated with a student who expresses regressive behaviors, advisors should never assume that a student's early major or career choice is the final word. Titley and Titley (1980) discovered that most college students express increasingly unspecific career choices as they near graduation. In addition, often students returning from semester breaks have faced disequilibrium. Therefore, after noting that changes are typical among undergraduates and acknowledging that more lengthy sessions may be needed, advisors may initiate appointments with decided students by asking whether the advisee is still committed to the original direction or other options are being considered.

Marcia's (2002) theory helps advisors understand that student career development seldom conforms to an orderly progression or a time line. Advisors familiar with it will recognize disequilibrating events and appreciate that regression can lead to developmental advances. This situation reinforces a basic tenet of developmental advising—that advising is a process, not an event.

DECISION MAKING AND CAREER ADVISING

King and Kitchener (1994) looked specifically at reflective decision making in the face of problems for which easy solutions or definitive answers are unavailable or arguable. They refer to these issues as ill-formed problems and consider the process of solving them "a neglected facet of critical thinking" (p. 1). Because a single, correct career choice does not exist, the answers to questions raised in the career development process may inspire debate among stakeholders, including the advisee, advisor, family members, and friends. Advisors who understand King and Kitchener's reflective judgment model have valuable insight into issues advisees are facing and strategies for helping to resolve ill-formed problems associated with career decisions.

Based on 15 years of research, King and Kitchener (1994) drew heavily from Perry's (1968) work. Their reflective judgment model contains seven stages with distinctive assumptions about the nature of problem solving that result in different problem-solving strategies among college students. King and Kitchener suggested specific strategies and interventions to move students forward in this developmental process. Evans, Forney, and Guido-DiBrito (1998) clustered these seven stages into three broad categories: prereflective thinkers (stages 1, 2, and 3); quasi-reflective thinkers (stages 4 and 5); and reflective thinkers (stages 6 and 7). Each stage is "posited to represent a more complex and effective form of justification, providing more inclusive and better integrated assumptions for evaluating and defending a point of view" (King & Kitchener, 1994, p. 13). Prereflective thinkers, like those in a dualistic stage, assume an absolute truth and that authorities have responsibility for imparting information to students. Quasi-reflective thinkers, like those at the multiplistic and relativistic phases, understand that not all knowledge is certain and that opinions do not constitute an argument. Reflective thinkers, like students who have reached the commitment stage, understand that knowledge must be actively constructed by one whose theoretical claims are dependent upon context and that conclusions must be open to reassessment and reevaluation.

Because King and Kitchener (1994) suggested that student decisions be challenged, they noted the importance of showing respect for all students, regardless of their problem-solving stage. Advisors should not blindly accept student declarations without challenging them with probing questions that uncover the processes that led to the decision and encouraging them to support their opinions and assumptions. For instance, advisors might ask students about the personal strengths that will benefit them in their career and ask them for examples of using them in the past. Even if a student seems to have a general sense of the duties required for a particular occupation, the advisor should ask whether the student is familiar with a typical day at the workplace and encourage job shadowing or informational interviewing. Addressing issues such as these places the responsibility for seeking and evaluating information on the student, which may inspire the advisee to reassess and reevaluate original assumptions.

To maintain a healthy, respectful relationship so that the advisee responds positively to advisor challenges, Galbraith (2003) recommended that advisors adopt a mentoring approach. Johnson (2006) noted that mentors enhance the mentee's self-esteem and competence by creating a durable relationship built on a foundation of trust and respect. By building such long-standing rapport, advisors can engage students in reflective visioning at a deeply personal level. For instance, the advisor may ask students to envision the lives they will lead if they choose specific occupations, and they can then encourage advisees to interview practitioners of these jobs.

King and Kitchener (1994) further recommended that students be offered many opportunities to reflect on problems through experiences in multiple settings. Career and orientation courses can offer opportunities through written assignments, including journaling. Learning communities, such as those at Ferris State University Care Exploration Learning Community (CARE) (www.ferris.edu/htmls/colleges/university/devcurriculum_care.htm) and the University of Wisconsin–Milwaukee residential living-learning community for freshmen titled "Creating Your Future: Exploring Major and Career Directions" (www4.uwm.edu/access_success/learning_communities.cfm), allow students to explore career and major options with their advisor via structured activities in a supportive peer community.

King and Kitchener's (1994) theory demonstrates the importance of reflection in the career decision-making process. King and Kitchener encourage advisors to provide multiple opportunities for student reflection within the advising relationship and to respond to student decision making with a balance of respectful support and challenge.

INDEPENDENT DECISION MAKING AND CAREER ADVISING

Chickering (1969) saw the movement toward independence and the development of mature relationships as developmental vectors. King and Kitchener (1994) noted that supporters of an individual can disagree about the best career decision for the individual. Advisors understand that students may rely on others while forming career decisions. Baxter Magolda and King (2004) showed how students develop into independent decision makers and made suggestions advisors can use to foster the development of independence in the career development process. Although King and Kitchener focused primarily on the cognitive aspects of decision making and offered suggestions for encouraging cognitive growth, Baxter Magolda focused on the role others play in the decision-making process.

Baxter Magolda and King (2004, 2008) explored the importance of self-authorship, the ability to generate values and identity internally rather than relying on the beliefs of others, as central to the development of authentic purpose among college students. According to Baxter Magolda and King (2008), advisors guiding "students to consider how their values, interests, skills and goals for further exploration affect academic and career choices" (p. 11) are key to fostering the development of self-authorship. Although believing that the advisor must be sympathetic and supporting, they agree with Marcia (2002) and Sanford (1966) that for development to occur, the advisor must challenge the advisee, noting that "there is an inherent tension in accepting students 'as they are' while encouraging them to transform their meaning making framework . . . " (Baxter Magolda & King, 2008, p. 11).

Baxter Magolda (2007) noted that, in the early stages of self-authorship, students who consult with others do not necessarily consider differing options carefully. She cautioned that encouraging students to consult a variety of sources does not mean that the students will carefully weigh all opinions or use valid criteria to assess the validity of each option. For instance, some students will give greater weight to an opinion about a major or career simply because it comes from an influential source (e.g., athletic coach or religious leader). These nonacademic advisors may not have an in-depth knowledge about academic majors or careers. Therefore, advisors should meet with advisees to help them reflect on the information they have gathered. To shape advisee decisions based on an effective use of all the information, advisors can ask students specifically how their strengths and abilities differ from those of the influential persons in their lives and how those differences might guide students down a different path than the one their elders have taken. Advisors can also ask students which sources of advice or information are most valid and the evidence that they used to make this determination.

Phalen (2005) suggested that Millennials differ from their predecessors in the third and sixth Chickering vectors (Chickering & Reisser, 1993): developing autonomy and purpose. Taylor, Harris, and Taylor (2004) noted that Millennials seek career advice from parents and that parents of college students are intensively involved in the students' career decision making. Because self-authorship is central to independent decision making, Baxter Magolda and King's (2004, 2008) work has particular application to the Millennial generation. Advisors can ask advisees the level of involvement their parents have had in shaping their career exploration and decision-making processes. They can encourage students to consider parental advice within the context of all the information students gathered as part of the career development process rather than as the only advice they should heed.

Baxter Magolda and King's (2004, 2008) work on self-authorship provides advisors with insight into the development of independent career decision making, and it may be especially relevant for Millennial students. Their work, along with that of King and Kitchener (1994), indicates that self-reflection is crucial to the development of self-authorship and that challenge as well as support is needed to develop autonomy and purpose.

ENGAGEMENT AND COLLABORATION

The developmental theories and approaches discussed primarily explain student behavior. Other theories and approaches have been created specifically to facilitate student development through student engagement and collaboration. By exploring these, advisors learn the role of engagement in fostering student development and see how career advising encourages student participation in the career development process.

The research of Astin (1965, 1984) and Kuh (2003) concerning student involvement and engagement provides a blueprint for proactive student development, including career decision making. Beginning in the 1960s, Astin (1965) showed that college environments have a direct effect on vocational choice because career decisions mirror the dominant major of the institutions they attend. Two decades later, Astin (1984) explored the role of student involvement on campus in undergraduate development, defining involvement as "the amount of physical and psychological energy that the student devotes to the academic experience" (p. 297). As a result of his work, Astin encouraged institutions to create climates that encourage student interest in campus activities.

Like Astin (1965, 1984), Kuh (2003) focused on the active role students play in their own development. He stated, "What students do during college counts more in terms of desired outcomes than who they are or even where they go to college" (p. 1). To assess the practices that foster student engagement, Kuh and others developed the National Survey of Student Engagement (NSSE) in 1999 (http://nsse.iub.edu). By 2008, the NSSE had surveyed more than 1,000 institutions of higher education about student participation in programs and services meant to increase student engagement in their own learning and development. The survey repeatedly found that seven practices, developed by Chickering and Gamson (1987), increase student engagement in learning and enhance student development. The highly rated institution

- Encourages contact between students and faculty
- Develops reciprocity and cooperation among students
- Encourages active learning
- Gives prompt feedback
- Emphasizes time on task
- Communicates high expectations
- Respects diverse talents and ways of learning

Such practices not only create a vibrant on-campus community, they foster intellectual development, mature decision making, and the acquisition of skills and competencies students will need in the world of work.

Some academic disciplines lend themselves easily to student-faculty collaborative research; they encourage faculty-student contact and fulfill Chickering and Gamson's (1987) other six principles as well. Such faculty-student connections foster the career development process by placing students in a challenging and competitive environment similar to the one they will discover on the job, thus helping them further develop the skills and competencies they will need in the work world. Advisors can encourage student involvement in joint research projects as a way to connect learners with faculty members at their institutions and with professional organizations within their disciplines. Advisors can also help students reflect on the experiences and the skills learned in the collaboration and articulate them to help students meet the demands of their chosen career.

Pascarella and Terenzini (2005) reported that successful students feel connected to advisors, faculty members, administrators, and peers in and out of the classroom, and that these students engage in educationally purposeful activities within this interconnected learning community. Involvement in academic-based, college-sponsored organizations develops reciprocity and cooperation among students while fostering skills and competencies they will use post-graduation. Participation in college-sponsored organizations also fosters intellectual development (Huang & Chang, 2004).

Advisors can encourage students to join clubs and organizations that sponsor career-directed activities of interest. The national business fraternity, Kappa Alpha Psi, or the international education honor society, Kappa Delta Pi, are just two examples of cocurricular entities that connect students, faculty members, and alumni as they maintain an academic focus through conferences, leadership training, and service activities. Huber, Hutchings, Gales, Miller, and Breen (2007) argued that advisors are responsible for purposefully integrating curricular and cocurricular activities in their recommendations and for encouraging students to seek connections among their own experiences.

Campbell and Nutt (2008) also believe that advisors play a key role in linking students with learning opportunities that foster engagement. Internships are a standard method for immersing students in the work environment of choice. They are potent learning experiences because through them students actively learn, receive prompt feedback, and understand the high expectations employers place on their employees. In addition to encouraging juniors and seniors to participate in internships, advisors should introduce job shadowing and service-learning opportunities to freshmen and sophomores.

APPLYING STUDENT DEVELOPMENT THEORY TO CAREER ADVISING

Understanding student development theory can enhance advisor practice and inform career advising. From the theories presented in this chapter, advisors can apply specific concepts to guide them as they support students in the career development process.

Developmental theory shows that career advising is a process, not an event. The process can be complex and recursive. Therefore, advisors must carefully build rapport with individual advisees, working with them to negotiate and define their relationship. Career advising is not a one-size-fits-all activity. Not only do individual students differ but individual students differ over time. As a result, advisors versed in student development theory create opportunities for multiple interactions or interventions throughout students' undergraduate careers. They expect students to regress and change direction as part of the career decision-making process; therefore, they keep in touch with their advisees, providing a balance of challenge and support, appreciating students' strengths, and noting weakly supported assumptions. Such interactions must be made in an atmosphere of trust, so advisors must foster mutual respect within the advising relationship.

Developmental theory shows that students make career decisions while negotiating other aspects of their lives. The process is inextricably bound with advisees' development of life purposes, values, relationships, and identities. From the first appointment, advisors who successfully help students through the career decision-making process seek to know all aspects of advisees' lives and encourage them to see career exploration and career decisions within the context of a comprehensive life plan. Advisees, especially Millennial students, will involve significant others (e.g., parents) in their career decisions. Advisors need to respect the views of advisees' inner circle while encouraging autonomous decision making.

Although students grow by engaging with multiple people, ideas, and experiences over time, the research of Astin (1965, 1984) and Kuh (2003) shows that students involved in such rich learning experiences do not necessarily integrate their new experiences with their own identities. Therefore, advisors should encourage verbal reflections or offer structured interventions, such as journaling, visioning, portfolio development, or discussions with peers, to make sure students fully process information and experiences.

Student development theory can enrich career advising programs and individual advisor's practice. It can help advisors understand students' cognitive, social, and identity development as it relates to major and career exploration. It can be used to create advising programs with meaningful interventions that encourage and foster students' career development. By providing a common conceptual base among practitioners and stakeholders, student development theory creates bridges that advisors and other professionals in academic and cocurricular programs can cross together in their quest to help students enhance the decision-making skills that will serve them in their lives and careers. Most important, through advisor application, student development theory can foster a nurturing and engaging learning community in which undergraduates grow to become active, contributing, creative, and responsible professionals in careers of their choice.

References

Astin, A. W. (1965). Effect of different college environments on the vocational choices of high aptitude students. *Journal of Counseling Psychology, 12,* 28–34.

Astin, A. W. (1984). Student involvement: A developmental theory for higher education. *Journal of College Student Personnel, 25,* 297–308.

Baxter Magolda, M. B. (2007). Self-authorship: The foundation for twenty-first century education. In P. S. Meszaros (Ed.), *Self-authorship: Advancing students' intellectual growth: No. 109. New directions for teaching and learning* (pp. 69–83). San Francisco: Jossey-Bass.

Baxter Magolda, M. B., & King, P. M. (Eds.). (2004). *Learning partnerships: Theories and models of practice to educate for self-authorship.* Sterling, VA: Stylus Press.

Baxter Magolda, M. B., & King, P. M. (2008). Toward reflective conversations: An advising approach that promotes self-authorship. *Peer Review, 10*(1), 8–11.

Campbell, S. M., & Nutt, C. (2008). Academic advising in the new global century: Supporting student engagement and learning outcomes achievement. *Peer Review, 10*(1), 4–7.

Chickering, A. W. (1969). *Education and identity.* San Francisco: Jossey-Bass.

Chickering, A. W., & Gamson, Z. F. (1987). Seven principles for good practice in undergraduate education. *The Wingspread Journal, 9*(2). Retrieved December 7, 2008, from http://wwww.johnsonfdn.org/Pulications/ConferenceReports/SevenPrinciples

Chickering, A. W., & Reisser, L. (1993). *Education and identity* (2nd ed.). San Francisco: Jossey-Bass.

Erikson, E. (1950). *Childhood and society.* Boston: W. W. Norton.

Evans, N., Forney, D., & Guido-DiBrito, F. (1998). *Student development in college: Theory, research, and practice.* San Francisco: Jossey-Bass.

Foubert, J. D., Nixon, M. L., Sisson, V. S., & Barnes, A. C. (2005). A longitudinal study of Chickering and Reisser's vectors: Exploring gender differences and implications for refining the theory. *Journal of College Student Development, 46,* 461–471.

Galbraith, M. W. (2003). Mentoring towards self-directedness. *Adult Learning, 14*(4), 9–11.

Hall, D. T. (2004). The protean career: A quarter-century journey. *Journal of Vocational Behavior, 65,* 1–13.

Huang, Y., & Chang, S. (2004). Academic and cocurricular involvement: Their relationship and the best combination for student growth. *Journal of College Student Development, 45,* 391–406.

Huber, M. T., Hutchings, P., Gales, R., Miller, R., & Breen, M. (2007). Leading initiatives for integrative learning. *Liberal Education, 93*(2), 46–51.

Johnson, W. B. (2006). *On being a mentor: A guide for higher education faculty.* Mahwah, NJ: Lawrence Earlbaum Associates.

Jones, H., & Newman, I. (1993, April). *A mosaic of diversity: Vocationally undecided students and the Perry scheme of intellectual and ethical development.* Paper presented at the annual meeting of the American Educational Research Association, Atlanta, GA.

King, P. M., & Kitchener, K. S. (1994). *Developing reflective judgment: Understanding and promoting intellectual growth and critical thinking in adolescents and adults.* San Francisco: Jossey-Bass.

Knefelkamp, L. L., & Slepitzka, R. (1976). A cognitive-developmental model of career development: An adaptation of the Perry scheme. *The Counseling Psychologist, 6*(3), 53–58.

Kuh, G. D. (2003). *The National Survey of Student Engagement: Conceptual framework and overview of psychometric properties.* Retrieved December 10, 2007, from http://nsse.iub.edu/pdf/conceptual_framework_2003.pdf

Laughlin, A., & Creamer, E. (2007). Engaging differences: Self-authorship and the decision-making process. In P. S. Meszaros (Ed.), *Self-authorship: Advancing students' intellectual growth: No. 9. New directions for teaching and learning* (pp. 43–51). San Francisco: Jossey-Bass.

Marcia, J. E. (2002). Identity and psychosocial development in adulthood. *Identity, 2*(1), 7–28.

Pascarella, E. T., & Terenzini P. T. (2005). *How college affects students: A third decade of research.* San Francisco: Jossey-Bass.

Perry, W. G., Jr. (1968). *Forms of intellectual and ethical development in the college years: A scheme.* New York: Rinehart & Winston.

Phalen, K. (2005, October). *Advising millennials: The good, the bad, and the parents.* Paper presented at the annual meeting of the National Academic Advising Association, Las Vegas, NV.

Sanford, N. (1966). *Self & society.* New York: Atherton Press.

Slowinski, P. T., & Hammock, W. K. (2003). *Undecided/open students.* Retrieved April 1, 2008, from http://www.nacada.ksu.edu/Clearinghouse/AdvisingIssues/adv_undeclared.htm

Stark, K. (2002, September 16). Advising undecided students: What works best? *The Mentor: An Academic Advising Journal, 4*(3). Retrieved March 15, 2008, from ww.psu.edu/dus/mentor/

Taylor, J., Harris, M. B., & Taylor, S. (2004). Parents have their say . . . about their college-aged children's career decisions. *NACE Journal, 64*(2). Retrieved March 15, 2008, from http://www.jobweb.com

Titley, W., & Titley, B. (1980). The major-changers: Are only the "undecided" undecided? *Journal of College Student Personnel, 21,* 293–298.

CHAPTER SIX

Diversity and Career Advising

Aaron H. Carlstrom, Marilyn S. Kaff, Karen R. Low

T he foci of career advising activities are to facilitate students' choice of
career and academic goals and subsequent development, implementation, and evaluation of plans to achieve their goals. In this pursuit, career
advising is often guided by traditional career development theories and activities, which emphasize student learning about self, options, and decision making, and then the use of that information to make an optimal choice.

However, for many students the exclusive use of traditional theories and
activities to understand their career development and to facilitate their career
planning is inadequate, because important issues connected with race/
ethnicity, disability status, sexual orientation, and gender are not appropriately addressed. Although there is limited knowledge about the validity of traditional career development approaches with racial/ethnic minority students,
LGBT students (i.e., lesbian, gay, bisexual, and transgender), and students
with disabilities, "[t]he assumption is that the relevance of career interventions can be increased by approaches that take into account" contextual factors (Byars-Winston & Fouad, 2006, p. 187).

Further, traditional career development theories and activities are based on
five cultural values, or key tenets, that may differ from the cultural, family, and
personal values and life experiences of students (Gysbers, Heppner, & Johnston,
2003). First, there is an emphasis on individuals making independent career
and life choices based on personal interests in contrast to making choices from
a relational or collectivist perspective (individualism and autonomy). Next,
the costs of pursuing certain career choices (e.g., paying tuition and not having an income while in college) are deemphasized (affluence). Further, limitations in the opportunity structure and subsequent restrictions in career choice
because of discrimination and prejudice in education and the workplace are
deemphasized (structure of opportunity open to all who strive). Fourth, work
is portrayed as the primary source of people's need fulfillment and identity,

and other life roles (e.g., partner or community member) are deemphasized (centrality of work in people's lives). Last, the linear, progressive, and rational aspects of the career development and planning process are emphasized versus work patterns that are nonlinear in progression (e.g., short-term employment based on job availability), or decision-making approaches that are nonlinear or intuitive (linearity, progressiveness, and rationality of the career development process). Thus, the extent to which students' values and experiences, whether experienced directly or through witnessing the experiences of family or community members, are inconsistent with these tenets, the exclusive use of traditional theories and activities is likely to be inadequate to facilitate students' career development and planning.

This does not mean that traditional theories and activities cannot be helpful when working with racial/ethnic minority students, LGBT students, students with disabilities, and female students; however, advisors need to evaluate the effectiveness and modify the use of these theories and activities within the context of students' experiences. When working with students from these groups traditional approaches should be used with *caution* and *flexibility*, based on an understanding about how students' experiences may differ from the underlying assumptions of traditional theories and activities. Although advisors should do this with *all* students, the issues addressed in this chapter are those more likely to affect racial/ethnic minority students, students with disabilities, LGBT students, and female students.

Therefore, the purpose of this chapter is to serve as a basic overview and introduction to the topic of diversity and career advising by highlighting some of the factors that may affect students' career development and planning connected with race/ethnicity, disability status, sexual orientation, and gender. Further, recommendations are provided about issues that should be addressed beyond those with traditional career planning approaches to facilitate the career development and planning of racial/ethnic minority students, LGBT students, students with disabilities, and female students.

The issues presented in this chapter are generalizations, and presented because students from these different groups are more likely to have these experiences than students who do not belong to these groups (e.g., students with disabilities are more likely to have limited career exploration experiences when they enter college compared to their non-disabled peers). However, these issues will not be true for every student from the specific group (e.g., some students with disabilities will come to college with a history of positive career exploration experiences). Further, students who do not belong to the groups presented may also experience the issues (e.g., students without disabilities may come to college with limited career exploration experiences). The salience of these issues for a specific student depends on the interaction of a number of factors: individual biological and personality factors, experiences within the family, and cultural and contextual factors (e.g., gender, race/ethnicity, disability status, sexual orientation, and socioeconomic status; Fouad & Bingham, 1995).

Further, it is important to be aware that within the broad social groups addressed in this chapter (i.e., racial/ethnic minority students, students with disabilities, LGBT students), there are specific social groups that differ from each other in significant and meaningful ways. In presenting four broad social groups the intent is to introduce some common career development issues that have a greater likelihood of being experienced by racial/ethnic minority students (compared to their White peers), LGBT students (compared to their heterosexual peers), students with disabilities (compared to their peers without disabilities), and female students (compared to their male peers). In essence, there is significant and meaningful diversity both within and between specific social groups, and flexibility and responsiveness to this diversity is essential for multicultural competency in career advising.

DIVERSITY IN HIGHER EDUCATION

The population of students in higher education became more diverse at the latter part of the twentieth century and the start of the twenty-first century. Over the past three decades there was a significant and meaningful increase in the number of students in higher education who are racial/ethnic minority students, students with disabilities, LGBT students, and women.

Racial/Ethnic Minority Students

The racial and ethnic diversity of students attending colleges and universities in the United States significantly increased over the past 30 years. As of 2004, approximately 31% of U.S. college students were racial/ethnic minority students, which was double the percentage from 1976 (U.S. Department of Education, National Center for Education Statistics [NCES], 2008). Further, racial/ethnic minority students represent even larger segments of the community college populations (Fassinger, 2008). As of the 2002–03 academic year, racial/ethnic minority students earned 27% of associate degrees, 22% of bachelor's degrees, 17% of master's degrees, 14% of doctoral degrees, and 24% of first-professional degrees (NCES, 2005).

Students with Disabilities

The number of college students with disabilities in the U.S. is estimated at 11%, which is a fivefold increase over the last three decades (NCES, 2006b), and about one-fifth of the U.S. population has a disability (Fassinger, 2008). The reported increase in college enrollment of students with disabilities is attributed to better diagnoses of disabilities during childhood and adolescence and higher expectations of students with disabilities (e.g., pursuing postsecondary education) connected with "mandated inclusive legislation which paved the way for equal opportunity and set the stage for encouraging professionals, families and youth to think in new ways about career goals" (Fabian & Liesener, 2005, p. 561).

The most prevalent disabilities reported by college students were orthopedic condition (25%), mental illness or depression (22%), and specific health impairment (17%). Men are more likely to report attention deficit disorders, and women more likely to report health impairments and mental illness or depression (NCES, 2006b).

LGBT Students

Although there are shortcomings to using the term *sexual orientation* (e.g., emphasis is placed on sexuality and other aspects of the person are ignored) (Perez, DeBord, & Bieschke, 2000), it is used here to indicate an attribute on which people differ and that affects career planning and development. Further, the acronym LGBT is used to indicate students who are lesbian women, gay men, bisexual men or women, or transgender persons. There is not complete agreement on including the T, for transgender, with LGB. Differences between sexual orientation and gender identity are recognized, but LGBT is used here because of the "historical, cultural, political, and psychological interrelatedness between sexual orientation and gender identity" (Chung, 2003, p. 79). See Pepper and Lorah (2008) for a discussion of career and workplace issues unique to transgender workers, such as transitioning at the workplace, difficult aspects of the job search, dealing with negative reactions of coworkers and supervisors, and deciding which bathroom to use in the workplace.

The exact numbers of LGBT students on college campuses is unknown. Most estimates of lesbian women and gay men in the general population vary between 1 and 15% (Savin-Williams & Ream, 2007; Sell, Wells, & Wypij, 1995). Gathering data on the number of LGBT students in the university setting is challenging because it requires students to reveal their sexual orientation. However, because of internalized negative stereotypes or the fear of being targeted with antigay prejudice and discrimination (Ender & Wilkie, 2000), LGBT students may be reluctant to reveal their sexual orientation. Despite this, LGBT students are becoming more visible on college campuses (Joslin, 2007).

Women

Women are entering higher education at greater rates, and earning a greater percentage of degrees than males. Between 1972 and 2006 the rate of women who entered four-year institutions immediately after high school increased faster than it did for men (NCES, 2007). As of 2004, women comprised approximately 57% of the students enrolled in degree-granting institutions in the U.S. (NCES, 2006a). Further, across all racial/ethnic groups, women earned more associate's (60%), bachelor's (57%), and master's (59%) degrees than men (NCES, 2005). However, within the STEM (i.e., science, technology, engineering, math) areas, 40% of doctorates earned by women are in the social, behavioral, and life sciences, whereas men earn the majority of doctorates in engineering, and the computer and physical sciences, fields associated with higher prestige and compensation (Fassinger, 2008).

ISSUES AFFECTING CAREER DEVELOPMENT AND PLANNING

It is important to be aware of how the experiences of racial/ethnic minority students, students with disabilities, LGBT students, and female students may differ from those assumed by traditional career development and planning activities. There are some ways in which students from these four groups are similar in how they differ from traditional career development assumptions, such as the experiences of educational and workplace discrimination, lack of access to role models and mentors who are similar, and the importance of factors other than interests in career choice. However, there are also ways in which students from these four groups are dissimilar in how they differ from traditional career development assumptions, such as acculturation and racial identity development (racial/ethnic minority students), lack of appropriate accommodations (students with disabilities), sexual identity management in the workplace (LGBT students), and managing multiple role responsibilities (female students).

Racial/Ethnic Minority Students

Encountering discrimination in education and work and having less access to role models, mentors, and good occupational information can negatively affect the career development and planning of racial/ethnic minority individuals. Further, although there are not racial/ethnic differences in career aspirations, attitudes, and behavior, there are racial/ethnic differences in career expectations, self-efficacy beliefs, and the importance of personal interests in making career choices. In addition, it is important for advisors to be aware of students' level of acculturation and racial identity development as a means of estimating the degree to which traditional career development activities need to be modified.

Discrimination and the World of Work. Racism is the "overarching barrier" (Fassinger, 2008, p. 259) to workplace achievement for racial/ethnic minority people in the United States. Examples of barriers connected with racism include (a) attending schools with inadequate resources, (b) low achievement expectations of racial/ethnic minority students, (c) lack of opportunities for career exploration, (d) lack of role models, mentors, and access to informal professional information and support networks, (e) negative consequences of tokenism, and (f) workplace discrimination in hiring, compensation, and advancement. The negative effects of racism on the workforce participation patterns of racial/ethnic minority workers include (a) significantly lower salaries than their White peers even when education, occupation, region of the country, and experience are controlled, (b) lower probability than White workers to be in STEM occupations, (c) African American and Latino workers are less likely to be managers and professionals than White workers, (d) greater likelihood of African Americans, Latinos, and American Indians earning college degrees in the social sciences and working in social service occupations (which are lower pay and lower status occupations) than White workers, and (e) greater likelihood to be temporarily employed, underemployed, or unemployed than White people.

Role Models, Mentors, and Occupational Information. It is difficult to distinguish between the effects of race/ethnicity and socioeconomic status (e.g., parental educational and occupational attainment, quality of K–12 education) on career development because these two factors are correlated in contemporary U.S. society (Fassinger, 2008). Workplace discrimination that results in the segregation of many racial/ethnic minority workers to a restricted range of occupations and work roles (e.g., semi- and low-skilled, low paying, low prestige, require minimal education and training; Fassinger, 2008) decreases the probability that racial/ethnic minority students will have role models and mentors in high pay and high prestige professions (e.g., STEM occupations), especially racially and ethnically similar role models and mentors. Role models and mentors are means to gain access to informal professional information, and support networks are important for career success and advancement (Fassinger, 2008). Further, role models and mentors, especially racially and ethnically similar role models and mentors, can help students build the confidence to pursue a career path, expand the occupations that students may consider as "open" to members of their racial/ethnic group, and provide support to help with the social and emotional consequences of confronting racial discrimination and barriers.

Segregated workforce participation patterns also serve to limit the exposure of racial/ethnic minority students to a range of quality information about the world of work. These negative consequences can be further compounded because racial/ethnic minority students are more likely to have no or limited exposure to career exploration activities in K–12 education (Fassinger, 2008), and participation in these activities is associated with the development of greater career aspirations for racial/ethnic minority students (Worthington, Flores, & Navarro, 2005). Racial/ethnic minority students are also less likely to be familiar with the traditional career decision-making process if their family and community members' work choices were characterized less by the implementation of a vocational self, and more by "short-term and disruptive employment in whatever field had an available opportunity" (Gysbers et al., 2003, p. 57) due to financial necessity and environmental barriers.

Interests, Aspirations, Attitudes, Behaviors, Expectations, and Self-Efficacy Beliefs. A series of meta-analyses concluded that there were not racial/ethnic differences in career interests, aspirations, or decision-making attitudes and behaviors (i.e., decision making self-efficacy, career maturity, career exploration behaviors) (Fouad & Byars-Winston, 2005). For example, all else being equal, a Mexican American advisee is just as likely to have high career goals and aspirations, and positive decision-making attitudes and behaviors, as her White classmates. However, the conclusions of individual studies in this area were mixed (Worthington et al., 2005), such as some evidence that Asian

Americans prefer more prestigious occupations than other racial/ethic groups (Miller & Brown, 2005), but this difference is probably due more to acculturation level than to racial/ethnic group membership. There are also family and contextual factors that appear to positively influence racial/ethnic minority students' aspirations: (a) family, kinship, peer, mentor, and general social support; (b) parental involvement with school activities; (c) school programs that facilitate student exploration of career opportunities; (d) acculturation level; (e) parental educational attainment for adolescents from families emigrated from Mexico; and (f) fathers' occupational status for African American students (Worthington et al., 2005).

Discrimination in education and work can also negatively affect the academic and career expectations and self-efficacy beliefs of racial/ethnic minority students. Although there were not racial/ethnic differences in interests, there was evidence that interests may play less of a role in making a career choice for racial/ethnic minority students than for White students. Factors such as barriers to education and work, confidence to perform the tasks associated with different occupations, and family influence may be more important in educational and career planning for racial/ethnic minority students than personal interests (Miller & Brown, 2005; Worthington et al., 2005).

Racial/ethnic minority students had lower expectations about attaining their academic and career goals, perceived greater barriers to their academic and career goals, and less confidence in their ability to cope with or manage those barriers (Byars-Winston & Fouad, 2006; Fassinger, 2008). These barriers can be about educational experience at college and entry to and success in the world of work. These factors may contribute to racial/ethnic minority students' narrowing their viable career options to "racially friendly" occupations, where the probability of encountering prejudice and discrimination is low (Miller & Brown, 2005), instead of selecting occupations that are a better match with their interests and goals. For example, all else being equal, an African American student is more likely than his White peer to perceive and encounter more career and educational barriers to his goal attainment, feel less confident to address those barriers, and have lower expectations that he will attain his career goals. Thus, the student may not pursue a high-aspiration career, not because he lacks interest or competence, but because of barriers, low self-efficacy to address those barriers, and thus decreased expectations about attaining his high aspiration academic and career goals.

Self-efficacy beliefs about being successful in different academic subjects and occupations also influence academic and career choices. Racial/ethnic minority students are less likely to have positive education and occupation self-efficacy beliefs, which is problematic because self-efficacy beliefs predict interests and may predict academic and career choices better than interests (Worthington et al., 2005). For example, a Native American student may be interested in science and math occupations, but she is more likely to have low self-efficacy for science and math occupations. This, in turn, could lead to lowered science and math interest and failing to choose science and math courses, academic majors, and career paths. Thus, the low science and math self-efficacy beliefs may have more influence on choice than the initial science and math interest.

Cultural Values, Acculturation, and Racial Identity Development. The tenets of individualism and autonomy and centrality of work in people's lives are incongruent with the important role of family and community in identity formation and making important life choices associated with the cultural values of many racial/ethnic minority groups. For example, (a) collectivism influences the career planning process of Asian Americans; (b) family influences, such as the preference to select occupations that are high in prestige, and where discrimination is less likely to be experienced, may be more important in career planning than personal interests for Asian Americans; (c) Native Americans place greater emphasis on family and community, both as a source of identity and as an influence on career planning; and (d) African Americans tend to value collectivism more than individualism, which has an effect on career development and planning (Miller & Brown, 2005). Further, family, kinship networks, and community are associated with positive academic and career development of racial/ethnic minority students: (a) family, peer, mentor, and kinship support positively affect school engagement attitudes, the importance placed on work, and academic persistence; and (b) family support and parental expectations positively affect the educational and career choices and development of African Americans (Miller & Brown, 2005; Worthington et al., 2005).

Acculturation is the extent to which people have adopted the beliefs, values, and behaviors of the dominant culture and maintained the beliefs, values, and behaviors of their culture of origin (Gysbers et al., 2003). Less acculturated individuals are more likely to adhere to traditional cultural values, compared to more acculturated people. For example, (a) Latino Americans who were more acculturated had career behaviors similar to their White peers, whereas the career attitudes, behaviors, and choice of those low in acculturation were influenced more by traditional cultural values, such as "allocentrism, familismo, simpatia, respeto and machismo" (Miller & Brown, 2005, p. 456); (b) highly acculturated Asian Americans considered a wider range of occupational choices, whereas less-acculturated Asian Americans were more likely to choose science and engineering occupations, make choices for reasons other than interests, and be less satisfied with their choice; and (c) Native Americans who were less acculturated emphasized community and family in making career decisions, whereas more acculturated Native Americans considered other factors, such as personal interests (Miller & Brown, 2005).

Racial identity development also influences career development and planning (Miller & Brown, 2005; Worthington et al., 2005) and can explain some of the within-group differences in the career development of racial/ethnic minority students. Racial identity development is similar to acculturation in that both involve race and ethnic-related beliefs, values, and behaviors, but racial identity development focuses on "understanding oneself in a racially oppressive environment" (Gysbers et al., 2003, p. 64). Racial/ethnic minority individuals with more developed racial identities are more likely to have more developed vocational identity, greater level of career maturity, and more confidence to make career decisions and set goals. However, there was not a consistent connection between racial identity development and career aspirations, although this finding varied based on racial/ethnic group and gender (Worthington et al., 2005). Further, it is hypothesized that students with less developed racial identities may lack adequate awareness of the role of race/ethnicity in the contemporary world of work (Gysbers et al., 2003), and thus not be prepared to address workplace discrimination and barriers.

Students with Disabilities

Students with disabilities encounter barriers and discrimination in education and work that negatively affect their career development and planning, such as lack of appropriate accommodations in higher education settings, and negative attitudes and discrimination from employers and coworkers. Further, students with disabilities are less likely to have had career exploration and work experiences prior to college, and access to role models and mentors (especially those with disabilities). Additionally, they are more likely to have lower career aspirations, expectations, and self-efficacy beliefs, and be less ready to make an optimal career choice.

Definitions, Legal Issues, and Differences in Higher Education. There is no single definition of disability because there are many different types of disabilities, each of which differentially affects people's functioning, both in terms of severity and the specific capacity affected (Fabian & Liesener, 2005). The Individuals with Disabilities Education Act (IDEA) lists 13 disability categories, such as orthopedic impairment, specific learning disability, and visual impairment (Gargiulo, 2009). Two civil rights laws (i.e., Section 504 of the 1973 Vocational Rehabilitation Act and the Americans with Disabilities Act [ADA]) do not list specific disabilities but establish the following criteria for a disability: "a physical or mental impairment that substantially limits one or more major life activities; a record of such an impairment; or being regarded as having such impairment" (U.S. Department of Justice, 2007, Section 12102, para. 2).

It is confusing for some students with disabilities and their families that IDEA is not applicable in higher education, because even though they qualified for special services in K–12 education under IDEA, they may not qualify for special services under the more stringent requirements in the adult system (Fabian & Liesener, 2005). In higher education, Section 504 and ADA provide for "equal access" to education for students with disabilities, although exactly how equal access applies to postsecondary instruction and transition to post-college life is much less clear (Brinckerhoff, McGuire, & Shaw, 2002). Fabian and Liesener (2005), Kosciulek (2003), and Fassinger (2008) address legislation relevant to the career and educational development of people with disabilities including IDEA, ADA, and Section 504.

Discrimination and the World of Work. Workforce participation patterns of people with disabilities are characterized by underrepresentation and job segregation (Fassinger, 2008). Compared to people without disabilities, people with disabilities are less likely to be employed full time, more likely to have low prestige and low-paying occupations, more likely to have episodic employment and involuntary job loss, and more likely to live below the poverty line. Employment difficulties of people with disabilities are worse for those with less education, more severe disabilities, women, and racial/ethnic minorities (Fabian & Liesener, 2005; Fassinger, 2008). Within higher education, students with disabilities have a greater chance of not graduating from college than their nondisabled peers, and students with disabilities who do graduate from college are less likely to graduate with a major in the STEM fields (Fabian & Liesener, 2005). Further, services and supports for students with disabilities have not kept pace with the dramatic influx of students to higher education. For example, students frequently find university programs lacking in the accommodations needed, often because instructors and advisors are unfamiliar with their needs and requirements (Lock & Layton, 2001). As a result, many students with disabilities are unable to successfully compete academically (Mull, Sitlington, & Alper, 2001), or simply leave before completing their planned program of study (Fairweather & Shaver, 1990–91; Lehmann, Davies, & Laurin, 2000).

Most people of working age with disabilities want to work (Fabian & Liesener, 2005), and thus the negative workforce participation patterns of people with disabilities are not attributable to a lack of motivation and desire. However, negative attitudes and discrimination from employers and coworkers are significant barriers to the hiring, tenure, and promotion of people with disabilities (Fabian & Liesener, 2005); one-fourth of people with disabilities who are employed experience direct job discrimination (Fassinger, 2008). Lack of employable skills is a barrier to work not only for people with disabilities in general, but also for people with disabilities who graduate college (Fassinger, 2008). Other barriers to employment for people with disabilities include lack of suitable jobs, lack of access to transportation to get to work, family responsibilities, and concern about losing disability benefits, especially access to health insurance, if they enter or reenter the workforce (Fabian & Liesener, 2005; Fassinger, 2008).

Career Exploration, Work Experiences, Role Models, and Mentors. Exposure to work experiences, role models, and career exploration activities can help develop positive, realistic academic and career-related self-efficacy beliefs, outcome expectations, interests, and attitudes for students with disabilities (Fabian & Liesener, 2005). However, many college students with disabilities had different academic and career development experiences than their nondisabled peers, which negatively affects their career planning and decision making. Students with disabilities often have limited knowledge about the world of work because they lacked exposure to career exploration activities in K–12 education. Lack of work-based learning experiences also decreases the chances that students with disabilities connect with role models and mentors (Fabian & Liesener, 2005; Fassinger, 2008). Further, given the invisible nature of some disabilities (e.g., learning disability), the workforce participation patterns of people with disabilities, and the barriers encountered by people with disabilities in education and the world of work, the probability is decreased that students with disabilities will have role models and mentors who have disabilities.

Interests, Aspirations, Motivation, Self-Efficacy Beliefs, and Outcome Expectations. The development of academic and career self-efficacy beliefs, outcome expectations, interests, and aspirations is important for the career development and planning of students with disabilities. Not only are self-efficacy beliefs positively associated with career choice, and interests for students with disabilities, they are also positively related to the ability to manage disability issues in a job interview (Fabian & Liesener, 2005). However, people with disabilities encounter several barriers (e.g., prejudice, negative social attitudes, and lowered expectations) to the development of positive self-efficacy beliefs, as well as outcome expectations, self-concept, aspirations, motivation, and sense of empowerment (Fabian & Liesener, 2005; Kosciulek, 2003). Not only do students with disabilities encounter prejudice, negative social attitudes, discrimination, and social isolation in K–12 education, these experiences often continue at college (Fabian & Liesener, 2005). Further, type of disability also influences the amount of negative thinking associated with making career transitions. People with a cognitive disability reported more negative thinking about making a career transition and more conflict with important others in their life in making a career decision than individuals with physical disabilities (Yanchak, Lease, & Strauser, 2005).

Career Maturity and Readiness to Make a Career Choice. Career maturity and readiness to make a career choice are important because they are associated with a clearer picture of one's career interests and goals and plans for how to achieve career goals. Students with disabilities often have very few or indistinct ideas about career paths and about how academic majors relate to occupational options. Often, important others in the students' lives (e.g., parents) made many of the important decisions about their future, and, therefore, they were more likely to have had fewer opportunities to develop decision-making skills (Fabian & Liesener, 2005), a situation that contributes to career development and planning difficulties (Kosciulek, 2003). In addition, limited work experience and exposure and limited participation with career education activities (Ender & Wilkie, 2000) contribute to students' reduced opportunities to practice decision making. Further, many students with disabilities may have been more concerned with making academic progress during their K–12 education than thinking about career goals and aspirations. The career maturity of students with disabilities is also influenced by the onset of the disability. People who started a career prior to the onset of their disability are more likely to choose occupations that are consistent with their career plans prior to the disability, whereas individuals who did not start to pursue a career prior to the onset of their disability (e.g., children) are more likely to have lower career maturity and to select occupations that reflect their parents' aspirations and socioeconomic status (Kosciulek, 2003).

LGBT Students

Discrimination in educational and workplace settings and lack of access to role models and mentors (especially LGBT role models and mentors) can negatively affect the career development and planning of LGBT students. Further, having LGBT role models and mentors not only can be beneficial for LGBT students in traditional ways but can also assist students as they navigate their sexual identity development and management. When working with LGBT students it is important to be aware of the influences on their expressed interests, the interaction between their career development and sexual identity development, and the issue of sexual identity management.

Discrimination and the World of Work. LGBT students live in a society that is often unreceptive and hostile. Thirty-seven states do not have laws to protect lesbian, gay, and bisexual K–12 students from discrimination because of their sexual orientation; 47 states do not have laws that protect transgender students from mistreatment; and LGBT workers have no federal protection from discrimination based on their sexual orientation or gender identity, although the results of opinion polls indicate an improvement in the outlook for LGBT workers (Fassinger, 2008). LGBT people experience antigay discrimination on campus and in the workplace. In one study of fraternity and sorority members, 3 to 6% reported they were gay or lesbian, 40% of those students came out to someone in their chapter, and 70% of those students reported experiencing homophobia or heterosexism within their own chapters (Case, 1996). These findings are consistent with other studies of U.S. university campuses (Rankin, Case, Windmeyer, Eberly, Hesp, et al., 2007; Sanlo, 2004). LGBT workers experience workplace discrimination, lack of domestic partner benefits, and disparity in wages compared to heterosexual workers (Fassinger, 2008).

Role Models and Mentors. LGBT role models and mentors can benefit the career development of LGBT students beyond the traditional benefits associated with role models and mentors. Some of the difficulty experienced with the coming out process is the fear of losing, or the actual loss of support and relationships with important others (e.g., family, friends, and religious institutions) (Ender & Wilkie, 2000). LGBT role models and mentors can help students build connections with the LGBT and professional communities.

In addition, the lack of LGBT role models, the lack of positive information about LGBT people in the broader society (Ender & Wilkie, 2000), and the societal barriers to having more "out" LGBT professionals makes it difficult for LGBT students to build positive sexual identities in general and specifically to consider a full range of occupational options as an LGBT individual. LGBT role models and mentors can help students build positive sexual identities and unlearn internalized negative stereotypes, learn about vocational sexual identity management and organizational climate evaluation, improve career development and occupation-specific self-efficacy and outcome expectations, serve as proof of successful career development of LGBT workers (Joslin, 2007), and challenge occupational stereotyping and broaden the occupations that students consider. LGBT professionals in different fields and LGBT campus faculty and staff can serve as role models and mentors (Joslin, 2007), and job shadowing with an LGBT professional can provide access to role models and mentors within an occupational field of interest.

Interests. Compared to heterosexual individuals, gay and lesbian people are more likely to have gender nontraditional interests (Gysbers et al., 2003). This can contribute to feelings of confusion or embarrassment (Nauta, Saucier, & Woodard, 2001). Therefore, if LGBT students follow socially prescribed messages about gender-appropriate interests and career plans but have gender nontraditional career interests, they are more likely to not pursue their gender nontraditional interests. This could contribute to career development difficulties, such as career indecision, restricting the career options considered, and decreased satisfaction. In addition, LGBT students at earlier stages of sexual identity development may not pursue their gender nontraditional career interests for fear that to do so may reveal their sexual identity. Some students worry that their sexual identity will be revealed in standardized testing and are therefore guarded when taking interest inventories, thus resulting in inaccurate assessment results (Fassinger, 1998). However, it is also important to note that lesbians, compared to gay men and heterosexual individuals, are more likely to pursue gender nontraditional careers (Gysbers et al., 2003).

Campus and workplace discrimination and hostility toward LGBT people can negatively affect students' career development by making safety a primary concern in career choice for LGBT students, as opposed to making choices based on fit with career interests and goals (Fassinger, 2008; Miller & Brown, 2005). Because of safety concerns, LGBT students may use occupational stereotyping, the limiting of occupational options considered viable to those occupations that students think are safe or friendly for LGBT workers (Fassinger, 2008; Miller & Brown, 2005) and eliminate occupational options that could lead to career satisfaction.

Sexual Identity Development. LGBT students' level of sexual identity development affects their career development, from influencing career choice and the development of interests, values, and skills, to influencing the job search process, professional relationships, and the relation between work and home (Gelberg & Chojnacki, 1996). Joslin (2007) noted that the sexual identity development models of Cass (1979), D'Augelli (1994), and Fassinger (1998) are frequently referenced in relation to LGBT students in the advising literature. Although there are various sexual identity development models, the following stages are found in many of the models: (a) individual's growing awareness of their sexual identity and orientation (i.e., lesbian, gay, bisexual), (b) exploration of the meaning of their sexual identity and orientation in their lives, (c) acceptance of their sexual identity and orientation, and (d) integration of their sexual identity and orientation with their other self-identities. Although the models posited by Cass, D'Augelli, and Fassinger address sexual orientation, they have been used to understand transgender identity development (e.g., Bilodeau & Renn, 2005), and the models are frequently used in the advising literature for both LGB and transgender students (Joslin, 2007).

For traditional-aged college students, college is the developmental period in which students continue to crystallize their vocational identity, make choices about educational and vocational paths, and implement an occupational choice (Super, Savickas, & Super, 1996). However, for LGBT students, college is also an important time in their sexual identity development (i.e., coming out process). For many LGBT students, college may be the time when they begin to explore or accept their sexual identity development because it is the first time they are away from the constraints, or perceived constraints, of their family. Thus, LGBT students may spend significantly more time and energy attempting to find an affirming community and to develop positive relationships (Ender & Wilkie, 2000) than their heterosexual peers who were able to begin addressing these developmental tasks at an earlier age. LGBT students also deal with the turmoil often associated with the coming out process (Fassinger, 2008), such as dealing with internalized negative stereotypes and self-acceptance; experiencing anxiety about being rejected, harassed, or discriminated against because of their sexuality; coping with feelings of isolation; and being concerned that family and important others may stop personal and financial support (Ender & Wilkie, 2000; Miller & Brown, 2005).

Given the time and energy necessary for LGBT students to successfully address the developmental tasks associated with sexual identity development within a society that is often rejecting and hostile to LGBT people, students—especially those at the earlier stages of sexual identity development—may tend to focus on sexual identity development more than career development (Croteau, Anderson, Distefano, & Kampa-Kokesch, 2000) and come to advising with delayed vocational development (Fassinger, 2008), such as presenting few or no career options (Miller & Brown, 2005). Further, LGBT students at lower levels of sexual identity development may spend less time on activities that facilitate awareness of academic and career interests, educational and occupational opportunities, and how to develop and implement academic and career plans. Therefore, if LGBT students' career development is delayed, or they are not fully engaged in career development activities, this does not necessarily indicate that they are chronically indecisive or unmotivated. It may indicate that they are focusing more time and energy on the developmental tasks associated with sexual identity development.

Sexual Identity Management. Since "most workplaces are rife with heterosexism and antigay prejudice" (Fassinger, 2008, p. 255), sexual identity management in the workplace and college is an important issue. Sexual identity management in the workplace involves the extent to which employees reveal that they are lesbian, gay, bisexual, or transgender at work. There are four strategies of vocational sexual identity management along a continuum ranging from not revealing one's sexual identity to being fully out in the workplace: passing (i.e., communicating to coworkers that you are heterosexual), covering (i.e., hiding one's sexual orientation from coworkers), implicitly out (i.e., being honest with coworkers about one's life but not labeling one's sexual orientation), and explicitly out (i.e., stating that one is lesbian, gay, bisexual, or transgender at work) (Griffin, 1992, in Gysbers et al., 2003). Passing can help employees avoid negative workplace experiences, such as discrimination, but it is also associated with negative personal consequences. However, revealing that one is lesbian, gay, bisexual, or transgender can also have negative career consequences (Miller & Brown, 2005).

Ethical and Legal Issues. Finally, it is important to highlight some ethical and legal issues connected to working with LGBT students. Some advisors may not wish to work with LGBT students for personal or religious reasons. However, in addition to their personal commitment to provide the most effective advising for all students, when working with LGBT students advisors should also be aware of the ethical and legal obligations. The first core value of the NACADA (2004) Statement of Core Values of Academic Advising is "[a]dvisors are responsible to the individuals they advise," and "[a]cademic advisors work to strengthen the importance, dignity, potential, and unique nature of each individual within the academic setting." Joslin (2007) applied the NACADA Core Values to working with LGBT students and elaborated on the ethical responsibilities of advisors' work with LGBT students.

There are also potential legal consequences for not providing assistance to all students. A salient case is *Bruff* v. *North Mississippi Health Services, Inc.*, 2001 (Hermann & Herlihy, 2006), in which a counselor was fired for refusing to counsel an LGBT client. The counselor indicated that the client's homosexuality was at variance with the counselor's religious beliefs. The federal court upheld the termination, noting that an employer's duty to provide reasonable accommodation for an employee's religious beliefs did not include refusing services because of a person's sexual orientation.

Women

Discrimination in educational and workplace settings, lack of access to female role models and mentors especially in STEM fields, and multiple role responsibilities negatively affect women's career development and planning. Further, it is important for advisors to be aware of the influence of gender role socialization on interest development and the role of both social and professional relationships on the girls' and women's career development and planning.

Discrimination and the World of Work. Over the past 30 years, there has been a dramatic increase (more than 70%) in the number of women employed between the ages of 25 and 55 years, and the odds that a woman will be employed during her life (90%) have also significantly increased (Fassinger, 2008). Despite these improvements there is still substantial inequality between men and women in the workplace, including "pervasive occupational segregation, underrepresentation in leadership positions, and inequities in compensation" (Fassinger, 2008, p. 253). For example, women earn only 80% of what their male peers make one year out of college, and this discrepancy continues to increase over time (i.e., women earn only 69% of what their male peers earn 10 years out of college) (Fassinger, 2008).

Fassinger (2008) summarized the work of Barnett and Hyde (2001), who, after reviewing the literature, concluded that the primary influence on women's occupational behavior was the workplace opportunity structure. For example, resources (e.g., educational scholarships and salaries) are distributed unequally between men and women, and the discrepancy in salaries is partially attributed to the segregation of women to a restricted range of occupations and work roles (i.e., nonleadership work roles) (Fassinger, 2008). Further, hostile educational and work environments (e.g., sexual harassment of female students and workers), informal social and information networks important for career advancement that exclude women, and the lack of professional female role models and mentors (Fassinger, 2008; Gysbers et al., 2003) also negatively affect women's career development and advancement.

Interests, Skills, and Self-Efficacy. Women's self-assessment of interests and skills is significantly influenced by factors other than vocational identity (e.g., gender role socialization, lack of female role models and mentors in gender nontraditional occupations and leadership positions, negative self-efficacy beliefs about STEM subjects and occupations, inaccurate underestimations of skills and abilities). Therefore, when working with female students the unmodified use of self-assessment of interests and skills can compromise career planning. Beginning early in childhood and continuing into adulthood, females and males are socialized about the occupations considered socially appropriate for women and men (i.e., gender role socialization) (Gysbers et al., 2003). Thus, the academic and career planning of students is deeply embedded in a gendered context.

Social and artistic interests, which are associated with female gender traditional occupations, tend to be the highest scores for women on interest assessments (Fouad, Ihle Helledy, & Metz, 2003). College women also choose careers that are more gender traditional than the careers they identified as wanting to pursue as high school seniors (Gysbers et al., 2003). This is consistent with the experiences of older women reentering the paid workforce, who often choose careers consistent with social interests and report lower levels of autonomy and assertiveness and more career indecision (Miller & Brown, 2005). Not only are women more likely to report interests consistent with traditional gender roles, but they also report lower self-efficacy beliefs for gender nontraditional occupations (e.g., STEM) and inaccurately underestimate their academic achievement in college (Gysbers et al., 2003). Also, in high school, girls take fewer math courses (Gysbers et al., 2003). External barriers can contribute to lower math self-efficacy beliefs, which contribute to math avoidance behaviors, which in turn lead to lower math self-efficacy, thus decreasing the probability of girls pursuing STEM majors and occupations. Further, the lack of female role models and mentors in STEM fields serves as a barrier to improving female students' math and science self-efficacy (Lent, Brown, & Hackett, 1996).

Therefore, the higher levels of social and artistic interests, compared to STEM interests, can result from decreased self-efficacy, inaccurate underestimation of skills, lack of female role models and mentors, and math avoidance (Gysbers et al., 2003; Lent et al., 1996), not from an accurate picture of female students' vocational identity. Thus, if female students report their highest interests in the social or artistic areas, this may reflect an artificially narrow range of interests based on gender role socialization, external barriers, and consequent lower self-efficacy, inaccurate underestimation of skills, and math avoidance, instead of a reflection of students' personal interests. Also, because social and artistic interests are associated with lower pay and lower-prestige occupations (Gysbers et al., 2003), the unmodified use of self-assessment of interests and skills in career planning can serve to maintain the status quo by encouraging women to pursue a narrow range of gender traditional careers.

Role of Relationships. Relationships, both social (e.g., with parents) and professional (e.g., with instructors), are important in the career development and planning of women. One way relationships are salient to women's career development and planning is the importance of the relational focus in girl's and women's development, which emphasizes the maintenance of relationships, as contrasted to the emphasis on separation, independence, and autonomy in boy's and men's development (Gysbers et al., 2003). For example, the value of positive relationships with coworkers may influence career choice more than the values of prestige and salaries, which tend to influence men's career choices (Gysbers et al., 2003). Further, some evidence supports that attachment to parents is associated with positive career development outcomes for women, and that women have greater awareness than men of the effect that their career decisions have on their family (Gysbers et al., 2003).

The importance of relationships on women's career development is further evidenced by the effect of college faculty on female students' experiences. For example, faculty feedback and judgment influences female students' career choice and perceptions of personal ability more than it influences that of their male peers (Fassinger, 2008). Thus, an academic environment that does not *actively* encourage female students' achievement, even though it does not discourage their achievement, is a "null environment" and considered "passive discrimination" (Fassinger, 2008, p. 258). This is especially salient in STEM academic areas.

The influence of relationships also affects women's aspirations and career plans. There is evidence that for some women one reason their career aspirations decrease between late high school and college is due to the increased time spent on dating and romantic relationships in college, which eventually leads to women giving greater importance to their husband's career development (Gysbers et al., 2003).

Multiple Role Responsibilities and Career Choice. Gender-role socialization promotes the expectation that women should assume responsibility for domestic roles as well as occupational roles, an expectation not held for men (Miller & Brown, 2005). This expectation has negative consequences for women, both professionally and psychologically. The range of potential career choices women consider may be restricted to those they or important others in their lives believe will allow them to manage home and work responsibilities (Miller & Brown, 2005), and the demands on women's time and energy to satisfy home and career responsibilities can also lead to increased levels of personal stress (Miller & Brown, 2005). However, the distribution of domestic responsibilities is shifting toward greater equality for heterosexual couples (Fassinger, 2008) and is more equal for lesbian couples, although differences in occupational sexual identity management can create work-home conflict for lesbian couples (Gysbers et al., 2003).

Multiple role responsibilities also affect the timing of women's choices to return to college. These women often base the timing of their decision to return to college on when it would be least disruptive to important others in their lives (e.g., partners, children, parents), as opposed to when they initially wanted to return (Miller & Brown, 2005). Also, women who left the paid workforce, often because of conflicts from multiple role responsibilities, and return, "have lower career aspirations and tend to choose lower level occupations than other women" (Miller & Brown, 2005, p. 452).

IMPLICATIONS FOR CAREER ADVISING

Although the focus of the Culturally Appropriate Career Counseling Model (CACCM; Byars-Winston & Fouad, 2006; Fouad & Bingham, 1995) is career *counseling* with racial/ethnic minority clients, it provides an effective framework to understand the implications for career *advising* with racial/ethnic minority students, as well as LBGT students, students with disabilities, and female students. The seven steps of the CACCM, modified for career advising, are (a) establish a culturally appropriate advising relationship with the student, (b) identify the student's career development and planning needs, (c) assess the effects of diversity issues, (d) set career advising goals that are culturally appropriate, (e) select and implement culturally appropriate career advising activities, (f) support the student in making a career planning decision, and (g) implement the plan and follow up with the student. Two case studies are presented in Appendix B to provide opportunities to apply these seven steps related to career advising and the content of this chapter. Presented along with the case studies are questions intended to facilitate discussion and to determine appropriate career advising goals and activities.

Byars-Winston and Fouad (2006) expanded the CACCM to include the skill of metacognitive awareness. It is important for advisors to develop metacognitive awareness in career advising because advisors' cultural contexts also influence the process and outcomes of career advising. There are three processes to developing metacognitive awareness. The first process is for advisors to develop a plan for working with a specific student that coincides with step one of the CACCM. At this point advisors could ask, "What are any gaps in my knowledge about the . . . (student's) context?" (p. 195). The second process coincides with steps two through four of the CACCM and involves advisors monitoring "how and to what aspects of . . . (student) information they are attending and what that reflects about their own cultural values and worldview" (p. 195). At this point advisors could ask: (a) "What is the . . . (student's) cultural context and what are my reactions to that?" (p. 195; Stage 2); (b) "Are there . . . (diversity issues) that I am emphasizing more than the . . . (student)?" (p. 195; Stage 3); and (c) "How will I respond if the . . . (student's) goals differ from my own?" (p. 195; Stage 4). The third process is for advisors to evaluate the effectiveness of career advising activities that coincide with steps five and six. At this point advisors could ask: (a) "On what basis am I determining how helpful . . . (the career advising activities) are?" (p. 195; Stage 5); and (b) "How culturally congruent are the . . . (career advising) outcomes with the . . . (student's) desired goals?" (p. 195; Stage 6). The 10 questions that Carlstrom (2005) applied to advising, based on Plummer's (1995) work for mental health counselors, can also be used to develop the skill of metacognitive awareness in career advising.

Step 1: Establish a Culturally Appropriate Advising Relationship with the Student

A culturally appropriate relationship in career advising is one in which the advisor is responsive and flexible to students' cultural norms and expectations of advising in general and to career planning specifically and suspends stereotypes and assumptions (Fouad & Bingham, 1995; Swanson & Fouad, 1999). The development and maintenance of a culturally appropriate advising relationship is important because it increases students' trust of advisors, which increases the likelihood that students will address diversity issues pertinent to their career planning (Fouad & Bingham, 1995)—a conversation students may find difficult, especially when advisor and student are culturally different.

Culturally appropriate advising relationships can be developed and maintained when advisors demonstrate their understanding of the career development issues associated with race/ethnicity, disability status, sexual orientation, and gender. Culturally appropriate advising relationships are also facilitated by assisting students with their initial concerns in career advising, listening empathically, and focusing on what students meant to communicate to guard against misinterpretation. Carlstrom (2005) provided an overview of a process for listening empathically and principles for focusing on meaning in multicultural advising relationships, based on the work of Bennett (1998) and Storti (1994). Further, Fassinger (2008) recommended that female students' academic and career achievement should be *actively* supported to avoid the creation of a "null environment," especially in the STEM fields, although this is also a good recommendation for career advising with racial/ethnic minority students, students with disabilities, and LGBT students.

In addition, the physical space should communicate that the office is safe for and supportive of all students. A display of materials that address the concerns of racial/ethnic minority students, students with disabilities, LGBT students, and female students communicates safety and support (e.g., the magazines *Careers & the disAbled*, and *Hispanic Career World*; brochures from the LGBT Student Resource Center, and the Women in Engineering Program). The use of inclusive language also facilitates achievement of this goal; the National Gay and Lesbian Journalists Association provides guidance about the accurate use of LGBT inclusive language (www.nlgja.org/resources/NLGJA_Stylebook.pdf). Further, the office should be accessible to students with disabilities.

Steps 2: Identify Career Development and Planning Needs

Next, the advisor collaborates with students to identify their career development and planning needs (e.g., select an academic major, obtain a job, get accepted to graduate school). To accomplish these goals the student may need to learn about self, options, decision making, networking, writing résumés, or interviewing.

Step 3: Assess Effects of Diversity Issues

Once students' career development and planning needs are identified, advisors draw on their knowledge of how diversity issues influence career planning and development and work collaboratively with students to (a) formulate working hypotheses about how diversity issues may have affected students' career development and planning, (b) test these hypotheses against students' experiences, and (c) reformulate the hypotheses accordingly. For example, when working with an African American male, the advisor could explore the student's experience, both direct and indirect, of discrimination in education and the workplace and further explore whether that experience negatively affected the student's expectations of career attainment. This step is important because it helps guard against the potential errors of ignoring diversity issues, ignoring individual experiences in career development and planning, or both.

Steps 4 and 5: Set Culturally Appropriate Career Advising Goals and Select and Implement Culturally Appropriate Career Advising Activities

When there is an understanding about the influence of diversity issues on students' career planning and development then culturally appropriate career advising goals and activities can be developed and selected, respectively. Career advising is likely to be unhelpful if there is disconnect between students' experiences, values, expectations, and needs, and the assumptions that underlie traditional career advising goals and activities (Gysbers et al., 2003). Therefore, explore the degree to which students' experiences, values, expectations, and needs align with those assumed by traditional career advising goals and activities, and modify career advising goals and activities accordingly. Further, advisors should not automatically view differences between students' experiences, values, expectations, and needs and those assumed by traditional career advising activities negatively (e.g., immature, lack of vocational identity, dependent decision-making style). Instead, advisors should seek to understand the differences to assist in making modifications that are in students' best interest. In this section, recommendations are presented for addressing diversity issues in career advising.

Assessing Degree of Modification Needed. To provide culturally appropriate career advising, advisors must address both traditional individual career development factors (e.g., interests, skills, work values, gathering occupational information, and decision making), and diversity issues that affect career development (e.g., discrimination, acculturation, self-efficacy to cope with barriers) (Fouad & Byars-Winston, 2005). Therefore, assessing the amount of modification needed to goals and activities is the first step in setting culturally appropriate career advising goals and selecting subsequent career advising activities.

There are a number of considerations advisors can review when determining the amount of modification needed. First, explore students' perceptions and experiences of discrimination, barriers, and opportunity in education and the workplace, especially related to race/ethnicity, disability status, sexual orientation, and gender. The experience of discrimination, barriers, and lack of opportunity challenge the traditional assumptions of the opportunity structure being open to all, work being central to people's lives, and the career development process occurring in a linear and progressive sequence.

Modifying career advising goals and activities to be consistent with students' cultural values, level of acculturation, and level of racial identity development improves the efficacy of career planning activities with racial/ethnic minority students (Miller & Brown, 2005; Worthington et al., 2005). Exploring both the role of family, community, and kinship networks in making career choices, and the relative importance given to family, community, and career in need fulfillment and identity development are important components of this process. More acculturated individuals may have less need for modified career advising goals and activities, but students who are less acculturated and adhere to traditional cultural values may benefit from career advising goals and activities modified to be congruent with traditional cultural values. For example, when working with a Mexican American student whose values are congruent with traditional cultural values that place importance on family in making decisions to select an academic major, it may be helpful to modify the traditional career decision-making approach, which emphasizes the role of personal interests and goals in making career choices, to include exploration of the role of the family in making important life decisions.

Similarly, it is important to evaluate the extent that female students have a relational perspective. When working with female students who have a relational perspective, advisors should value the relational perspective (Gysbers et al., 2003), listen empathically to the role and meaning that both career and social development have in students' lives, and integrate both into the career advising process (Miller & Brown, 2005). Further it is important to assess the extent to which female students experience support from family, peers, supervisors, and instructors to pursue their academic and career goals, multiple role conflict, and a "null environment," especially if they have gender nontraditional goals.

It is also important to develop a comprehensive, active, and systematic career plan with students with disabilities during their first year of college, which in addition to traditional career development activities also includes the development of empowerment, self-advocacy, and decision-making skills and enhances autonomy (Ender & Wilkie, 2000; Friehe, Aune, & Leuenberger, 1996; Kosciulek, 2003). These activities can facilitate career maturity and choice, and as Grandin and Duffy (2004) noted, unless students with disabilities receive this kind of support, they are very likely to be unemployed or underemployed upon graduation. Disabilities should not be the primary focus of advising, but instead disabilities should be understood as risk factors to students' career development within contemporary social and physical environments, and recommendations should focus on modifications needed so students can succeed. Advisors should learn how students perceive their disabilities and about the personal and environmental barriers encountered, especially those contributing to academic and career development difficulties (Fabian & Liesener, 2005; Kosciulek, 2003). This is a person-in-environment model of disability (i.e., modify the environment), compared to a medical model (i.e., change the person) (Fabian & Liesener, 2005).

When working with LGBT students, it can be helpful to understand where students are in their sexual identity development. Students who are further along in their sexual identity development may require less modification in career advising activities and goals. However, students in the earlier stages may need to wait until they have more time and energy to devote to career exploration activities before they focus on academic and career planning, and may benefit from referrals to other resources and supports on campus to help them address the challenges of sexual identity development (e.g., LGBTQ student organization, women's center, counseling center). Advisors should help normalize students' potential experience of delayed career development by discussing the amount of time and energy that both developmental processes require, and assist students in exploring the interplay between sexual identity development and career development (Joslin, 2007).

Dealing with Barriers and Discrimination. In addition to exploring students' experience of barriers and discrimination, assess their plans, self-efficacy (i.e., do they believe they can successfully implement the plan), and outcome expectations (i.e., do they believe that the successful implementation of the plan will result in a desirable outcome) to deal with barriers and discrimination. Helping students develop plans and build realistic self-efficacy beliefs and outcome expectations for dealing with education and workplace barriers and discrimination can be facilitated by discussing student strengths; developing problem-solving skills; modifying self-talk to counter internalized negative societal stereotypes and gender role socialization; connecting with role models and mentors; participating in campus programs, student organizations, and work-based learning experiences; and experiencing success at college (Gysbers et al., 2003).

Another way to help students prepare to deal with barriers and discrimination is to help them learn about legal rights and issues (e.g., affirmative action policies and procedures, legal and illegal interview questions, and legal rights in the workplace). Further, students with disabilities need to learn about the kinds of accommodations needed to succeed in the workplace. Helping students learn about legal issues will probably require collaboration with different offices on campus (e.g., disability support services, Office of Affirmative Action, legal services office, career and employment services). Both Reilly and Davis (2005) and Briel and Getzel (2005) address legal issues associated with academic and career concerns of students with disabilities.

Evaluate Organizational Climate. One way to decrease the experience of barriers and discrimination is to work for organizations supportive of racial/ethnic minority, female, and LGBT employees and employees with disabilities. Helping students learn to evaluate potential employers during the job search and interview process can assist with this. Students can start to develop this skill during college by evaluating their own campus. For example, LGBT students could evaluate the institutional policies of the college (e.g., domestic partner benefits, published nondiscrimination policies); visibility of LGBT people on campus; and resources allocated for LGBT concerns, activities, and services (Joslin, 2007; Miller & Brown, 2005). Gysbers et al. (2003) provide a set of questions women can use to evaluate the work environment (e.g., "Are your skills and interests being actively promoted and developed within the organization?," p. 96), and also recommend practicing job interviewing as a means to help women learn to recognize hostile or unsupportive work environments.

Role Models, Mentors, Social Support, and Professional Networks. Advisors should address with students the need to build social support and professional networks. Students can receive social support from family, kinship networks, other students, role models, mentors, and college faculty and staff. Further, student participation in campus programs and student groups can facilitate both the experience of social support and the development of professional networks. Campus programs and organizations in which students can become involved include campus programs where the focus is the academic and career development of racial/ethnic minority students, students with disabilities, or female students (e.g., Women in Engineering and Science program); student organizations that have a professional focus (e.g., multicultural business student organization, National Society of Black Engineers); and student organizations that have a diversity focus (e.g., Hispanic American Leadership Organization, Asian American Student Union, Queer Straight Alliance).

Student participation in campus programs and organizations can increase student access to role models and mentors who are culturally similar and in gender nontraditional work roles and occupations. Role models and mentors can be professionals, including faculty. For LGBT students, a role model or mentor who is LGBT can help them learn about sexual identity management in the workplace. Role models and mentors can also be helpful to address acculturation in career development and planning. For example, connecting an Asian American student with a low level of acculturation with an Asian American role model or mentor who is highly acculturated could help the student learn bicultural competencies, consider a broader range of occupations, and learn about workplace dynamics (Miller & Brown, 2005).

Given the history of discrimination in education and work and the location of some colleges, access to role models and mentors who are culturally similar to racial/ethnic minority students, students with disabilities, LGBT students, and female students, especially in STEM fields, could be difficult (Fassinger, 2008). In addition, it is necessary for LGBT professionals, professionals who are LGBT allies, and professionals with some types of disabilities to self-identify if they are going to be asked to serve as mentors and role models. This requires that advisors be aware of potential role models and mentors, which could be facilitated through collaboration and consultation with other offices on campus (e.g., alumni relations, career and employment services, disability support services, office of multicultural affairs).

Gaining Information About the World of Work. Advisors should facilitate student access to a broad range of quality information about the world of work (Fabian & Liesener, 2005). Teaching students how to use this information in the career decision-making process will also be helpful, although it is important to respect potential personal or cultural differences in decision-making strategies.

Work-based learning experiences (e.g., part-time employment, internships, practicum experiences, service learning, job shadowing), participation in campus programs and organizations, and connecting with role models and mentors can also help students gain exposure to a broad range of information about the world of work and help with the decision-making process. Further, work-based learning experiences can help students network with potential employers, role models, and mentors; develop academic and career plans; develop job skills relevant for future employment; and develop skills and positive self-efficacy beliefs and outcomes expectations to deal with workplace discrimination. To increase the efficacy of work-based learning experiences, advisors can assist students in linking work experiences to students' interests and academic major.

When working with students with disabilities, be aware that students may need accommodations for accessing occupational information and for work-based learning experiences. To identify opportunities for work-based learning experiences, advisors may need to collaborate with other offices on campus (e.g., career and employment services). Advisors can also consult with disability support services to help students obtain accommodations and accessible information. Universal design for instruction is relevant to this issue (see Scott and McGuire, 2005).

Interests and Personal Goals. The use of interests and personal goals, whether assessed formally or informally, is a central feature of traditional career development and planning activities, and formal interest assessment is one way to expose students to a broad range of occupational options. Further, using interests and goals when working with students is a way to focus on student strengths instead of limitations (Kosciulek, 2003), and helping students find a major that matches their interests, instead of their limitations, can facilitate academic success (Ender & Wilkie, 2000). However, discrimination and barriers in education and work limit students' exposure to the world of work. In these cases self-assessment of interests and personal goals may reflect this narrow exposure more than students' vocational identity. Therefore, even though many traditional career advising approaches begin with interest assessment, advisors should consider activities that effectively expose students to a broad range of options prior to interest assessment. Effective activities include exploring online and print sources of academic and career information, connecting with role models and mentors (Worthington et al., 2005), participating in work and volunteer experiences, and participating in student programs and organizations. Also, personal and cultural values should be integrated into the use of self-assessment of interests, skills, and goals. The role of family and community in decision making should be considered and discussed when using interests in the academic and career planning process (Worthington et al., 2005) with students who have collectivist or relational perspectives.

When working with students with disabilities, advisors should inquire when the onset of a student's disability was, and evaluate the effect that might have on students' interests and clarity of career plans and the information and concerns students consider when making a decision (Kosciulek, 2003). Further, when reviewing self-assessment results, advisors should be responsive to how students' disabilities may interact with the format of the results and potentially cause difficulty in the students' understanding of the information. For example, many students with learning disabilities have difficulty with short-term memory, reading rates, comprehension, and visual processing (Ender & Wilkie, 2000). Therefore, advisors should check the extent to which students understand career self-assessment results.

Advisors should not ignore students' interests and goals that are gender nontraditional by only highlighting and discussing interests and goals that are gender traditional. If an LGBT student reports low levels of career interests or few career interests, it could be helpful to explore the extent to which this is an accurate representation of the student's interests or whether the student neglected to endorse certain interests because they were gender nontraditional (Gysbers et al., 2003). It is important to provide female students with accurate information about the costs (e.g., lower compensation, restricted range of opportunity, distress) of limiting academic and career choices to gender traditional careers and roles, and the benefits of pursuing math and science (e.g., higher compensation, broader range of opportunity, increased self-efficacy). Further, Gysbers et al. (2003) present strategies to increase female students' participation in math and science (e.g., helping them find innovative programs to develop math and science skills).

For LGBT students, safety issues and subsequent occupational stereotyping may influence the interests students express or the occupational options students pursue. Racial/ethnic minority students may also select career paths based on occupations they perceive as racially friendly and having fewer barriers to entry and advancement. Thus, it could be beneficial to address these issues with students before they complete career self-assessment in order to encourage a broader range of expressed options. Exploring the extent to which these issues potentially restrict students' expressed career interests, plans, and choices could enhance students' vocational identity. The goal is not to dismiss students' concerns about safety and career advancement, but to help them develop awareness of the full range of interests and occupational options.

Financial difficulties and stress can also influence students' expressed interests and goals. If students' current financial circumstances and concerns appear to have a disproportionate influence on their academic and career choice, it could be helpful to refer students to campus resources that may be able to assist with financial difficulties (e.g., Office of Student Financial Assistance, Office of Student Life) and financial stress (e.g., counseling center), as well as reviewing academic and occupational opportunities that may better fit their interests and goals.

Self-Efficacy and Outcome Expectations. Assessment of students' self-efficacy beliefs and outcome expectations about different academic subjects and occupations should be integrated with assessment of interests and goals. Advisors should explore with students the extent to which their experiences either positively or negatively affected the development of self-efficacy beliefs, self-concepts, and outcome expectations. Experiences that contribute to the development of positive self-efficacy, self-concept, and outcome expectations include having teachers with high academic expectations for all students; receiving quality career education in high school; and having opportunities for work experience. Experiences that contribute to negative self-efficacy, self-concepts, and outcomes expectations include encountering negative attitudes, prejudice, and low expectations; having limited opportunities to make decisions about the future; and lack of exposure to role models and mentors. If students have low self-efficacy beliefs and outcome expectations, steps should be taken to help students develop positive self-efficacy beliefs and outcome expectations and the corresponding skills. If students' self-efficacy beliefs are negative, advisors should consider encouraging students to not declare an academic major before participating in activities that could improve their self-efficacy. Further, advisors can explore with students the extent to which negative self-efficacy beliefs developed due to the internalization of negative societal stereotypes associated with race/ethnicity, sexual orientation, disability status, and gender role socialization.

When working with female students, the following activities can help positively alter negative self-efficacy and outcome expectation beliefs and broaden the range of interests and goals: (a) sharing information about the negative effects of gender role socialization; (b) actively supporting the choice of gender

nontraditional academic and career plans; (c) encouraging students to participate in gender nontraditional work-based learning experiences in supportive
environments; and (d) connecting students with female role models and mentors who are in gender nontraditional occupations and work roles (Gysbers
et al., 2003). Further, helping students learn to write strong résumés and to
present themselves as highly qualified in job interviews can help students
accurately and confidently present their abilities in the job search process;
referral to the career and employment office on campus could also facilitate
development of these skills.

Self-Advocacy and Problem-Solving Skills. It is important that students with
disabilities develop self-advocacy and problem-solving skills because they will
need to learn how to address their disability and needed accommodations
in the job search and negotiation process (Friehe et al., 1996). Advisors can
assist students with disabilities in developing these skills by supporting them
in the process of sharing with their instructors the accommodations needed
(Ender & Wilkie, 2000). Facilitating students' connection with the office of
Disability Support Services and gathering information about campus, workplace, and community networks that provide support is a way to help students develop a sense of empowerment through increased self-reliance, social
connection, and support (Kosciulek, 2003).

Briel and Getzel (2005) address how to disclose a disability throughout the
employment process, from the cover letter to after a person starts the job. They
also address the pros and cons of disclosing a disability at different points in
the internship or employment process. For example, although never disclosing
one's disability keeps it private, this approach also results in not being protected from discrimination under ADA. Briel and Wehman (2005) provide questions that advisors could review with students with disabilities to determine
whether disclosure of a disability may be necessary or beneficial, such as "Will
my compensatory strategies (e.g., the use of adaptive software or assistive technology) change the traditional way of getting the job done?" (p. 300). Finally,
Burgstahler (2005) addresses the role of assistive technologies in fostering success in college and career of people with disabilities and the different technologies for various types of disabilities (e.g., mobility, speech, hearing, and health
impairments; low vision; blindness; specific learning disabilities).

Sexual Identity Management. Since LGBT students must manage how much
of their sexual identity they reveal at work while still maintaining a sense of
personal integrity and congruence, advisors need to address workplace sexual identity management with LGBT students. Advisors should explore with
students the extent to which they reveal their sexual orientation during the
job search and interview process (Joslin, 2007). For example, students need
to decide whether or not to include membership in LGBT affiliated student
organizations on their résumé (Ender & Wilkie, 2000). Advisors should also
review with students their plans for sexual identity management in the workplace, the potential positive and negative consequences of their plan, and

the development of coping strategies for dealing with the potential negative consequences of their plan (e.g., building social support networks) (Miller & Brown, 2005). Students' plans for sexual identity management in the workplace will differ by where they are in their sexual identity development, their comfort with risk-taking, and their occupation. Further, it is important for advisors to remember that the goal of these conversations is not to impose the advisor's comfort level with risk-taking, but to help students make informed decisions, learn to evaluate the outcomes of their decisions, and develop coping strategies for potential negative consequences of others' reactions.

Work-Home Conflicts and Multiple Role Responsibilities. Advisors can discuss issues of work-home conflict and multiple role responsibilities with female students (Miller & Brown, 2005) and facilitate students' exploration of the balance they want to have between work and career, help students problem solve to create the balance they want, and address with students how to counter gender-role socialization messages that promote unequal and unrealistic expectations for women. For nontraditionally aged female college students, it is also important to address workplace discrimination in hiring and advancement due to both age and sex (Miller & Brown, 2005).

Step 6: Support the Student to Make a Career Planning Decision

During this step, students make a career planning decision (e.g., declare chemistry as a major, decide to accept a job offer). After making a decision, some students may recycle through the career decision-making process to address different career development and planning needs. Recycling through the process may indicate a preference for a circular decision-making style, and advisors should be flexible and responsive to this style even though it does not reflect the linear style associated with traditional career development and planning activities (Fouad & Bingham, 1995; Gysbers et al., 2003).

Step 7: Implement the Plan and Follow-Up

After students implement the career planning decision made in step six, it can be helpful for advisors to follow up with students. Although this may be easier to accomplish with students who advisors continue to work with at the college, it can still be helpful to follow up with graduates. For example, students with disabilities may benefit from advisors checking in with them even after graduation (Kosciulek, 2003).

SUMMARY

In order to provide career advising that is responsive to all contemporary college students, advisors need to explore the degree which students' experiences, values, expectations, and needs are similar and dissimilar to those assumed by traditional career development theories and activities and make appropriate modifications. Thus, developing career advising goals and selecting career advising activities should be understood as a cultural activity, not as a neutral activity, and therefore addressing diversity in career advising is not practiced as an add-on but is integrated throughout the career advising process with all students.

For example, many students' career planning benefits from the input and support of important others in their lives, and therefore, career advising goals and activities based on the assumption that autonomous career choices, separate from one's family, are the most beneficial need to be evaluated for consistency with students' experience, values, expectations, and needs. Goals and activities that assume affluence need to be modified when students' current (e.g., need to work to pay for tuition and to support family) and future (e.g., a gay male seeking employment with a company that provides domestic partner benefits) financial concerns are a significant factor in their career planning. Further, the opportunity structure in education and work is often restricted because of discrimination and barriers for racial/ethnic minority students, students with disabilities, LGBT students, and female students, a factor that challenges goals and activities that assume the opportunity structure is open to all who strive. Career advising approaches that assume that work is central in people's lives for need fulfillment and identity need to be modified when LGBT students are in earlier stages of sexual identity development and need to focus on sexual identity development more than career development. Activities based on the assumption that career development and planning is linear, progressive, and rational may need to be modified for students who value an intuitive decision-making style, or if they or their family made career decisions based more on job availability and financial difficulties than congruence with personal interests and goals.

Further, advisors should monitor their own reactions, cultural context, and competence when helping students with career planning, especially students with whom they are culturally different. Developing and maintaining multicultural competence in advising involves ongoing and intentional learning, including interaction with people one is culturally different from (both professionally and personally), seeking professional consultation and supervision, attending professional development seminars, and remaining current on the literature.

References

Bennett, M. J. (1998). Overcoming the golden rule: Sympathy and empathy. In M. J. Bennett (Ed.), *Basic concepts of intercultural communication* (pp. 191–214). Yarmouth, ME: Intercultural Press.

Bilodeau, B. L., & Renn, K. A. (2005). Analysis of LGBT identity development models and implications for practice. *New Directions for Student Services, 111*, 25–39.

Briel, L. W., & Getzel, E. E. (2005). Internships and field experiences. In E. E. Getzel & P. Wehman (Eds.), *Going to college: Expanding opportunities for people with disabilities*. (pp. 271–290). Baltimore: Paul H. Brookes.

Briel, L. W., & Wehman, P. (2005). Career planning and placement. In E. E. Getzel & P. Wehman (Eds.), *Going to college: Expanding opportunities for people with disabilities* (pp. 291–305). Baltimore: Paul H. Brookes.

Brinckerhoff, L. C., McGuire, J. M., & Shaw, S. F. (2002). *Postsecondary education and transition for students with learning disabilities* (2nd ed.). Austin, TX: PRO-ED.

Burgstahler, S. (2005). The role of technology in preparing for college and careers. In E. E. Getzel & P. Wehman (Eds.), *Going to college: Expanding opportunities for people with disabilities* (pp. 179–198). Baltimore: Paul H. Brookes.

Byars-Winston, A. M., & Fouad, N. A. (2006). Metacognition and multicultural competence: Expanding the Culturally Appropriate Career Counseling Model. *The Career Development Quarterly, 54,* 187–201.

Carlstrom, A. H. (2005, December). Preparing for multicultural advising relationships. *Academic Advising Today, 28*(4), 1, 8.

Case, D. N. (1996). A glimpse of the invisible membership: A national survey of lesbi-gay Greek members. *Perspectives, 23,* 5–8.

Cass, V. C. (1979). Homosexual identity formation: A theoretical model. *Journal of Homosexuality, 4,* 219–235.

Chung, Y. B. (2003). Career counseling with lesbian, gay, bisexual, and transgendered persons: The next decade. *The Career Development Quarterly, 52,* 78–86.

Comas-Diaz, L., & Jacobsen, F. M. (1991). Ethnocultural transference and counter-transference in the therapeutic dyad. *American Journal of Orthopsychiatry, 61,* 392–402.

Croteau, J. M., Anderson, M. Z., Distefano, T. M., & Kampa-Kokesch, S. (2000). Lesbian, gay, and bisexual vocational psychology: Reviewing foundations and planning construction. In R. M. Perez, K. DeBord, & K. J. Bieschke (Eds.), *Handbook of counseling and therapy with lesbian, gay, and bisexual clients* (pp. 383–408). Washington, DC: American Psychological Association.

D'Augelli, A. R. (1994). Identity development and sexual orientation: Toward a model of lesbian, gay, and bisexual development. In E. J. Trickett, R. J. Watts, & D. Birman (Eds.), *Human diversity: Perspectives on people in context* (pp. 312–333). San Francisco: Jossey-Bass.

Ender, S. C., & Wilkie, C. J. (2000). Advising students with special needs. In V. N. Gordon & W. R. Habley (Eds.), *Academic advising: A comprehensive handbook* (pp. 118–143). San Francisco: Jossey-Bass.

Fabian, E. S., & Liesener, J. L. (2005). Promoting the career potential of youth with disabilities. In S. D. Brown & R. W. Lent (Eds.), *Career development and counseling: Putting theory and research to work* (pp. 551–572). New York: Wiley.

Fairweather, J. S., & Shaver, D. M. (1990–91). Making the transition to postsecondary education and training. *Exceptional Children, 57,* 264–270.

Fassinger, R. E. (1998). Lesbian, gay, and bisexual identity and student development theory. In R. L. Sanlo (Ed.), *Working with lesbian, gay, bisexual, and transgender college students: A handbook for faculty and administrators* (pp. 13–22). Westport, CT: Greenwood Press.

Fassinger, R. E. (2008). Workplace diversity and public policy: Challenges and opportunities for psychology. *American Psychologist, 63,* 252–268.

Fouad, N. A., & Bingham, R. (1995). Career counseling with racial/ethnic minorities. In W. B. Walsh & S. H. Osipow (Eds.), *Handbook of vocational psychology* (2nd ed., pp. 331–366). Hillsdale, NJ: Erlbaum.

Fouad, N. A., & Byars-Winston, A. M. (2005). Cultural context of career choice: Meta-analysis of race/ethnicity differences. *The Career Development Quarterly, 53*, 223–233.

Fouad, N. A., Ihle Helledy, K., & Metz, A. J. (2003). Effective strategies for career counseling with women. In M. Kopala & M. E. Keitel (Eds.), *Handbook of counseling women* (pp. 131–151). Thousand Oaks, CA: Sage.

Friehe, M., Aune, B., & Leuenberger, J. (1996). Career service needs of college students with disabilities. *The Career Development Quarterly, 44*, 289–300.

Gargiulo, R. M. (2009). *Special education in contemporary society: An introduction to exceptionality*. Thousand Oaks, CA: Sage.

Gelberg, S., & Chojnacki, J. T. (1996). *Career and life planning with gay, lesbian, and bisexual persons*. Alexandria, VA: American Counseling Association.

Gysbers, N. C., Heppner, M. J., & Johnston, J. A. (2003). *Career counseling: Process, issues, and techniques* (2nd ed.). Boston: Allyn and Bacon.

Grandin, T., & Duffy, K. (2004). *Developing talents: Careers for individuals with Asperger syndrome and high-functioning autism*. Shawnee Mission, KS: Autism Asperger Publishing.

Hermann, M. A., & Herlihy, B. R. (2006). Legal and ethical implications of refusing to counsel homosexual clients. *Journal of Counseling & Development, 84*, 414–418.

Joslin, J. (2007). Lesbians, gay, bisexual, transgender, and queer students. In L. Huff & P. Jordan (Eds.), *Advising special student populations: Adult learners, community college students LGBTQ students, multicultural students, students on probation, undecided students* (Monograph No. 17; pp. 87–99). Manhattan, KS: National Academic Advising Association.

Kosciulek, J. (2003). An empowerment approach to career counseling with people with disabilities. In N. C. Gysbers, M. J. Heppner, & J. A. Johnston, *Career counseling: Process, issues, and techniques* (2nd ed., pp. 139–153). Boston: Allyn and Bacon.

Lehmann, J. P., Davies, T. G., & Laurin, K. M. (2000). Listening to student voices about postsecondary education. *TEACHING Exceptional Children, 32*(5), 60–65.

Lent, R. W., Brown, S. D., & Hackett, G. (1996). Career development from a social cognitive perspective. In D. Brown, L. Brooks, and Associates (Eds.), *Career choice and development* (3rd ed., pp. 373–421). San Francisco: Jossey-Bass.

Lock, R. H., & Layton, C. A. (2001). Succeeding in postsecondary ed through self-advocacy. *TEACHING Exceptional Children, 34*(2), 66–71.

Miller, M. J., & Brown, S. D. (2005). Counseling for career choice: Implications for improving interventions and working with diverse populations. In S. D. Brown & R. W. Lent (Eds.), *Career development and counseling: Putting theory and research to work* (pp. 441–465). New York: Wiley.

Mull, C., Sitlington, P. L., & Alper, S. (2001). Postsecondary education for students with learning disabilities: A synthesis of the literature. *Exceptional Children, 68*(1), 97–118.

NACADA. (2004). *NACADA statement of core values of academic advising*. Retrieved December 15, 2008, from the NACADA Clearinghouse of Academic Advising Resources Web site: http://www.nacada.ksu.edu/Clearinghouse/AdvisingIssues/Core-Values.htm

Nauta, M. M., Saucier, A. M., & Woodard, L. E. (2001). Interpersonal influences on students' academic and career decisions: The impact of sexual orientation. *The Career Development Quarterly*, *49*, 352–362.

Pepper, S. M., & Lorah, P. (2008). Career issues and workplace considerations for the transsexual community: Bridging a gap of knowledge for career counselors and mental health care providers. *The Career Development Quarterly*, *56*, 330–343.

Perez, R. M., DeBord, K. A., & Bieschke, K. J. (2000). Introduction: The challenge of awareness, knowledge, and action. In R. M. Perez, K. A. DeBord, & K. J. Bieschke (Eds.), *Handbook of counseling and psychotherapy with lesbian, gay, and bisexual clients* (pp. 3–8). Washington, DC: American Psychological Association.

Plummer, D. L. (1995). The therapist as gatekeeper in multicultural counseling: Understanding ourselves as persons of culture. *Journal of Psychological Practice*, *1*, 30–35.

Rankin, S. R., Case, D. N., Windmeyer, S. L., Eberly, C. G., Hesp, G. A., Miller, G., & Molasso, B. (2007). *Experiences of LGBT people in fraternities and sororities: From 1960 to 2007*. Charlotte, NC: Lambda 10 Project.

Reilly, V. J., & Davis, T. (2005). Understanding the regulatory environment. In E. E. Getzel & P. Wehman (Eds.), *Going to college: Expanding opportunities for people with disabilities* (pp. 25–48). Baltimore: Paul H. Brookes.

Sanlo, R. (2004). Lesbian, gay, and bisexual college students: Risk, resiliency, and retention. *Journal of College Student Retention: Research, Theory, and Practice*, *6*(1), 97–110.

Savin-Williams, R. C., & Ream, G. L. (2007). Prevalence and stability of sexual orientation components during adolescence and young adulthood. *Archives of Sexual Behavior*, *36*, 385–394.

Scott, S. S., & McGuire, J. M. (2005). Implementing universal design for instruction to promote inclusive college teaching. In E. E. Getzel & P. Wehman (Eds.), *Going to college: Expanding opportunities for people with disabilities* (pp. 119–138). Baltimore: Paul H. Brookes.

Sell, R. L., Wells, J. A., & Wypij, D. (1995). The prevalence of homosexual behavior and attraction in the United States, the United Kingdom and France: Results of national population-based samples. *Archives of Sexual Behavior*, *24*, 235–248.

Storti, C. (1994). *Cross-cultural dialogues: 74 brief encounters with cultural difference*. Boston: Intercultural Press.

Super, D. E., Savickas, M. L., & Super, C. M. (1996). The life-span, life-space approach to careers. In D. Brown, L. Brooks, & Associates (Eds.), *Career choice and development* (3rd ed., pp. 121–178). San Francisco: Jossey-Bass.

Swanson, J. L., & Fouad, N. A. (1999). *Career theory and practice: Learning through case studies*. Thousand Oaks, CA: Sage.

U.S. Department of Education, National Center for Educational Statistics. (2005). *Postsecondary institutions in the United States: Fall 2003 and degrees and other awards conferred: 2002–03* (NCES 2005–154). Retrieved December 15, 2008, from http://nces.ed.gov/fastfacts/display.asp?id = 72

U.S. Department of Education, National Center for Education Statistics. (2006a). *Digest of education statistics, 2005* (NCES 2006–005), Chapter 3. Retrieved December 15, 2008, from http://nces.ed.gov/fastfacts/display.asp?id = 98

U.S. Department of Education, National Center for Education Statistics. (2006b). *Profile of undergraduates in U.S. postsecondary education institutions: 2003–04* (NCES 2006–184). Retrieved December 15, 2008, from http://nces.ed.gov/fastfacts/ display.asp?id = 60

U.S. Department of Education, National Center for Education Statistics. (2007). *The condition of education 2007* (NCES 2007–064, Indicator 24). Retrieved December 15, 2008, from http://nces.ed.gov/programs/coe/2008/section3/indicator24.asp

U.S. Department of Education, National Center for Education Statistics. (2008). *Digest of education statistics, 2007* (NCES 2008–022), Chapter 3. Retrieved December 15, 2008, from http://nces.ed.gov/programs/digest/d07/ch_3.asp

U.S. Department of Justice. (2007). *Americans with Disabilities Act of 1990*. Retrieved December 15, 2008, from http://www.ada.gov/pubs/ada.htm

Worthington, R. L., Flores, L.Y., & Navarro, R.L. (2005). Career development in context: Research with People of Color. In S. D. Brown & R. W. Lent (Eds.), *Career development and counseling: Putting theory and research to work* (pp. 225–252). New York: Wiley.

Yanchak, K. V., Lease, S. H., & Strauser, D. R. (2005). Relation of disability type and career thoughts to vocational identity. *Rehabilitation Counseling Bulletin, 48*(3), 130–138.

CHAPTER SEVEN

Information Resources to Enhance Career Advising

Darrin L. Carr, Susan A. Epstein

M aking career decisions can be daunting, but individuals who make such decisions may use information resources in many ways to help them choose among career alternatives. In fact, the planful decision-making model described by Harris-Bowlsbey, Riley-Dikel, and Sampson (2002) emphasizes that information resources are central to every step involved in making career decisions. Career information resources can help college students learn about themselves, choose appropriate college majors and academic institutions, identify interesting job titles and industries, transition successfully to other career fields, or master effective job search strategies. Academic advisors can facilitate the use of career information in the decision-making processes in various ways; as Gordon (2006) notes, advisors' most important role with career information "is to teach students how to obtain, evaluate, and use it" (p. 74).

This chapter describes the nature and use of information in career planning and decision making, and how academic advisors can use various resources to help students. Via sample scenarios of academic advisors working with students in postsecondary education settings, we hope to motivate advisors to use career resources effectively, and to illustrate the responsibilities advisors and students have in the advising process. Each case describes how resources can be used within the framework of the cognitive information processing approach (Sampson, Reardon, Peterson, & Lenz, 2004). In addition, we address several topics related to using information in the career planning process, such as identifying quality resources and accessibility for people with disabilities. By the end of the chapter, we hope that academic advisors will understand why information must be part of any successful career decision and learn how to use career resources with their students for maximum effectiveness.

INFORMATION IN CAREER PLANNING AND DECISION MAKING

Words such as *data, details*, and *facts* describe bits of information that can lead to knowledge and wisdom, but they must be structured and integrated into some type of framework to be useful. Information needed for career decision making is no exception to this reality—its effectiveness requires some action on the part of those who make it available to others (Epstein & Lenz, 2008). The process of making information usable involves such concepts as standards, evaluation, management, analysis, and systems, which may seem "boring" to advisors whose main focus is using resources with their advisees. A basic understanding of these concepts, however, can greatly increase advisors' effectiveness in helping students with their career concerns—they can select appropriate career resources for specific students and make career information accessible and useful for them. Thus, we hope to bring these concepts alive with concrete examples throughout the chapter that demonstrate how the concepts can facilitate advisors' efforts to use career information wisely.

Using career information has been an integral part of career development interventions since the beginning of the 20th century, as the United States moved from an agricultural to an industrial economy. Frank Parsons, often referred to as the father of the vocational guidance movement, included information-seeking activities in his vocational counseling approach to help individuals make vocational choices. For example, he felt that statistics from the U.S. Census could provide valuable employment outlook and salary information (Parsons, 1909) and that biographies of people in various careers, observation of workers in various settings, and descriptions of various occupations would be effective resources for gathering the information needed to make appropriate choices (Niles & Harris-Bowlsbey, 2005). Parsons also believed in a systematic approach to career interventions and created a classification of industries to illustrate the world of work.

Like Parsons, national and international governments and organizations have long recognized the value of classification systems for organizing industrial and occupational data to make it usable. Classifications of industries, occupations, and educational programs, developed at the governmental and organizational levels throughout the 20th century (see Exhibit 7.1), have provided frameworks and standards for organizing and analyzing economic activity, occupational data, and academic achievement. Classifications such as the Standard Industrial Classification (SIC), *Dictionary of Occupational Titles* (DOT) system, and International Standard Classification of Education (ISCED) have evolved into online databases and other systems used worldwide in a variety of career information resources. Information technology itself, like classification systems, has improved access to career data that people use to make decisions; the Internet especially has affected many aspects of electronic data gathering, management, production, and delivery. For example, physical media formats such as audiotapes, videotapes, and compact discs have largely been replaced by widely available resources such as podcasts, streaming videos, and interactive Web sites. Career Web sites, databases, and software offer a variety of possible formats for career information, in addition to the print resources that continue to be produced, but also present many challenges of identifying quality resources and managing career resource collections.

The current career resource panorama can best be described as rapidly changing, with government funding waxing and waning and vendors of information and assessments emerging, merging, and disappearing. The resources listed in this chapter today may not be available tomorrow; likewise new resources will appear over time. In the United States and Canada, career information from government sources, professional associations, and long-established publishers is taken for granted. Information resources, however, are often limited in countries that do not focus on career development in public policy,

---

Exhibit 7.1. Information Organization and Classification Systems.

Classification of Instructional Programs (CIP)

The Classification of Instructional Programs (CIP) is a taxonomy (hierarchy) developed by the U.S. Department of Education's National Center for Education Statistics (NCES). The CIP consists of primarily postsecondary instructional programs and descriptions, and can be used to track, assess, and report fields of study and program completions activity.

North American Industry Classification System (NAICS)

The North American Industrial Classification System (NAICS), a hierarchy that consists of 20 broad industrial sectors, was developed jointly by the U.S., Canada, and Mexico in order to more effectively compare industrial activity and statistics among the three nations. The NAICS uses six-digit codes to describe various types of businesses, associations, government entities, and other organizations in the United States and across North America.

RIASEC Hexagon

The RIASEC hexagon is a valid model that can be used to describe an individual's interests and work, occupational, and leisure environments. The model is intuitive, improves students' schema of the world of work, and is used in several assessments, including the Self-Directed Search. It is less helpful, however, for organizing collections of information for easy reference.

Standard Occupational Classification System (SOC)

The Standard Occupational Classification System (SOC) is a hierarchical schema consisting of over 820 specific occupations with details on job duties, skills, education, and experience. Specific occupations are categorized into 23 major groups, as well as minor groups and broad occupations. The SOC was developed by the U.S. federal government to assign codes to workers in various occupations to facilitate the collection, calculation, and dissemination of occupational statistics.

or that have less-developed economies. With all the uncertainty, however, standards of quality and organizational schemas for career information and resources have remained fairly stable and should be employed as much as possible to increase usability. Epstein and Lenz (2008) can be consulted for a more in-depth discussion of developing and managing career resources.

CAREER DECISION MAKING AND THE DATA-INFORMATION-KNOWLEDGE-WISDOM HIERARCHY

Before continuing with the discussion of career information, we should note that the concept of "information" has been addressed and defined in various ways by professionals in different domains. In the career development field, Niles and Harris-Bowlsbey (2005) articulated a process of turning career data into information, and both the information science and the knowledge management fields developed what has come to be known as the data-information-knowledge-wisdom (DIKW) hierarchy to describe the relationships among data, information, knowledge, and wisdom (Ackoff, 1989; Cleveland, 1982; Zeleny, 1987, as cited by Sharma, 2008). Through an understanding of these various information models, academic advisors can provide students with a framework for using information resources in the context of career decision making.

According to Niles and Harris-Bowlsbey (2005), and based on the work of Tiedeman and O'Hara (1963), when a student understands and selects a collection of occupational or educational facts in order to make informed decisions, these facts, or data, have become information. This process consists of three steps: identifying personal characteristics and career preferences; selecting and organizing options, based on both internal and external criteria; and researching selected options. Throughout these steps, career information resources are central to the process and will be used repeatedly at varying levels of intensity. Students turn data into information when they "make sense out of what can be an overload of data about occupations, schools, and other training options, financial aid and so on" (Niles & Harris-Bowlsbey, 2005, p.195).

How does the DIKW hierarchy relate to career information, resources, and choices? The first element, data (knowing what), describes what Niles and Harris-Bowlsbey (2005) call a "collection of facts about occupational and educational opportunities" (p. 176); the second and third elements—information (knowing which) and knowledge (knowing where and how)—relate to selecting important facts and using them to make career choices. Wisdom, the fourth element, goes beyond the Niles and Harris-Bowlsbey framework to address the questions of when information can help in making a particular career decision, and why or why not. Steele (2006) emphasizes that the wisdom stage is where academic advisors help students "process the human considerations in relationship to academic and career issues" (p. 51). Advisors who understand the DIKW hierarchy in the context of career decision making will be more likely to use information resources wisely with their students. We will return to this concept of wisdom throughout the chapter, as academic advisors must continually evaluate the level of career development intervention that they can appropriately provide.

Ultimately, the primary goal for those involved with career development interventions is to understand how selected data about occupations, educational options, and other career concerns can be sifted from a variety of resources to make knowledgeable and wise career choices. An effective academic advisor models good information-seeking, integration, and decision-making skills to an advisee, while providing specific information for the student's immediate need. Methods of modeling skills can include writing an individual learning plan to create a customized plan of action, creating preprinted "recipes" for answering common career questions (guides, lists, activities), asking whether the information obtained meets quality criteria, and checking whether the information obtained has met the student's needs.

CAREER INFORMATION RESOURCES IN STUDENTS' ACADEMIC PLANNING

Students often have limited conceptualizations of the world of work and their occupational options. When asked about occupations with which they are familiar, students will often list those from prime-time TV, such as lawyers, doctors, and crime scene investigators. Unfortunately, these fictionalized depictions are not always accurate and usually provide more misinformation than facts; for example, most lawyers spend much more time reading and writing than arguing dramatic court room cases. When asked about their parents' real-world occupations, students may vaguely reply "business" or "education" without much depth or detail on work duties. In spite of decades of career education efforts, students' occupational schema may be shaped more by the passive consumption of mass media rather than active exploration of the world of work. It is the role of the academic advisor to encourage active exploration that enhances students' schema of occupational information so they can understand relationships among occupations, thereby making more fully informed career decisions.

Several authors have commented on the importance of information in career advising. Bullock, Reardon, and Lenz (2007) noted that career advising consists of helping students, "use information to make educational and occupational decisions" (p. 195). Furthermore, Gordon (2006) asserted that a role of academic advisors is "to assist students in gathering and processing the information needed to engage in realistic academically related career planning" (p. 8). Others have described career advising as a process that involves informal or formal assessment, or both, to determine student needs, then implementing various strategies for finding information (Krumboltz, 1993;

Sampson et al., 2004). In short, career advising without information about self and options is not possible.

INFORMATION GATHERING AND USAGE ROLES AND RESPONSIBILITIES

In successful career development interventions, the responsibility for gathering data and using career information resources belongs to both the academic advisor and the student, with advisors modeling effective research strategies that students can emulate and adopt. Gordon (2006) sees the advisor in a teaching role, encouraging students to learn from the process of finding resources, completing research, and analyzing what they have learned, and Steele (2006) feels academic advisors can use online communication tools to "address better their students' various learning styles" (p. 55). In addition to their role as teachers, advisors also select information resources "that conform to the guidelines provided by professional associations" (Niles & Harris-Bowlsbey, 2005, p. 177) and work with students to help them differentiate levels of quality so that they may be able to select quality resources for themselves. Academic advisors should make the selected information resources available to students by organizing them in a user-friendly manner and providing any help needed to access the resources. Later in the chapter we discuss concerns related to managing career resources and making them accessible.

Perhaps the most challenging part of the academic advisor's role relates to the concept of wisdom. Advisors facilitate the student's selection of the most appropriate data from the highest quality information resources and process of using the data to make decisions; however, throughout this process, they should be able to recognize when the data, information, and knowledge a student has is not enough to solve a career problem (Epstein & Lenz, 2008). Academic advisors must then exhibit their wisdom and make an appropriate referral to a career counselor or others. Gordon (2006) includes the ability of academic advisors to make referrals in her list of career-advising competencies because it "is an extremely important aspect of career advising" (p. 35). Examples of when referrals to career counseling services might be appropriate will be illustrated later in this chapter.

Academic advisees often depend on their advisors to facilitate their choice of major, as well as other types of career development decisions. According to Gordon (2006), students can "take an active role in their learning and evaluate how and what they are learning in the context of making career-related decisions" (p. 35). Motivation to take responsibility for their own career choices may be increased by the effective use of career information, which can broaden an awareness of available options (Sampson et al., 2004). Niles and Harris-Bowlsbey (2005) discussed decision-making responsibilities in depth, noting that students must make a commitment to gather and process career data and subsequently make their own informed career decisions.

USING CAREER RESOURCES: CASE EXAMPLES

One approach that can help academic advisors assess needs and choose information resources that meet those needs is the cognitive information processing approach to career decision making (Sampson et al., 2004). This approach, described in Chapter Three, emphasizes key content and process elements in advising college students about career decisions. Content to be included is appraisal of what students *know* about themselves (e.g., values, interests, skills, work preferences) and their options (e.g., majors or programs of study, occupations, leisure activities). It is also important to understand what a student has *done,* as a student's information needs may differ at various stages of the decision-making process (Peterson, Sampson, & Reardon, 1991). Finally, consider a student's *readiness* for career decision making in terms of personal capability (e.g., internal psychological resources) and the complexity (e.g., external social, economic, and other factors) of the career problem (Sampson et al., 2004).

Sampson's (2008) four-step model for promoting effective use of assessment and information resources can facilitate the advising process. This model includes (a) *understanding* the student's readiness, what the student needs to *know* and what student needs to *do* to make a career decision; (b) *recommending* appropriate assessments and information that fit readiness and needs; (c) *orienting* the students to the assessment or resource; and (d) *following up* with students to determine whether the resource has been properly used and has met their needs.

While understanding students' readiness, effective advisors recognize when career information is not enough to help students make their decisions. They know when to refer advisees who have low capability for career problem solving or highly complex career problems to other professionals (e.g., career counselors, mental health counselors, physicians). Effective advisors also recommend assessments and information they are qualified to use. In addition, the prudent advisor takes time to orient students to information resources by modeling information-seeking behavior, explaining the use of specific resources, describing resource strengths and limitations, and encouraging critical analysis of information. Finally, they always follow up with students, reinforcing independent information-seeking behavior and checking whether the information resource met students' needs.

We shall explore this four-step process by presenting and reviewing four hypothetical cases. The first two cases are relatively straightforward, in that the readiness for career decision making is high and the students' requests for information are narrowly defined. The second two cases describe students with lower readiness for career decision making, where additional assessment and referral may be necessary to resolve their academic and career problems. Information resources used in all four cases can be easily referenced in Exhibit 7.2.

Exhibit 7.2. Sample Information Resources.

Occupations

Bureau of Labor Statistics Occupational Employment Statistics

Census Bureau's Current Population Survey

Career Opportunities in (and/or another series)

Chronicle Guidance Briefs

http://www.chronicleguidance.com

Occupational Outlook Handbook (OOH)

Occupational Outlook Quarterly (OOQ)

O*NET

Salary and relocation Web sites

Education, Training, and Experience

Department of Labor: Bureau of Apprenticeship and Training

http://www.doleta.gov/OA/sainformation.cfm

Educational Opportunities Finder

Gradschools.com

http://www.gradschools.com

Internship Series from the Career Education Institutes

Military Careers

http://www.todaysmilitary.com

The Peterson's Internships (print and Web resources for undergraduate and graduate training)

Vault Guide to Top Internships

Industry, Employers, and Employment

Career Onestop

http://www.careeronestop.org

Dun & Bradstreet's Career Guide

Hoover's Handbook of American Business

National Trade and Professional Associations

O'Dwyers Public Relations Directory

Official Museums Directory

Plunkett's Directories

Places Rated Almanac

http://www.placesratedbooks.com/

(Continued)

Sperling's BestPlaces

http://www.bestplaces.net

Exercises and Assessments

The Holland Party exercise (RIASEC hexagon)

Self-Directed Search: assessment booklet and finder booklets

Computer-assisted career guidance systems (see Exhibit 7.4 for selected systems)

Institutionally Created Resources

List of majors by Holland code

Match major Sheets

http://www.career.fsu.edu/occupations/matchmajor/index.html

Resource guides (e.g., résumé writing, interviewing)

What Can I Do with a Major?

http://career.utk.edu/students/majors.asp

Accessibility Software

JAWS screen reader or Magic screen magnifier

http://www.freedomscientific.com/

ZoomText screen magnifier

http://www.aisquared.com/

Case 1: Luis—Choosing an Internship

Luis is a 20-year-old, male, Hispanic American. A junior majoring in English with an emphasis in creative writing, Luis is deciding what kind of internship to pursue. He appears confident, yet unsure about how to pursue an internship.

	Dialogue	*Commentary*
Luis	Hi, I was thinking I should maybe do an internship or something to get some experience . . .	The advisee is unsure about the internship process, so he is seeking help from his academic advisor.
Advisor	Yes, you can gain skills and knowledge, and the experience can help you know whether that type of work is a good match for your interests. You can also make some good networking contacts.	The advisor *understands* that Luis needs confirmation for his idea by stating many documented benefits of doing an internship.

Luis	Yeah, the only thing is, I don't know what type of internship I want. There are so many possibilities out there and I want to try them all. But I don't have any idea how to find out what's possible.	The student's primary concern is revealed. He is an English major, but is interested in many kinds of work.
Advisor	Well, editing or writing would be obvious matches for you, being an English major with a creative writing emphasis, but let's look at other possibilities too. Here's a *match-major sheet*, where you can see sample occupations and work settings for English majors. Once you know more about what kind of internship you want, I can show you how to find possible sites.	The advisor *recommends* a match-major sheet (see Exhibit 7.3) to help Luis first expand and then narrow his options. Some "major-to-occupation" matches are more direct than others; even for "direct" matches, many occupations have specializations and require decision making by students. Selecting the type of employer can also make the process challenging for students, with their limited knowledge of the world of work.
Luis	(looking at the match major sheet) Wow, it would be great to get some experience as a researcher or a public relations manager for a museum or arts foundation.	Seeing actual names of occupations and industries encourages students to think divergently and select the most appealing ones.
Advisor	Well, now you'll have to identify cultural organizations where you could do research or public relations. One way is through print and online directories, which are usually organized by type of industry. Some contain actual internships and others can identify possible employers that may have internships. For those, you'll have to check each employer Web site to see if they actually offer internships.	The advisor *orients* the student by broadening the industry designation to prepare him in case the actual words *museums* and *arts foundations* do not appear in indexes or pull-down lists. The North American Industrial Classification System (NAICS) codes may also be used in both print and online directories.
Luis	Where can I get these directories?	The advisor *understands* the student is ready to do the necessary research.

(Continued)

	Dialogue	Commentary
Advisor	I have one here in the office, our career center's library has some, and there are some online. Online directories sometimes are free, but many cost money—paid for by our college's library. There are general directories such as *Vault's Internship Guide*, *Hoovers Handbook*, *Plunkett's*, and *Dun & Bradstreet*, then specialized ones, such as the *History Internship Book*, the *Official Museums Directory*, and *O'Dwyer's PR Directory of Public Relations Firms*. Let's look at this one first to get an idea of how they work.	After describing places where directories may be found and noting that not all information on the Web is free, the advisor helps the student understand how directories work in print and online (e.g., pull-down categories and keyword search strategies). Depending on the directory's indexes or search features, internship sites may be identified by city, size and type of organization, products and services, and other criteria.

The advisor and student together look at introductory pages, including the table of contents, and indexes. The student immediately points out several possibilities.

	Dialogue	Commentary
Advisor	How does this information look to you?	The advisor *follows up* to check whether the resource is fulfilling the student's needs.
Luis	This is great! What else is there?	The student's need is met; actual internship opportunities and employers motivate the student to continue work.
Advisor	Well, you could conduct information interviews with professionals who do work you might like. Here's a guide on how to contact them and what questions you might ask.	Sources for interviewees include alumni databases, campus or local job fairs, and professional associations.
Luis	And then I'll have to go through an application process, won't I?	The student realizes applying for internships is similar to applying for jobs.
Advisor	Yes, you can use books and guides to write résumé and cover letters. You also may want to watch a workshop on interviewing skills on our career center's Web site.	Job search preparation resources are available in many formats through libraries, career centers, and workforce organizations.
Luis	I saw on Facebook that some experts will help you write your résumés.	The student tests the idea of getting advice and help via online resources.

Advisor	That might be OK, but you always need to check on the person's credentials—the Internet has both disreputable and honest individuals claiming to be career experts. More important, learning to write your own résumé will prepare you for future interviews and job hunts. Remember, employers are going to ask you questions based on your résumé and the only "expert" in the room will be you!	The student should verify credentials (background and/or experience in human resources or career planning) *and* advice via independent sources. In the end, any advice obtained from various resources must be evaluated by the student.
Luis	Yeah, I'll remember that. OK, I think I've got a lot to do!	The student has the tools he needs to do research.
Advisor	Well, if you get stuck in the process, let me know.	The advisor leaves the door open for future contact.

Exhibit 7.3. Matching Majors to Occupations and Work Settings.

English

Sample Occupations

Please ask a career advisor for help in identifying resources for the following occupations and job titles. Note that some of these options may require an advanced degree.

Administrative officer	Film editor	Novelist/writer
Advertising occupations	Foreign service officer	Personnel director
Archivist	Freelance writer	Playwright
Author	Grant writer	Proofreader
Bibliographer	Information industry occupations	Public relations manager
Bookkeeper	Information manager/scientist	Public relations specialist
Broadcasting/comm. occupations	Interpreter/translator	Radio/television coordinator
Columnist	Job analyst	
Community relations worker	Journalist	Reporter
	Lawyer	Screenwriter
Computer systems analyst	Librarian	Speech writer
Copywriter	Library assistant	Teacher/professor
Critic	Literary agent	Technical writer
Editor	Magazine publisher	Translator
Education occupations	Newspaper editor	Underwriter

(Continued)

Sample Work Settings

Advertising	Federal agencies	Private industry and business
Aircraft industry	Financial institutions	
Banks	Food products organization	Public relations departments and firms
Book publishers		
Businesses	Junior colleges	Public service organizations
Broadcast media/radio	Legal firms	
Chemical and drug companies	Libraries	Publishing houses
	Local school boards	Schools
Colleges	Local and state government	Television/motion pictures
Commercial/specialty magazines		
	Magazine publishers	Theater
Company/independent newsletters	Museums	Trade publications
	Newspapers	Travel and tourism
Corporate communications departments	Office equipment companies	Universities
Educational institutions	Philanthropic foundations	

Students considering internships will be at different stages of the career decision-making process; thus, academic advisors need to make a variety of resources available to them. For those students who have not yet decided what type of internship or organizations they want to pursue, resources such as career center guides that relate majors to occupations (see the FSU Match Major Pages at http://www.career.fsu.edu/occupations/matchmajor/index.html and the *What Can I Do with a Major?* resource available in print or online at http://career.utk.edu/students/majors.asp), books such as the McGraw-Hill series (*Opportunities in* or *Careers in*) and computer-assisted career guidance systems (see Exhibit 7.4) may help students narrow their internship options. Directories of internship opportunities may be general, such as *Peterson's Internships* or the *Vault Guide to Top Internships*, or very specific, such as the *Internship Series* produced by the Career Education Institutes, which includes titles focused on internships in history, advertising, human rights, law and policy, and media, among others.

Students may also use directories that list organizations in specific industries to identify possible internship sites. Directories of this nature may either contain an overview of many industries or focus on only one industry or group of related industries. University career centers and libraries will typically have this kind of directory in print or digital format. Industries in the overview type of directory are sometimes organized according to the North

Exhibit 7.4. Sample Computer-Assisted Career Guidance Systems.

Career Information System (CIS)

CIS is published by intoCareers, an outreach unit of the University of Oregon. CIS is available in standalone versions for PCs and Macintosh and via the Internet. This product is licensed by over 15 states and at 7,000 sites. Learn more at http://cis.uoregon.edu/.

Choices Planner CT

Published by Bridges, Inc., Choices Planner CT combines traditional features of assessment and career/education information delivery with planning and jour-naling tools in an individualized portfolio. More about Choices and other career information products for children and adults can be found at http://www .bridges.com.

DISCOVER

Published by ACT, DISCOVER is available via standalone CD-ROM and Internet versions for high school students, college students, and adults. Ask for a free 30-day trial and learn more about Discover at http://www.act.org/discover/.

SIGI 3

SIGI 3 is an Internet-based system published by Valpar International. Following this work of Katz (1993), SIGI 3 focuses on clarifying work values as a basis for making career choices. Learn more about SIGI 3 at http://www.valparint.com/.

MyPlan

Unlike the systems listed above, MyPlan is a newcomer to the CACG arena. This site appears to work on a fee-per-service basis, charging for the various assessments provided. One interesting note is that paid advertising appears to be displayed alongside occupational information. Learn more at http://www .myplan.com.

American Industrial Classification System (NAICS, 2008), which consists of 20 broad industrial sectors and uses six-digit codes to describe various types of businesses, associations, government entities, and other organizations. Using these codes can sometimes make the research process easier for stu-dents. After identifying potential internship sites, students then need to research each organization to determine whether they offer internships. Ways to learn about individual organizations, as well as to discover internship opportunities, include reviewing organizational Web sites, conducting infor-mation interviews with alumni or professional association acquaintances, and attending college or local business career expositions.

Case 2: Jolie—Senior, Deciding Between Finding a Job and Going to Grad School

Jolie is a 21-year-old, first-generation African American student whose parents are Haitian. She experiences a good deal of self-imposed pressure to succeed for her family.

	Dialogue	Commentary
Jolie	Can you help? I graduate next semester and don't know if I should get a master's degree or not.	The student appears ambivalent about going to graduate school. This may be due to a lack of occupational knowledge or some other cause.
Advisor	What are your eventual career plans?	The advisor attempts to *understand* what the student knows about herself and the firmness of her career goal.
Jolie	To be director of a chemistry lab that does cancer research. Maybe some work experience will be better for me?	The student has a very specific career goal, so the advisor recognizes her need for occupational information. Less specific career goals may indicate the need for a referral to career counselor.
Advisor	Well, first let's see if graduate school makes sense for you by finding out the educational requirements for lab managers. Then you can also check on outlook and salaries. The first step on your action plan is to review online resources with occupational data.	The advisor *recommends* occupational information, such as the *OOH* and *O*NET* (described later in the chapter), professional association brochures and Web sites, and occupational brief and book series.
Jolie	Hmm, I see from this Web site that lab management is a big growth occupation nationally these days, especially in the pharmaceutical field. I'll have to look at this more to see what the outlook is for Georgia and North Carolina.	The student becomes aware that occupational outlook data are available from the U.S. government (e.g., the *Occupational Employment Statistics, Current Population Survey,* and the *Occupational Outlook Quarterly*) at national, state, and local levels.
Advisor	That's good; just remember that outlook may change, depending on the economy, laws, disasters, and so on.	The advisor continues to *orient* the student on the nature and use of these resources (i.e., data collection might also be faulty—but outlook data effectively tracks general trends).

Jolie	Someone told me that people with master's degrees don't make much more than if you just have a bachelor's.	Many students question the "return on investment" of attending graduate school.
Advisor	Well, that's part of weighing the pros and cons of going to graduate school. Several books and articles address these issues, including the salary benefits of getting a master's degree. You'll have to compare the money you can make with how and where you want to live in the future.	Salary information is available for many occupations; it can play a major role in career decisions and quality of life issues, including choosing a major, going to graduate school, and accepting job offers. Resources for cost of life and quality of life include Sperling's http://www.bestplaces.net or *Places Rated Almanac.*
Jolie	Yeah, that stuff's important while you're going to graduate school, too, isn't it?	The student worries about being a "broke" graduate student.
Advisor	Yes, but first let's look at some resources for researching graduate school, including how to pay for it.	Advisor returns the focus to the next steps in the decision-making process; adds to action plan.
Jolie	That's one of my biggest concerns.	Cost may keep many students from considering graduate studies.
Advisor	I know—it is for most students looking at graduate school. I have one directory here, but career services and the library have both print and electronic resources with information on assistantships, fellowships, grants, and scholarships.	Advisors often need to help students separate issues of where to attend graduate school and how to pay for it. If information doesn't seem to help the process, the student may need a referral to a career counselor.

The advisor and Jolie review the graduate school directory.

Advisor	What do you think now that you have reviewed this information?	The advisor *follows up*, asking whether the information meets the student's needs.
Jolie	Great—that makes me feel much better . . . there are many programs that vary in cost. . . .	The student confirms that she is ready to continue with the process.
Advisor	OK, so the next step will be to decide which program and research you want to focus on, and create a list of universities that meet your criteria. These Web sites and other resources should help you identify programs, then you'll have to research the faculty and departments to evaluate	The advisor *recommends* resources such as Peterson's guides in print and on the Web, the Classification of Instructional Programs (CIP), and graduate school expos and brochures. Faculty also often post their vitas and syllabi on department Web sites. The advisor

(Continued)

	Dialogue	Commentary
	each of the programs. The library's databases might be useful to see who publishes most frequently in the chemistry journals.	*orients* the student by mentioning that some programs are heavily marketed, which is not the same as being a good match for the student's needs.
Jolie	OK, I'll get started right away on finding out more about lab managers.	The student knows to start with first step on the individualized action plan.

Students consider attending graduate school for many reasons, including to satisfy parental expectations or occupational aspirations, to avoid finding a job, or simply to learn more about their field of study. Making this decision requires a variety of career resources, which will be primarily of two types: those that address the issue of whether or not to attend graduate school, and those that help students decide which graduate programs are best for them. Often a large aspect of the first issue concerns the financial challenges of going to graduate school. Resources on Web sites such as http://www .petersons.com and http://gradschool.com, guides created by career centers, and books and articles that discuss costs and benefits of graduate school can help students decide whether or not graduate school is the next step in their careers. Many of these same types of resources, as well as "in-person" resources such as career fairs, campus visits, and information interviews, can also assist students with determining the type of graduate program best suited to their particular career goals.

Case 3: Lynn—Choosing a Major: Part 1, Understanding Needs and Recommending Resources

An 18-year-old, first-year student who is undecided about a major, Lynn arrives at the advising center's office well groomed and in trendy clothes but looking a bit nervous. Obviously popular, Lynn's cell phone keeps vibrating with calls and text messages from friends.

	Dialogue	Commentary
Lynn	Hi, the computer won't let me schedule classes for next semester! It told me to see my academic advisor . . .	Students often procrastinate as a way of coping with anxiety surrounding decision making. Institutional rules sometimes "force" them to choose a major.
Advisor	Well, welcome! You need to choose a major . . . what have you done so far?	A warm greeting, but an open-ended question that begins to *understand* the student's needs and assess readiness for career decision making.

Lynn	Nothing really . . . I've been putting it off. I don't really know what I want to do and what majors fit me. *I can't make decisions like this by myself.* My friend told me she took some test here that told her what to do.	The student confirms avoidance behavior and expresses both lack of self-knowledge and options knowledge. Her negative self-talk about her decision-making ability undermines her self-confidence, feeds feelings of anxiety and helplessness, and promotes further inaction. Lynn appears to be looking to an external source for an easy answer from the "magic test." If Lynn's negative self-talk continues, a referral to a career or mental health counselor may be needed.
Advisor	Well Lynn, I'm glad you decided to come in today and start solving this problem for yourself. I'm also happy your friend found her work here helpful. But instead of "tests," we call our exercises "assessments." Tests can be passed or failed, but assessments help you learn more about your values, interests, and skills—there are no right or wrong answers!What do you hope to gain from an assessment?	The advisor positively reinforces the student for her action and places responsibility for problem solving with the student. The advisor also gently corrects the student's use of the word *test* in favor of the more accurate term *assessment*. This helps the student place self-assessment exercises in the proper context and reduces any stress that may come with the term *test*.
Lynn	Well, I hope the assessment will tell me my major.	The student's statement again suggests a somewhat mechanistic and simplistic understanding of the goal of assessment.
Advisor	Our assessments can suggest majors and occupations about which you can learn. Many students think an assessment will narrow down their choices. But in reality it may give you more choices to explore than you could possibly imagine. In short, the assessment will broaden your options, not narrow them down.	Again, the advisor gently challenges the student's prior assumptions about the purpose of assessment.
Lynn	So you mean I'm still going to have to decide what to do? The assessment is only going to suggest some options for me to explore further? How will I learn about these options?	The student acknowledges responsibility for decision making, but still experiences confusion about exploring options and decision making.

(Continued)

	Dialogue	Commentary
Advisor	Yes, Lynn. I think you will find our Holland Party exercise can help you identify options you can explore. We can also help you find information you need for the options suggested.	The advisor *recommends* a helpful exercise that emphasizes the student's knowledge of self and ability to make choices. The student is also reassured that support is available in researching her options. This can serve to reduce anxiety in decision making.
Lynn	OK . . . where do we start?	The student is ready to begin exploration of self-knowledge through assessment.

Best practice in assessment employs empirically supported instruments that have been found to be reliable and valid and that are used in an appropriate and ethical manner by advisors. Specialized skills, training, experience, and supervision are required to administer most assessments, including career assessments. Vendors of assessments also abide by ethical codes and guidelines of associations (e.g., American Psychological Association) and sell assessments only to users with appropriate professional credentials. However, there are also many opportunities to make mistakes in assessment, including (but not limited to) (a) selecting an inappropriate assessment for a student's needs, (b) injecting cultural bias when working with students different from the assessment's normative group, and (c) misinterpretation of results. Academic advisors should tread carefully into the world of assessment and seek training and supervision from qualified colleagues.

For the reasons already described, this chapter includes assessments that can be used by any academic advisor to assist a student exploring knowledge of self and options. One method of assessment is to simply ask the student directly about values, interests, and skills. For example, a simple prompt such as, "What three things that are most important to you in all of life?" is usually sufficient to begin a conversation about values as they relate to education and occupational choices. Often students struggle to reply to one or more of these types of questions. This difficulty is not surprising, as being asked, "Who are you?" is not a daily occurrence. To spare students the discomfort of "not knowing," some may be tempted to provide simple, homemade checklists of items to support the student in verbalizing their values, interests, and skills. However, difficulties replying to simple open-ended questions about values, interests, or skills are diagnostic of a student's limited self-knowledge. Such difficulties suggest that additional assessment and exploration in these areas could be helpful to the decision-making process.

Interests can be simply defined as what one enjoys or more specifically as the locus of an individual's psychological world and the environment.

Holland (1973) defined vocational interests as "the expression of personality in work, hobbies, recreational activities, and preferences" (p. 7). Holland, identified as one of the most influential theorists in career assessment (Borgen, 1991; Brown & Brooks, 1996; Isaacson & Brown, 1997), championed the notion that clients are active shapers of their careers and should be active participants in the career advising process (Borgen, 1991; Reardon & Lenz, 1998). The RIASEC hexagon model (see Figure 7.1) and the Self-Directed

Holland's Hexagon

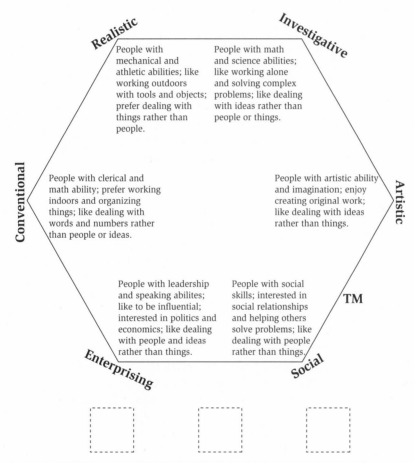

Realistic
People with mechanical and athletic abilities; like working outdoors with tools and objects; prefer dealing with things rather than people.

Investigative
People with math and science abilities; like working alone and solving complex problems; like dealing with ideas rather than people or things.

Conventional
People with clerical and math ability; prefer working indoors and organizing things; like dealing with words and numbers rather than people or ideas.

Artistic
People with artistic ability and imagination; enjoy creating original work; like dealing with ideas rather than things.

Enterprising
People with leadership and speaking abilites; like to be influential; interested in politics and economics; like dealing with people and ideas rather than things.

Social
People with social skills; interested in social relationships and helping others solve problems; like dealing with people rather than things.

TM

Adapted From: Holland, J. H. (1992). *Making Vocational Choices* (2nd edition). Odessa, FL: Psychological Assessment Resources, Inc.

Figure 7.1 The Holland Party.

Search (SDS; Holland, 1994) are powerful yet easy-to-use tools that students and advisors can use to quickly assess vocational interests and find matching occupational, educational, and leisure environments to explore.

The RIASEC hexagon has become an icon of vocational psychology (Borgen, 1991) (see Chapter Three). The six interest and environment types of *realistic, investigative, artistic, social, enterprising,* and *conventional* are ordered so that adjacent types are assumed to be more similar in interests and vocational pursuits than opposite. One method of asking students to express their interests is to use an exercise such as the Holland Party (see Figure 7.1). The students' expressed Holland code can then be used to review a list of college majors categorized by one Holland code. For example, majors categorized under the realistic type might include mechanical engineering and graphic design, whereas social majors might include child development and music therapy.

This is an efficient yet theoretically grounded method of identifying interest areas and matching programs of study. For more details matching Holland codes to majors see the *Educational Opportunities Finder* (Rosen, Holmberg, & Holland, 1997). The next case illustrates how this exercise might work by resuming the dialogue between Lynn and her advisor.

Case 3: Lynn—Choosing a Major, Part 2, Orienting Students and Following Up

	Dialogue	*Commentary*
Lynn	Okay . . . where do we start?	The student is ready to begin exploration of self-knowledge through assessment.
Advisor	I'd like you to look at this worksheet. Pretend you are at a party in a room with six corners and six walls. In each corner is a distinct group of people. Please tell me who you would hang out with first, second, and third by writing the first letter of each group's name in the three boxes below.	The advisor *orients* Lynn to the exercise, purposefully setting up a party so that the focus is on an enjoyable and relaxed atmosphere.
Lynn	Okay, I like the social, enterprising, and artistic groups (writes S E A on the worksheet).	Lynn projects her self-concept onto the groups and selects the three most similar to her interests.

Advisor	Great! So now you have a three-letter code known as the Holland code, which we'll talk about in a bit. What led you to hang out with the social people first?	The advisor asks for Lynn's decision-making process. Note that Lynn could also have been asked to think aloud while selecting the three groups so the advisor could monitor her negative career thinking.
Lynn	I like to meet people and learn about them. Their desire to help others seems like me too.	
Advisor	Now look at the realistic people hanging out on the other side of the room. What led you to not choose them?	The advisor begins to teach Lynn about the structure of the Holland hexagon.
Lynn	Well they are the total *opposite* of the social people! They like to work alone and with things instead of others.	Lynn picks up on the intuitive order of the hexagon.
Advisor	Exactly! You understand a major feature of what we call the Holland or RIASEC hexagon. Peoples' interests have been found by John Holland to fit these six main types. He also indicated that leisure, education, and occupation environments can be categorized in the same way. People will be happier and more productive when they are in education and work environments that match their interests. What kind of occupations do you think social people would want to pursue?	The advisor praises the student and describes some fundamental concepts of Holland's theory. This is followed by a question to Lynn that begins to bridge the gap between interests and occupations and eventually majors.
Lynn	Teaching, counseling, social work. . . .	The student lists some common social occupations.
Advisor	Exactly! Those are some good examples. Now what kind of occupations do you think the realistic people would pursue?	The advisor continues to build the student's schema.

(Continued)

	Dialogue	Commentary
Lynn	Plumbers, carpenters, firefighters, forest rangers. . . .	Lynn is quite bright, realizing that a wide variety of people like to use their hands and bodies, work outside, and manipulate tools.
Advisor	Right! Now let's look at your enterprising and artistic codes and their opposites . . .	The advisor continues explaining the hexagon and building the student's schema for the world of work.

Lynn and her advisor quickly work through discussing the remainder of the hexagon.

	Dialogue	Commentary
Lynn	OK . . . so now I know what my Holland code is, and some occupations I might pursue: I still don't know my major.	The student has not quite made the connection yet between interests and majors.
Advisor	We'll take a look at this handout; it lists all of the majors at Big State University categorized by one Holland code.	The advisor has roughly categorized the university's majors by matching it to the closest option in the *Educational Opportunities Finder* (Rosen et al., 1997). This booklet lists 750 post-secondary fields of study by their three-letter Holland code.
Lynn	Cool! So I should look at my three letters to figure out what to major in?	The student connects interests to majors.
Advisor	Yes, take a look at each of the majors below your three Holland types. For each major, put a star next to the ones that sound appealing, a question mark next to the ones that you don't know anything about, and mark through the ones you know would not be a good fit for you.	The advisor asks Lynn to actively process the list of majors that match her Holland code. A drawback of this technique is that Lynn may eliminate or include options based on stereotype or misinformation. However, it does help narrow down the list to a manageable number of options that match her interests.

Lynn reviews and marks the list of majors as suggested by the advisor.

	Dialogue	Commentary
Lynn	Some of these majors like psychology and social work I had thought of before. . . . But I have at least five new majors I hadn't considered.	The face validity of the process is confirmed by the presence of majors Lynn has previously considered. This external validation of previously considered options can also reduce anxiety and increases decision-making confidence.

Advisor	Good! How do you feel about what you've learned using this exercise?	The advisor *follows up* on the experience.
Lynn	I'm feeling a little less anxious. I've moved forward, at least I have some options now. But how do I choose among these?	If the experience is not a success, the advisor may have misunderstood the student's needs or readiness for career decision making. A referral to a career counselor may also be appropriate after repeated unsuccessful attempts.
Advisor	Well, Lynn, now the fun part of exploring your options begins . . .	Lynn and the advisor visit a Web site such as http://www.academic-guide.fsu.edu/index.html, which helps her learn about her options. Information interviews with faculty and students in possible majors, as well as additional visits with her advisor, may be required for Lynn to narrow her options and make a final choice.

A more formal method of assessing and matching Lynn's interests to her education, occupation, and leisure options would be to administer the Self-Directed Search (SDS; Holland, 1994). The SDS, a simulated career counseling activity, is the outcome of almost 40 years of theory building and assessment development by John Holland (Reardon & Lenz, 1998). It can be used by students either with or without the intervention of an advisor. This activity is an accessible, economical, easy-to-use, and powerful intervention to improve students' schema of self-knowledge and options.

The SDS allows individuals to both express and assess their vocational interests. This tool is available in various reading levels, age versions, and media formats (e.g., print, computer-based, and Internet-based). By using the printed lists of occupations, educational programs, and leisure activities, students can identify options matching their Holland code types. In turn, the options identified in these booklets are easily searchable by classification systems (e.g., *Dictionary of Occupational Titles* or Classification of Instructional Programs).

Returning to case 3, Lynn has chosen to major in psychology but remains uncertain about what to do with her major after graduation. By taking the SDS, Lynn will identify and make plans to explore the occupations of school counselor, music therapist, and interpreter.

Case 3: Lynn—Choosing a Major: Part 3, Connecting Majors to Occupations

	Dialogue	*Commentary*
Advisor	Well Lynn it's good to see you . . . how is psychology as a major?	
Lynn	I'm really enjoying my classes this semester. It's such a relief to know what I'm going to get my degree in, but now I'm worried about something else. I'm sure you can help me solve it, though . . .	The student continues to rely on others for support. If this is a pattern causing problems for Lynn, a referral to another professional may be in order.
Advisor	I'm certain *you* can solve it, but I'm happy to give you some pointers along the way.	The advisor reminds the student of who is responsible for decision making.
Lynn	Well, I would like to find out what I can do with a degree in psychology.	The student assertively states a concrete request for information.
Advisor	There are a large number of occupations you can pursue in psychology, Lynn. Would you like to take a more formal interest assessment to identify occupations that might be related to your degree and will also fit you and your interests?	*Understanding* that Lynn needs some additional work bridging her self-knowledge to occupational options, the advisor suggests a more formal assessment.
Lynn	Sure. It will be interesting to see if my career options match my major. I'm learning about "testing" too right now in class, so this should be fun.	The student makes a connection between her academic work and personal life. These connections are necessary for the development of "wisdom."

The advisor orients the student to the Self-Directed Search following the guidelines suggested by Sampson (2008). Lynn completes the SDS in about 20 minutes. The follow-up with Lynn indicates that she found the assessment valuable and helpful.

It is now time to link Lynn's self-knowledge with her options via information resources. Since Lynn has three occupations she is interested in exploring, the strategic academic advisor will begin with more general resources that describe the world of work. Two such sources are the *O*NET* and the *Occupational Outlook Handbook*, both of which are supported by the U.S. Department of Labor.

The *O*NET* (Occupational Information Network) is an expansive database of information on over 800 occupations, organized by the Standard Occupational Classification system and updated quarterly with a sophisticated survey methodology. A comprehensive overview of the *O*NET* program may be found at http://www.online.onetcenter.org/help.onet. The content model for the database covers worker characteristics, worker requirements, experience requirements, occupational requirements, workforce characteristics, and occupation-specific information, and uses data collected from both businesses and workers. In its raw form, the 277 data elements collected for each occupation within the system may overwhelm even sophisticated career decision makers. Fortunately, several products have been created by the government and private vendors that turn the data in this system to useable information. Among these are *O*NET Online* and the *O*NET Dictionary of Occupational Titles* (JIST Works, 2007).

O*NET Online (http://online.onetcenter.org/) is the Web presence for *O*NET*, in which all information is searchable by multiple classification systems, text keyword, interests, and many other methods. Although this is an invaluable information resource and free of charge, it could be a bit intimidating for students, given its somewhat sparse user interface. This perhaps reflects the government's strategy of focusing on providing high-quality data and allowing private vendors to focus on the process of transforming *O*NET* data to information through "value added" print materials and computer software systems.

The *O*NET Dictionary of Occupational Titles* (JIST Works, 2007) is an example of such a value-added product. This printed reference book is, according to its introduction, "easier to use than it looks" (p. iii). For each occupation a concise description is provided, along with data on tasks, work values, personality type (e.g., Holland code type), required skills and abilities, work activities and conditions, and the amount of time usually required for entry. In addition to an alphabetical listing of occupations, this resource is indexed by *O*NET* number, interest areas, education and training requirements, earnings, growth, number of openings, and related military jobs. Cross references are also provided for other occupational information resources such as the retired *Dictionary of Occupational Titles* coding system and the current *Occupational Outlook Handbook*.

If *O*NET* is a dictionary, then the *Occupational Outlook Handbook* (*OOH*, JIST Works, 2008; http://www.bls.gov/OCO/) is more like an encyclopedia. Covering about 250 occupational titles, or about 9 out of 10 jobs in the economy, approximately two pages of information are presented in prose form for each occupation. The standard organizational scheme for each includes significant points, nature of work, training, qualifications and advancement, employment, job outlook, and earnings, among other headings. Like the *O*NET,* the *OOH* is available at no charge online, where it can be searched via multiple methods. Print versions are also available directly from the federal government or from third-party vendors.

The *OOH* and other occupational outlook resources should be used appropriately in the career decision-making process, and academic advisors play a pivotal role. For example, a 1% growth rate for an occupation is very different when the base employment is 1,000 or 1,000,000 people. It is the advisor's task to help students take the next step and ask, "How many people are currently employed in the occupation?" and to distinguish between big growth and fast growth in occupations (Reardon, Lenz, Sampson, & Peterson, 2006). Although outlook can provide valuable information, one only has to think of the structural shifts in the economy following the rapid adoption of the Internet or tragic events of September 11, 2001 to realize that it can be hard to predict the future. Instead of overemphasizing outlook, advisors can encourage students and their families to focus on trends in science, technology, and culture. Emphasizing trends that may affect career decisions over the next 10 years instead of numbers depicting percentage change and base employment allows the advisor to help students transform knowledge into wisdom.

In addition to the *O*NET* and *OOH*, a computer-assisted career guidance (CACG) system would be a good, comprehensive resource for Lynn to explore her occupations of interest. Developed in the 1960s, CACG systems have converged over intervening decades to be very similar in the information and tools they contain. What remain unique are the theories underlying each system's assessments and connection to occupations (Harris-Bowlsbey & Sampson, 2001). Today, most systems contain print and multimedia information on several hundred occupations, which can be filtered based upon assessment results. CACG systems are also cross-indexed via classification tables to provide connections between occupations, related programs of study (i.e., majors), and institutions offering these programs of study. Some systems now include opportunities for users to share their own experiences in career exploration via "Web 2.0" tools such as blogging.

Examples of current systems in the marketplace are presented in Exhibit 7.4. These systems often base their occupational, education and training, and other career resource information from data in the public domain collected by the federal government (e.g., *O*NET*). Some vendors also customize their systems for major purchasers, such as state departments of education and workforce development. Therefore, before purchasing a CACG system, check whether the system can be purchased or subscribed to at a discount through state education and workforce offices. Some systems may even be available for free use! The Association of Computer-based Systems for Career Information (ACSCI) is also a good source of information for evaluating and selecting CACG systems (see Exhibit 7.4).

Professional associations and labor organizations are also an invaluable resource for career information, keeping in mind that professional and craft workers have a vested interest in promoting their chosen occupations. A good way of identifying these associations and organizations is by using a directory such as the *National Trade and Professional Associations,* or the free acronym index to association titles currently available at http://www.association-execs.com/. Associations may provide information in the form of Web sites, brochures, and social networking opportunities on occupations, trends in the field, and sometimes even scholarship competitions. Membership directories can also facilitate students conducting information interviews to benefit from the wisdom of workers at varying career stages. These interviews can provide a "reality check" that balances knowledge gained from print or online information resources, and may also evolve into internships and other work opportunities. Students should also take advantage of career center and alumni association databases to identify professionals for information interviews and other career opportunities.

Case 4: Mark—A College "Drop-out"

Mark is a 19-year-old, Caucasian male. Dressed in tattered jeans, he carries a motorcycle helmet. His hands are somewhat weather-beaten and his fingernails have grease beneath them.

	Dialogue	Commentary
Mark	Hey, I need to drop all of my classes.	The student makes a concrete request.
Advisor	I can help you with that, since you can still withdraw without a dean's signature. But what is leading you to withdraw from classes?	The advisor acknowledges the student's request, but an open-ended question gently probes for the reason for the withdrawal request in an attempt to better *understand* his needs.
Mark	It's my second year here at Big State University and I just don't feel like I belong. I don't want to do the homework and I hate my classes.	The student responds with powerful feelings, reflecting both isolation from and dislike of his current environment.
Advisor	So you feel like you don't belong here and you aren't very motivated to do the class work. Do you think Big State University is a poor fit or do you think that college in general is not a good option for you?	The advisor reflects the student's feelings, but clarifies the student's problem in terms of knowledge of self and options.
Mark	I didn't want to come here or to any college. I only came here last year because my older brother graduated from Big State and my parents wanted me to come here too. I wanted to become an auto mechanic but no one listened to me. I'm stuck here and no one cares!	The student admits that college is not for him; rather he felt pressured into it based on external conflict with family members. He does have an occupational aspiration—auto mechanic—which has been deferred due to this external conflict. Referral to a career or mental health counselor may be appropriate.

(Continued)

	Dialogue	Commentary
Advisor	Wow, you sound pretty angry about not getting to become an auto mechanic. Do you like to work on motorcycles too?	The advisor reflects the student's obvious anger over being "stuck" in college, and acknowledges his motorcycle helmet.
Mark	Yeah I guess I am angry. I really get into working on my bike, but it doesn't help me do my schoolwork.	The student makes the connection between his anger, coping behavior of working on his motorcycle, and lack of time and motivation for schoolwork.
Advisor	Before you decide to withdraw today, would you like to review some information on training opportunities for auto mechanics? I can also show you how to learn what mechanics do and how much money they might earn.	The advisor suggests that the student makes an informed decision about withdrawal from college based on information about his occupational aspiration of becoming a mechanic.
Mark	Sure! No one has ever taken my goal of being a mechanic seriously before.	The advisor, by understanding the student's needs, has tapped the motivation intrinsic to vocational interests.
Advisor	Great! Well, you have several options for becoming an auto mechanic, including a two-year technical school, apprenticeship, or military training. You could also transfer to PolyTech College, which offers a bachelor's degree in automotive design. Let me show you what we have in these books and on the computer. . . .	The advisor describes several non-bachelor's degree training options and a college transfer option using a variety of resources. After reviewing his options, Mark decides to withdraw from school and pursue training at a two-year technical school in his hometown.

Mark is not an uncommon student. Nationwide, only some 56% of first-time, full-time degree-seeking students complete a bachelor's degree within six years of enrolling in college (NCHEMS, 2006). What happens to the 44% who do not graduate? Students progress slowly through or leave college for a variety of reasons, including poor academic performance, financial difficulties, family dysfunction, and physical or mental health problems. Upon leaving college, many are burdened with student loans or other debts that require repayment. College may also represent a student's last chance to receive services such as health care that can be difficult or impossible to obtain later in the "real world" marketplace.

Thus, academic advisors have a responsibility to facilitate a smooth transition out of college for students like Mark, regardless of whether they graduate or withdraw from classes. A primary goal should be to help students keep options open for later continuation of their education and training. For example, students often do not follow institutional procedures for withdrawal, which contributes to failure of several courses and elimination of future academic options. It is also important to help withdrawing students clarify their vocational identities, and provide resources on education and training alternatives to the four-year degree. That is, students should move toward a career goal rather than simply "run away" from college. If deemed necessary, advisors should consider possible referral to other institutional or community resources (e.g., counseling center).

An example of such a resource is the community college, which is usually well equipped to help students remediate deficits in academic skills. Apprenticeship is also a centuries-old method of learning well-paying, skilled occupations. These programs, which are often administered by labor unions, comprise a combination of formal classroom training and on-the-job, supervised experience. A list of state apprenticeship Web sites can be found at the U.S. Department of Labor's Web site at http://www.doleta.gov/OA/sainformation.cfm. Community workforce development services can also be an invaluable source of information and services. Colloquially known as "the unemployment" office, these organizations provide a much wider variety of career planning and employment services than processing unemployment insurance claims. Job seekers of all skill levels and needs can usually find helpful information and assistance at these "one stop" centers. More information on workforce development may be found at http://www.careeronestop.org.

Enlistment in a branch of the armed forces is a common option pursued by students leaving college before graduation. The military's emphasis on vocational training is clear from the title of "Career Advisor" presently used by many of its recruiters. In fact, current career assessments are derived partially from the military's efforts to screen and place large numbers of inductees during World War I (Zytowski & Swanson, 1994). The armed forces continue this tradition through use of aptitude and interest assessments during the recruiting process. The Department of Defense also invests significant resources in providing information on the various military occupational specialties available to enlistees. Information on these occupational specialties is available at http://www.todaysmilitary.com.

It should be emphasized that the military is not an "easy out" for students from the responsibility of career decision making, as continuous training and improvement is expected of all military personnel. Although military service can be an option for students whose personalities and values fit a more hierarchical, authority-driven environment, the organizational cultures of the separate branches and occupational specialties can vary widely. As with all career decisions, individuals considering the military should fully explore their knowledge of self and their options by using a variety information sources before making a decision about enlistment.

MANAGEMENT AND ACCESSIBILITY OF CAREER INFORMATION

Career resources range greatly in quality and may be in many formats, which sometimes presents challenges for those who select them and make them available to others. Questions such as "Does the producer of this resource have the credentials needed to present information on this topic?" and "Is the presentation of occupational or other data clear, organized, and simple, without distracting graphics, complicated charts, or incomprehensible vocabulary?" come up frequently. Professional associations and other organizations (see Exhibit 7.5) have created standards to help advisors select resources for students in the most appropriate formats and at the appropriate reading levels. Various perspectives on these issues are also discussed in the works of the Canadian Career Information Association (2004), Epstein and Lenz (2008), Gordon (2006), Harris-Bowlsbey et al. (2002), Osborn and Zunker (2006), and Schutt and Finkle (2008). In their presentations, many of these authors include lists of criteria or questions to consider when evaluating career resources.

Exhibit 7.5. Associations and Groups Working with Career Information Resources.

America's Career Network Association (ACRNA)

ACRNA is a nonprofit organization dedicated to ensuring that all individuals have the knowledge and skills necessary to make fully informed career decisions. Members include career professionals, as well as vendors of career information. Topics addressed by ACRNA include influencing career development-related public policy, serving ex-offenders, and developing national guidelines for personal and social development, educational achievement and lifelong learning, and career management. Learn more about ACRNA at http://www.acrna.net.

Association of Computer-Based Systems for Career Information (ACSCI)

ACSCI is an organization of entities that develop, manage, or distribute career information and services to individuals who are interested in such activities. This group has created standards for the development and delivery of career information systems, as well as consumer checklists for evaluating systems. Visit http://www.acsci.org/ to learn more.

Career Resource Managers Association (CRMA)

CRMA is an organization for career resource librarians and other career professionals who manage information resources. Holding meetings twice yearly,

CRMA provides networking and including guest speakers, resource sharing, and discussion groups. Active for over 10 years, CRMA is based in the New England region. Learn more about CRMA at http://www.crmaonline.org/.

Canadian Career Information Association (CCIA)

Formed in 1975, CCIA brings together groups and individuals who share a common interest in the development, distribution, and use of career resources. Educational institutions, libraries, businesses, government and community organizations, students, and private practitioners interested in career-related information for client and professional use can join CCIA. Support information, such as the practical, 148-page guide *Developing a Career Information Centre* (5th ed.), is also available for purchase. Visit http://www.ccia-acadop.ca/ to learn more about CCIA.

National Associations of Colleges and Employers (NACE)

NACE provides leadership in the career development and employment process of college students and alumni to both employers and institutions of higher education. NACE serves its members by providing networking opportunities, ethical guidelines, and standards for best practices, research, and shared online information services through NACELink. Learn more about NACE and its member services at http://www.naceweb.org/.

National Career Development Association (NCDA)

A division of the American Counseling Association (ACA), NCDA promotes the career development of all people over the life span. NCDA supports professional development activities, publications, research, public information, professional standards, advocacy, and recognition for achievement and service for professionals involved in career development. Interested parties can learn about NCDA resources at http://www.ncda.org/.

Once resources have been selected for quality and appropriateness, the issue of making them available to users must be addressed; simply having quality career information resources will be meaningless unless they are organized effectively for easy identification and retrieval. Whether in-house or online, resources should be arranged in a schema that allows for logical searching in the context of the service provided. Niles and Harris-Bowlsbey (2005) mention that resources may be organized by format (type), content, step in the career planning process, or audience (life role). Both the National Association of Colleges and Employers (NACE) and the Florida State University Career Center have independently developed organizational schemas that combine career planning process and content. The NACE standards for career information and career information categories may be found at http://www.naceweb.org/standards/standards_2.htm#2B. An example of the FSU schema as used for online resources is at http://www.career.fsu.edu/library/links.html.

Managing career resources, whether they be print or electronic, in-house or online, requires time, attention to detail, and a long-term commitment. As mentioned earlier in this chapter, information technology and the producers of career resources are constantly evolving, and career resources become dated or cease to meet the current needs of students. Setting up simple procedures and systems to manage the acquisition, organization, and weeding of resources can assure that, over time, advisors and students have the best career information available. More information on developing quality career resources, managing them effectively, and making them accessible to users may be found in works by the Canadian Career Information Association (2004), Epstein and Lenz (2008), and Sampson et al. (2004).

Accessibility must especially be considered when meeting the needs of persons with disabilities. In accordance with the Americans with Disabilities Act of 1990, information and services must be accessible to individuals with a wide variety of disabilities via reasonable accommodations. People with visual disabilities are most commonly thought of when considering information accessibility. However, other kinds of disabilities must also be accommodated when delivering career information.

A first step for working with people with visual disabilities is to note the availability of accessible versions of information on all print publications. Furthermore, making print publications available in accessibly designed Web sites is a simple way of serving individuals with visual disabilities. Although some basic text to speech software is available in modern computer operating systems, individuals with visual disabilities often require a more sophisticated screen reading system such as JAWS or screen magnifying software such as ZoomText or Magic. When purchasing specific software applications (e.g., computer-assisted career guidance software or Web-based assessments), it is important to include accessibility and compatibility with accessibility utilities as evaluation criteria.

People with other disabilities should also be considered. For example, individuals who are deaf or hearing impaired could benefit from closed captioning of library videos or online streaming videos. Also, people with motor disabilities, who might use wheelchairs, should be accommodated when designing workspaces and shelving for information resources. Some students with learning disabilities might require a quiet workspace where they can work without distraction, while others may need a room where they can read aloud or listen to audio recordings of information without disturbing others.

Regardless of in-house planning for accommodations, it is important to also partner with the on-campus resource center for students with disabilities and the campus library. Not only are these offices good sources of referrals to the academic advising office, but they also can work with academic advisors and students to ensure accessibility of information resources with a minimum of expense and effort. See Ettinger (2008) and Lulgjuraj and Hartley (2004) for a more substantial discussion of providing career services to people with disabilities.

SUMMARY

Career information has come a long way since Frank Parsons began using career information at the beginning of the 20th century. Today the amount of information can be overwhelming for both advisors and students unless it is properly organized, managed, and accessible. Fortunately, organizational systems such as the SOC, NAICS, and CIP can enhance academic advisor and student knowledge about occupations, industries, and educational programs and institutions. The RIASEC hexagon can also help students identify and organize vocational interests so they can be easily matched to congruent occupational, educational, and leisure environments. Working within these organizational systems can create more sophisticated personal schemas for both advisors and students that may lead to better, more informed career decisions.

The cognitive information processing approach is one method of conceptualizing career decision making and the delivery of career services. Focusing on what students need to *know* about themselves and their options, what they need to *do* in the career decision-making process, and how they are *thinking* about themselves and their decisions will help advisors deliver services efficiently and make appropriate referrals. However, not all students have sufficient *readiness* to benefit from career information, given their limited capability or the complexity of their career problems. Students with low readiness (e.g., low capability and high problem complexity) are good candidates for referral to career counselors and other professionals for services. For these students, information will most likely not be enough to solve their career problems.

For those students who are ready to benefit from career information, Sampson's (2008) four-step model that promotes the effective use of assessment and information resources can further facilitate the advising process and provide a convenient method of using career information. First, the advisor *understands* a student's needs, including knowledge of self, knowledge of options, and readiness for career decision making. Second, the advisor *recommends* information resources that fit the student's needs. Third, the advisor *orients* the student to the information resource, and fourth, the advisor *follows up* with the student to see whether needs have been met.

Although using career information when advising students can be a demanding task, the management of career information resources can be equally challenging. Given the abundance of publishers of career information, a basic information collection covering occupational information, education and training information, simple assessment exercises, and institutionally created "home-grown" information resources can be created at minimal cost. Careful planning and significant effort, however, are required to maintain information collections that are current and of high quality. It is also important that information resources be accessible to all students regardless of disability.

The goal of the academic advisor is not only to provide access to *data* and *information*, but also to facilitate the acquisition of *knowledge*. But perhaps most important, academic advisors have a role to play in helping students develop *wisdom* and when to employ information as part of the decision-making process. Knowing "why" information is or is not important in decision making is a critical skill that students must learn in order be successful, not only in their careers but also as citizens in a healthy, functioning society.

References

Ackoff, R. (1989). From data to wisdom. *Journal of Applied Systems Analysis, 16,* 3–9.

Borgen, F. (1991). Megatrends and milestones in vocational behavior: A 20-year counseling psychology retrospective. *Journal of Vocational Behavior, 39,* 263–290.

Brown, D., & Brooks, L. (Eds.). (1996). *Career choice and development* (3rd ed.). San Francisco: Jossey-Bass.

Bullock, E. E., Reardon, R. C., & Lenz, J. G. (2007). Planning good academic and career decisions. In G. L. Kramer (Ed.), *Fostering student success in the campus community* (pp. 193–213). San Francisco: Jossey-Bass.

Canadian Career Information Association. (2004). *Developing a career information centre* (5th ed.). Toronto, ON: CCIA/ACADOP.

Cleveland, H. (1982, December). Information as resource. *The Futurist, 16*(6), 34–39.

Epstein, S., & Lenz, J. (2008). *Developing and managing career resources.* Broken Arrow, OK: National Career Development Association.

Ettinger, J. (2008). Serving diverse populations. In D. A. Shutt, Jr. (Ed.), *How to plan and develop a career center* (2nd ed., pp. 105–118). New York: Ferguson Publishing.

Harris-Bowlsbey, J., Riley-Dikel, M., & Sampson, J. P., Jr. (Eds.). (2002). *The Internet: A tool for career planning* (2nd ed.). Tulsa, OK: National Career Development Association.

Harris-Bowlsbey, J., & Sampson, J. P., Jr. (2001). Computer-based career planning systems: Dreams and realities. *The Career Development Quarterly, 49,* 250–260.

Gordon, V. N. (2006). *Career advising: An academic advisor's guide.* San Francisco: Jossey-Bass.

Holland, J. L. (1973). *Making vocational choices: A theory of careers.* Englewood Cliffs, NJ: Prentice Hall.

Holland, J. L. (1994). *Self-Directed Search Form R* (4th ed.). Lutz, FL: PAR.

Isaacson, L. E., & Brown, D. (1997). *Career information, career counseling, and career development* (6th ed.). Boston: Allyn & Bacon.

JIST Works. (2007). *O*NET dictionary of occupational titles* (4th ed.). Indianapolis, IN: JIST Publishing.

JIST Works. (2008). *Occupational outlook handbook* (2008–2009 ed.). Indianapolis, IN: JIST Publishing.

Katz, M. R. (1993). *Computer-assisted career decision making.* Hillsdale, NJ: Lawrence Erlbaum.

Krumboltz, J. D. (1993). Integrating career and personal counseling. *The Career Development Quarterly, 42,* 143–148.

Lulgjuraj, B., & Hartley, S. L. (2004, June). Breaking barriers: Career centers reaching out to students with disabilities. *Career Convergence.* Retrieved May 5, 2008, from http://www.ncda.org

NAICS. (2008). *The history of NAICS*. Retrieved May 16, 2008, from http://www.naics
.com/info.htm

NCHEMS. (2006). *Graduation rates six-year graduation rates of bachelor's students—
2006*. Retrieved June 23, 2008 from http://www.higheredinfo.org

Niles, S. G., & Harris-Bowlsbey, J. (2005). *Career development interventions in the 21st
century* (2nd ed.). Upper Saddle River, NJ: Pearson Education.

Osborn, D., & Zunker, V. (2006). *Using assessment results for career development*
(7th ed.). Belmont, CA: Thomson Brooks/Cole.

Parsons, F. (1909). *Choosing a vocation*. Boston: Houghton Mifflin.

Peterson, G. W., Sampson, J. P., Jr., & Reardon, R. C. (1991). *Career development and
services: A cognitive approach*. Belmont, CA: Brooks/Cole.

Reardon, R. C., & Lenz, J. G. (1998). *The Self-Directed Search and related Holland
career materials: A practitioner's guide*. Odessa, FL: Psychological Assessment
Resources.

Reardon, R. C., Lenz, J. G., Sampson, J. P., Jr., & Peterson, G. W. (2006). *Career development and planning: A comprehensive approach* (2nd ed.). Mason, OH: Thomson.

Rosen, D., Holmberg, K., & Holland, J. (1997). *The educational opportunities finder*.
Lutz, FL: PAR.

Sampson, J. P., Jr. (2008). *Designing and implementing career programs: A handbook
for effective practice*. Broken Arrow, OK: National Career Development Association.

Sampson, J. P., Jr., Reardon, R. C., Peterson, G. W., & Lenz, J. G. (2004). *Career counseling and services: A cognitive information processing approach*. Belmont, CA:
Brooks/Cole.

Schutt, D. A., Jr., & Finkle, J. (2008). Critical center resources. In D. A. Schutt, Jr.
(Ed.). *How to plan and develop a career center* (2nd ed., pp. 53–71). New York:
Ferguson Publishing.

Sharma, N. (2008). *The origin of the data information knowledge wisdom hierarchy*.
Retrieved May 5, 2008, from http://www-personal.si.umich.edu/ ~ nsharma/dikw_
origin.htm

Steele, G. (2006). Five possible work profiles for full-time academic advisors. *NACADA
Journal, 26*(2), 48–52.

Tiedeman, D. V., & O'Hara, R. P. (1963). *Career development: Choice and adjustment*.
Princeton, NJ: College Entrance Examination Board.

Zytowski, D. G., & Swanson, J. L. (1994). Parsons' contribution to career assessment.
Journal of Career Development, 20, 305–310.

CHAPTER EIGHT

Career Advising

A Framework for Practice

Joanne K. Damminger

Higher education is focused on the development of the whole student, including body, mind, emotion, and spirit, and must assist in moving students toward attainable goals (Fried, 2006). One major goal for many students attending higher education is to improve their lives and chances for employment. According to Fried (2006), obtaining a better job and enhancing career possibilities are ranked as top reasons students attend college. This is affirmed by the annual survey conducted by the Higher Education Research Institute at the University of California at Los Angeles (Pryor, Hurtado, Sharkness, & Korn, 2008) that found 52% of the students surveyed indicated they selected a certain college because graduates from that institution obtain good jobs. Since students place primary importance on securing good jobs as a result of their education, institutions of higher education must dedicate practices, time, and resources to assist students in exploring career opportunities, making career decisions, and preparing for life after college. One way to assist students in exploring themselves, majors, careers, and their futures after college is through career advising. Career advising plays a critical role in the curriculum of academic advising.

The curriculum of advising is designed to aid students' growth and development by creating a teaching-learning relationship that helps students manage college-level learning and build a successful educational plan (Darling & Woodside, 2007). Gordon (2006) emphasizes that career advising focuses on the informational nature of advising and the need to help students see the connection between educational decisions and careers. Through the career advising process students are helped to connect self-awareness, including interests, values, abilities, and learning preferences, to their academic choices and future career plans. As students meet with advisors to discuss course selection and completion of academic programs, students are helped to discover who they are, the major that is the best fit for them, the courses appropriate for the major, and how these choices correlate with their future career aspirations.

The goal of this chapter is to inform advisors how to apply the concepts of career advising in academic advising. It presents a seven-step process for career advising. The step-by-step career advising process is designed to aid advisors as they increase students' awareness of self-exploration and the role it plays in informed decision making that can positively affect educational success and attainment of future career goals. The chapter also presents student and advisor responsibilities and intended student learning outcomes related to integrated career and academic advising, and highlights how advisors help students integrate course, major, and career information to set goals; make academic and career decisions; and develop plans to accomplish goals and decisions.

THE CAREER ADVISING PROCESS

Career advising is an extremely important component of success within the higher education system, as it assists students in integrating the processes of identity development, knowledge acquisition, and learning through experience and action. According to Gordon (2006), "All students need career advising, even those who enter college decided on an academic major" (p. 5). However, few students recognize the importance of advising, and for many students advising is synonymous with course selection. This type of prescriptive advising often lacks working relationships and does not provide a lasting connection between advisors and advisees. Career advising, integrated into academic advising, can provide both and help students see where they are, where they want to go in the future, and how to get there. The steps of career advising help students learn about themselves, investigate options, make informed decisions, and realize the meaning of their education (Stone, 2008).

Steps in the career advising process overlap the steps of personal counseling and career counseling but are unique in the way they assist students in connecting educational choices with future plans. Gordon (2006) laid the groundwork for applying the career advising process to practice with the 3-I Process: inform, inquire, and integrate. The seven steps of the career advising process expand on the good work of Gordon and are presented under the framework of the 3-I Process. In addition, as part of the process, students are assisted in making informed decisions, setting goals based on the decisions, and developing plans to achieve the goals.

The steps of career advising are presented sequentially for ease of understanding; however, advisors may find that in working with some students the steps are not sequential, and may move in and out of the steps based on individual student need. Some students may be guided to complete one step and move to the next, but may revisit a step if they need more information, resources for exploration, or time for reflection. Yet advisors may move through the steps seamlessly when they work with students, as some advisees are ready and need to move from one step to another in the advising process and may not need to revisit steps. Still other students may not need to spend time on each step. Advisors' use of attentive listening and open-ended questioning will aid in assessing where students are and steps needed to assist students in their academic and career planning. Advisors determine what students need and the types of recommendations to discuss with students based on information provided by students throughout the process. Advisors' competencies are important in effectively applying the steps in the career advising process to facilitate students' planning and development.

The Seven Steps of Career Advising

The seven steps of the career advising process, listed under the umbrella of Gordon's (2006) 3-I Process, include the following:

Inquire

1. Establish rapport and build a working relationship with the student.

2. Determine the student's knowledge base and assess the student's career advising needs.

Inform

3. Explain and help the student understand the connections among self-awareness, educational choices, occupational information, and academic and career planning.

4. Explain and help the student select interventions to assist in self-, major, and career exploration and career planning.

5. Set career advising goals with the student.

Integrate

6. Review and integrate gathered information (including interpretation of exploration results) and create a career plan to achieve the student's goals.

7. Evaluate plans and accomplishments, determine any short- or long-term follow-up with the student, and offer continuing support.

As the initial steps of the career advising process, Steps 1 and 2 involve advisors gathering information during the inquiry (Gordon, 2006) phase of the career advising process. As part of these steps, advisors (a) establish rapport, (b) determine students' questions and concerns, (c) assess students' needs, and (d) prepare students to collect and receive information in the next phase. During Steps 3, 4, and 5, advisors seek to inform (Gordon, 2006) advisees about (a) exploring their personal characteristics (e.g., interests, values, and abilities), (b) gaining educational information about courses, majors, and transferable skills, and (c) gathering occupational information about the world of work and future career possibilities. Steps 6 and 7 constitute the integrate (Gordon, 2006) phase of career advising. These steps emphasize the important role advisors play in (a) helping students integrate personal, educational, and occupational information to successfully complete their academic major and enter their chosen occupation, and (b) determining any additional information or assistance needed by students.

Step 1: Establish rapport and build a working relationship with the student. Building a working relationship with the student is extremely important in any advising session and is one of the most valuable building blocks for effective career advising. A trusting and open relationship with a student that is grounded in mutual respect is key to effective advising (Folsom, 2008). The career advising relationship allows an advisee to feel comfortable and to value the career advisor as a professional to whom he or she can turn for advice now and in the future. A career advising relationship can be initiated by casual conversation that helps advisees relax and puts them at ease. While escorting students to an office or greeting them, dialogue about their day or semester can help make students feel comfortable as they learn that the advisor is approachable and interested in their well-being. The advisor might initiate this by greeting the advisee with "Hello, I am glad you came for advising today." The advisor might then ask, "How is your semester going? What are you thinking about today that I can help you with?"

Helping an advisee relax and communicate relevant information facilitates progress in an advising session. According to Herr, Cramer, and Niles (2004), successful advising is dependent on the advisor's ability to establish a therapeutic and helpful environment in which the advisor demonstrates respect for the advisee, empathic understanding, genuineness, and the willingness to engage in dialogue about the situations, issues, or questions presented. It is vital that when advisees leave advising sessions they know that the advisor cares about them as individuals and that the conversation can extend beyond making academic choices.

Step 2: Determine the student's knowledge base and assess the student's career advising needs. Step 1 in the career advising process can easily lead to Step 2 as the advisor comments about the student's responses to introductory questions and moves to assess need. This step is important to ascertain the student's thoughts, questions, and concerns and to determine what the student is asking and what is needed. Thoughtful questions communicate to the student that the advisor wants to be helpful and spark conversation about why a student has come for advising. This approach also emphasizes that advising questions and concerns are often developmental, and advising sessions are helpful and engaging sessions.

The use of open-ended questions that require students to engage in conversation, avoiding one-word responses (e.g., "yes," "no"), is very helpful in gathering information about students' thoughts and needs. Students often verbalize their needs related to course selection; however, open-ended questions can help advisors ascertain how much students really know about themselves and their major and how that awareness can be helpful in decision making. Students' thoughts about interests, abilities, and values can assist the advisor in determining whether there are issues that might affect students' ability to make informed decisions, such as a lack information.

Students' current ideas about courses they enjoy, electives they want to explore, what they are going to do with their major, and other thoughts about postgraduation are instrumental in integrating career advising in advising sessions. Sharing this type of information can lead to discussions about using free electives to build a minor or area of concentration, or to study an area of interest even if unrelated to the major. Discussions such as these help students see the relevance of their perceptions of themselves to their academic program and future plans.

Advising is most productive if it meets students where they are in the advising process, and helps them recognize what is needed to get where they want to go. In working with students, advisors need to consider students' developmental level, maturity, preparedness, and decision-making competencies. Students often are unaware of the gaps in their decision making and self-identity, and will be dependent on career advising to help them address critical issues that enhance or inhibit their academic and career development and choices.

Let's look at the case of Katie to illustrate application of the career advising process.

Katie's Quandary

Katie seeks advising to choose courses for the following semester. She is an undeclared first-semester freshman, and she has no idea what major she wants to study. She knows she has to select a major next year, but she just seems to get more and more confused as there are many things she wants to do. Her immediate concern is the courses she should take as an undeclared student. Katie is doing well in her psychology class, but she does not know the kinds of careers that involve psychology. Education interests her, but she does not really have patience with children. Her dad was a business major and she could do that, but she is not great at math and she needs two math courses to even apply to business. She really does not know the major to choose or the kind of job she would want as a result. Therefore, she has no idea how to choose courses for the next semester.

In meeting with Katie, the advisor would greet her warmly and ask what brings her to advising (Step 1). The advisor would ask a series of questions to ascertain Katie's knowledge base, needs, and issues about which she has questions or is unsure. Comments and questions might include, "I understand that your major concern today is the classes that you will take next semester." "We are going to create a list of courses for you, but as you think about choosing courses, what subjects do you enjoy most?" "What interests you?" "What do you see as your strengths?" As Katie and her advisor discuss the selection of courses, the advisor might ask, "In what ways do these courses relate to your interests, values, strengths, and skills?" As Katie talks about choosing courses for the next semester, the advisor assesses Katie's need for self-assessment for her to learn more about herself, possible majors, and careers. Katie's concerns also indicate the need for her to learn about occupational possibilities related to her areas of interest. The advisor assures Katie that together they can select courses that will relate to the various majors in which she is interested and then points out to Katie the benefits to her gathering personal, educational, and occupational information.

Step 3: Explain and help the student to understand the connections among self-awareness, educational choices, occupational information, and academic and career planning. Step 3 involves interactions between the advisor and advisee to help the student realize that the choices made each semester have an impact on one's future. The advisor's role is to enhance the student's awareness of the need to connect information about oneself and the chosen program of study with the occupational information gathered. This step moves the advisor and student into the *inform* phase of career advising (Gordon, 2006). As students explore, increase self-knowledge, and make decisions about how to progress toward their degree, the advisor's role is to help students see how decisions they make each semester relate to their short- and long-term goals, both during and after college. This often does not happen naturally because even though students come to college to get a better job, they have not given thoughtful consideration to their academic and career goals (McCalla-Wriggins, 2000). This is often missing in academic advising, as once students are assisted with choosing courses for the upcoming semester, the conversation ends. Step 3 enables students to know that such connections exist and there are resources to help them.

Step 3 in the career advising process is critical in helping students see that the answers they seek about well-matched majors and occupations are often within themselves and what they know and learn about themselves. Most students, even those in declared majors, need to increase their self-awareness and reflect on what they enjoy doing (interests), what they are good at doing (abilities), and what is important to them (values). This stage in the process can also help students learn where connections between their self-awareness and their choices are missing, as well as help them learn ways to enhance the connections.

Step 3 is invaluable in helping students realize that they do not need to make academic and career decisions in a vacuum. There are many resources to help them; however, many students may not be aware of these resources. Interventions can be planned to assist students in verifying that their choice of majors is congruent with their interests, values, abilities, strengths, and learning preferences and will lead to appropriate career choices. In addition, various resources and interventions can assist students in learning about job outlook, salary expectations, nature of work, and the work environment associated with various careers being considered.

The application of Step 3 can be demonstrated in the vignette about Katie. The advisor has several options in assisting Katie. The advisor may begin by assuring Katie that she is not alone in her confusion about majors and related careers. Many students are unsure of their major and what to do with it. However, Katie does not have to determine this on her own because there are many resources to help her explore and learn about herself, majors, and related careers. The advisor may explain that once students understand more about their interests, values, and abilities, they can begin to see how self-awareness will help them explore majors that are congruent with these characteristics, thus leading to career options that are interesting and satisfying. Katie can be helped to relax as the advisor explains that this type of exploration is extremely helpful, and learning more about oneself can lead to more informed decisions about majors and careers.

Step 4: Explain and help the student select interventions to assist in self-, major, and career exploration and career planning. In Step 4, advisors explain and help students select resources and interventions from the myriad available to assist students to explore and learn about themselves, majors, and careers (e.g., inventories, computer-assisted systems, internships, job shadowing, informational interviewing, field experiences). As part of this step, students are recommended resources and interventions to explore information about themselves and their career aspirations to make informed choices. Exploratory resources can be helpful in making short-term decisions about courses and major, and also setting long-term goals regarding entrance to the workplace or graduate school. Advisors who are not knowledgeable about such interventions and resources can refer advisees to appropriate campus offices (e.g., career center, counseling center). Advisors less experienced with exploratory resources can also keep a list of such resources readily available to offer to students. It is important to remember that recommended resources must be appropriate for advisees' developmental stage and their particular needs (Gordon, 2006).

Many students may be hesitant to invest time and energy in the types of activities and interventions explained in this step; however, advisors can help students understand that the effort will be worthwhile and is necessary for creating a satisfying and attainable career plan (Gore & Metz, 2008). Suggested exploratory interventions often begin with inventories, paper or electronic, to help students learn about themselves—for example, their interests, values, abilities, strengths, and learning preferences. Students should be encouraged to begin with resources to learn about themselves and then expand to exploration of majors and careers. Students will benefit from using resources that are most interesting, accessible, and manageable for them. Examples of resources for increasing self-awareness are John Holland's Self-Directed Search (SDS, www.self-directed-search.com/), the Career Occupational Preference System (COPSystem, www.edits.net/career.html), the Strong Interest Inventory (www.cpp.com/products/strong/index.asp), the Learning Connections Inventory (www.lcrinfo.com), and comprehensive online career planning systems such as DISCOVER (www.act.org/discover/) and MyRoad (MyRoad.com).

In addition to self-exploration, an important part of preparing for life after college is an awareness of the world of work and occupations. Integrating career advising in advising sessions can provide suggestions for multiple resources to research occupational information that can facilitate informed decision making. With this in mind, it becomes incumbent on advisors to assist students in exploring occupational information and learning about current trends in the workplace that can have an impact on employability, job outlook, and successful job searching. Referral to occupational resources such as the *Occupational Outlook Handbook* (www.bls.gov/oco) and the *O*NET* (www.onetcenter.org), as well as referral to career centers, can be most useful. In addition to providing students assistance in learning about themselves, online career planning systems (e.g., DISCOVER, MyRoad) can be helpful with exploring majors and careers. Advisors can maintain their own library of resources or refer students to the resources available on campus.

Most students will also benefit from learning about the resources to assist with experiences prior to graduation (e.g., part-time jobs, internships, field experiences). The number of credits that can be earned, if any, and helpful resources to assist with this process may be available in each academic department or college. On- and off-campus experiences (e.g., federal and institutional work study jobs) may be beneficial for occupational exploration as well. Students who are considering graduate school immediately after the baccalaureate experience may need to explore programs, complete applications, and secure recommendations, as well as seek graduate assistantships and other opportunities.

Information about various resources to explore what it is like in the workplace can be offered individually or in a group setting to an entire class, workshop audience, or specific student group. As noted by Gore and Metz (2008), group career advising can be very effective, but it should include a follow-up, one-on-one session with an advisor to personally discuss academic and future plans.

Advisors should be knowledgeable about the resources available on their campus. Advisors must be sure to recommend appropriate resources based on students' needs and willingness to use particular methods of investigation (e.g., computer, paper). Advisors also need to know how to assist students in turning data about themselves into information and career action plans (Pyle, 2001). Advisors who are not knowledgeable regarding the interpretation of exploratory techniques may seek professional development related to this or refer students to the appropriate campus offices. It is important that advisors who do not have expertise with specific assessments refer to appropriate campus professionals. In advising it is important that materials are appropriate for advisees; advisors are knowledgeable about students, institutional information, and the materials they suggest; and advisors are sensitive to ethical and cultural issues surrounding the advising process (Folsom, 2008).

In the case of Katie, the advisor would spend time explaining various types of self-assessment and exploration interventions and resources that could assist Katie in learning about her own interests, values, and abilities. The advisor may make recommendations based on knowledge of Katie and her needs or preferences. Also, the advisor might ask Katie, "Which instruments or resources interest you the most?" "Do you prefer paper or online tools?" "Would you like to complete the instruments and then return for a follow-up appointment to interpret the results and discuss what you have learned?" "What other information do you need to begin?"

Step 5: Set career advising goals with the student. Once an advisor has helped students to see the connection between academic choices and future career plans, it is important to move into the goal-setting stage of the career advising process. This step in the process includes the need for advisee, with assistance from the advisor, to set attainable goals, determine interventions that the student will complete, and arrange for follow-up advising sessions.

McCalla-Wriggins (2000) suggests that helping students to establish clear goals in the advising process is critical. Students' willingness to accomplish the necessary work and remain committed to the attainment of goals is also important. Advisees must be aware that more than one career advising session may be required to accomplish the goals they set. In addition, goals set by students must address both academic decisions and decisions about future career planning. Students' goals should be specific, measurable, attainable, realistic, and timely. The goals set in the career advising session must be student-driven, as attempts by the advisor to impose goals on the advisee will prove ineffective.

An advisor and advisee can set goals for current and future advising sessions by first briefly summarizing the discussion of the present advising session and reviewing what the student learned and is willing to do as next steps to gather self-, educational, and occupational information needed for decision making. It is important that these goals include both the information needed to pursue or continue in an academic program and the understanding of how academic decisions fit into plans for graduation and steps beyond. The following are examples of possible goals: (a) choosing courses for the next semester based on received information, (b) planning to participate in self-assessment, (c) using resources to explore majors and careers, (d) investigating minors, concentrations, and certifications, and (e) investigating internship and job searching information. Goal setting is extremely important in all advising sessions, as it is vital that students accept responsibility in the advising process and make a commitment to their personal decision making.

Advisors may find it very helpful in Step 5 to summarize students' goals at the conclusion of the advising session. Affirming with students that goals are accurate and that students are willing to work toward the goals is important. Restating goals for the advisee affords the advisor the opportunity to assure that the set goals are clear, feasible, and agreeable to the advisee.

In the case of Katie, the advisor could review the discussion about the need to explore self and majors to make relevant decisions about academic majors and careers. The advisor could briefly review the interventions and resources discussed in the advising session and those Katie decided to use. The advisor might then summarize and review with Katie the following goals to see whether they are accurate and attainable for Katie:

1. Choose courses required of the majors that are being considered or register for courses that would provide exploration of the various majors.

2. Use specific interventions to explore Katie's interests, values, and abilities and how they relate to the majors being considered.

3. Explore resources with information about the majors being considered to learn about them and related careers.

4. Return for a follow-up advising session to discuss the information she gathered and to initiate decision making.

The discussion and interpretation noted in the fourth goal focuses on an important component of self-, major, and career exploration. This interpretation helps students become knowledgeable of the results and their meaning for the individual student.

Step 6: Review and integrate gathered information (including interpretation of exploration results) and create a career plan to achieve the student's goals. One of the most important components of the career advising process is to help students turn "data into information" (Niles & Harris-Bowlsbey, 2009, p. 194) and to make sense of gathered information. Interpretation of self-assessment and exploratory instruments is critical to learning and the career planning process. "Interpretation includes looking at objective data and inferring meaning" (Damminger, 2007, p. 67). Many full-time advisors are experienced in interpretation; those who are not can refer to the appropriate campus offices.

Interpretation of self-, major, and career information often involves meeting with students in follow-up appointments after they have completed activities or interventions to review what they learned about their own interests, values, abilities, strengths, learning preferences, majors, or careers. With the guidance of the advisor, students can begin to integrate this knowledge to choose courses and majors and determine future career possibilities. Both advisors and advisees need to consider the results of students' exploration and discuss students' thoughts about the information. It is very important that students learn the connections in information about themselves and the choices they are considering. The interpretation of the results of self-assessment and exploratory interventions and resources can be completed in a group setting, but should be followed by a one-on-one meeting with each student to be most effective (Gore & Metz, 2008). Examples of questions to consider include: Will their choices utilize their strengths and appeal to their interests? Are they willing to develop skills that need strengthening for success in the areas they are considering? These are critical issues for discussion and reflection.

It can be very helpful during this step of career planning to consider the data from various interventions and experiences as a student decides how she or he can prepare to successfully enter, be satisfied, and be sustained in possible occupations. The use of the information reviewed in the interpretation could be compared to a funnel in that students are encouraged to gather lots of information from various sources in the exploration process. Then students consider all of the information to determine the most relevant for their future steps (Fornell as cited in Yin, 2003). This "funnel" process can assist students in narrowing their focus and arriving at informed decisions after considering information gathered in the exploratory steps of career advising. When students are ready to make decisions regarding the steps they need to take to accomplish their goals, the actions decided on become part of their career plan.

Students' planned actions can be noted on a career plan. One example of a career plan is the College Level Individualized Career Plan (see Exhibit 8.1). An individualized career plan can help both the advisor and student document a student's interests, values, and abilities, as well as the activities a student plans to complete to accomplish his or her career goals. A written career plan provides a list of activities that a student would like to accomplish to complete the requirements of their major and graduate, and to take their next career steps. In addition, a career plan can help students be intentional in how they plan for the future, and it can serve as a commitment regarding what they are willing to do to achieve their goals. Not all students will engage in creating a written career plan; however, the written plan can be helpful to many.

Exhibit 8.1. College Level Individualized Career Plan (CLICP).
An individualized career plan is intended to assist in educational and career decisions leading to increased success during and after college.

Part 1: Personal Data

Name _____

Address _____

City, State, Zip _____

Date of Birth _____

Phone _____

E-mail _____

Part 2: Career Daydreams

List the careers you have been thinking about since an early age. Be sure to include your most recent thoughts.

Part 3: Results of Assessments

	Inventory	Date Administered	Results
Achievement			
Career Interests			
Career Values			
Learning Patterns			
Other			

Part 4: Interests and What You Like

Part 5: Values that are Important

_____

Part 6: Career Activities to Meet Goals

_____ Choose a major or affirm current declared major

_____ Create an academic plan, by semester, to complete courses
for my degree in _____ (list
major/minors/concentrations)

_____ Take a variety of courses to increase exposure to possible career areas

_____ Achieve the highest GPA possible

_____ Develop a working relationship with at least one professor a semester

_____ Begin creating a personal network

_____ Complete the following self-assessment inventories:
_____

_____ Explore the following majors, minors, concentrations, and
specializations: _____

_____ Explore the following occupations:
_____

_____ Visit the career center

_____ Attend career fairs

_____ Seek internships

_____ Obtain a part-time job related to desired major

_____ Become involved on campus (e.g. campus organizations, clubs)

_____ Study abroad

_____ Participate in service learning

_____ Volunteer in the community

_____ Develop leadership skills

_____ Explore graduate programs

_____ Create a résumé

_____ Practice interviewing skills

_____ Learn about traditional and online job searching

Other _____
_____

Other _____
_____

Another example of a type of plan is an Individual Learning Plan (ILP), which is based on the cognitive information processing approach (Sampson, Reardon, Peterson, & Lenz, 2004), and its development is a step in delivering career services. The ILP includes goals, activities, purposes or outcomes for activities, time commitment, and prioritization of activities. There are a variety of types of career plans that can be used to help students in their academic and career planning. Advisors can determine the plan that best meets their students' needs and facilitates career actions by students.

Step 6 can be challenging, as some students leave Steps 4 and 5, intending to explore, and they fail to conduct the exploration or do not return for the interpretation and integration of the results of the interventions and assessments. These students may lack information to plan appropriately for their futures and may resurface in their senior year to revisit previous steps in the career advising process.

When considering Katie's situation, Step 6 would most likely take place in a follow-up appointment. The advisor would review the results of Katie's exploration and interpret and explain any information that might not be clearly understood. Advisor comments might include these: "Regarding your interest in choosing a well-matched major, today in the career advising session we reviewed a good deal of information that you gathered about yourself, your values, skills, interests, and preferences as well as a few careers that are interesting to you." "What are your thoughts about the majors that seem best-matched for you when considering the information you collected?" The advisor might continue, "As we discuss your thoughts, it might be helpful for you to create a career plan of what you would like and need to do to prepare for applying to this major, completing the major in four years, and developing transferable skills for the occupations that are of interest to you." If agreeable, Katie, working with the advisor, would use a career plan to determine next steps for her. After working on the plan, the advisor he might conclude with, "How reasonable is this plan for you to meet your goals?" and "Let's discuss anything that needs additional clarification."

Step 7: Evaluate plans and accomplishments, determine any short- or long-term follow-up with the student, and offer continuing support. Step 7 will naturally flow from the previous steps if the former steps have been successful. In other words, if an advisor has been effective in establishing rapport and providing information, resources, and career planning, students will consider additional follow-up that might be recommended. Some students might need to continue the exploration they started and perhaps visit the advisor in the next few weeks, and others may not need another appointment until it is time to choose courses for the following semester. Advisors may recommend that students continue to meet if, for example, advisees do not have enough information to make informed decisions about their educational program or career. Students may return for additional support and may want to revisit the steps of career advising as new issues or opportunities arise. In addition, some students may choose to meet again just to report progress with their career plans.

As part of Step 7, students will evaluate the extent to which they have accomplished their goals set as part of the career advising process. For accomplished goals, students can move on in their program and career. For goals that have not been accomplished, students may need to continue working toward the goals, make adjustments in the steps to achieve the goals, or revise the goals.

At the conclusion of Step 7, students should feel a sense of accomplishment and have a sense of direction with respect to their academic program and career. They should have the information they need to move forward with their educational and career plans.

In the case of Katie, this advising session might conclude with the advisor asking whether Katie has the information that she needs to take exploratory courses and continue to consider majors. A possible question might be: "What additional assistance or information do you need?" The advisor might discuss any future exploration that could benefit Katie and help her meet her goals. The advisor may ask if Katie would like to set up a follow-up appointment to discuss her progress at mid-semester. The advisor might ask, "Would you like to schedule a follow-up appointment to discuss your thoughts about majors and careers in a few months?" The advisor could remind Katie that she is available if Katie needs assistance prior to their next meeting. As a result of career advising Katie will have increased her awareness about various majors that are interesting to her and how her attributes match those majors. She may also have learned about areas that she needs to develop to be successful in various majors, and that additional exploration of careers related to her possible majors would be beneficial and may include various options (e.g., Internet-career resources, informational interviews, internships) that can be discussed in future visits with the advisor.

STUDENT RESPONSIBILITIES IN CAREER ADVISING

Career advising is grounded in the belief that it is a dynamic, interactive process that calls for participation and responsibilities on part of the student and the academic advisor. Mutual participation is paramount as each plays a critical role in the career advising process. Herr et al. (2004) stated, "If the counselor [advisor] assumes all responsibility for participation, the interview [advising session] is nothing more than advice giving" (p. 540). Effective career advising, like academic advising, is a joint partnership between the advisor and student. However, it is ultimately students' responsibility for making decisions about both academic and career goals (Council for the Advancement of Standards [CAS], 2005). Advisors can support and facilitate students' career and academic planning and decision making; however, students are responsible for their decisions and taking advantage of learning opportunities.

Each part in the career advising process and related steps requires a commitment of time and effort on the part of the student. Students need to reserve time to prepare for and attend advising sessions, and to complete the follow-up agreed to in the session. In addition, it is imperative that students reflect on awareness of self, majors, occupations, and decision making for the process to be internalized and beneficial. Students are also responsible to pursue learning experiences in and out of the classroom (e.g., job shadowing, internships, part-time employment, and informational interviews). Students need to commit to use resources intended to lead to the desired goals and learning outcomes.

ADVISOR RESPONSIBILITIES IN CAREER ADVISING

According to CAS (2005), the advising process is the shared responsibility of both students and advisors. Advisor responsibilities related to career advising are similar to those of academic advisors with an additional emphasis on referral to others on campus if they are not trained in various self-exploratory and career resources on campus or career advising interventions. In addition, advisors who make career advising an integral part of academic advising need to have an understanding of relevant student development, student learning, and career development theory. Advisors are required to have a thorough knowledge of an institution's academic programs, requirements, majors, minors, certifications, support services, and institutional policies and procedures. Also, advisors need to remain current regarding trends in advising and should seek professional development opportunities (CAS, 2005). As with academic advising, it is equally important that advisors understand their student population (Folsom, 2008).

Advisors who integrate career advising into academic advising have the ability to increase students' awareness of the connections between academic and career choices. To assist with this, advisors need to have knowledge of the resources to help students learn more about themselves, majors, and career options. It is important that advisors provide high-quality information and resources to help students learn who they are, what they want to attain, and how to accomplish it. Advisors should also provide information about the current work world and resources that students can use to explore this information. One of the most difficult advisor responsibilities related to career advising may be the need for advisors to assist advisees in making meaningful use of gathered information (Niles & Harris-Bowlsbey, 2009). Those who are not well versed in such resources, interpretation, and processing of acquired data can provide referrals to appropriate campus offices.

STUDENT LEARNING OUTCOMES FOR CAREER ADVISING

Student learning outcomes provide the foundation for career advising, and many outcomes overlap with intended outcomes for academic advising (Burton Nelson, 2006). Hamrick, Evans, and Schuh (2002) outline five clusters of outcomes that society and students can expect as a result of the higher education experience. Three are related to outcomes of career advising, including (a) educated persons—recognizing the importance of lifelong learning and the interrelationship of education to one's life; (b) skilled workers—colleges prepare students for the workforce, help them to learn related skills, and identify options; and (c) life skills managers—the ability to manage one's life and provide the quality life desired. Higher education has a responsibility to assist students with accomplishing these student learning outcomes, and career advising can play a critical role. Integrating career advising into academic advising encourages students to reflect on and realize the connections between the educational choices made and their application to life during and after college.

According to CAS (2005), the outcomes for advising are grouped into several categories relevant for career advising. The related CAS categories include (a) intellectual growth, (b) personal and educational goals, (c) enhanced self-esteem, (d) realistic self-appraisal, (e) clarified values, (f) career choices, (g) meaningful interpersonal relationships, (h) collaboration, and (i) satisfying and productive lifestyles. A review of these advising categories builds an even stronger case for integrating career advising into academic advising.

Through career and academic advising, students can be assisted in accomplishing learning outcomes listed in the CAS (2005) Standards. Student learning outcomes that can be achieved through career advising include the following:

1. Enhance decision-making skills
2. Learn about themselves, including their interests, values, abilities, and learning preferences, and utilize this awareness in decision making
3. Reflect on personal values and lifestyle values and recognize their relevance in academic and career decisions
4. Understand there is a connection between academic decisions and career planning
5. Set academic and career goals
6. Create action plans to accomplish academic and career goals
7. Learn about and use resources to explore majors, occupations, graduate opportunities, and the changing workplace
8. Increase awareness of learning opportunities (e.g., service learning, on- and off-campus jobs, internships, career courses, job shadowing, and coop and field experiences)
9. Engage in the institution in meaningful ways as a result of interactions with career advisors and consideration for others' points of view (CAS, 2005)

Additional career advising outcomes may be more general and relate to the mission of an institution. These include outcomes related to (a) leadership development, (b) organization/planning skills, (c) critical thinking and problem-solving skills, and (d) relationship building. Grounding higher education practice in the attainment of student learning outcomes is of utmost importance. Specific student learning outcomes will vary from campus to campus as they link to campus and departmental missions and reflect the learning intentions of a particular institution.

SUMMARY

One of the goals of higher education is to focus on learning as a complex, holistic experience that pervades the entire college experience (American College Personnel Association & National Association of Student Personnel Administrators, 2004). In *Learning Reconsidered 2*, Fried (2006) explains that an important concept for higher education is that when learning is powerful and transformational, it can change the way students think about themselves, how they learn, and the world around them. This is the type of learning that must be emphasized for all students. Career advising fosters transformational learning, and helps students integrate the choices they make today with plans for the future. In addition, career advising encourages students to choose courses, create opportunities, experience the work world through fieldwork and internships, and create action plans that will lead to success during and after college.

Integrating career and academic advising is not a new concept. Career advising needs to be integrated into the advising process and not merely viewed as an add-on for some students. This is a call to action for all advisors to incorporate career advising as an integral part of their academic advising for all students. It is paramount that advisors assist students in gathering personal, educational, and occupational information as they navigate their academic program. Advisors are encouraged to assist students in recognizing that the most engaging learning takes place when it is seen in the context of their lives (Fried, 2006). When advisors successfully integrate career and academic advising and use the step-by-step approach to career advising in their daily practice, students benefit as a result of enhanced academic and career development and planning.

Career advising integrated in academic advising helps students build their own futures and make the most of their educational experiences. In so doing, academic advisors encourage students to design their own journey—a journey that helps students link their understanding of themselves, the surrounding world, and their vision for the future.

References

American College Personnel Association (ACPA) & National Association of Student Personnel Administrators (NASPA). (2004). *Learning reconsidered: A campus-wide focus on the student experience*. Washington, DC: Authors.

Burton Nelson, D. (2006). *Career advisors: A new breed*. Retrieved November 3, 2007, from NACADA Clearinghouse of Academic Advising Resources Web site http://www.nacada.ksu.edu/clearinghouse/adviisngissues/career-advisors.htm

Council for the Advancement of Standards (CAS). (2005). *Academic advising: CAS standards and guidelines*. Retrieved March 17, 2008, from http://www.nacada.ksu.edu/Clearinghouse/Research_Related/CASStandardsForAdvising.pdf

Damminger, J. K. (2007). Self-Assessment: Relevance and value in first-year advising. In M. S. Hunter, B. McCalla-Wriggins, & E. R. White (Eds.), *Academic advising: New insights for teaching and learning in the first year* (Monograph No. 46 [National Resource Center]; Monograph No. 14 [National Academic Advising

Association]; pp. 59–69). Columbia, SC: University of South Carolina, National Resource Center for The First-Year Experience and Students in Transition.

Darling, R. A., & Woodside, M. (2007). The academic advisor as teacher: First-year transitions. In M. S. Hunter, B. McCalla-Wriggins, & E. R. White (Eds.), *Academic advising: New insights for teaching and learning in the first year* (Monograph No. 46 [National Resource Center]; Monograph No. 14 [National Academic Advising Association]; pp. 5–17). Columbia, SC: University of South Carolina, National Resource Center for the First-Year Experience and Students in Transition.

Folsom, P. (2008). Tools and resources for advisors. In V. N. Gordon, W. R. Habley, & T. J. Grites (Eds.), *Academic advising: A comprehensive handbook* (2nd ed., pp. 323–341). San Francisco: Jossey-Bass.

Fried, J. (2006). Rethinking learning. In R. P. Keeling (Ed.), *Learning reconsidered 2: A practical guide to implementing a campus-wide focus on the students experience* (pp. 3–9). Washington, DC: ACPA, ACUHO-I, ACUI, NACADA, NACA, NASPA, NIRSA.

Gordon, V. N. (2006). *Career advising: An academic advisor's guide.* San Francisco: Jossey-Bass.

Gore, P. A., & Metz, J. (2008). Foundations: Advising for career and life planning. In V. N. Gordon, W. R. Habley, & T. J. Grites (Eds.), *Academic advising: A comprehensive handbook* (2nd ed., pp. 103–117). San Francisco: Jossey-Bass.

Hamrick, R. A., Evans, N. J., & Schuh, J. H. (2002). *Foundations of student affairs practice: How philosophy, theory and research strengthen educational outcomes.* San Francisco: Jossey-Bass.

Herr, E. L., Cramer, S. H., & Niles, S. G. (2004). *Career guidance and counseling through the lifespan: Systematic approaches* (6th ed.). Boston: Pearson Education.

McCalla-Wriggins, B. (2000). Integrating academic advising and career and life planning. In V. N. Gordon, W. R. Habley, & Associates (Eds.), *Academic advising: A comprehensive handbook* (pp. 162–176). San Francisco: Jossey-Bass.

Niles, S. G., & Harris-Bowlsbey, J. (2009). *Career development interventions for the 21st century* (3rd ed.). Upper Saddle River, NJ: Pearson Education.

Pryor, J. H., Hurtado, S., Sharkness, J., & Korn, W. S. (2008). *The American freshman: National norms for fall 2007* (HERI Research Brief). Los Angeles: Higher Education Research Institute.

Pyle, K. R. (2001). Career counseling in an information age: The promise of high touch in a high tech age. *Career Planning and Adult Development Journal, 16*(3). Retrieved on March 27, 2008, from http://www.careertrainer.com/Request. jsp?lView = ViewArticle&Article = OID%3A111930&Page = OID%3A111933

Sampson, J. P., Jr., Reardon, R. C., Peterson, G. W., & Lenz, J. G. (2004). *Career counseling & services: A cognitive information processing approach.* Belmont, CA: Brooks/Cole.

Stone, C. (2008, Spring). College, career and academic counseling: Tools for social change. *National Career Development Association Career Developments, 24*(2), 16–17.

Yin, S. (2003, December 10). Know thyself. *The Chronicle of Higher Education.* Retrieved December 10, 2008, from http://chronicle.com/jobs/2003/12/ 2003121001c.htm

CHAPTER NINE

Integrated Career and Academic Advising Programs

Dorothy Burton Nelson, Betsy McCalla-Wriggins

According to national surveys, students attend college in the hope for a better job (Astin, 2007). In order to increase the probability that they will obtain a better job, all students need some assistance. According to Gordon (2006), all college students are involved in various stages of career and academic planning. In addition, support mechanisms should be in place to promote student success and progress in college coursework.

Some decided students select an academic major based on self-knowledge and an accurate understanding of academic and career options, but they may not be aware of ways to enhance their collegiate experience to increase either employment or graduate school options after graduation. Other decided students may have committed to a major with limited information about degree options, the relationship of academic requirements to personal skills, and the connection of interests, values, and personality to career possibilities associated with the major. Undecided students may be similar to the second group of decided students and are operating with limited or even inaccurate information. Still other undecided students may be interested in so many options that they have difficulty making a choice. A third group of undecided students may know exactly what they want and why, but have not been accepted into their major of choice. These students may also have limited knowledge of the options to consider if acceptance into their desired major does not occur.

Since students are continually making curricular and extracurricular choices, they need information about themselves, academic and career options, and strategies to enhance job and graduate school opportunities to make informed decisions. Advisors are uniquely positioned within the academic community to assist all students in this process of making these important academic and career decisions. If this assistance is not available through the advising process, students may seek information from other sources that are not as reliable (Gordon, 2006).

Integrating self-knowledge with academic and career options can be overwhelming for a student, but having clearly defined "places" within the institution where students can go to receive assistance can be extremely helpful and make the process more manageable. Students do not see the separateness of academic advising and career advising, so institutions need to explore and implement ways to integrate them. According to an ACT (2008) survey, the earlier students engage in discussions and activities to help them clarify career goals and develop plans, the greater their satisfaction with college.

There are many ways to integrate career advising in academic advising. In this chapter, we describe the similarities and differences between academic advising and career advising and both informal and formal approaches for this integration. In addition, we discuss the advantages, disadvantages, and strategies for achieving both informal and formal integration. Finally, we describe the process for planning for a formal approach to integrating academic and career advising.

ACADEMIC AND CAREER ADVISING: SIMILARITIES AND DIFFERENCES

A key factor in the process of integrating academic and career advising is to understand the similarities and differences between academic and career advising. One framework to describe these issues is to review the three elements included in advisor development programs: conceptual, informational, and relational (Ford, 2007). The conceptual component includes what an individual needs to understand. Academic advisors often have a foundation in academic advising and student development theories. Career advisors use student development and career development theories in their work with students. Student development theories are common to both groups, and in an integrated unit, foundations of academic advising and career development theories are important for advisors' work with students. The informational component relates to what individuals need to know. This is where there may be the most significant differences between academic and career advising. Academic advisors are very familiar with the academic options offered at their institution, including general education requirements, majors, GPA, and other specific degree requirements. In addition, academic advisors know institutional policies, procedures, deadlines, and how to navigate the bureaucracy. Career advisors may also have some general institutional knowledge, but they will have specific information about careers, the world of work, and strategies to obtain employment. Skills in the relational component are how individuals need to behave. These behaviors are the same for all advisors, including, for example, listening, reflecting, caring, communicating, questioning, and referring.

Academic advising is "based in the teaching and learning mission of higher education, and is a series of intentional interactions with a curriculum, a pedagogy, and a set of student learning outcomes. Academic advising synthesizes and contextualizes students' educational experiences within the frameworks of their aspirations, abilities and lives to extend learning beyond campus boundaries and timeframes" (National Academic Advising Association, 2006). According to this statement, there is a natural connection between academic pursuits and career-related topics. Substituting "academic and career advising" for "academic advising" in the above statement makes explicit the purpose of an integrated approach.

A curriculum, a pedagogy, and learning outcomes are essential to both academic and career advising. The curriculum answers the following question: What do students need to know about themselves, academic and career options, obtaining meaningful employment, and applying to graduate school? Pedagogy addresses the following question: What methods will be used to engage students in learning about these topics? Student learning outcomes address the question: How will students demonstrate they have learned the knowledge identified in the curriculum?

As noted, there are differences in academic and career advising, but the similarities provide a strong foundation from which institutions can frame options for the integration of the two. Integrating academic and career advising empowers students and the goal is to enhance student learning and development. Integrating career and academic advising will work best when customized to the campus and can be accomplished either informally or formally.

INFORMAL INTEGRATION OF ACADEMIC AND CAREER ADVISING

Informal efforts can be described as those planned and implemented by individuals and that occur independent of the institution's organization or culture. Informal programs can be initiated by a single advisor, a group of advisors, or by collaborative efforts among faculty advisors, full-time advisors, and other faculty and academic and student affairs professionals. Integrating academic and career advising through informal efforts is truly limited only by the imagination of those involved.

The Individual Approach

Any faculty or full-time advisor can take the initiative to integrate academic and career advising in interactions with students. This can be accomplished by one person within a department or by several advisors within a unit. It may begin by reaching out to career services to seek more information about career options for a specific major, expanding internship possibilities, asking others on campus to identify self-assessment resources for students, or seeking answers to student questions after their participation in a career event. Once informal integration is initiated, advisors may need to enhance this knowledge with respect to career theories and career information. This can be as formal as additional course work or as informal as meeting with those in the career services area. Regardless of the method, it is important advisors know the resources available to support them in providing both academic and career advising for their students.

The Collaborative Approach

Collaborating with others on campus to provide an integrated approach to academic and career advising can take multiple forms. Special events, resources, and classroom presentations are three types of activities that illustrate the collaborative approach.

Special Events. An event that sets the stage for integrating academic and career advising co-sponsored by multiple units is pre-orientation "interviews." Parents and students are invited to campus to meet with faculty, full-time academic advisors, and career services staff. The interviews are structured panel discussions, followed by audience questions/answers, which are followed by small group and individual discussions. Parents and students leave knowing where to obtain more information and how to proceed before students start classes. Topics focus on structure of the college major and expectations of academic preparation and performance (e.g., study skills, time management), internship opportunities and associated occupations, and personal characteristics of students who successfully complete the curriculum. According to Wilson (2006), pre-orientation interviews have been quite effective in improving freshman-to-sophomore persistence. This particular activity is especially attractive to academic departments, as students are more likely to think through their decisions and make changes before becoming a part of the department's entering cohort. Students and parents have time to ask questions, process the information, and adjust decisions, as compared to fast-paced orientation programs where information sessions cover many aspects of campus life in the time allowed.

Co-hosting a "college majors and minors fair" is similar in structure to career fairs. Department heads and faculty advisors from academic units display information about their majors for recruiting purposes. Displaying graphics of related career and occupational opportunities, employing agencies, and of workers in the field augments academic information. Career staff can add an additional element to departmental displays by adding information about personality types and characteristics associated with satisfaction in the field. Business and industry representatives may attend college major fairs with hiring or recruiting intentions, but are asked to participate further by posting "academic criteria" in their displays, noting the most attractive or commonly sought college major(s), the required skills and experience, and recommendations for résumé writing and interviewing. Quite often, companies are willing to hire students before graduation, thus affording the company and the student time to determine whether there is a good fit. The educational value of early job experiences cannot be provided through college lecture courses, and part-time work in the field of interest should, logically, increase student interest in the classroom.

Integrating information in topical workshops can be used to target specific groups of students. Student organizations, college residence halls, specific majors, or off-campus sites are intact "groups" that can be considered for workshop planning. For instance, for kinesiology majors, advisors and career staff could present academic and career information, in workshop format, addressing "Careers in the Health Field." Career staff would guide activities involving informal assessment and discussion of personality, interests, abilities, and values associated with occupations and careers, followed by academic advisors discussing the demands and standards expected in the associated majors. A workshop on "The Secrets of Success" could be useful for students in campus housing who are experiencing academic difficulty. Career staff could present information on successful people in various occupations and the skills required for success in the workplace. Academic advisors could address those same skills and discuss their relevance in classroom success (e.g., good attendance, arriving on time, time management skills, organizational skills, effective leadership and communication skills, involvement in extracurricular activities). The expertise of career staff and academic advisors blends well in these types of activities, and the benefits of students making informed decisions about academic work goes beyond the college years.

Resources. Another informal collaborative approach to integrating academic and career advising is in the development and sharing of resources. "Requirements for . . . major," "what can I do with a major in . . . ?," "your personalized academic and career plan," "jobs for people who love to travel," "volunteer your way to a career," "résumé-building activities," and "applying to graduate school" are examples of resources that can be collaboratively created, placed on the Web, and linked to from multiple home pages. Engaging colleagues in brainstorming the resources needed, determining what is available and how those can be shared, developing those unique to the institution, and utilizing technology to make them accessible to prospective and current students as well as to alumni benefits everyone.

Classroom Presentations. This informal approach to providing groups of students with integrated academic and career advising has the added benefit of reaching larger numbers of students. "Don't Cancel That Class!" is an event that takes place in the classroom for any given subject, with academic advising and career staff as class presenters. Course instructors plan for the presentation to be given at times when they travel, attend meetings, or any other time they would otherwise cancel class. The presentation focuses on the structure of the curriculum and its associated career and occupational options, skills for the field, emerging work trends, and traditional and nontraditional employers of workers with that particular college major. For example, the presentation in a math class would address careers in math, courses in the curriculum that are key in skill development for certain jobs, the math skills sought by various companies, and what the future holds for math majors. Students in the class are directed to Web sites for more information and are invited to schedule appointments for engaging in career advising or for discussing individual concerns and opportunities.

Making presentations in First-Year Experience (FYE) courses can also help students understand early in their college experience that learning about themselves is a foundation to making informed academic and career decisions. Faculty teaching FYE courses at Rowan University are invited to bring their class to the Career and Academic Planning Center. During this visit students learn about the services provided by the center and also sign on to the computers to take one or two self-assessment inventories. They are then encouraged to make an appointment with an advisor to further explore their options. FYE courses at some institutions actually include a self-assessment unit.

Other class presentation options are in basic writing courses taught during the first year. Most institutions require one or two writing courses, and these provide opportunities for students to explore academic and career options. A topic for a paper in the first basic writing course could focus on self-assessment, the foundation for making academic and career decisions. In the second writing course, a research paper is often required. Students could identify several career fields of interest and then research the academic preparation required, as well as specific job qualifications. In courses, collaborative presentations by academic advisors and career services staff could provide students with information to develop these topics and expose them to other resources on campus. The other advantage of this approach is that it has some personal relevance for the students. The more students can make meaning of their academic experiences, the more successful they will be.

Advantages, Disadvantages, and Strategies to Achieve Informal Integration

There are both advantages and disadvantages to the informal approach to integrating academic and career advising. An advantage of the informal approach is that faculty and full-time advisors can provide both academic and career advising to their students without any mandate from a department, college, or institution. Individuals can also collaborate on activities that integrate academic and career advising, and these collaborations often create positive, supportive relationships that transfer to other collaborative efforts on campus. It is important to reemphasize that the informal approach provides exciting opportunities for creativity and collaboration to enhance students' academic and career development and planning.

One disadvantage of the informal approach is that only those students working with the individual advisors or in the classes, or both, will have the benefit of the integrated approach and, therefore, systemic and transformational change at the unit, college, or institution most likely will not occur.

Since these informal approaches are often person specific, there is no guarantee of continuity in providing students with this integrated approach if the individuals who do so leave the institution.

Even with the disadvantages of the informal approach, there is much to be gained from considering and implementing this approach. For the individual advisor, integrating career advising in academic advising requires a foundational understanding of career development needs of college students and how to apply that understanding in meetings with students. Career development theory courses or formal education programs would facilitate the acquisition of this new knowledge. Other options for learning career development theory and techniques may be through activities of a professional organization (e.g., the National Career Development Association), through networking with other advisors (from universities who have established programs of integrated career and academic advising), and from subscriptions to professional journals (e.g., the *Journal of Career Development, The Career Development Quarterly,* and the *NACADA Journal*).

Obtaining information on specific occupations and the job market can be challenging because there are multiple sources of information. The staff in career services will be able to describe what is available on campus and which of the multiple resources are most helpful, relevant, and used by students. There is not any one resource that will meet the needs of all students, so it is important to identify several options. Chapter Seven focuses on resources for assisting students through career advising.

The strategies in the individual approach often naturally lead to the development of collaborative efforts. As an individual advisor reaches out to and collaborates with the staff in career services, it may become apparent to both that continuing conversations and sharing of information can be extremely helpful. When academic and career advising are separate functions, students meeting with an academic advisor often ask this question: "What can I do with this major?" For students meeting with a career advisor, the question is: "What majors prepare me for this career and what courses could I consider to investigate those options?" During these conversations, the need to provide answers to both of these questions may become apparent. Working together to address these student questions may create the need and desire to move to a more formal integration of academic and career advising.

FORMAL INTEGRATION OF ACADEMIC AND CAREER ADVISING

Formal integration involves a unit, college, or institution recognizing the need and value of having advisors provide both academic and career advising to the students. In this approach, students know that in the designated unit or college or across the entire institution they can expect to receive support in making both academic and career decisions from their advisors. As in the informal approach, there is no one approach that fits all institutions.

An understanding of variations of this formal approach may be instructive to those considering this approach to integration.

The method for integrating career and academic advising to the greatest degree possible is to have a one-stop center with fully cross-trained advisors that provide all students with academic and career advising. Advisors are hired based on their knowledge and experience in facilitating both academic and career decision making and students' academic and career development. The center may be staffed by full-time advisors as well as faculty advisors who serve on a release time or rotating basis. They are housed in one centralized unit, and provide campuswide academic and career advising. Administrators and faculty who recognize the need for hiring cross-trained advisors will, by their support, optimize program benefits and outcomes. Cross-trained advisors who anticipate and intrusively address student concerns, academic and career-related, can have a positive impact on the culture and outcomes of advising. In this approach, all advisors provide both academic and career advising in an integrated way. Activities and events are naturally focused on career and academic advising, at critical times during the semester, in strategic formats. Most one-stop advising centers incorporate an electronic infrastructure for providing students easy access to academic and career information and for interacting with advisors.

Career and academic advising in a one-stop model targets critical timing issues, student career goals, academic and curricular dynamics, and integrates career and academic issues with the ultimate purpose of preparing the student for graduating from the university and entering the world of gainful employment. Integrated career and academic advising in a one-stop, centralized location will provide ongoing support for students. Though much is required of the institution to achieve such a unit, the benefits to students are well worth the investments.

A variation of the formal approach described above is a one-stop center that has responsibility for a specific student population or populations. Many institutions have created these centers to serve undeclared students and those who have changed their major. Other centers are created for a specific college to serve those majors. Advisors, either full-time or faculty or a combination of both, in these centers provide both academic and career advising for selected groups of students and may also serve as a resource for other advisors on campus.

A third variation of the formal approach is when the academic advising and career services staff are located in the same physical space and report to the same administrator but maintain all or some of their separate and distinct responsibilities. Referrals between the two are more easily facilitated by virtue of the shared space and often there is a common resource room or library. With both the second and third variations of the formal approach, advisors in other units on campus may or may not integrate academic and career advising in their work with students.

Another formal approach is a faculty-based advising model in which all faculty advisors integrate academic and career advising in student sessions.

There may be an administrator who coordinates academic advising and career services at the institutional level, but the faculty advisors work with students individually as they make academic and career decisions.

Appendix A of the *Handbook* provides descriptions of nine institutions and centers that demonstrate a formally integrated approach to academic and career advising. Table 9.1 presents three additional examples of formal integration of career and academic advising.

It is important to note that all of the collaborative events, resources, and classroom activities described in the section on informal integration can become formal and ongoing. The purpose of this integration is to enhance students' academic and career planning and preparation for the future. Additional formal activities that further demonstrate this integrated approach are credit courses (e.g., Careers for Psychology Majors). The College of Business at Rowan University has also implemented an intrusive advising and career development plan created for all their majors. Faculty and the staff in the Career and Academic Planning Center established very specific assignments for students at freshmen, junior, and senior levels to engage in curricular-based activities that support informed academic and career decision making.

Advantages and Disadvantages of the Formal Approach

The primary advantage of the formal approaches for integrating academic and career advising is that more students will receive services through this more holistic approach and that integration will continue even when staff leave or change positions. When larger numbers of students are affected, there is also a greater probability that retention and graduation rates will improve. Integrating academic and career advising also empowers advisors with additional resources to assist students. By helping students see the connections between academic and career choices, advisors are able to provide more information and support. Being involved in an integrated approach requires advisors to enhance their knowledge and skills, provides more variety in their day-to-day activities, and may lead to increased professional development opportunities. All of these are desirable outcomes and can lead to not only increased student satisfaction and success, but also increased employee morale.

Disadvantages to a formal integrated approach are quite limited and normally revolve around students who are not advised through that approach. For an undeclared student accustomed to discussing both academic and career issues with his/her advisor, there may be some reluctance to move to the major advisor if the integrated approach is not followed in that department.

Steps in the Formal Integration of Academic and Career Advising

A primary goal in integrating career and academic advising is to guide students in making rational, informed career decisions, while developing and implementing realistic academic plans. That goal can be met through a variety

Table 9.1. NACADA Outstanding Advising Program Award Winners

Institution Type and Example	Valencia Community College (two-year)	Indiana University-Purdue University (four-year)	Principia College (private)
Model type	Unified cross-campus system (LifeMap) and Atlas online learning community.	Integrated campus center for advising and career counseling located in University College.	Fully integrated campus center (Office of Academic and Career Advising) with career advisors.
Staff involved and training	College faculty advisors trained in career advising. Student support staff in admissions and financial aid offices are cross-trained in career advising to man campus "answer centers."	Academic advisors and career counselors housed together. Separate positions, but with cross-training available through 1) a career resource binder for academic advisors, and 2) campuswide conference on integrating career and academic planning.	In 2003, the Academic Advising Center (AAC) and Career Development Center (CDC) were merged into a single unit, now known as the office of Academic and Career Advising (ACA); practitioners hired as career advisors.
Physical location	Faculty offices and campus answer centers along with district offices and online "virtual" office.	Centralized advising center.	Centralized career advising office.
Target population and services provided	All students. Career and educational planning. Resource assistance and online access to services.	All freshmen. Major/career connections information sheets, a first-year seminar course for exploratory students, and a career development textbook.	New students and students who have not declared a major.
Achievements/awards	Increased fall to spring persistence for first time in college students and credit hours completed. Valencia ranked #1 among community colleges in the United States in the number of associate degrees awarded, and #4 in associate degrees awarded to Hispanic students.	University College has been nationally recognized by U.S. News and World Report for its work with first-year students. Since 2001 the University College Advising Center has been the recipient of four NACADA Outstanding Program Awards.	Principia College achieved significant improvements in student contact rates, faculty engagement, new program components, and cost-efficiencies.

Source: National Academic Advising Association (2008).

Outstanding advising program awards (1984–2008 award winners and certificates of merit). http://www.nacada.ksu.edu/Awards/Outstanding_Program.htm

of methods and each campus has unique features that should be considered when deciding on how and to what degree programs will be integrated. However, there are key steps to follow to increase the probability that the integration of academic and career advising will proceed smoothly.

Develop a Rationale and Vision. Establishing the rationale and vision for the integration of academic and career advising is an important first step. As part of the process, it is important to assess the institution with respect to integration by addressing the following questions: How are students currently being served and what needs to be improved? How will the institution's culture and values, as well as organizational structure and politics, affect this change? Will the integration occur at the institutional level or within a specific division, college, or unit? These discussions of a rationale and vision for formal integration may begin at a grassroots level, within the context of a strategic plan or accreditation process, as a result of an external review process, or through the development of a mission statement for academic and career advising. Once the rationale and vision are developed, a decision must be made about moving to the formal integration of academic and career advising.

Obtain Support. Obtaining the support of the administrator in charge of these affected units is a critical next step in the formal integration of academic and career advising and the development of an integrated program. If the integrated approach is within a college or division, the key administrator will probably have been involved in the development of the rationale and vision, as well as in the decision to move forward. If the integration is going to be institutionwide, and especially if the affected units report to two different divisions, the support may need to come from an administrator above the division level. Once this support is obtained, consideration needs to be given to where this newly created unit should be placed in the organizational structure to most effectively serve the students for which it is created. Integrated units may report to either Academic Affairs or Student Affairs, and each institution must make the determination that is best for their specific campus. If both divisions actively endorse and have equal resources to support the integrated approach, placing the integrated unit within academic affairs can facilitate collaborative efforts with faculty. This can be especially valuable if integrating academic and career advising activities into the curriculum is also a goal.

Plan the Integration Process. Planning the process for formally integrating academic and career advising is the next step. There are multiple approaches to this integration, and creating a program development team or a task force to investigate and explore the various options is an effective strategy. Representatives of the academic advising and career staff, faculty, students, and administrators should be included on this task force or development team. Another effective strategy for managing this change process (Sanaghan, Goldstein, & Gavel, 2007) is to select a "transition manager" who can identify the key stakeholders and their places and roles in the organizational structure.

If this strategy is selected, the transition manager needs to be well respected on campus and especially by those most affected by this change. This person could also serve as chair of the task force or development team if that process is chosen. Regardless of the method selected, it is important that the process be characterized as open, honest, and transparent and that all involved commit to the shared vision.

Determining who has final decision-making authority is an important issue that needs to be addressed at the very beginning of the process. If a team is created, it is important to determine whether it is an advisory or recommending body and, if so, to whom do they present their recommendations. If the team is a decision-making body, it is important to know the parameters of making decisions for the integrated program. For example, determination must be made on how recommendations or decisions will be made: all agree or by majority rule. Although consensus is certainly desirable, it is not likely to occur in all areas. Having a protocol in place for ultimate decision making at the onset will facilitate this process.

Identify the Tasks. All good plans begin with a detailed list of the tasks to be completed. To integrate career and academic advising, the team must identify tasks related to who, what, when, where, how, and why. The team should identify these tasks and other issues in order to know the obstacles, plan the strategies, and anticipate the need for adjustments.

Review Rationale and Create the Structure. The first task in this phase of the process is to review the problems identified in the first step where the rationale for integrating academic and career advising was established. The next task is to define the specific benefits expected from integrating the career and academic advising and to develop an organizational structure with specific position descriptions that supports those anticipated benefits and resolves the identified problems. In many integrated units and programs, there are common academic and career advising responsibilities all staff assume, and each person also has some unique responsibilities. The numbers of students served, the numbers and types of services offered, and the number of staff in this integrated unit impact the structure created. Examples of structures in various types of integrated units are included in the exemplary practices section in Appendix A of the *Handbook*. With more institutions moving to a formally integrated approach, it can be very helpful to contact those who have been part of a process to integrate academic and career advising and to learn from their experiences.

Determine Staffing. In identifying the unit's personnel, there are several questions to be answered. Who will direct the program and how will that selection be made? How many advisors will be necessary for a highly functioning unit? Will the unit be staffed with full-time advisors or a combination of full-time and faculty advisors? How will advisors be selected? What educational backgrounds are important? Will the staff be expected to have previous training and experience with both career and academic advising? If the staff joining this integrated unit has different pay levels and titles, how will that be managed? How will job responsibilities change? Where are the matches of the current staff and the newly created position descriptions? What is missing and how will those responsibilities be addressed?

Defining the roles of support staff is also important. One factor in determining the number of support staff will be the number of advising staff, the student caseload, and the types of services offered by the integrated unit. Support staff may include graduate assistants, student workers, and administrative and professional support personnel. How many of each will be determined not only by the factors mentioned above but also by policies and procedures, student traffic-flow and management, appointment scheduling, method of documentation and record-keeping, the size and complexities of the unit budget, and the number and complexity of technology resources.

Determine Needs and Options for Professional Development. Once the structure has been created, specific position descriptions developed, and the determination made about who will staff the formally integrated center, it is time to identify the professional development needs of the staff. Providing professional development opportunities as part of the planning process instead of waiting until the center is actually established makes clear that a new structure will be a reality. It may also reinforce the similarities between academic and career advising, recognize and value the specific knowledge each staff member brings to the unit, and create opportunities for discussions about this new future of an academic and career advising program. Visiting an institution that has a formally integrated academic and career advising unit is another option that supports professional development.

Professional development needs to be a priority not only through the planning and implementation process but also ongoing, with resources allocated in each budget cycle. Additional specific topics included in professional development are the conceptual, informational, and relational elements noted earlier. Learning how to develop an academic and career advising curriculum, determine the most effective pedagogy, and establish student learning outcomes for academic and career advising are also important elements of a professional development program.

Advisors also need to know how to set personal and professional goals and how to evaluate their goals at the end of a specified period. Advisor goals should include how they will address career and academic advising practices, their plans to address unique needs of special populations, development of their own interpersonal styles, and professional growth.

Professional associations (e.g., NACADA, FYE, National Association of Colleges and Employers, and NCDA) provide a multitude of opportunities for networking with other professionals, as well as enhancing knowledge and skills. Local, regional, and national conferences, print and electronic resources, and webinars sponsored by these organizations are examples of professional development opportunities for advisors to learn more about integrated career and academic advising programs.

Develop the Assessment Plan. An important task in the planning stage is to develop an assessment plan. This should include process and student learning outcomes assessment, as well as a personnel evaluation system for staff. It may be helpful to begin with the process and student learning outcomes assessment component before implementing the staff evaluation component. This recognizes that professional development experiences are going to be provided and that new knowledge and skills may need to be developed. An extensive discussion of the assessment process is presented in Chapter Twelve.

Establish a Time Line. When determining a date for the establishment of this newly integrated unit, there must be sufficient time to consider and make decisions about the relevant issues. If there is a physical move involved, the target date must accommodate the packing, unpacking, and setting up furniture, materials, equipment, and other resources. If space is being renovated, that adds another consideration to the schedule. During summer or semester break may be the best possibility for this transition; however, each institution has unique needs, so the academic calendar should be consulted before making the decision about a date when this integrated unit will be fully operational. Once that date has been established, the process of back mapping all the specific decisions and tasks can be very instrumental in keeping the integration on schedule. The mapping process also illustrates the relationship of all the tasks and decisions, which can be extremely helpful if adjustments have to be made.

Determine the Unit Location and Name. The actual physical location for the formally integrated academic and career advising unit is important. This determination is influenced by the goals and objectives of the integrated unit. Questions to be considered include the following: How much space will be necessary? Will advisors need office space to accommodate small groups? Will there be a need for smart classrooms, computer labs, resource rooms, and interview rooms for employers? Where will students wait to see their advisors? How much storage space is required? Reviewing the current space of the separate offices that will be integrated may provide some guidance, but new initiatives may be created by this integrated unit. Anticipating and providing for those future needs also reinforces the expectations that this unit will serve students better. Whatever is included should be directly tied to meeting program goals and objectives.

Another consideration for the campus location of this integrated unit is that, if possible, the units being integrated should move into totally different space from areas those units are currently occupying. Moving into new space has some psychological advantages that can support the staff as they interact in this new structure. It prevents one group from feeling as though their space has been invaded and the other group from feeling like intruders. The physical location should also be in an area of high student traffic and accessible to all. An off-the-beaten-path location may result in the program being a well-hidden secret.

The name of this unit also is an important consideration. At one medium-sized college, the first name for the integrated unit providing academic and career advising for undeclared and change of major students and career advising for all students and alumni was Advising and Career Services. Even though there was extensive publicity and ongoing communication to the campus community about the office and its newly integrated services, it was discovered two years after integration that many students, staff, and faculty had the perception that there were no longer career services on campus. Through the use of feedback systems with stakeholders on campus, the name was then changed to the Career and Academic Planning Center. Although a number of institutions use Career and Academic Planning (CAP) as the name for their integrated center, there are many other possibilities. Using focus groups of students, staff, faculty, and employers can be an effective method to test different options and determine one that fits.

Acknowledge Feelings. For those who are leading and involved in the process of making this integrated unit a reality, it is very important to understand that those affected by this change may experience a variety of feelings. There will be some who will eagerly participate in the process, support the changes, and enthusiastically move into new ways of working. Others may appear to agree with the concepts and to support movement to a unit that provides both academic and career advising, but in reality they are not ready or eager to change. Change that has an impact on the way a person perceives his or her status, level of control, power, relationships, turf, or responsibilities can elicit strong negative feelings. Some people are uncomfortable with and fear any change whereas others may be fearful that they will not be able to do what is expected of them in the future. In an effort to protect their status quo, people sometimes engage in behaviors that are counterproductive.

There is no absolute method to address these issues, but one way to be proactive in managing these concerns is to meet with each person being affected by this change early in the planning process. Asking questions about their thoughts, feelings, concerns and fears, suggestions, and goals can help identify and address some of these issues. Depending on how much the person asking the questions is trusted will determine the degree to which persons disclose their concerns; however, carefully listening to those answers may provide insights that can then be incorporated into the plan. These conversations may also result in the individual exploring other campus opportunities or in helping these individuals clarify and identify options that better support their goals.

Being aware that these undercurrents may exist can alert a leader if questionable behaviors are observed. Addressing the person demonstrating inappropriate behaviors from the very beginning is critical and sends a message to others that unprofessional behavior will not be tolerated. This may appear harsh, but too often one person with a negative attitude can have significant impact on the interactions of the entire group and the services students receive.

Provide Resources. The best plans will not occur if the appropriate resources are not available both in the creation of a formally integrated academic and career advising unit and in the subsequent budget cycles. These include salary, non-salary, and physical plant resources. One way to determine the resources needed is to look at the current level of resources for the units as they currently exist, review the mission statement of the integrated unit to determine the additional services to be provided, and project the resources required to meet the goals. This process should also include a review of current services to determine whether there are more effective and efficient ways to deliver a service. Technology can enhance and make more efficient many services but may create a need for a staff member with expertise in that area to manage those resources. If a computer lab is part of this unit, replacement costs for the computers and printers need to be anticipated and provided. Another way to assess resource needs is to talk with directors of integrated units at other institutions.

Implement the Plan. Once all the tasks listed above have been completed, the plan is ready to be implemented. It is important to recognize that this is the time when some of those feelings described earlier may become apparent. Those who may have verbally supported this initiative, but who internally hoped it would not actually happen, may attempt to delay or derail movement toward the implementation.

Review, Assess, and Make Adjustments. Once the unit is operational, periodic conversations about how the integrated program is operating are important. This does not imply that the units may be separated again, but these are checkpoints to determine that implementation is on target in meeting goals and objectives. New processes, procedures, and services need to be given sufficient time to determine their viability, but if a particular issue needs immediate resolution, a decision should be made then. The formal assessment plan developed during the task identification stage also needs to be implemented as scheduled. That process can be very instructive regarding the areas that are working well and those that need adjustments.

SUMMARY

Successfully integrating career and academic advising requires focus on positive outcomes that benefit students, advisors, institutions, communities, and society at large. Successfully integrating programs begins with the question, "What can be provided for students that will culminate in academic success and satisfying entry into the world of work?" followed by the question, "Through what means and methods can that best be provided?"

As described in this chapter, there are multiple ways to answer those questions, but integrating academic advising and career advising is an important component of any approach. A single advisor can provide great information during a single advising session, or campus units can provide meaningful career and academic advising events, or instructors/professors may involve students in career-related experiences as they progress through their coursework, learning first-hand about occupational dynamics, or advisors can provide academic and career advising through formally integrated units. Delivering academic and career advising through all formats available enhances the opportunity for students to find relevance and meaning from their college experiences as they prepare for the future. Institutions that invest the necessary resources in integrated career and academic advising programs make a strong statement of their core values. It is a statement that focuses on academic and career-related experiences to encourage students as they make meaningful, life-changing decisions to support their development as people and professionals.

References

ACT. (2008). *The economic benefits of academic and career preparation.* Iowa City, IA: Author. (ERIC Document Reproduction Service No. ED501272)

Astin, A. W. (2007). *The American freshmen: National norms for Fall 2006.* Los Angeles: Higher Education Research Institute.

Ford, S. S. (2007). *The essential steps for developing the content of an effective advisor training and development program.* Retrieved December 14, 2008, from the NACADA Clearinghouse of Academic Advising Resources Web site: http://www.nacada.ksu.edu/Clearinghouse/AdvisingIssues/Adv-Trng-Steps.htm

Gordon, V. N. (2006). *Career advising: An academic advisor's guide.* San Francisco: Jossey-Bass.

National Academic Advising Association. (2006). *NACADA concept of academic advising.* Retrieved October 20, 2008, http://www.nacada.ksu.edu/Clearinghouse/AdvisingIssues/Concept-Advising.htm

National Academic Advising Association. (2008). *Outstanding advising program awards* (1984–2008 award winners and certificates of merit). Retrieved October 20, 2008, http://www.nacada.ksu.edu/Awards/Outstanding_Program.htm

Sanaghan, P. H., Goldstein, L., & Gavel, K. D. (2007). *Presidential transitions: It's not just the position, it's the transition.* Portsmouth, NH: Greenwood.

Wilson, S. (2006). Improving retention and success: A case study approach for practical results. *Journal of College Student Retention, 7,* 245–261.

CHAPTER TEN

Career Advising with Undecided Students

Catherine A. Buyarski

The numbers of undecided students on any campus can be very large, particularly when the types and range of career and major indecision are considered. The complex and diverse needs of students who are exploring majors and careers can be challenging for advisors, and these challenges often keep exploratory students in the front of their minds (Lewallen, 1993).

For over 20 years, it has consistently been reported that between 20% and 50% of all entering students are undecided about academic major and career (Anderson, Creamer, & Cross, 1989; Gordon, 1995b; McCalla-Wriggins, 2000). Many other students will become major changers or experience periods of indecision during the college years (McCalla-Wriggins, 2000; Steele, 1994). In addition, between 50% and 70% of all college students change their major at least once before they graduate (Titley, Titley, & Wolf, 1976). In many ways, being exploratory or undecided can be considered the norm rather than the exception (Lewallen, 1993).

Although all students will benefit from career advising, undecided students are often the focus of advising that incorporates career exploration and decision making because of the need to commit to a program of study in order to make progress toward a degree, as well as the supposition that students who have made a commitment to a major or career goal are more likely to persist to graduation. Understanding exploratory students and providing appropriate career advising is important for any campus. Many higher education professionals argue that undecided students are in need of specialized programs and services because of their propensity to be attrition-prone (Lewallen, 1994). In general, researchers have argued that having decided upon a vocational goal increases student commitment to collegiate study (Fralick, 1993; Lewallen, 1994; Hull-Banks, Robinson Kurpius, Befort, Sollenberger, Foley Nicpon, & Huser, 2005). For example, in a study of over 4,000 students at a midwestern institution, Dennis (2008) found differences between freshman to sophomore year retention and graduation rates for undecided and decided students (although there was no difference in GPA). As an indicator of retention, Ting (1997) found that having long-term goals significantly predicted academic performance.

Caution must be exercised when making connections between major and career indecision and persistence. Pascarella and Terenzini (2005) and Lewallen (1993) posit that causation between major or career decision and persistence cannot be inferred due to the complexity of the educational process. Students engage in a wide array of educational experiences that affect persistence and graduation. Enrollment and participation in an academic major is just one factor, and the impact of enrollment in a particular academic department may result in differences in access to faculty and advisors, intellectual engagement, and interaction with peers—all of which are shown to positively impact enrollment and graduation. Therefore, advising to address major and career decision making should be considered one component of effective methods for enhancing student success and retention.

Beyond issues of retention, most students indicate that they enroll in college to pursue vocational goals (Astin, 2007), which points to career decision making being of paramount important to students and, therefore, it must be a focus of advisors. Grounded in the assumption that student success is defined by assisting students in reaching their academic and career goals, this chapter provides an examination of two primary topics related to career advising for undecided students. First, an exploration of who undecided students are leads to a presentation of established typologies of undecided. Second, the chapter discusses career advising strategies and interventions for assisting undecided students. Both are intended to assist advisors in understanding the career advising needs of students and enhancing their ability to meet those needs.

The terms *exploratory* and *undecided* are often used interchangeably to describe student populations who have not declared a major. For many, the term *exploratory* is generally preferred because it brings forth the importance of the action that is associated with career development and decision making whereas the term *undecided* assigns a label to a temporary state of indecision. Gordon (2007a) uses *undecided* to describe students who are "unwilling, unable, or unready to make educational and/or vocational decisions" (p. x). In this chapter, Gordon's definition is expanded to describe students who are in need of career advising in order to assist with major and career decision making.

UNDERSTANDING UNDECIDED STUDENTS

Given the large number of students on any campus who are exploring majors and careers, it is important to have an in-depth understanding of the characteristics of these students so that effective advising can be provided. Although typologies of undecided students have been created and serve to help understand this student population, it is necessary to recognize the nuances and limitations of any classification system.

First, it must be recognized that being exploratory is a naturally occurring phenomenon faced by most students at some point in their collegiate experience. For many students, career choice is not a pressing concern at college entry, and the number of potential majors at some institutions can be overwhelming. This is particularly true for students who have had little exposure to major and career exploration in high school (Lewallen, 1993). Exposure to ideas, fields of studies, and careers coupled with increasing self-understanding may result in continued reflection, exploration, and decision making about academic and career opportunities. In fact, several studies have found undecided and decided students are more alike than different (Anderson et al., 1989; Ashby, Wall, & Osipow, 1966; Gordon, 1981; Newman, Fuqua, & Minger, 1990).

Second, undecided students are generally identified by declared majors (or lack thereof) in an institution's student record system; this method of identification is limited in that there are always students who have declared or changed majors but have not completed the steps needed to make this change part of their academic record. A declared major does not indicate that a student is no longer exploring major and career choices. Students may have been forced to declare a major through factors such as institutional policy or parental pressure when, in reality, they are still considering academic and career options. In contrast, some institutions will not allow students to declare a major at entry or during their first semester or year of enrollment (Gordon, 1995a, 2007b). Further, students often need to engage in career exploration within fields of study. A student who is interested in biology or has shown potential for success in the biological sciences may need assistance in fully exploring this interest or aptitude, or both, in relation to collegiate study and the world of work.

Finally, underpinning any definition of undecided students are issues of student development. Developmental theories can assist advisors in understanding why students are undecided. In their work on developmental vectors Chickering and Reisser (1993) show that creating a sense of purpose, which is the foundation of career choice, is a developmental task faced in the latter part of a student's college experience. Because of the close association between identity development and career choice, Odom (2005) stated, "Most traditional-aged students are being true to the developmental task of this stage, needing to answer Who am I? before they can tackle Where am I going" (p. 124). Therefore, being asked to select a major upon entry to an institution is often challenging and early decision making may need to undergo constant reevaluation as students continue to develop an understanding of themselves. Similarly, cognitive development theories, such as Perry's (1970) scheme of intellectual development, show that first-year students are dualistic in their thinking and tend to look for simplistic answers from authoritative sources, such as academic advisors (Gordon, 1995a). Dualistic thinking makes understanding the complexity of the world of work difficult at best. As students move through stages of cognitive development, they become more able to complete exploration of themselves and the world of work. Finally, identity development theories for special populations (Atkinson, Morten, & Sue, 1993;

D'Augelli, 1994; Belenky, Clinchy, Goldberger, & Tarule, 1986; Phinney, 1990) can provide insight into how diverse populations of students may approach career decision making within the context of their racial, ethnic, gender, or sexual identity. In addition to providing a context of major and career indecision, student development theory can help in determining students' readiness to participate in and benefit from career advising and programs.

Caution must be exercised when using definitions and typologies of students to determine who is and who is not in need of career advising; it is far better to acknowledge that all students will need career advising at some point in their college experience (Gordon, 2006). This includes students who enter undecided about a major, those who voluntarily change their major once enrolled, and those who are forced to change their major due to reasons such as competitive admissions. All students, regardless of where they are in the career decision-making process, need guidance in considering how their academic choices may affect their goals. Because of the complexity of the population of undecided students, an understanding of the types of undecided students can assist advisors in developing appropriate interventions to meet the diverse career needs of these students.

Types of Undecided Students

Research on the characteristics of major and career indecision is voluminous and spans well over 80 years. As discussed by Gordon (1981, 1995a, 1995b, 2007a, 2007b), variables studied in relation to major and career indecision include personality traits, psychological factors (e.g., locus of control and identity), decision making, avoidance behavior, social and moral attitudes, risk-taking, anxiety, psychological problems, and cross-cultural differences. Whereas early frameworks sought to provide a dichotomy between career decision and indecision, models have now moved to a multidimensional continuum (Savickas, 1995). Undecided students are often placed along this multidimensional continuum of career decision–indecision in combination with other characteristics. The findings from a number of studies (Anderson et al., 1989; Fuqua & Hartman, 1983; Hull-Banks et al., 2005) provide invaluable information on understanding undecided students and, for the academic advisor, the most relevant findings are those which cluster characteristics of undecided students into subtypes. These subtypes provide academic advisors with a framework through which to understand students and provide appropriate interventions.

Subtypes of Undecided Students

Gordon (1998) presents a comprehensive review of 15 major studies of undecided students. This chapter discusses three of the frameworks she presents, each providing a differing view of undecided students. These frameworks are included to highlight the complexity of identifying characteristics of students experiencing career indecision in conjunction with additional factors (e.g., problem solving and anxiety). The frameworks include the works of Savickas and Jarjoura (1991), who focused on establishing categories of career indecision;

Larson, Heppner, Ham, and Dugan (1988), who added the additional variable of problem solving to career indecision; and Newman et al. (1990), who examined career decision status and anxiety. Finally, the chapter presents the overarching typology that emerged from Gordon's analysis of the studies on characteristics of undecided students. Each framework provides a somewhat different perspective that, when understood collectively, can assist academic advisors in theoretically understanding the complexity of career decision making and, more practically, engage in appropriate career advising conversations and interventions.

Categories of Career Indecision. The Career Decision Scale (Osipow, Carney, Winer, Yanico, & Koschier, 1976) was originally developed as an instrument to assess a client's level of indecision and the reasons for this indecision. The research of Savickas and Jarjoura (1991) sought to use cluster analysis to move the instrument from trait identification to being able to identify types of undecided students. Of the five types identified, the first three deal with career development tasks associated with exploration. The final two types focus more on problems that impede a person's ability to work through career decision-making tasks.

Students who are implementing are those who are typically labeled as *decided* students. They report no problems with career decision making, have an occupational objective in mind, and appear to be moving forward on implementing career plans. Students who are *specifying choice through advanced exploration* have identified a preference for an occupational field and are looking for additional information on careers related to their major, how to choose between career alternatives, or how to implement their career choice. In the third type, *crystallizing a preference* through broad exploration, students need more knowledge about themselves and the world of work so that they can determine a career choice. Students who are *unrealistic or learning to compromise* are blocked by the pressure of trying to choose the perfect choice from among multiple interests and career choices, or are experiencing a block in pursuing their ideal career choice. Finally, students who are *indecisive or learning to make decisions* are experiencing high levels of anxiety and are overwhelmed by the career decision-making process.

Career Indecision and Problem Solving. The research of Larson et al. (1988) used established career status inventories along with a problem-solving assessment and individual interviews to attempt to define a typology of undecided students. Assuming that career decision-making status in the freshman year is relatively unsteady due to continued exploration of self and the world of work, the sample for their study consisted primarily of sophomore students. The result of their cluster analysis was the identification of four subtypes of undecided students. Painless avoiders were the least informed about career planning activities and the least involved in career problem-solving activities. They rated themselves negatively on their ability to problem-solve, indicating a lack of confidence and avoidance of problem-solving attitudes and behaviors. Despite having more career information than even decided students, informed indecisives showed lack of confidence and avoidance of problems, factors most likely to be related to their career indecision. Confident but uninformed students reported high levels of confidence in their problem-solving abilities but lacked information about career decision-making. The fourth group, uninformed, lacked some career-planning information and scored moderately on the problem-solving inventory. This typology is useful in its assessment of both the need for career-related information and the student's ability to engage in productive problem-solving behaviors.

Career Decision Status and Anxiety. Through investigating the career choice of community college students, Newman et al. (1990) focused on assessing career decision status and indicators of anxiety. The results identified six types of students: undecided—serious, undecided—not serious, decided—uncomfortable, decided—somewhat comfortable, decided—moderately comfortable, and decided—very comfortable. This framework highlighted that choosing a major or career is not an absolute indicator of career decision-making status; a student's sense of confidence and ease with that decision are critical as well.

The most important finding of their study was that students who report having made a career choice but are feeling relatively uncomfortable experience career indecision similar to that of undecided students. Similarly, students who were undecided but did not see this indecision as a serious problem experienced the same low levels of anxiety as decided students who felt relatively comfortable with their choice. Therefore, career decision alone cannot be used as an indicator of whether or not a student is in need of career decision-making assistance. This typology brings to light the importance of examining a student's level of anxiety or discomfort when discussing career options.

Gordon's Subtypes of Decided and Undecided Students. Based on a review of 15 studies of undecided students, Gordon (1998) identified common characteristics that arose from the profiles presented. Career decision status was used as the framework around which the subtypes were organized; three categories of decided students and four categories of undecided types emerged. Table 10.1 presents a summary of the typology presented by Gordon and adapted by Steele (2003).

This small sampling of frameworks for understanding career decision and indecision illustrates that a list of characteristics to identify undecided students in need of career advising does not exist. Students are complex beings and, as would be expected, any decisions they make are equally multifaceted. Therefore, it is critical for any advisor to understand the complexity of the decision-making process and the multiple factors affecting exploration of self and the world of work. The frameworks presented offer a way to broadly understand where students lie on a continuum of career decision making, as well as issues such as problem solving and anxiety that may need to be addressed in an advising session.

Table 10.1. Subtypes of Decided and Undecided Students

Subtypes	Characteristics
Very decided	These students feel good about themselves, believe they have personal control over their lives, and see themselves as making good decisions regarding their future. While they are capable of implementing choices or making plans, it may still be necessary for advisors to review the exploration process with them.
Somewhat decided	These students have some doubts about their decision and have higher levels of trait anxiety and lower levels of self-clarity, decisiveness, and self-esteem. They may have made premature choices because of external pressures. By taking time to encourage these students to explore their concerns, advisors can in the long-run help these students confirm their original choice or identify a well-grounded alternative.
Unstable undecided	These students exhibit high goal instability, a high level of anxiety, and lack of confidence in their ability to perform adequately. They may also experience ambivalence about their choice and believe that since a sincere decision has been made there is no reason to seek help to confirm or to change their direction. Advising strategies would include discussing the student's career development history allied with the goal of improving his or her decision-making skills.
Tentatively undecided	These students feel comfortable with themselves, have a strong sense of personal esteem, and are more vocationally mature. They may exhibit a vocational direction and are often intuitive decision makers. They do not perceive barriers to achieving goals and are confident that a decision will be made when it feels right. Advisors can help these students establish a plan to explore and discuss the relationships of values to work and non-work tasks and concerns about commitment.
Developmentally undecided	These students are dealing with the normal developmental tasks involved in the major/career decision-making process. They need to gather pertinent information about themselves and the world of work and develop decision-making skills. They may be "multipotential," that is, interested in and competent to succeed in many areas. Advising strategies would include traditional psycho-educational and career planning interventions.
Seriously undecided	These students have low levels of vocational identity, self-clarity, and self-esteem. They have limited knowledge of educational and occupational alternatives and may be looking for the "perfect" choice. They may be seeking occupational information to support that choice. In addition to traditional psycho-educational and career planning interventions, advisors may need to refer these students to personal counseling due to the scope of their problems.

(Continued)

Table 10.1. *(Continued)*

Chronically indecisive	These students have excessive anxiety that permeates many facets of their lives. They are often distressed, unclear about their career options, and depend on others' assistance and approval when making decisions. Advisors may need to refer these students to long-term counseling rather than doing academic and career advising with them.

Source: From Steele, G. (2003). A research-based approach to working with undecided students: A case study illustration. *NACADA Journal, 23*, 10–20. Adapted with permission.

Undecided Versus Indecision

As can be seen from the typologies presented, undecided students are often referred to on a continuum of decidedness or as being in contrast with students with declared majors. The dichotomy of undecided versus decided must be carefully considered. Students who are "decided" may still be exploring major and career options. The act of writing a major in a blank on an admission form or recording a major in a student record system may not be a true indication of commitment to a particular field of study or career path. Further, undecided students are typically considered to be at various stages of the career exploration and decision-making process. "Career indecision," on the other hand, most often refers to a state that stems from psychological issues such as anxiety that lead to a person being unable to make decisions (Fuqua & Hartman, 1983). It is critically important that advisors are able to identify those students who are undecided versus those who are experiencing indecision, thereby requiring more counseling-based interventions.

Almost every advisor has probably met with at least one student for whom all approaches to assisting with career decision making met with resistance from the student or failed. Arguing that most career indecision typologies focus on assisting students working through normal developmental tasks, Fuqua and Hartman (1983) sought to classify career decision making in a way that recognized it as more psychologically complex. They pursued this line of inquiry in an attempt to identify students who could not be assisted through regular, developmentally appropriate career interventions; these students, therefore, need to be referred for psychological counseling before they will be ready to engage in career decision making. Acknowledging that few formal assessment techniques for identifying students who face more complex psychological issues exist, Fuqua and Hartman (1983) presented three dimensions of career indecision, each of which identifies underlying reasons for difficulties with the career process.

The first dimension, *developmental*, refers to students who exhibit career immaturity that stems from the normal development process. Students in this dimension need assistance with self-exploration, evaluation of career alternatives, and effective decision making. In the second dimension, *acute situational indecision*, students are undecided due to an environmental stressor, which in many cases causes increased levels of anxiety. Environmental stressors may include institutional policies and procedures that force (or the student perceives as forcing) them to make a career decision prematurely. Similarly, students who have not adequately moved through the career decision-making process may experience tremendous pressure upon graduation from college. The issue is the student's inappropriate response to the stressor. Students in this dimension need counseling support focused on problem solving in order to develop appropriate reactions to the environmental stressor. The third dimension, *chronic career indecision*, refers to a psychological or behavioral dysfunction including anxiety, issues with self-perception, or an external locus of control. Students in this dimension need to engage in a more therapeutic relationship during which the underlying issue can be addressed for career issues to be resolved.

Career decision making is clearly a complex, nonlinear process in which academic advisors need to understand a variety of variables and student characteristics when seeking to provide career advising. By developing knowledge of the multiple frameworks for career decision making, advisors will be better equipped to facilitate career decision making. Further, advisors will be able to recognize when a student's career indecision needs to be supported by working with a professional counselor.

Groups of Undecided College Students

In addition to considering the individual characteristics of undecided students through the use of subtypes, students can be grouped by a variety of factors such as class standing and ability. These groupings can be helpful when used in conjunction with the typologies of undecided to develop effective intervention strategies (Gordon, 2007a). By grouping undecided students, academic and career advising for specific populations can be enhanced to include relevant career decision-making strategies. Further, providing support for specific categories of students can be a way to effectively and efficiently engage resources to support undecided students. Three categories of undecided students are discussed here: undecided students in their first year of enrollment, major changers, and undecided students in differing ability groups.

The first year of college enrollment is characterized by transition and change. The developmental tasks associated with successfully navigating a new phase of life and a new educational environment can be overwhelming. Odom (2005) argued that the issue of developing an understanding of self is as closely related to entering college as it is important to the career advising process. Gordon (1995a) noted that interest in choosing a major often takes a back seat to other pressures associated with the novelty of the college environment, including meeting different people, learning new study skills, and living in campus housing.

There are three primary career advising needs of first-year students (Gordon, 1995a). First, entering students are often in need of information about themselves, academic fields of study, and occupational opportunities. Second, many traditional-aged first-year students have not mastered the developmental tasks associated with decision making. Finally, students may experience self-conflicts as they embark on identity development. These can be conflicts between values and goals such as a desire for a good salary but interest in relatively low-paying careers. Or a student may experience an interest-ability conflict, for instance, by showing high interest in a major or career but lacking the ability to succeed in that area; the reverse may be true as well. Or a self-conflict may arise as a result of external pressures from significant others that are in opposition to a student's true interests and goals. These issues may also be exhibited by students who change their major from that which they declared at matriculation.

Another important category of undecided students is students who enter college with a declared major but change their minds during the college experience. Major changers are estimated to represent up to 75% of all college students (Gordon, 2007a). As noted previously, even students who report having decided on a major are in need of career advising because of several factors. Some students make initial decisions that are unrealistic given their precollege preparation or aptitude for a certain area of study. Others make premature major and career decisions because of lack of information about themselves and the world of work or pressure from family members. Still others are forced to reconsider their academic and career goals because they are not admitted to competitive or restricted programs of study. Often the challenge of competitive grade point averages for entry into academic programs, unwise course decision making, and restrictions on the time and money available to continue college enrollment complicate the process of exploring and changing majors (Mayhall & Burg, 2002). Theophilides, Tereznini, and Lorang (1984) argued that the first year is a testing ground for academic abilities that may result in a change of majors. The findings of their study suggest that weak academic performance may be an indicator of either lack of interest in a declared major or a mismatch between a declared major and academic ability. Steele, Kennedy, and Gordon (1993) found that upper-class major changers who participated in targeted career advising interventions were more likely to be retained and graduate.

Major changing may also be tied to career self-efficacy (Nauta, 2007). Students who were satisfied with their major, as shown by persistence in that major over time, had high levels of career decision self-efficacy, possibly stemming from the confidence gained from making what is perceived to be a difficult decision. Nauta noted that experiencing dissatisfaction with a major (as shown by lack of persistence in a declared field of study) can be seen by students as a failure leading students to perceive themselves as ineffective decision makers. Further, students who are dissatisfied with their major experience high levels of career decision-making anxiety, possibly because they perceive themselves as being locked into a major and having to choose among unsatisfactory career alternatives. Academic advisors are well positioned to help students assess their satisfaction with a declared major.

Gordon (2007a) also categorized major changers and provided recommendations for advising strategies to assist each group of students (see Table 10.2).

Given the propensity for students to engage in major changing, it is critical that students have access to appropriate career advising interventions to guide them through the process of clarifying their interests, skills, and values and determining how these match with alternative majors and careers. Although few formal programs exist to identify and assist the various types of students who will engage in major changing (Steele, 1994), many campuses have programs to assist students who fall on the ends of the spectrum of academic ability (e.g., developmental education, honors programs).

Programs that assist groups of students of varying academic ability can provide a vehicle through which to engage students in career advising. On one

Table 10.2. Types of Major Changers

Type of Major Changer	Description	Recommendations for Advising Support
Drifters	Recognize early that their initial choice is wrong but are reluctant to seek assistance to explore other options.	Recognize these students exist; provide information on majors and assistance in conducting an orderly exploration of alternatives.
Closet changers	Change their major but tell no institutional representative. Enroll in courses for a new major with no guidance from an advisor.	Encourage students to confirm their choice of new major through the proper institutional channels. Provide course enrollment assistance.
Externals	Change majors frequently and seek advice from anyone who will engage with them.	Help engage in productive exploration and decision-making strategies.
Up-tighters	Often denied admission to restricted majors and are unable or unwilling to explore alternatives.	Validate the feelings of rejection and loss of goal identity. Assist in identifying values and interests that led them to the initial major so as to guide exploration of alternatives.
Experts	Rarely request assistance even when initial choice of major is unrealistic. Continue on path even though it is not realistic.	Use sensitivity to guide the exploration of alternatives. Be encouraging and nonjudgmental. Sometimes only institutional policy will force a student to change majors.
Systematics	Acknowledge that a change of major is needed. Engage in productive exploration and decision-making activities.	These students are the ideal; ultimately every student should be guided to become a systematic.

Source: From Gordon, V. N. (2007a). *The undecided college student: An academic and career advising challenge (2nd ed.).* Springfield, IL: Charles C. Thomas. Adapted with permission.

end of the spectrum, underprepared students may lack the prerequisite skills to be successful in an academic major or they may not perform to the level needed to enter a field of study. Unfortunately, Ashby et al. (1966) found that students with poor academic preparation were more decided than their college-ready peers. Therefore, clear assessment of interests, skills, and knowledge of majors and careers becomes critically important. When working with academically underprepared students, advisors should be ready to face issues related to disappointment and grief associated with students' lack of ability to enter their chosen major or career (Beatty, 1994), or the extended length of time to degree as a result of the need to take additional preparatory classes.

On the other end of the ability spectrum are high-ability undecided students. Indecision for these students may be associated with the overwhelming opportunities available to them. In addition, due to the increase in early college enrollment programs, high-ability students may find themselves engaged in major and career exploration at a very young age, a situation that increases the role of developmental challenges affecting career decision making, including the role of outside authority figures such as parents and lack of identity formation (Beatty, 1994). High-ability students may make premature career decisions based on success in a field of study or have difficulty with decision making due to the pressure to excel in all areas (Gordon, 2007a). Career advising for high-ability students needs to focus on values and interest clarification to assist in helping the student find a major and career match in the sea of opportunities.

ADVISING THE UNDECIDED STUDENT

The types of undecided students illustrate the importance of providing sound career advising for this student population. As part of conversations about academic planning, advisors are most often the institutional representative with whom a student will discuss major and career options. Gordon (2007b) indicated that the most effective and preferred method of helping students through the career decision-making process is one-on-one interaction with an academic or career advisor who is "knowledgeable, competent, and dedicated" (p. 187). Further, she posits that while some advisors focus exclusively on working with undecided students, all advisors will encounter students who are making career decisions. Therefore, it is incumbent upon advisors to have developed the knowledge and skills to serve undecided students well. Advisors must be proactive in introducing and working through career exploration and decision making with all students.

For far too many undecided students, conversations about career options arise out of situational pressures (e.g., early registration periods, credit hour limitations at which students are required to declare a major, or denial of admission to an academic program). At each of these points, the urgency of needing to declare a major can undermine the importance of engaging in the career decision-making process. Therefore, it is critically important that academic advisors have a thorough understanding of this process and assist students in working through career exploration and decision making in a purposeful manner. An understanding of the career decision-making process will ensure that academic advisors guide students through a comprehensive exploration of themselves and career options; it is also essential that advisors share their knowledge of the process with students so that they can understand that choosing a major and setting career goals does not happen in one 30-minute advising appointment (Bogenschutz, 1994).

As part of the career decision-making process, advisors need knowledge of curricula so that they can recommend courses in which a student might explore majors and explain how these exploratory courses may apply to general education requirements. Advisors also need knowledge of general career information including how careers are clustered by occupational type and how an occupation can be accessed through a variety of majors (Gordon, 2007a). The University College Advising Center at Indiana University-Purdue University Indianapolis developed a series of Major Career Connection Sheets that provide advisors and students with easy access to exploring the relationship between majors and careers (http://uc.iupui.edu/students/academics/mccs.asp). In addition, many institutions developed "What Can I Do with the Major in . . . ?" resources (e.g., Match Major Website developed by Florida State University, http://www.career.fsu.edu/occupations/matchmajor/index.html).

Advisors also need to have knowledge of their role in the career advising process. As stated by Gordon (2006), "Academic advisors are not expected to be career counselors but to assist students in gathering and processing the information needed to engage in academically related career planning" (p. 8). If one views academic advising and career counseling on a continuum with each professional's unique skills and knowledge at each end, it becomes apparent that there is a large middle section of the continuum in which academic advising and career counseling intersect. Advisors, particularly those assisting undecided students, need to understand that it is critical for them to utilize advising skills such as listening, questioning, and guiding to venture into the basics of major and career exploration while maintaining solid relationships with their career counseling professionals who will serve as a key resource for referral to the persons with the highly specialized knowledge and skills associated with career counseling. The developmental model of academic advising provides a solid framework for working with undecided students in need of career advising.

Developmental Advising for Undecided Students

In 1972, O'Banion proposed a developmental model of academic advising that focused on the relationships among life, career, and academic planning. This model identifies five elements of the advising process: exploration of life goals, vocational goals, program choice, course choice, and scheduling options. These five elements are presented in a linear fashion, which implies that academic decisions are based on vocational goals and career planning is based in life goals. This highly integrated model of career and academic planning suggests that academic advising is a logical setting for career advising, particularly with undecided students who need to explore life and vocational goals before they are able to engage in sound academic planning.

Habley (1994) added specificity regarding the needs of undecided students to the developmental advising model by outlining the specific tasks associated with each of the stages presented by O'Banion (1972). Table 10.3 illustrates the addition of Habley's (1994) tasks for undecided students as framed by the developmental advising model. These tasks provide advisors with concrete topics of discussion for academic advisors and undecided students.

Clearly, advisors who are assisting undecided students need to spend the most time engaged in Habley's (1994) tasks one through seven, including assisting students in identifying values, abilities, and interests, exploring the world of work, and consideration of fields of study that will support career and life goals. It is important to note that these processes, although mapped as linear, are often recurring. Students may revisit previous tasks or engage in several tasks concurrently as they use the exploration process to clarify information about themselves and the world of work. Advisors should be prepared to facilitate this recurring process as well as to assure students of its normalcy.

Table 10.3. Career Exploration Tasks at Each Stage of Developmental Advising

Exploration of life goals	Task 1: Awareness of individual values, abilities, and interests
	Task 2: Clarification of life goals based on awareness of individual values, abilities, and interests
Exploration of career goals	Task 3: Exploration of relationship between life and career goals
	Task 4: Exploration of aspects of the world of work
	Task 5: Clarification of career goals
Exploration of educational goals	Task 6: Exploration of educational combinations leading to life and career goals
	Task 7: Selection of appropriate educational combinations
Selection of courses	Task 8: Exploration of elective courses to enhance goal achievement
	Task 9: Sequencing and selection of courses
Course scheduling	Task 10: Scheduling of courses
	Task 11: Evaluation of experiences for confirmation or redirection of plans

Source: From, Habley, W. R. (1994). Administrative approaches to advising undecided students. In V. Gordon (Ed.), *Issues in advising the undecided college student.* (Monograph No. 15, pp. 17–23). Columbia, SC: University of South Carolina, National Resource Center for The Freshman Year Experience. Adapted with permission.

Appreciative Advising as a Tool for Major and Career Exploration

Drawing on a number of different fields of study including appreciative inquiry and developmental advising, Bloom and Martin (2002) explored the idea of using appreciative techniques to enhance academic advising and help students reach their fullest potential. "Appreciative advising is the intentional collaborative practice of asking positive, open-ended questions that helps students optimize their educational experiences and achieve their dreams, goals, and potentials. It is perhaps the best example of a fully student-centered approach to student development" (Bloom, Hutson, & He, 2008b). This approach to advising integrates academic and career planning and places emphasis on optimizing students' dreams by building on the strengths they possess to assist in making these dreams a reality. As such, it offers a sound framework upon which advisors can begin the process of major and career exploration with undecided students. In addition, because of the positive focus of the approach, it has tremendous potential for use with major changers who may be struggling to find strengths on which to build a career.

The appreciative advising approach includes six stages: disarm, discover, dream, design, deliver, and don't settle (Bloom, Hutson, & He, 2008a). The first three stages are particularly useful for working with undecided students, including major changers. The disarm phase focuses on creating a safe and welcoming environment for students. This is a key step in working with undecided students who need a secure environment in which to talk about themselves as well as any anxiety they have about choosing a major and career. Advisors can set the stage by welcoming the student with a smile, calling the student by name, and expressing sincere appreciation for the student's engagement in the advising process. The discover phase is devoted to helping students identify their positive core, that is the strengths, passions, and values they want to ensure are carried into their future life and career endeavors. Advisors facilitate discovery through the use of positive open-ended questions that address students' interests, strengths, and passions. Advisors must engage in active listening and ask clarifying questions in order to ensure they understand the exact nature of the information students are offering. In the dream phase, students formulate a vision of what they might become. In this stage, students may not use specific language related to majors or careers because they may be describing life goals. Again, careful listening and clarifying questions are important. Advisors should help students make connections between the information shared in the discover phase and remind students to be open to multiple realities of their future—there is rarely one path to a goal. The discover and dream phases are particularly useful when working with major changers as they allow students to verbalize why they embarked upon their first major, as well as to redirect their core strengths and passions to new paths for achieving their goals. This positive approach can assist students in redirecting their career interests.

Matching major and career options with a student's dream is the goal of the design phase. In the design phase, the advisor will assist the student in devising incremental and achievable goals and, therefore, the focus becomes finding majors and careers that match the student's dreams. In this phase, advisors model how to make informed decisions through exploration of options. In addition, in the design phase advisors will help the student engage in use of campus resources for learning more about majors and careers. Once a major and career decision has been made, the student will embark on the deliver phase in which she or he will take action steps toward meeting the learning goals and skill development outcomes needed to succeed in the chosen field of study and career. Finally, as a student begins to achieve some of the goals set, the advisor will be there to encourage the student to raise his or her own internal bar of expectations—the heart and soul of the final phase, don't settle. Academic advisors are important in helping students see beyond what they may believe is the ceiling of their potential.

At the University of North Carolina-Greensboro (Bloom et al., 2008a), prenursing students must earn a cumulative 2.0 GPA after the first semester to remain a prenursing major, and after completing 30 semester hours must maintain a 2.7 GPA. Students who do not meet these requirements must declare a different major. Beginning with a pilot program in spring 2005, students who did not earn first semester GPAs high enough for this very competitive program were advised by an advisor skilled in appreciative advising. Since the program was introduced, students who experienced appreciative advising were more likely to change their major, be retained to the next year, and earned higher GPAs in the next term than previous cohorts of prenursing students who did not experience appreciative advising. These findings suggest that the use of appreciative advising techniques can be a powerful way to assist students in exploring themselves and college majors congruent with their skills, abilities, and interests.

Programs and Services to Assist Undecided Students

Although individual advising is a very effective way to assist undecided students, there are other programs and services that can serve this population. By clearly delineating the outcomes of career interventions for undecided students, alternative delivery methods can be both effective and efficient. For example, with a well-defined curriculum, group interventions such as workshops or courses can provide an efficient method of teaching large numbers of students about career decision making while classroom interaction with peers enhances the effectiveness of the program. It is important that campuses carefully assess the needs of their students, available resources, and learning outcomes for career advising when making decisions about programs and services for undecided students.

Career Exploration Courses. First-year seminar courses that integrate major and career exploration into topics of college transitions and success can be an intervention to engage students who do not declare a major upon entry to the institution. These courses often use exploration of self as a gateway to providing students with support and information to make the transition to college as well as to explore majors and careers. Similarly, themed learning communities for first-year students can provide students with the opportunity to explore majors and careers through a block of courses taught around a theme of interest (e.g., the environment, the economy, and social justice). For undecided students, the curricular theme can allow a student to find a major and career within an area of personal interest. As noted earlier, even first-year students who have declared a major may need career advising and, in this case, the curricular theme can provide an opportunity to fine-tune career goals.

Many campuses offer a seminar course that leads students through the career decision-making process. Class assignments require students to complete career assessments, complete research on majors and careers of interest, and engage in activities such as informational interviewing and job shadowing. Career courses should be structured in a way so as to offer assistance to students at various stages in their college career. For example, if a campus has a credit hour limit at which a student must declare a major, offering a career course a semester or two prior to the deadline may be an effective way to uphold a campus policy while providing support for undecided students. Having these courses cotaught by academic advisors and career counselors can effectively integrate academic and career planning in a targeted seminar.

Courses that serve as an introduction to majors are also a vehicle to assist students with career exploration and decision making. This can take the format of a course specifically designed for students who have declared a major in a field of study. In such courses students learn about the academic curriculum, have opportunities for co-curricular learning (e.g., service learning and undergraduate research), and explore career paths for students holding degrees in that major. For example, at Indiana University-Purdue University Indianapolis all psychology majors are required to take an introductory course in which they explore their reasons for choosing a major in psychology, explore curricular options and requirements, construct a four-year academic plan, and develop career goals. Alternately, academic and career information can be shared in introductory courses taken by all students (e.g., sociology or chemistry course). Students who enroll in a general education course to fulfill graduation requirements may not realize the exciting career opportunities in that field of study. Introductory courses can be a suitable place to help students make connections between their learning and the world of work.

Specialized Programs for Undecided Students. There are also many ways to creatively meet the needs of undecided students through specialized programs. These programs can be a way to meet the needs of large numbers of students and make effective use of limited resources. Further, specialized programs allow for high levels of student engagement in the career advising process by allowing students to gain information on themselves, academic majors, and potential careers through interaction with a variety of people and resources.

Major and career fairs can help undecided students explore available options on campus and learn more about how majors are related to the world of work.

Involving career services professionals and alumni in these fairs can broaden the focus beyond academic fields of study to include career information.

Information about academic programs can be disseminated through a variety of mechanisms. Departmental Web sites that include both academic and career information can assist students in considering a major from both perspectives. Departmental open houses provide an excellent forum where students can meet faculty, learn about academic options, and discuss career paths associated with degree programs. Similarly, workshops sponsored by academic departments can serve as introductions to programs of study. A coordinated campuswide approach to offering a comprehensive program of informational workshops and open houses could be offered prior to early registration periods and create a strong focus on exploring academic and career options.

Alumni can provide outstanding information that allows students to see how academic majors lead to careers. An alumni mentoring program can match students interested in a field of study with graduates in the same major working in different careers. Alumni speakers, panels, and networking events offer students the opportunity to meet alumni and learn about career options and pathways. Students often appreciate learning about majors and careers from persons who have walked in their shoes.

Online Career Information and Programs. The complexity of students' lives coupled with increasing reliance on technology leads many students to online programs and services. Serving undecided students through technology is gaining prominence on many campuses. Ball State University and Richard Stockton College of New Jersey provide two examples of how undecided students can be assisted through technology.

Ball State University's Quest program (http://www.bsu.edu/students/careers/quest/) is an online program that allows students to match their personality and interests to Ball State majors and careers. The program also identifies Ball State University courses that support further exploration and study of an academic major. Students can take an interest inventory, complete a commercial personality assessment, or begin by learning more about majors, careers, or workplace skills. The program is self-paced and provides information on how to access additional resources at the institution.

Similarly, Richard Stockton College of New Jersey offers students an online workbook for choosing a major (http://loki.stockton.edu/ ~ stk16973/pages/home.htm). Linked to the college career center's online career assessment tool, this workbook provides a thorough presentation and discussion on being undecided and exploring potential majors and careers. Students are asked to complete several reflective writings to prepare them for interpreting the results of a career assessment and meeting with an advisor. Information is presented on how to gather information on majors through workshops, informational interviewing, and talking with faculty.

Administrative Structures. Administrative structures are a consideration in serving undecided students. One structural way of meeting the needs of undecided students is to assign undecided students to advisors who have expertise in this area. This can be implemented through a special advising center for undecided students or by having specially trained advisors in a general advising center. Specialized advising centers for undecided students are identified by various names including University Division, University Studies Program, General Education Student Program, and Pre-Majors Advising (National Academic Advising Association, n.d.). In general, all provide students with access to advisors who have in-depth knowledge of career decision making, familiarity with a wide variety of academic and career resources, and skills to facilitate major and career exploration. On some campuses, undecided students are assigned to specific advisors in a general advising center (e.g., campuswide advising center, advising center in the largest academic school, school of liberal arts). If undecided students are served as part of a larger student population, it is important to ensure that undecided students feel supported and that their decision to engage in more exploration prior to committing to a major is celebrated, not minimized.

McCalla-Wriggins (2000) provided a thorough discussion of formal and informal structures to provide support for career advising. The most comprehensive and challenging of the organizational structures is a complete integration of academic advising and career services units. In this structure academic advisors and career counselors work in the same unit and may conduct both activities so that individual conversations with students involve decision making around academic planning and major and career options. This can be very fruitful for undecided students for whom the issues are very tightly connected. In addition, addressing both the academic and career development needs of undecided students highlights the importance of the holistic career-decision-making model. At Indiana University-Purdue University Indianapolis, this structure is implemented by having several academic advisors who serve jointly as career counselors. These advisors/career counselors bring expertise and experience on career planning to the entire unit; they are responsible for assisting other academic advisors in their continued understanding of career development. Joint academic advisors/career counselors are key members of the instructional team for first-year seminars for undecided students. Students are well-served by the seamless conversations and expertise of the staff in these positions.

Gordon (2007b) indicates that regardless of the administrative structure of academic advising and career counseling, the programs must focus on collaboration. A collaborative approach to serving both the academic and career planning needs of students will help ensure that students are engaged in holistic thinking about their future.

ENGAGING IN CAREER ADVISING FOR UNDECIDED STUDENTS

This chapter highlights the importance of providing career advising to undecided students of all types—from those who have not declared a major at matriculation to those who find themselves in situations requiring reconsideration of their original major and career goals. Advisors are well served by understanding the characteristics and types of undecided students and using this knowledge to engage students in appropriate conversations and interventions for career advising. Knowledge of the career decision-making process, curricula across majors, and general career information will ensure that advisors can assist students in thorough exploration of themselves, academic majors, and career opportunities. When working individually with students, advisors can apply developmental advising approaches and use the positive techniques offered by the appreciative advising approach. In addition to individual interventions, first-year seminar courses, career courses, and administrative structures can be designed to meet the unique needs of undecided students. The large numbers of students who will be undecided at some point in their college career, coupled with a rapidly changing world of work, require that advisors be adept in facilitating the career decision-making process with all students.

All advisors are strongly encouraged to become familiar with the nature of undecided students and career indecision. Further, advisors should be familiar with the resources on their campuses that support career decision making, including career counseling, psychological counseling, programs and services in academic departments, and experiential learning opportunities. Finally, advisors should develop a repertoire of questions that can serve to guide a student through an exploration of themselves, academic programs, and the world of work. Appendix C at the end of the book presents two cases that apply the concepts and content of this chapter.

References

Anderson, B. C., Creamer, D. C., & Cross, L. H. (1989). Undecided, multiple change, and decided students: How different are they? *NACADA Journal, 9*(1), 46–50.

Ashby, J. C., Wall, H. W., & Osipow, S. H. (1966). Vocational certainty and indecision in college freshmen. *The Personnel and Guidance Journal, 44*, 1037–1041.

Astin, A. W. (2007). *The American freshman: National norms for fall 2006.* Los Angeles: Higher Education Research Institute.

Atkinson, D. R., Morten, G., & Sue, D. W. (Eds.). (1993). *Counseling American minorities: A cross cultural perspective* (3rd ed.). Dubuque, IA: Brown.

Beatty, J. D. (1994). Advising special groups within the undecided student population. In V. Gordon (Ed.), *Issues in advising the undecided college student* (Monograph No. 15, pp. 67–83). Columbia, SC: University of South Carolina, National Resource Center for the Freshman Year Experience.

Belenky, M. F., Clinchy, B. M., Goldberer, N. R., & Tarule, J. M. (1986). *Women's ways of knowing: The development of self, voice, and mind.* New York: Basic Books.

Bloom, J. L., Hutson, B. L., & He, Y. (2008a). *The appreciative advising revolution.* Champaign, IL: Stipes Publishing.

Bloom, J. L., Hutson, B. L., & He, Y. (2008b). *How can you empower your students to optimize their educational opportunities?* Retrieved November 30, 2008, from http://www.appreciativeadvising.net

Bloom, J. L., & Martin, N. (2002, August 29). Incorporating appreciative inquiry into academic advising. *The Mentor: An Academic Advising Journal, 4*(3). Retrieved May 9, 2008, from http://www.psu.edu/dus/mentor

Bogenschutz, M. (1994). Career advising for the undecided student. In V. Gordon (Ed.), *Issues in advising the undecided college student* (Monograph No. 15, pp. 49–58). Columbia, SC: University of South Carolina, National Resource Center for the Freshman Year Experience.

Chickering, A. W., & Reisser, L. (1993). *Education and identity* (2nd ed.). San Francisco: Jossey-Bass.

D'Augelli, A. R. (1994). Identity development and sexual orientation: Toward a model of lesbian, gay, and bisexual development. In E. J. Trickett, R. J. Watts, & D. Birman (Eds.), *Human diversity: Perspectives on people in context* (pp. 312–333). San Francisco: Jossey-Bass.

Dennis, B. D. (2008). Retaining exploratory students: A comparison study of decided and undecided college students. *Dissertation Abstracts International, 68*(12-A), 4498.

Fralick, M. A. (1993). College success: A study of positive and negative attrition. *Community College Review, 20*(5), 29–39.

Fuqua, D. R. & Hartman, B. W. (1983). Differential diagnosis and treatment of career indecision. *The Personnel and Guidance Journal, 62,* 27–29.

Gordon, V. N. (1981). The undecided student: A developmental perspective. *The Personnel and Guidance Journal, 59,* 433–439.

Gordon, V. N. (1995a). Advising undecided first-year students. In M. L. Upcraft & G. L. Kramer (Eds.), *First-year academic advising patterns in the present, pathways to the future* (Monograph No. 18, pp. 93–100). Columbia, SC: University of South Carolina, National Resource Center for The Freshman Experience.

Gordon, V. N. (1995b). *The undecided college student: An academic and career advising challenge* (2nd ed.). Springfield, IL: Charles C. Thomas.

Gordon, V. N. (1998). Career decidedness types: A literature review. *The Career Development Quarterly, 46,* 386–403.

Gordon, V. N. (2006). *Career advising: An academic advisor's guide.* San Francisco: Jossey-Bass.

Gordon, V. N. (2007a). *The undecided college student: An academic and career advising challenge* (3rd ed.). Springfield, IL: Charles C. Thomas.

Gordon, V. N. (2007b). Undecided students: A special population. In L. Huff & P. Jordon (Eds.), *Advising special student populations: Adult learners, community college students, LGBTQ students, multicultural students, students on probation, undecided students* (Monograph No. 27, pp. 187–233). Manhattan, KS: NACADA.

Habley, W. R. (1994). Administrative approaches to advising undecided students. In V. Gordon (Ed.), *Issues in advising the undecided college student* (Monograph No. 15, pp. 17–23). Columbia, SC: University of South Carolina, National Resource Center for the Freshman Year Experience.

Hull-Banks, E., Robinson Kurpius, S.E., Befort, C., Sollenberger, S., Foley Nicpon, M., & Huser, L. (2005). Career goals and retention-related factors among college freshmen. *Journal of Career Development, 32,* 16–30.

Larson, L. M., Heppner, P. P., Ham, T., & Dugan, K. (1988). Investigating multiple subtypes of career indecision through cluster analysis. *Journal of Counseling Psychology*, *35*, 439–446.

Lewallen, W. C. (1993). The impact of being "undecided" on college-student persistence. *Journal of College Student Development*, *34*, 103–112.

Lewallen, W. C. (1994). A profile of undecided college students. In V. Gordon (Ed.), *Issues in advising the undecided college student* (Monograph No. 15, pp. 5–16). Columbia, SC: University of South Carolina, National Resource Center for the Freshman Year Experience.

Mayhall, J., & Burg, J. E. (2002). Solution-focused advising with undecided students. *NACADA Journal*, *22*(1), 76–82.

McCalla-Wriggins, B. (2000). Integrating academic advising and career and life planning. In V. N. Gordon & W. R. Habley (Eds.), *Academic advising: A comprehensive handbook* (pp. 162–176). San Francisco: Jossey-Bass.

National Academic Advising Association. (n.d.). *Frequently asked questions from Academic advising: Collaborations to foster retention*. Retrieved October 19, 2008, from the NACADA Clearinghouse of Academic Advising Resources Web site: http://www.nacada.ksu.edu/Clearinghouse/AdvisingIssues/adv_undeclared.htm

Nauta, M. M. (2007). Assessing college students' satisfaction with their academic majors. *Journal of Career Assessment*, *15*, 446–462.

Newman, J. L., Fuqua, D. R., & Minger, C. (1990). Further evidence for the use of career subtypes in defining career status. *The Career Development Quarterly*, *39*, 178–188.

O'Banion, T. (1972). An academic advising model. *Junior College Journal*, *42* (6), 62–69.

Odom, J. E. (2005). A comprehensive program to facilitate the career development of first-year undecided students. In P. A. Gore, Jr. (Ed.), *Facilitating the career development of students in transition* (Monograph No. 43, pp. 123–135). Columbia, SC: University of South Carolina, National Resource Center for The First-Year Experience and Students in Transition.

Osipow, S. H., Carney, C. G., Winer, J., Yanico, B., & Koschier, M. (1976). *The career decision scale* (3rd rev.). Columbus, OH: Marathon Consulting and Press.

Pascarella, E. T., & Terenzini, P. T. (2005). *How college affects students: A third decade of research*. San Francisco: Jossey-Bass.

Perry, W. (1970). *Forms of intellectual and ethical development in the college years*. New York: Holt, Rinehart & Winston.

Phinney, J. S. (1990). Ethnic identity in adolescents and adults: Review of research. *Psychological Bulletin*, *180*, 499–514.

Savickas, M. L. (1995). Constructivist counseling for career indecision. *The Career Development Quarterly*, *43*, 363–373.

Savickas, M. L., & Jarjoura, D. (1991). The career decision scale as a type indicator. *Journal of Counseling Psychology*, *38*, 85–90.

Steele, G. E. (1994). Major-changers: A special type of undecided student. In V. Gordon (Ed.), *Issues in advising the undecided college student* (Monograph No. 15, pp. 85–92). Columbia, SC: University of South Carolina, National Resource Center for the Freshman Year Experience.

Steele, G. (2003). A research-based approach to working with undecided students: A case study illustration. *NACADA Journal, 23*(1&2), 10–20.

Steele, G. E., Kennedy, G. J., & Gordon, V. N. (1992). The retention of major changers: A longitudinal study. *Journal of College Student Development, 34*, 58–62.

Theophilides, C., Terenzini, P., & Lorang, W. (1984). Freshmen and sophomore experiences and changes in major field. *Review of Higher Education, 7*, 261–298.

Ting, S. R. (1997). Estimating academic success in the 1st year of college for specially admitted white students: A model combining cognitive and psychosocial predictors. *Journal of College Student Development, 38*, 401–409.

Titley, R. M., Titley, B. S., & Wolf, W. (1976). The major changers: Continuity and discontinuity in the career process. *Journal of Vocational Behavior, 8*, 105–111.

CHAPTER ELEVEN

Career Advising with Specific Student Populations

Peggy Jordan, Terri Blevins

In institutions of higher learning, effective academic advisors are skilled in weaving career advising into academic advising. According to Burton Nelson (2006), "Content of the advising sessions can be considered bi-faceted: (1) educational/academic planning, and (2) career/life planning" (p. 1). In addition to focusing on these areas, it is important for advisors to consider the diversity of student populations in providing career advising. These special populations of students may share similar backgrounds, characteristics, needs, and propensities. Some students may belong to two or more special groups of students. Awareness of the characteristics of these groups can help advisors develop specific programs to assist these students with career and academic planning. However, it must be remembered that each student has individual characteristics and needs that always take precedence over general characteristics of a group. Awareness of commonalities within special student groups simply offers advisors a beginning framework from which to build their working relationship with the student. In providing career advising to students, any student, regardless of the specific population to which he or she belongs, may fit at any point of the continuum from undecided to decided.

Although there are numerous special student populations, this chapter outlines the characteristics and needs, challenges, and recommendations for career advising with the following: military students and students in military families, honors students, underprepared students, second-year students, adult learners, transfer students, and student athletes. In addition, all students fall into a cohort of individuals from their generation, and these cohorts may approach college and careers differently.

GENERATIONAL ISSUES

There are differences among generations that are important to consider in advising students. Coomes and DeBard (2004) stated, "each generation has its own biography, a biography that tells the story of how the personality of the generation is shaped and how this subsequently shapes other generations" (p. 8). A brief discussion is presented of the characteristics of three generations, and how these characteristics might affect the career advising when working with members of each group. The focus is on millennial students because it is the largest generational group currently attending colleges and universities (Howe & Strauss, 2000).

Baby Boomers

Born in the years between 1942 and 1960, Baby Boomers were born at the end of World War II. Primarily raised by stay-at-home moms, they grew up in the age of civil rights and women's rights. Although they had a great deal of homework, they had almost unlimited time for playing outside and limited time watching television. This particular group is very materialistic and highly educated. "It was members of this group, as returning adult learners, who were responsible for significant enrollment growth" (Coomes & DeBard, 2004, p. 11) in higher education. Many boomers came to college in the 1960s, and while they were protesting outside the classroom, they were also focused on learning inside the classroom (El-Shamy, 2004). Boomers like a linear approach; they like to focus on content. Boomers work hard, for long hours, and they are very process-focused; they strive for personal gratification. As students, boomers will be likely to want a lot for their money, expect quality education, and expect a challenging curriculum.

Generation X

Generation X, born between 1961 and 1981, is the most racially diverse in United States history (Sutaria, 2007). They are a skeptical group, have little faith in institutions, and are anti-government and anti-authority. Members of Generation X view themselves as consumers, and they want college to be convenient, be flexible, and offer online services. They are very self-reliant, cynical, and impatient. In addition, those who make up Generation X may lack interpersonal skills, and want relevance in coursework. They also want a nice balance between work and school and life. This generation also feels the pressure of a lot of debt and a lack of opportunity in the job market, exacerbated by Baby Boomers retiring later in life and the instability of the job market.

Millennial Generation

The current generation of young adults is different in many ways from previous generations. Known as "Millennials," the generation born between 1979 and 1994 is a very large generation, only slightly smaller than the Baby Boomers.

They have come of age watching current events literally as they happen. They have protective parents who are actively involved in their academic and career and social success (often referred to as "helicopter parents"). Millennials typically have a multitude of experiences and adventures, but have most likely not held a job.

Communication among and with millennials is very different from earlier generations. Millenials are familiar with and use many electronic tools—Google, Facebook, Yahoo, e-mail, text messaging, and instant messenger. Most millenials cannot remember a time before Internet.

Millennials expect a large variety of learning options and more services from institutions—and they expect them quickly (Howe & Strauss, 2000). On the whole, millennials prefer to learn by doing and interacting; they almost never read the directions. In the academic world, they are more engaged by games, simulations, case studies, and hands-on experiences. Millenials want flexible time, convenience, and customization for them personally. In the academic world, they want continuous monitoring and coaching, not assessment and feedback. They have no tolerance for delays and expect things instantly.

Millenials also tend to be motivated, good at multitasking, and "prolific communicators" (Howe & Strauss, 2000). They not only like video supplements to the curriculum, they expect them; conversely, they also like and expect face-to-face time with professors and advisors (Sweeney, 2006). They are, as a group, hard-working and interested in helping others. According to Howe and Strauss (2000) "Millenial students are (1) conventionally motivated, (2) structured rule followers, (3) protected and sheltered, (4) cooperative and team-oriented, (5) talented achievers, and (6) confident and optimistic about their futures" (p. 23). They are often less mature than students of 10 years ago, because they are close to and rely very heavily on their parents. They can also have a difficult time making a decision, because making a decision means giving up the alternative, something millenials hate to do.

The implications for career advising are that millenials expect advisors to be knowledgeable about careers and the process of selecting a career, and be able to provide data, resources, and information to both millenials and their parents. Advisors must also be able to communicate policies to millenials and their parents. These students will be interested in service learning, community projects, and mentoring programs. Advisors can encourage millenials to explore careers by shadowing experiences, volunteer projects, and internships. Millenials will expect quick responses to questions, and seem to need a lot of feedback; they expect access to services and information 24/7.

MILITARY STUDENTS AND STUDENTS IN MILITARY FAMILIES

Military students include those who are veterans or on active military duty, and many complete courses online from distant locations, including Iraq. The group also includes spouses and dependents of active military members.

Students who are veterans of war zones in Iraq and Afghanistan are usually more mature than traditional-age students. They have endured more hardship and witnessed more suffering and death than most students. These experiences can make it challenging to relate and fit in to a relatively carefree college environment (Ely, 2008). According to Rocker (2007), advisors may initially see these students as very goal oriented; however, the dropout rate of veterans is high. The reason for dropping out is that veterans, although they want a degree, may not know how to accomplish that goal. Ely (2008) noted that veterans develop highly specialized skills in the military; however, they often do not know how to translate those skills into a career or degree plan. Advisors can help veterans make that transition.

The population of active duty military personnel is estimated to be 1.6 million, with over 1.9 million family members in the United States (Hoshmand & Hoshmand, 2007). The 1.02 million individuals in the Reserve and National Guard and their families, who total 1.15 million, make a sizable population. Since the majority of military members are younger than age 35 (Hoshmand & Hoshmand, 2007), many of them seek courses and degrees through colleges and universities. Students who are on active military duty may choose to complete courses online from distant locations. Spouses and dependents of active military members may either enroll in on-campus or online classes.

Challenges

The primary challenges for military students and those working with military students are their frequent moves and deployments. The General Accounting Office (2001) estimated military families relocate on average every one to two years. This makes it difficult for advisors to establish relationships with military students. At many higher education institutions, there is a relative lack of interest in military students because they are seen as a transient population. These are students who may not be at the same institution from the start to finish of their degree. There may also be hesitation to be involved with military students because of ideological ambivalence toward war (Hoshmand & Hoshmand, 2007).

Many states have articulation agreements within their states and a few states have articulation agreements with neighboring states. There is no national articulation agreement, however, which means military students have no guarantee the courses they successfully complete at one institution will transfer to a subsequent institution. Further, they have no idea if the courses required for a degree plan from one institution will even apply toward their degree at another institution. Since military family members frequently have no idea where they will be relocated, these students do not have the option of contacting potential transfer institutions to plan their degrees. Advisors can still support and encourage military students' career exploration. At the same time, advisors can offer general information about the types of courses usually required for various degrees.

Career Advising of Military Students and Students of Military Families

Support groups are helpful for students who are in the military or have family members in the military because their circumstances are often unique. It is difficult for someone not associated with the military to identify with the special challenges they face. Sponsoring or at least visiting a support group is a way advisors can develop a better understanding and connection to military students. Students benefit when colleges and universities have advisors with information about the resources available for military students. Because these resources are subject to change, advisors must stay current with the changes. Career advising of veterans and their families without acknowledging the hurdles these students face can undermine the trust military students have in their advisor.

Because students serving in the military may be deployed to distant locations, having a connection to an advisor for career advising may help them persist as they make use of many of the online courses available at colleges and universities. Career information and career exploration tools should also be provided online by the institution. A dedicated online advisor can be an essential resource to keep online military students on track with their academic goals and to aid in resolving administrative problems these students cannot handle with a trip to campus. Hoshmand and Hoshmand (2007) referred to a "continuum of care" for military families that includes collaboration among community agencies and professionals. This "continuum of care" can be extended to the college or university community, in which offices, including career and academic advising, collaborate to meet the needs of military students and their families.

A Veterans Transition Center located at the University of Minnesota (see http://blog.lib.umn.edu/vtc/vtc) offers veterans a friendly atmosphere where they can talk with other veterans about college and military experiences. While helping veterans acclimate to the college climate, they are also provided mentors within their field of study and have opportunities to network and obtain information about future employment. Another program called "Boots to Books" is offered at Citrus College in Glendora, California (Fisher, 2008). It is a class taken for academic credit that teaches military students and their family members how to transfer their military experiences into positive choices in civilian life.

HONORS STUDENTS

Honors students have been found to be more prepared for class, ask more questions, volunteer for community service, participate in co-curricular activities, have jobs on campus, be more conscientious, and be more open to new experiences as compared to non-honors students (Long & Lange, 2002). Honors students may be on scholarship for exceptional ability in academics, athletics, fine arts, or leadership. They may not have scholarships but are highly motivated by academic challenges. Honors students may have average ability but because of exceptional effort have been successful in rigorous courses that require additional academic effort. There is tremendous pressure on honors students to succeed. Sometimes this is self-imposed, but with some honors students the pressure is exerted by parents, teachers, and even advisors (Digby, 2007). Parents for a variety of reasons may have high aspirations for their children and place on them inordinate demands directly or subtly. Professors may have high expectations for students with high ability because students' success makes the program or the institution look good. Even advisors may lack sensitivity when honors students do not live up to their potential.

While diverse in most every other way, many honors students have in common multipotentiality (Blackburn & Erickson, 1986; Greene, 2006; McDonald, 2003), the ability to accomplish and take pleasure in many things. They often have numerous options both in ability and in interest. Although they may be able to succeed in multiple areas, they may lack direction and have difficulty narrowing their choices. McDonald (2003) stressed that honors students are no different developmentally than other students and must be encouraged to struggle with the same developmental tasks as their age mates.

Challenges

Honors students may seem to have limitless potential, but they often have multiple and sometimes incompatible goals (McDonald, 2003). College students who go to their advisor saying, "I want to be a neurosurgeon, an architect, and an opera singer" will probably be met with a deep sigh. It is sometimes difficult for bright, high-achieving students to limit themselves to one or two goals. Even more difficult for them may be to choose their most important goal out of a list of 20 to 50 things they want to accomplish. For students who have been told most of their life they can do anything, they may need a time to grieve over not being able to do everything.

Too often honors students are directed toward a limited number of career options that are prestigious and require a high level of academic ability to achieve (Colangelo, 2003). These include medicine, engineering, law, and business. Some honors students are best served by choosing fields of study that allow ample time for them to devote free time to their myriad interests.

Consider the case of Sara, who was a student who seemed to excel in all she did. She was exceptionally gifted in math and science. Sara was also a competitive gymnast, a creative writer, and a talented visual artist. She was passionate about a variety of political topics. Sara had very supportive parents who sold their home and bought a smaller one to support Sara's talents. They were excited about her prospects in the medical field. After two semesters in college, Sara decided to pursue a bachelor's degree in visual art. Talking with her advisor, Sara confessed that she disliked math and science. She also resented the time required to earn superior grades in such classes. Sara longed for time to tackle new challenges. She had no interest in a medical career but was afraid of betraying her parents if she followed her interest in visual art.

After listening to Sara, her advisor encouraged Sara to share her feelings with her parents. It sounded as though Sara's parents had always tried to follow Sara's interests, rather than lead them. Sara had already visited medical facilities to observe the work setting and talked with medical doctors in practice and in research settings before coming to her advisor for help with her career. She also had a mentor in her newly chosen field of visual art. Sara needed encouragement to trust herself. She also needed coaching on how to talk with her parents, who were very supportive of her new career decision.

Perfectionism, often a characteristic of honors students, can be a positive or a negative attribute (Delisle, 1986). When perfectionism propels students toward mastery of material and exemplary accomplishments, it is a powerfully positive trait. However, when perfectionism drives a student to constant dissatisfaction with his or her own work, it impedes progress and is debilitating. Not making a mistake becomes the goal, rather than high performance. Perfectionism can also affect career decisions when honors students avoid challenging courses for fear of earning a grade of B or strive to make the "perfect" career decision and are plagued with self-doubt. It is up to the advisor to help honors students adequately explore careers.

As an example, consider Greg, who was a sophomore, had changed majors twice, and was anxious about his inability to settle on a career goal or major. He had explored careers ranging from construction engineering, nursing, secondary education, and medical school. Greg told his advisors he had interests in so many things it was impossible to commit to one career. His advisor assured Greg that making a decision now would not rule out additional decisions in the future. His advisor also talked with Greg about how his interests could tie into multiple careers. Science and math were the common ties that allowed Greg to chose a major but keep his options open so he could do a variety of things in the future. Advisors can help perfectionistic honors students' progress by reassuring them that no career decision is unchangeable. Letting these students know they continue to have options can give them the courage to make a decision.

It is also important to mention some cultures may not interpret high academic achievement in the same manner as the majority population. In particular high-achieving Black students often feel the need to hide their intelligence to fit in socially with peers (Fries-Britt, 2000). At other times, Black students may find it necessary to prove they are smart because of biased thinking from the majority population. It is especially important for Black honors students to encounter peers with whom they can identify and enjoy similar interests. According to Fries-Britt (2000), "Faculty can be instrumental in helping black students blend their racial and intellectual identities by creating conditions in and outside of the classroom that reinforce and support the development of a strong sense of self"(p. 63). On the other hand, Asian honors students may be more likely to follow career advice of parents or other family members because they belong to a collectivistic culture (Santrock, 2007). These students may value decisions that serve the family, so their decisions may be strongly influenced not by individual goals but by family goals or needs.

Career Advising of Honors Students

Although honors students may enter college with career goals in mind, career advising should not be dismissive of these students' needs. Inquiry concerning how decisions about career were made, whose guidance was received, and what exploration the student made are all important areas to cover and to insure they do not foreclose too early (Greene, 2006). Career decisions, especially of honors students, should be couched in terms of a lifelong process. Honors students should be guided to think in terms of their values, personality traits, leisure activities, balancing multiple roles, and the fact that they will likely see hundreds of new occupations emerge in their lifetime.

Although traditional assessment tools may be used with honors students, advisors should also encourage self-reflection and experiential learning. Mentors should be obtained to encourage the widest range of exploration possible. Honors students must also learn how to prioritize their interests so they can begin to make appropriate choices concerning career, major, and courses (Greene, 2006).

In career advising of honors students, it is helpful to provide small group career discussions for honors students as these students are often struggling with similar issues and can benefit from hearing how their peers resolve some of these dilemmas. Also, encouraging career exploration and having access to the most current changes in occupational trends and employment opportunities can be helpful to honors students. Since honors students are, at times, behind their peers in social development, being familiar with students' identity development can be helpful in working with the students. In addition, being knowledgeable of this can be useful in helping students separate appropriately from parental directives.

UNDERPREPARED STUDENTS

Underprepared students may lack academic preparation in math, reading, or writing (Makela, 2006). This may occur for a variety of reasons. Some students attend secondary schools that are not financially able to offer college preparatory classes. Other students attend schools that afford high-quality college preparatory classes, but the students did not apply themselves. Some students are adults who did well in college preparatory classes, but because of time, have forgotten pertinent information. Still other students deal with specific learning disabilities that interfere with one or more areas of academic performance.

Many underprepared students start their higher education at a community college, because almost all community colleges offer developmental courses in reading, writing, and math (Kozeracki & Brooks, 2006). According to Byrd and MacDonald (2005), 41% of students entering community colleges and 29% of all students entering college are underprepared in one or more basic skill areas of reading, writing, or math. Although underprepared students are as diverse as their reasons for underpreparedness, Johannessen (2003) reported that disproportionately high numbers of underprepared students come from low socioeconomic status (SES) families, ethnic minorities, and linguistic minority families. One explanation for this is that low SES and minority students often attend underfunded elementary and secondary schools with outdated equipment, a shortage of text books, and run-down buildings (Berk, 2007). These students are also placed in lower academic tracks by the time they reach junior high school. Dobelle (2006) noted that students' readiness for college is positively correlated with the wealth of their home communities. Students who attend poorer elementary and secondary schools not only are less likely to have parents who attended college, they also more often had teachers who displayed a lowered expectation for their success.

Nonacademic characteristics of underprepared students include lack of study skills, low self-esteem, and low self-regulatory strategies (Makela, 2006). Grimes (1997) found underprepared students had a more external locus of control, meaning they perceived themselves to have less control over their environments and felt less responsibility for their actions. She also found underprepared students took less advantage of free tutorial services and demonstrated less persistence in second semester completion than their more prepared college classmates. In addition, underprepared students may not be economically prepared for college. If financial aid is delayed or if they have unforeseen financial hardships (e.g., car trouble, medical bills, increase in the cost of gasoline), these students may see no other option than withdrawing from college.

Challenges

One of the biggest challenges for underprepared students is their low academic self-esteem. Not only do they lack confidence in their own success, they also compare their accomplishments with others and lower their expectations further (House, 1995). These students also lack the foundation skills required in the college curriculum (Tritelli, 2003). This may add as much as two full semesters of coursework in pre-college level courses to their degree. If underprepared students are not actively engaged in career exploration, they may have difficulty persisting until they are enrolled in courses that actually apply to a degree. It is essential for advisors to help underprepared students focus on and develop career goals.

In addition, underprepared students often have adult responsibilities of work, family, and other activities that demand their time and resources (Smittle, 2003). They can easily become overwhelmed with life issues competing for their time and money. Students are well served by advisors who continually remind students of the long-term effect of their academic decisions.

Sometimes underprepared students' initial career goal is unrealistic. Interaction with an advisor can help redirect them and keep them from dropping out of college. Collaboration between academic advisors and developmental teachers, as part of career advising, can help students set goals and make connections between the classes they are taking and their career goals.

Career Advising of Underprepared Students

It is up to advisors to reinforce skills underprepared students have and teach skills needed to be successful in college. Career advising with underprepared students early in their academic career will assist students in goal setting and exploration of career fields. Some underprepared students are motivated to attend college because they want to improve their own lives and the future of their children. By showing students the impact their behavior has on their grades, knowledge, and overall lives, academic advisors can begin to help underprepared students take control of their future. Career advising should be initiated early and often to influence students who may not otherwise think about careers until much later. Making even tentative decisions about careers can also help underprepared students persist in college (Byrd & McDonald, 2005).

Consider Lucy, a first-semester Native American student, who saw her advisor when she wanted to withdraw from a developmental math class. Although Lucy's grades were mostly Bs, by the tenth week of a 16-week course she was convinced she would fail the course. Lucy explained she was told by teachers in elementary school she could not do math. She had subsequently avoided math classes as much as possible. Lucy's advisor talked with her about her goals. Lucy wanted a better life for herself and her future children than she had experienced. Her parents were laborers, and Lucy had no idea what career path she wanted to follow. Her advisor assured Lucy she would need her current math class for any career she pursued. Her advisor recommended that Lucy visit a number of student clubs on campus and take career assessments. She also introduced Lucy to a peer mentoring program with several active Native American students.

It is imperative for advisors providing career advising and developmental teachers to work together. Information about goal setting, careers, and majors should be incorporated into the developmental coursework, with advisors presenting to developmental classes and developmental teachers making reading and writing assignments in areas of career exploration. Outreach to this group of students is important because they are less likely to seek career information. All students need to see a relationship between the courses they are taking and the goals that brought them to higher education. For underprepared students, those goals may be ill defined. They may see education as a way to make more money, improve their lifestyle, or get out of an unsatisfying job. They often have not focused specifically on a career. Helping students develop and clarify their goals and develop plans to meet their goals is an important part of career advising for underprepared students.

Underprepared students also carry with them many nonacademic problems (Smittle, 2003). Their affective needs as well as cognitive needs must be addressed. If the needs are greater than the teacher or advisor can manage, resources must be available to refer students for further assistance (e.g., counselor or psychologist on campus or in the community). Our Lady of the Lake University, in San Antonio, Texas, received a grant in 2006 to offer personal coaching services to all first-year and transfer students, many of whom were

underprepared for college (Farrell, 2007). The goal was to motivate and counsel students, including helping students navigate the public welfare system
or intervening with parents who did not understand the financial resources
needed to complete a college degree. According to Farrell (2007), "During
weekly meetings, coaches encourage students and help them connect those
goals to their daily habits and actions. They often ask questions to determine
what roadblocks the students might face" (p. 45). Personal coaching and
career advising can play an integral role in helping students overcome barriers
that prevent them from reaching their goals.

In career advising of underprepared students, it is imperative that advisors
working with underprepared students focus on the whole student's needs and
goals rather than just academic needs. Helping underprepared students make connections to resources on campus, and encouraging students to join campus clubs
and attend college functions, especially in areas the student expressed career
interest, can be helpful in their career and academic development. In addition,
academic advisors should be proactive in setting up appointments with developmental students to address students' career needs. Advisors can also teach students to take personal responsibility for academic and career decisions. Finally,
academic advisors can use community resources as well as college resources to
provide career exploration opportunities for underprepared students.

SECOND-YEAR STUDENTS

First-year students have been investigated and discussed in the literature
for many years. Within the last five to ten years there has been a growing
awareness of the need for special programs for sophomore students. Lipka
(2006) noted that the "sophomore slump" is a 50-year-old diagnosis that has
no widely prescribed treatment. Gahagan and Hunter (2006) described the
sophomore slump as a time when second-year students "lack motivation, feel
disconnected, and flounder academically" (p. 18). Gump (2007) described
the sophomore slump as "decreasing interest, declining grades, increasing
absences, and ultimately, dropping out altogether" (p. 111).

Graunke and Woosley (2005) found two issues linked to academic success
of second-year students. These were commitment to an academic major and
satisfaction with their interactions with faculty members. Second-year students who were uncertain about their goals and academic major had lower
grade point averages and were more likely to drop out of college (Schaller,
2005). Students who are completely undecided after their first year of college have difficulty sustaining their focus on another year of general education requirements. Gump (2007) proposed that the goals of general education
courses may actually exacerbate some of the negative effects some sophomores experience. Students often see general education as irrelevant and are
less likely to be engaged in those courses than in courses selected based on
interest. Added to that is the fact that many students delay taking general
education courses they perceive as most difficult until their sophomore year.

If students are able to connect a rationale to successful completion of general education courses (e.g., like they are a step closer to meeting major/career goals), they are more likely to persist in college. When advising students it is important to check where they are in the process of career exploration and decision making. Students who have completed two semesters of college should be strongly encouraged, if not required, to visit the career center or meet with an academic advisor for career advising.

Challenges

According to Evenbeck, Boston, DuVivier, and Hallberg (2000), sophomore slump is a stronger factor in attrition in colleges that have less selective admissions. These institutions also have lower graduation rates. Since most community colleges have open admissions, they would be expected to have the largest populations of sophomore students who become disengaged from education. Gump (2007) identified challenges with second-year students as lack of interest, falling grades, absences, and disengagement from class even when present. Another issue faced by second-year students is conflict over identity (Tobolowsky & Cox, 2007). While the first year of college is filled with the new experiences and the excitement of being away from home and family, the second year of college may have more pressure and anxiety about commitments. Schaller (2007) offered the following insight on college sophomores: "individuals deconstruct their past definitions of self but have yet to construct a new definition of self" (p. 7). Second-year students are faced with deciding on careers and majors, values, and lifestyle preferences. It is up to advisors to provide these students with avenues of exploration. Boivin, Fountain, and Baylis (2000) described the sophomore slump as largely a developmental issue. Advisors must be knowledgeable of student development theories in order to discern where a student's development lies and what experiences may enhance a healthy transition to the next level.

Career Advising for Second-Year Students

Although most colleges and universities have freshman orientation programs, few have special programs for sophomores. Keeping students connected to college through the sophomore year is important. This can be initiated through a sophomore trip or dinner, having sophomore officers on a leadership council, creating publications specific to sophomores, or having peer mentors for second-year students. Every institution is different and has its own unique needs. Of the institutions offering second-year programs, Tobolowsky and Cox (2007) found that most focused on career planning and major selection. Talking directly with students is the most effective way to determine the specific services second-year students need.

As an example of a second-year student, consider Kelly who completed her first year of college as a music major. She struggled her sophomore year as she looked more closely at music as a career. Kelly changed to a special admissions program in speech pathology but was underprepared to meet the stringent admission requirements. She was frustrated and, as a result, talked to her advisor about dropping out of college. Her advisor talked with Kelly about the things she liked to do as well as her areas of interest. Kelly enjoyed young children, and had considered entering elementary education. She decided against it because of the low pay and perceived lack of advancement potential. Her advisor was able to share with Kelly additional career avenues stemming from elementary education, including school counselor, school administrator, school psychometrist, school psychologist, and speech pathologist. Kelly's advisor suggested elementary education could be a way to strengthen Kelly's grade point average and work experience. In addition, it could help finance her ultimate goal of a master's degree in speech pathology.

A national survey was conducted in 2005 to learn about and understand specific programs being offered to sophomores (Tobolowsky & Cox, 2007). Of the 382 institutions polled, 36 reported sophomore initiatives. Several colleges have sophomore mentors or dedicated sophomore advisors. Beloit College developed one of the first sophomore-year initiative programs (Flanagan, 2007). It was built on the foundation of their first-year program, but allowed students to work more independently than first-year students. It includes a Major Exploration and Declaration Fair in which student opportunities are highlighted, including internships, field experiences, and domestic and study abroad programs. Colorado College in Colorado Springs, Colorado, developed a program titled Sophomore Jump (Stockenberg, 2007). The advising program was enhanced for sophomores to make sure they set goals and were ready to declare majors appropriate to those goals. Career advising raises questions to stimulate students to think about how their academic plan relates to their work and personal lives. Reflection is also considered very important for these students. Existing programs already available on campus are specifically packaged for second-year students. A faculty-sophomore dinner series was initiated during which featured faculty members engaged sophomores in conversation about careers and majors.

In career advising of second-year students, it is important to have an understanding of the normal career development of second-year students to stimulate and enhance their development. In addition, offering focused career information and exploration can enhance the career and academic planning of second-year students. As part of career advising, second-year students can benefit from opportunities to interact with faculty members outside of class so they can develop mentoring relationships with faculty members in the students' major academic area. Finally, opportunities can be provided for second-year students to learn about their identity development and ways to use this knowledge to enhance their career development.

ADULT STUDENTS

Adult students are growing in numbers across college campuses, and are described as learners who either delayed entry into higher education or have been away from formal education for at least two years. Many institutions are using age 25 and older as a basis for defining adult students (Eriksen et al., 1986). According to the *Digest of Educational Statistics* (Plisko, 2007), 38.7% or almost 7 million students enrolled in postsecondary institutions are 25 years old or older. From 1990 to 2005, there was an 18% increase in enrollment of students over age 25 and older. According to Brown (2002),

> There are several trends that are responsible for the growing numbers of adult students. The linear life course—education, work, retirement—is increasingly rare as people change jobs, retrain voluntarily or involuntarily, and enter the workforce at various times. In addition, the changing workplace—by now a familiar litany of economic, demographic, organizational, and social changes— has created the need to develop life-long learning programs that meet the needs of learners in a kaleidoscope of contexts. (p. 68)

The workplace is changing rapidly, and adults can no longer spend an entire career in one organization. Also, early retirement can result in a career change, as many adults live longer and are in better health and want to continue to work (Brown, 2002). In addition to this, there are many life changes that may stimulate adults to return to higher education.

Adult students are a very diverse group, at very different stages of life, and they present many unique challenges for academic advisors. Adult students may be women, returning to college after raising a family; others may be displaced workers, who need to transition "from the industrial to the information age" (Bland, 2004, p. 6). Still others may be retiring from one career and anticipating another career. Some are adults who could not afford college when they were younger and are seeking to "enhance their skills and abilities" (Bland, 2004, p. 6) or seeking to fulfill a lifelong dream of obtaining a college education. Or they may be motivated to return to college due to a "nonevent" (e.g., a promotion that did not happen, a job they did not get, which went to a less experienced but more educated colleague) (Schlossberg, 1984).

Challenges

Consider Andrea's situation as she is in her advisor's office for their initial appointment. Andrea tells the advisor that she wants to major in business or something "marketable." She left college, she says, after two years because of a marriage and an unplanned pregnancy. Her baby is now in school, leaving Andrea anxious to resume and complete her college education. The advisor looks at Andrea's transcript and comments that Andrea will need to complete some additional prerequisites before enrolling in the upper division business classes. She gives Andrea a list of these classes, and then notices Andrea's expression. Andrea comments that these classes sound really boring. The advisor gives Andrea a copy of the course schedule for the semester, and asks which classes sound interesting to Andrea. Andrea points to a literature class, several American Studies classes, and a history class. The advisor notes that none of those classes will apply to her business degree. At this point, the advisor decides to have a discussion with Andrea about her career interests to see if they can find a major that is a better fit for Andrea. In this discussion, the advisor realizes that Andrea is more interested in a liberal arts degree, but that Andrea cannot determine how that degree would eventually get her a job. Andrea states that she cannot really afford to go to college just for the "fun of it" but would at least like to take classes that are interesting to her. Andrea and the advisor discuss the various skills developed in liberal arts classes, and the kinds of occupations that might be open to someone with a degree in American Studies or English.

On one hand, it would seem that adult learners, being older and having been in the workplace with some life experiences, would have a good working knowledge of careers and the career planning process, and would have very specific career goals. However, just the opposite seems to be the case. Hughey and Hunt (2006) noted that most adults are "pre-occupationally illiterate, meaning that they have a knowledge of only a small percentage of existing occupations in the current job market" (p. 1). They also may not be aware of new and emerging job trends and opportunities. Consequently, it is important to give adult learners information on the current job market to enhance their knowledge of the options and opportunities available to them.

Also, many adult students may have entered the job market at a young age, instead of going to college, or after leaving college without finishing a degree. They may have had little opportunity to explore career options, but may have simply fallen into or settled for a job. They may have had little or no opportunity to assess their own skills, interests, abilities, and strengths, and how these factors relate to career satisfaction. Opportunities to spend time in self-reflection and to participate in self-assessment exercises may affect their career choices and area of study.

Adult students have responsibilities they must balance against the demands of education. Adult students have numerous characteristics that advisors might categorize as risk factors (e.g., lack of time, lack of money, lack of information, scheduling problems, child-care issues, being away from formal education for a time, and transportation problems). Many are also working at least part-time while attending class. They may be experiencing some degree of anxiety related to their return to the classroom; often, they are afraid that they will be slower than their younger counterparts or that they will lack skills related to technology or research. These issues can create huge barriers to learning. Advisors can be instrumental to adult learners' success by making sure students are connected to campus and community services. Advisors further strengthen this tie by helping adult learners associate their current sacrifices and challenges to achieving their career and life goals.

Career Advising for Adult Students

To facilitate career advising with adult students, advisors need to understand adult students' motivation for enrolling in higher education, and, to the extent possible or desired by students, assist them in addressing the challenges to remaining enrolled. Career change is one of the most common reasons that adults return to higher education (Walther & Ritchie, 1998). Advisors need to be knowledgeable about emerging careers and job opportunities, and be able to assist adult students in locating and making effective use of good, concise, concrete information about resources available to them. Advisors working with adult students should be aware of the "constant change and uncertainty" (Kerka, 1995, p. 5) in the workplace and the impact of that change on their adult students.

Academic advisors need to be prepared to work with adult students on finding a major, and helping them understand how their degree will be useful in the workplace. Many adult students may want to pursue a major because that major has known career opportunities; however, the subject matter may or may not be of interest. Or they may be decided on a career but have no idea about the majors that would lend themselves to the career. Helping adult students see and understand the wide range of opportunities for a variety of majors may be relevant to them. Advisors can assist adult students to understand the difference between education and job training which may also help the adult students find that path to career satisfaction. It may be important to help adult students see how a combination of experience and education can help them, and how their experience and skills, coupled with the requirements of their major, can translate to other careers. Advisors need to be familiar with and utilize a variety of career inventories that can assist adult students in discovering their strengths, interests, values, and abilities or refer to professionals on campus.

In addition to career issues, advisors may need to work with adult students to help them find a balance in their responsibilities of work, classes, and family, and be able to help their adult students find appropriate resources to address and manage these issues. Because adult students are more likely to be nontraditional students and live off campus, and thus spend less time on campus, they will need opportunities to find a sense of community and involvement on the campus. They may also need assistance in managing and understanding the culture of the institution.

In career advising of adult students, it may be helpful to assist adult students to reduce or minimize the impact of barriers and challenges to students' success. This could be accomplished, in part, by assisting adult students to find and use resources to address a variety of issues that potentially have an impact on their education (e.g., time and money issues; balancing family, work, and classes). In addition, advisors may note high levels of anxiety about returning to school. In such cases, it would be important to be knowledgeable of and recommend appropriate resources to enhance students' success. Also, helping adult students find a sense of community and engagement with their institution is an important role for advisors. Finally, advisors serve as advocates for adult students to address and be responsive to their career and academic needs in the context of their lives.

TRANSFER STUDENTS

Transfer students are students who begin higher education at one institution and transfer to a different institution. Although these students have at least some higher education experience, the experience at one institution may be vastly different from their experience at another institution. Often, these students are transferring from a community college to a four-year institution, but some may transfer from one four-year institution to another or to a community college. In addition, some students may transfer multiple times. Even though there are various reasons for transferring, these students do have some commonalities that can be useful for an advisor to understand when working with them on career planning issues (Holaday, 2005).

Students may transfer because the school they are attending does not offer the degree they are seeking, or they may have completed requirements for a two-year degree and wish to continue at a four-year institution (Grites, 2004). Also, students may not have initially been admissible at the institution of their choice. They may want to be closer to home or farther away from home. They may be transferring because they want a smaller institution or a larger institution. Another possibility is that they were originally a student athlete and found themselves not competitive, chose not to compete, or have the opportunity to pursue their sport at a different institution. It may be that they did not get along with a roommate, or they want to be with a significant other (Withem, 2007). Whatever the reasons for the transfer, this group of students has some very special challenges.

Challenges

Consider the case of Scott who makes an appointment with his advisor at the midpoint in the semester. The advisor notices that Scott is frustrated. Scott tells the advisor that he is struggling in his computer science classes, that he does not seem to have as much math background as the other students, and they are using a language with which he is unfamiliar. Scott completed the prerequisite courses at the local community college; however, he does not think they covered as much material in his beginning C class. He is considering dropping all of his classes and changing his major, even though he really liked the computer science classes that he took at his community college. As the advisor visits with Scott, he senses that Scott has not made any friends on this campus. He also learns that Scott has not talked with the professor and that he is unaware of the tutoring lab on campus where he can get some additional help with the programming languages. The advisor encourages Scott to talk with his professor and to visit the tutoring lab. In addition, he indicated that he hoped Scott would continue with this semester, so as not to lose all the credits for this semester. Scott then tells the advisor that he is already working as a programmer but he is using a different programming language. In order to advance with his current company, he needs a college degree. The advisor takes this opportunity to begin a discussion of the different majors that are associated with computer technology and describes some of the differences in the coursework. They discuss the other major options and how his current coursework would apply to each of those options. The advisor tells Scott that if he switches to one of the business degrees, not as much math would be required, and the programming language that Scott is more familiar with is the one required. He would have to take some lower division prerequisites in business; however, he might be able to test out of some of those, since he has had some business management and marketing experience. Scott seems happier with this plan, and thinks he might also be able to test out of statistics and one other required class.

Transfer students often experience "transfer shock" (Hills, 1965), which is a decline in grade point average during their first semester at an institution. Transfer students, at least in one study, were found to be more likely to be on academic probation than continuing "native students" (Graham & Dallam, 1986), although their grade point average issues tend to right themselves after a semester or two. Transfer shock may vary in severity; therefore, institutions need to be very much aware of the transfer student population and be prepared to offer resources to help them make successful transitions.

Also, transfer students may have difficulty with the adjustment process, including the academic, social, and psychological aspects (Kim, 2001), due to the differences in institutions. This may be particularly true for minority students. Advisors should be able to clearly communicate their institutional policies on transfers and clarify how and if the transfer institution can fit into the student's career goals.

Career Advising of Transfer Students

Providing programs specifically designed for transfer students can be very helpful. Transfer students often experience anxiety related to transfer of credits and how the credits will apply toward their intended degree. Communication between professionals at institutions, when possible, can smooth the transfer process, particularly between two- and four-year institutions. Working together with other institutions on articulated agreements and understanding of degree requirements, credits, and course equivalency standards can facilitate the process.

Making sure that transfer students have correct degree information is an important role of advisors. Requirements vary from one institution to another, and transfer students often have to make up credits or requirements in a short amount of time. Being knowledgeable about courses that are acceptable substitutions, about opportunities for testing out of courses, or other ways of filling in the gaps left by transferring can shorten the path and lessen the stress for many transfer students. Sometimes, being an advocate for the transfer student with departments and colleges becomes necessary. This is also an opportune time for advisors to make sure students are pursuing degrees that will ultimately meet their career and life goals.

It may be important to address with transfer students the difference between a job training program and an academic program. Students need to understand that a major may be good preparation for a career or advanced degree, but it may not be the specific job training they are seeking. They may also be able to get the same job with a different degree, one that may be able to use more of their credits from other institutions.

Students transferring from two-year institutions to four-year institutions will also need an understanding of the differences between lower division and upper division work and the requirements of specific majors. They need opportunities to discuss their career goals and discover the different majors that will prepare them for meeting those career goals. Helping students understand exactly how credits from their former institution apply to their current degree plan can alleviate some of the stress of transfer. Supporting transfer students and helping them achieve professional and personal goals and offering opportunities for career exploration and mentoring can help alleviate transfer shock and enhance the transition for transfer students.

An integrated approach to career and academic advising for transfer students should involve the development of career programs specifically targeting these students. At times, it may be helpful for advisors to encourage transfer students to explore multiple degree options, and help them find the best fit for their interests, values, abilities, strengths, and goals, while also making the best use of the credits they have already completed. Finally, communicating issues and concerns relative to transfer students with academic advisors from other institutions can be helpful to these students.

STUDENT ATHLETES

Student athletes come to college with the same developmental and emotional issues as other college students their age; however, student athletes face additional pressures and concerns that can make career planning with a student athlete an even greater challenge. Student athletes must balance conflicting demands of their athletic schedules with their academic schedules. They must also deal with relationships with family, teammates, coaches, and friends (Howard-Hamilton & Villegas, 2008). According to Hollis (2001), advisors should understand student athletes' constant conflict between meeting athletic and academic demands.

Challenges

Consider the case of John, who is a scholarship athlete on the basketball team. In previous meetings with his advisor, he seems uninterested in career planning, as his career plan is to finish his eligibility at this institution and then play professionally. His only concern, and that of his coach, is to schedule classes from mid-morning to early afternoon, so that he can arrive at practice early. He tells his advisor that he really likes history and literature, but he does not have time to do all of the reading. As a result, any major that does not require a lot of reading is fine with him. However, at the beginning of his junior year, a bad accident ends John's playing career, at least for that season and maybe permanently. John is distraught; he cannot imagine the end of his playing career, and he cannot see himself in any other kind of a job. The advisor meets with John, and discusses some options with him. The advisor suggests that John might want to complete an online career system, available in the career center, to determine his interests, values, and skills. She also suggests that while John is rehabilitating might be the time to explore other opportunities and develop some new skills that might also be useful in professional athletics. She arranges for John to visit with a professor in mass communications about opportunities in broadcasting and public relations. She also arranges for him to shadow the play-by-play announcer at several basketball games. The academic advisor also gives him information about majors and how his current coursework would apply to these degree areas. She encourages John to research careers that are connected with professional athletics in some way.

Parham (1993) identified six areas of challenges confronting today's student athletes. These included balancing athletics and academics; balancing social activities with athletic participation; balancing athletic success or lack of success with maintaining mental equilibrium; balancing physical health with injury; balancing the demands of the many complex relationships of coaches, team, family, and friends; and dealing with the end of their college career. The need to juggle demands of the sport with time for classes, social activities, studying, and team meetings may prevent student athletes from pursuing a visit to the career center or scheduling an appointment with an advisor for career advising. Bringing career advising to the student athlete and being creative about exposing the athlete to career possibilities is extremely important.

"Research suggests that participation in collegiate sports (and sports in general) has many positive effects on an individual's . . . development" (Shurts & Shoffner, 2004, p. 96) but can also lead to difficulties in other areas, particularly career development. Furthermore, student athletes "progress more slowly in their career development than do their non-athlete peers" (Shurts & Shoffner, 2004, p. 98) possibly stemming from the isolation caused by participating in college athletics. The intensity with which student athletes pursue their sport can lead to identity foreclosure, which means student athletes commit to their sport at an early age without exploring the other options available to them (Marcia, 1966). This can also be associated with relying on others to make decisions for them. Student athletes have spent a great deal of time and effort focused on their sport; they may not have spent much time developing competence in other areas. Student athletes may also view their options as limited, basically because the commitment to sport may be viewed as the only viable career option (Martens & Lee, 1998).

Career Advising of Student Athletes

Student athletes have specific needs for career advising. They have often devoted a lot of time from a very young age to developing competency in a single sport, and very little time to planning for life beyond their participation in that sport. Clearly, they need to develop an understanding of the career development process, the options available to them, and how their interests and capabilities can be applied to an occupation, both inside or outside of their sport.

Advisors should be prepared, at least initially, for some resistance from the student athlete to career planning and the career development process, especially for those who have identity foreclosure. Many student athletes are committed to pursuing a career in professional sports; they may not be able to visualize any other outcome. Advisors may need to focus on working with student athletes to identify opportunities and interests they have in addition to their sport, or that they might consider upon retirement from their sport. Advisors may also need to help students understand and work through the many variables that can affect their athletic career, both positively and negatively (e.g., injury, lack of opportunity, or having the opportunity to leave college before completing their degree because of the professional draft). In addition, advisors should help the student athletes prepare for both events that happen and "nonevents" (Schlossberg, 1984), events they expect to happen but do not.

Student athletes experience several barriers to the career development process. Time to explore other careers and interests can be a problem. Often a student is encouraged to pick a major based on factors other than the student's interest or ability (e.g., ease of course scheduling, low teacher-student ratio, majors that are perceived as easier or more flexible) so that the athlete can achieve academic success and still spend the majority of time on the sport. In addition to this, NCAA requirements that a student athlete must make progress toward a degree may inhibit the student athlete's ability to change majors.

Due to time constraints, many athletes will not have the opportunity to explore careers in the traditional manner (e.g., shadowing, trying out different courses). Their schedules are more rigid, and they may also have less time to develop hobbies and interests outside of their sport. Providing some creative opportunities and interventions may be helpful. By designing learning opportunities that will broaden their knowledge base and suggesting ways that their special skills may apply to other career choices may be helpful.

Martens and Lee (1998) suggested a life-career development view, which requires professionals to consider them as athletes, and also as the unique individual they are and "rather than approaching their career development in terms of a sport/non-sport dichotomy, it makes sense to mindfully integrate their athletic identity at all stages of the process" (p. 130). Understanding that the student athlete's sport is central to his or her identity at this stage, and using that in the career planning process, may help athletes feel "less anxious about the future and the career development process" (p. 130). Developing an alternative plan does not mean an athlete will have to give up the sport entirely but will only broaden one's opportunities.

Student athletes may also need assistance with developing decision-making skills and critical thinking strategies. They have a very structured life and schedule, dictated by a variety of systems (e.g., coaches, the NCAA, the athletic department) and may require help learning to think for themselves rather than as a part of a team. Obtaining information about options, the planning process, and developing helpful networks can also be important for student athletes. Student athletes also need to develop the necessary skills for writing a résumé, interviewing, and learning how to "take what they've learned as an athlete" (Martens & Lee, 1998, p. 132) and use it to further their career.

SUMMARY

Gordon (2006) stated, "It is always dangerous to generalize about specific groups of students since individuals often differ within a group even though environmental and cultural differences are similar" (p. 51). Understanding similarities of students who are members of specific groups can improve career advising by helping advisors understand the unique concerns and strengths of each student. This information can help advisors implement programs and services, based on the needs of specific groups of students that may be most useful to the individual student.

The consistent theme evident in working with specific student populations is the need for clear communication and a strong connection with faculty members and academic advisors. Advisors should look at the programs and services provided by their institutions to see whether they meet the needs of all students. If the career needs of specific populations of students are not being adequately met, advisors should advocate for the implementation of programs to meet students' career needs. In summary, advisors in all colleges and universities can strive to establish creative venues to stimulate career advising, promote student reflection, and enhance students' personal and professional development to meet the academic and career needs of all students.

References

Berk, L. E. (2007). *Development through the lifespan* (4th ed.). New York: Pearson Education.

Blackburn, A. C., & Erickson, D. B. (1986). Predictable crises of the gifted student. *Journal of Counseling & Development, 64*, 587–589.

Bland, S. M. (2004). Advising adults: Telling or coaching? *Adult Learning, 14*(2), 6–9.

Boivin, M., Fountain, G. A., & Baylis, B. (2000). Meeting the challenges of the sophomore year. In L. A. Schreiner & J. Pattengale (Eds.), *Visible solutions for invisible students: Helping sophomores succeed* (Monograph No. 31, pp. 1–18). Columbia, SC: National Resource Center for the First-Year Experience and Students in Transition, University of South Carolina.

Brown, S. M. (2002). Strategies that contribute to nontraditional/adult student development and persistence. *PAACE Journal of Lifelong Learning, 11*, 67–76.

Burton Nelson, D. (2006). *Career advisors: A new breed*. Retrieved August 12, 2008, from NACADA Clearinghouse of Academic Advising Resources Web site: http://www.nacada.ksu.edu/Clearinghouse/AdvisingIssues/career-advisors.htm

Byrd, K. L., & MacDonald, G. (2005). Defining college readiness from the inside out: First-generation college student perspectives. *Community College Review, 33*(1), 22–37.

Colangelo, N. (2003). Counseling gifted students. In N. Colangelo & G. A. Davis (Eds.), *Handbook of gifted education* (3rd ed., pp. 373–387). Boston: Allyn & Bacon.

Coomes, M., & DeBard, R. (2004). A generational approach to understanding students. *New Directions for Student Services, 106,* 5–16.

Delisle, J. R. (1986). Death with honors: Suicide among gifted adolescents. *Journal of Counseling & Development, 64,* 558–560.

Digby, J. (2007). Advising honors students. *Academic Advising Today, 30*(3). Retrieved July 10, 2008, from http://www.nacada.ksu.edu/AAT/NW30_3

Dobelle, E. (2006). Reform for college readiness. *Connection: The Journal of the New England Board of Higher Education, 20*(4), 9–10.

El-Shamy, S. (2004). *How to design and deliver training for the new and emerging generations.* San Francisco: Pfeiffer.

Ely, M. B. (2008, July 30). Veterans in college: What advisers should expect. *The Mentor: An Academic Advising Journal, 1*(1). Retrieved August 12, 2008, from http://www.psu.edu/dus/mentor

Eriksen, J., LeClaire, J., Murray, M., Mann, C., Webb, M., Polson, C., et al. (1986). *Advising adult learners* (NACADA Task Force Report No. 2). Manhattan, KS: National Academic Advising Association.

Evenbeck, S. E., Boston, M., DuVivier, R. S., & Hallberg, K. (2000). Institutional approaches to helping sophomores. In L.A. Schreiner & J. Pattengale (Eds.), *Visible solutions for invisible students: Helping sophomores succeed* (Monograph No. 31, pp. 79–87). Columbia, SC: National Resource Center for the First-Year Experience and Students in Transition, University of South Carolina.

Farrell, E. (2007). Some colleges provide success coaches for students. *The Education Digest, 73*(3), 44–47.

Fisher, M. (2008, June 16). California college program aims to help vets: Adjusting to college and civilian life is goal. *Community College Week, 20,* 25–26.

Flanagan, W. J. (2007). The sophomore-year initiative (SYI) program at Beloit College. In B.F. Tobolowsky & B.E. Cox (Eds.), *Shedding light on sophomores: An exploration of the second college year* (Monograph No. 47, pp. 49–61). Columbia, SC: National Resource Center for The First-Year Experience & Student in Transition, University of South Carolina.

Fries-Britt, S. (2000). Identity development of high-ability black collegians. *New Directions for Teaching and Learning, 82*(1), 55–65.

Gahagan, J., & Hunter, M. S. (2006). The second-year experience: Turning attention to the academy's middle children. *About Campus, 11*(3), 17–22.

General Accounting Office. (2001). *Military personnel: Longer time between moves related to higher satisfaction and retention.* Briefing report (GAO-01–841) to the Chairman and Ranking Minority Member, Subcommittee on Appropriation, U.S. Senate. Washington, DC: Author.

Gordon, V. N. (2006). *Career advising: An academic advisor's guide.* San Francisco: Jossey-Bass.

Graham, S., & Dallam, J. (1986). Academic probation as a measure of performance: Contrasting transfer students to native students. *Community/Junior College Quarterly of Research and Practice, 10,* 23–34.

Graunke, S. S., & Woosley, S. A. (2005). An exploration of the factors that affect the academic success of college sophomores. *College Student Journal, 39,* 367–376.

Greene, M. J. (2006). Helping build lives: Career and life development of gifted and talented students. *Professional School Counseling, 10,* 34–48.

Grimes, S. (1997). Underprepared community college students: Characteristics, persistence, and academic success. *Community College Journal of Research & Practice, 21,* 47–56.

Grites, T. (2004, September). Advising transfer students. *Academic Advising Today, 27*(3). Retrieved December 3, 2008, from http://www.nacada.ksu.edu/AAT/NW27_3.htm#16

Gump, S. E. (2007). Classroom research in a general education course: Exploring implications through an investigation of the sophomore slump. *Journal of General Education, 56,* 105–125.

Hills, J. (1965). Transfer shock: The academic performance of the junior college transfer. *Journal of Experimental Education, 33,* 201–216.

Holaday, T. (2005, February). Diversity in transfer. *Academic Advising Today, 28*(1). Retrieved December 3, 2008, from http://www.nacada.ksu.edu/AAT/NW28_1.htm#5

Hollis, L. P. (2001). Service ace? Which academic services and resources truly benefit student-athletes. *Journal of College Student Retention, 3,* 265–284.

Hoshmand, L. T., & Hoshmand, A. L. (2007). Support for military families and communities. *Journal of Community Psychology, 35,* 171–180.

House, J. D. (1995). The predictive relationship between academic self-concept, achievement expectancies, and grade performance in college calculus. *Journal of Social Psychology, 135,* 111–112.

Howard-Hamilton, M., & Villegas, H. (2008). Student development theory. In A. Leslie-Toogood & E. Gill (Eds.), *Advising student-athletes: A collaborative approach to success* (Monograph No. 18, pp. 111–119). Manhattan, KS: NACADA.

Howe, N., & Strauss, W. (2000). *Millennials rising: The next great generation.* New York: Vintage Books.

Hughey, K., & Hunt, J. (2006, October). *Facilitating students' career development and planning: Using career theory to inform and enhance advising.* Session presented at the annual conference of the National Academic Advising Association, Indianapolis, IN.

Johannessen, L. R. (2003). Achieving success for the "resistant" student. *Clearing House, 77*(1), 6–13.

Kerka, S. (1995). *Adult career counseling in a new age.* (ERIC Document Reproduction Service No. ED389881). Retrieved August 3, 2008, from http://www.ericdigests.org/1996-3/age.htm

Kim, K. (2001). *Trends and issues in transfer.* (ERIC Document Reproduction Service No. ED456869). Retrieved August 3, 2008, from http://www.ericdigests.org/2002-2/transfer.htm

Kozeracki, C. A., & Brooks, J. B. (2006). Emerging institutional support for developmental education. In B. K. Townsend & K. J. Dougherty (Eds.), *Community College Missions in the 21st Century* (pp. 63–73). New Directions for Community Colleges, no. 136. San Francisco: Jossey-Bass.

Lipka, S. (2006, September 1). After the freshman bubble pops. *The Chronicle of Higher Education,* p. 42.

Long, E. C., & Lange, S. (2002). An exploratory study: A comparison of honors and non-honors students. *The National Honors Report*, *23*(2), 20–30.

Makela, J. P. (2006, June). *Advising community college students: Exploring traditional and emerging theory*. Champaign, IL: Office of Community College Research and Leadership, College of Education, University of Illinois-Champaign.

Marcia, J. (1966). Development and validation of ego-identity status. *Journal of Personality and Social Psychology*, *3*, 551–558.

Martens, M. P., & Lee, F. K. (1998). Promoting life-career development in the student athlete: How can career centers help? *Journal of Career Development*, *25*, 123–134.

McDonald, M. L. (2003). Advising high-ability business students. *NACADA Journal*, *23*(1 & 2), 58–65.

Parham, W. D. (1993). The intercollegiate athlete: A 1990s profile. *The Counseling Psychologist*, *21*, 411–429.

Plisko, V. (2007, July). *Digest of education statistics: 2006* (NCES 2007–017). Washington, DC: National Center for Education Statistics, U.S. Department of Education, Institute for Education Sciences. Retrieved January 9, 2009, from http://nces.ed.gov/programs/digest/d06/

Rocker, M. G. (2007). From Iraq to the classroom. *University of Minnesota News*. Retrieved August 17, 2008, at http://www1umn.edu/umnnews

Santrock, J. W. (2007). *A topical approach to life-span development*. New York: McGraw-Hill.

Schaller, M. A. (2005). Wandering and wondering: Traversing the uneven terrain of the second college year. *About Campus*, *10*(3), 17–24.

Schaller, M. A. (2007). The development of college sophomores. In B. F. Tobolowsky & B. E. Cox (Eds.), *Shedding light on sophomores: An exploration of the second college year* (Monograph No. 47, pp. 1–11). Columbia, SC: University of South Carolina, National Resource Center for the First-Year Experience & Students in Transition.

Shurts, W. M., & Shoffner, M. F. (2004). Providing career counseling for collegiate student-athletes: A learning theory approach. *Journal of Career Development*, *31*, 95–109.

Schlossberg, N. K. (1984). *Counseling adults in transitions*. New York: Springer.

Smittle, P. (2003). Principles for effective teaching in developmental education. *Journal of Developmental Education*, *26*(3), 10–16.

Stockenberg, J. T. (2007). The sophomore jump program at Colorado College. In B. F. Tobolowsky & B. E. Cox (Eds.), *Shedding light on sophomores: An exploration of the second college year* (Monograph No. 47, pp. 63–73). Columbia, SC: University of South Carolina, National Resource Center for the First-Year Experience & Students in Transition.

Sutaria, D. (2007, October). How to work with Generation X (born between 1965 and 1980). *CareerQuest Newsletter*. Retrieved November 20, 2008, from http://www.careerquestcentral.com/newsletter/oct07.html

Sweeney, R. (2006). *Millennial behaviors & demographics*. Retrieved April 3, 2008, from library1.njit.edu/staff-folders/sweeney/Millennials/Article-Millennial-Behaviors.doc

Tobolowsky, B. F., & Cox, B. E. (Eds.) (2007). *Shedding light on sophomores: An exploration of the second college year* (Monograph No. 47). Columbia, SC: University of South Carolina, National Resource Center for The First-Year Experience & Students in Transition.

Tritelli, D. (2003, Winter). From the editor. *Peer Review, 5*(2), 3. Retrieved August 12, 2008, from http://findarticles.com/p/articles/mi_qa4115/is_200401/ai_n9465323

Walther, E. S., & Ritchie, W. F. (1998, April 15). Counseling the adult college student. *Selfhelp Magazine*. Retrieved April 3, 2008, from http://www.selfhelpmagazine. com/article/node/108

Withem, R. D. (2007). The ignored population: Transfer students. *The Mentor: An Academic Advising Journal, 9*(2). Retrieved April 3, 2008, from www.psu. edu/dus/mentor/

CHAPTER TWELVE

Evaluation and Assessment in Career Advising

Rich Robbins

Evaluation and assessment of all components of higher education have become major foci of various external entities, such as regents' boards, state and regional governing boards, and accreditation agencies. While academic and student service units in the past may have conducted evaluation and assessment to ensure that programmatic goals were being achieved and students' needs were being met (Upcraft & Schuh, 1996), external expectations are now requiring assessment practices to, at least in part, justify the existence of such units, given the financial restraints many institutions are facing. Moreover, being proactive with evaluation and assessment provides real data on which to base innovations, justifications, and requests, and, as a result, may place an institution in a favorable position with external entities. However, higher education is also acknowledging that student learning is an individualized and complex process (Campbell, Nutt, Robbins, Kirk-Kuwaye, & Higa, 2005), and traditional ways of understanding student learning through simple summative evaluation cannot reflect this complexity. Maki (2002) suggests that this "institutional curiosity" (p. 3), the desire to investigate issues of student learning from multiple perspectives, may be the most compelling reason to perform assessment in higher education. The goals of evaluation and assessment for career advising thus include program effectiveness, program improvement, student learning, and accountability.

Still, despite these earnest goals of demonstrating effectiveness and evidencing student learning and success, evaluation and assessment are often viewed as negative processes focusing on performance and accountability only. With student learning and student success as primary objectives, which in turn can demonstrate both advisor and programmatic effectiveness, it is important to note that the true purpose of evaluation and assessment is consistent improvement. Thus, before embarking on evaluation and assessment of career advising, all involved should be educated on the positive reasons for conducting evaluation and assessment and the constructive ways in which the results will be used to inform data-driven decisions.

It is imperative to note at this point that much of the information presented in this chapter is borrowed from or relates to the academic advising literature. This is appropriate in that career advising is an integral part of academic advising, and the evaluative and assessment practices utilized for academic advising are those utilized for the career advising component as well.

EVALUATION VERSUS ASSESSMENT: AN OVERVIEW

Although the terms are often used interchangeably (e.g., Creamer & Scott, 2000; Cuseo, 2008; Lynch, 2000; Troxel, 2008), there are specific distinctions between evaluation and assessment in higher education. Simply put, evaluation is a discrete judgment of value or worth (Creamer & Scott, 2000) typically performed episodically on an individual, while assessment is a continuous, systematic process of collecting, reflecting upon, and utilizing information gathered from multiple data collection techniques, focusing on the improvement of student learning and development (Angelo, 1995; Ewell, 2000; Marchese, 1993; Palomba, 1999; Pellegrino, Chudowsky, & Glaser, 2001) which entails the mastery of student learning outcomes by students. Further, assessment can be performed at the institutional level, the programmatic level, and the advising experience level (Maki, 2004). In the case of career advising, evaluation focuses on the performance of the individual advisor, while assessment's larger focus is on the career advising program and services overall, primarily in regard to assessment of student learning outcomes. Evaluation of individual advisor performance may indeed be included as part of an overall assessment process designed to measure outcomes, but evaluation tends to be episodic and individually focused whereas assessment should be conducted at the programmatic level as a continuous process imbedded in the culture. This is not to say that evaluation does not continue to be an important process; evaluation alone, however, is no longer sufficient. Both evaluation and assessment are necessary to provide evidence of effectiveness and success in all areas of higher education, including career advising.

The information presented throughout this chapter regarding both evaluation and assessment is neither exclusive nor exhaustive. The goal is to provide a general sense of the different processes and measurements used for evaluation and assessment of career advising as well as the types of and uses for the resulting data. Although some specific examples and several resources for evaluative instruments are offered, these are presented for illustrative purposes only and should not be considered as the only methods to use or even the best methods to use when performing evaluation and assessment for career advising. There is no single magic bullet evaluative instrument or assessment measure; rather, when embarking on an evaluation or assessment process for career advising, one should identify the most significant and important outcomes to examine based on the specific program at a specific campus working with a specific student population in a specific geopolitical, financial, and accreditation climate.

OUTCOMES OF CAREER ADVISING

Regardless of whether career advising is being evaluated or assessed, the specific phenomena being evaluated or assessed are the outcomes of career advising: those resulting events and facts that are the most important for measuring based on the individual mission, goals, and needs of career advising. These outcomes are in the form of process and delivery outcomes, student learning outcomes, and career advisor learning outcomes.

Process and delivery outcomes are statements that articulate the expectations regarding *how* career advising is delivered and *what* information should be delivered *during* the career advising experience (adapted from Campbell et al., 2005). These outcomes are anchored in the career advising interaction, and are concerned with what occurs and what information is exchanged during that interaction. These outcomes are typically measured through student satisfaction instrument items, which are discussed further in the chapter.

Student learning outcomes are statements that articulate what students are expected to know, do, and value *as a result of* involvement in the career advising experience (adapted from Campbell et al., 2005). As such, they measure students' cognitive learning (what they know), behavioral learning (what they do), and affective learning (what they value or appreciate) that result from the career advising interaction. For example, a student may learn the curricular requirements to be eligible to participate in an internship (cognitive learning), the student may schedule an appointment and complete an interest inventory (behavioral learning), and the student may appreciate the value of networking in achieving their career goals (affective learning) as results of career advising.

A third type of outcome resulting from the career advising process is one that has been rarely examined in evaluation and assessment processes of career advising, and even more rarely discussed in the literature—the advisor learning outcome. Just as it is important to determine what students learn, do, and appreciate as a result of career advising, knowing what the advisor also takes away from the experience may also be important. Therefore, paralleling the types of student learning outcomes described above are advisor learning outcomes on the cognitive, behavioral, and affective dimensions—knowledge the advisor cognitively takes away or learns from the career advising interaction, behaviors the advisor performs as a result of the career advising interaction, and what the advisor comes to value or appreciate as a result of the career advising interaction. For example, the advisor may realize that being current on the latest job placement statistics is important (cognitive); the advisor may research these statistics (behavioral); and the advisor may appreciate the fact that having such information is important to meet students' needs (affective) as results of the career advising interaction.

It is important to consider process and delivery, student learning, and career advisor learning outcomes when evaluating and assessing career advising because these different types of outcomes are both complementary to and interdependent of one another. For example, the degrees to which student learning and advisor learning occur are, in part, due to the processes involved in the delivery of career advising. In order to measure that learning has occurred as a result of career advising, what was involved in the career advising process and how information was delivered must be known. The specific student learning and advisor learning outcomes related to career advising and identified as most important to be assessed are entirely dependent on the mission and goals of the individual advising program.

IDENTIFYING MEASURABLE OUTCOMES: MISSION AND GOALS

So how does one identify the outcomes most relevant and important to evaluate and assess? The ideal place to start is the mission of the advising unit relative to both the institutional mission and local goals for career advising. Having a clearly delineated mission statement and specified programmatic goals allows for evaluation and assessment to be performed more effectively (Campbell, 2008; White, 2000). When discussing a mission statement, one must start with value statements and vision statements from which the mission follows. A *value statement* is a declaration of what is considered important in regard to career advising (e.g., "Career advising at X University is an integral part of students' successes") whereas a *vision* is the statement of the aspiration for career advising at the institution (e.g., "The career advising program at X University aspires to be the recognized model for career advising regionally").

Based on the definition of a mission statement for academic advising in general (Campbell et al., 2005), a mission statement for career advising reflects the specific purpose of career advising on the campus and serves as the roadmap to achieve the vision and affirm the stated values for career advising (e.g., "The mission of career advising at X University is to assist students in realizing their fullest potential and achieving their career goals by offering superior career guidance and preparation to our students"). It needs to be descriptive regarding the career advising program, those it serves, and how it serves its clients. It should also be reflective of the institutional mission statement, which is likewise a descriptive statement indicating what the institution is about, whom it serves, and how it serves them. The Council for the Advancement of Standards (CAS, 2006) suggests that mission statements incorporate both student learning and student development, and be consistent with the mission and goals of the institution.

Goals are derived from the local mission statement and identify exactly what the program should achieve by describing how the values, vision, and mission will be enacted. Goal statements are more specific than mission statements (e.g., "Career advising at X University is based on developmental, vocational, and learning theories" or "Career advising at X University is responsive to the developmental and demographic profiles of the student population").

Following from the goals are objectives, which articulate expectations about how career advising is provided (e.g., "Career advising at X University supports the role of the academic experience in achieving career goals"). It is from the identified objectives that specific measurable process and delivery outcomes, student learning outcomes, and advisor learning outcomes are derived. If no agreed-upon values, vision, mission, goals, and resulting objectives for career advising exist, these should be developed. However, even in the absence of these, there are probably desired outcomes for career advising that can be identified. Therefore, although the ideal process in identifying desired outcomes for career advising is to begin with values and work through vision, mission, goals, and objectives to identified desired outcomes, it is important to start with what exists to begin the assessment process. That is, the assessment process can begin based on the articulation of desired outcomes if that is all that has been identified, and the development of the objectives, goals, and mission can occur while at the same time moving forward with the measurement of the process and delivery and student learning and advisor learning outcomes (Wiggens & McTighe, 2006).

There are other resources that can assist in the identification of process and delivery outcomes and student learning outcomes for career advising as well. According to Gordon (2006), career advising involves assisting students to understand how their academic interests, personal interests, individual abilities, and personal values relate to possible careers they are considering, and in aligning these academic and career goals. These identified outcomes could serve as process and delivery outcomes for the career advising interaction, as well as student learning outcomes. Gordon further identifies various advisor competencies that could be transformed into process and delivery outcomes, as well as desired outcomes of the career advising process, thus serving as student learning outcomes. Additional resources to help identify process and delivery outcomes and student learning outcomes for career advising include the CAS (2006) Standards for Academic Advising, and the National Association of Colleges and Employers (NACE, 2006) Professional Standards for College and University Career Services. The former includes specific outcomes for career advising as a component of academic advising; the latter includes identified outcomes for career advising as part of career services. These standards can easily be transformed into outcome statements. However, these should not be used just for the sake of having stated some measurable outcomes; they should only be used as outcome statements for career advising if they truly reflect the mission and goals of the specific advising program.

This brings us to so-called "best practices" for career advising. The term "best practices" is currently a popular buzz term in higher education. But how does one determine best practices without evaluation and assessment? So many "best practices" are based on common practices among institutions (especially among peer institutions or institutions of similar type), on recommendations from the literature regarding effective practices, or on presentations at conferences or workshops. However, without true evaluation and assessment of effectiveness, any given practice is not truly a "best practice." Moreover, what is a "best practice" at one institution or with one student cohort may not be an appropriate or effective practice at another institution or even within the same institution with different students. True best practices for any given career advising program must be based on evaluation and assessment locally rather than on external sources.

TYPES OF MEASUREMENT AND DATA

Once the mission, goals, and desired outcomes have been identified for career advising, the challenge lies in measuring whether or not the outcomes have been met. The next step is to determine who or what will be assessed and the data that will be gathered. It is important to understand that a survey is not the only way to gather evaluative or assessment data. Not all process and delivery outcomes, student learning outcomes, or advisor learning outcomes involved in the career advising process can be fully measured or understood by a simple survey. It is therefore necessary to identify multiple methods of measurement to engage the range of outcome data resulting from evaluation and assessment of career advising by using qualitative, quantitative, direct, and indirect measurements and data.

Qualitative measures result in data being described in words, such as responses to open-ended questions about the career advising experience. Qualitative measurement is exploratory, with information emerging from the process in the form of rich, in-depth responses to questions. The interpretation of the data is subjective and inductive. Qualitative methods should be utilized when little is known about the topic being evaluated or assessed or when closed-ended items (e.g., multiple-choice items, scaled items) that would yield data in numerical (quantitative) form cannot yet be determined. Qualitative methods may include, for example, focus groups, case studies, and naturalistic observation; the key is that the emerging information is the result of responses to open-ended inquiry. Examples of such open-ended questions are "What did you like best about your career advising experience?" "What did you like least about your career advising experience?" "If you could change one thing about your career advising experience, what would it be?" Qualitative items can also be developed in a more focused format relative to the stated goals for career advising. For example, if one career advising goal is "to provide accurate curricular information that relates to the student's career goals," a qualitative question could be stated as "What is your opinion about the information you received regarding the selection of courses appropriate for your career goals?" Such a question is still open-ended, yet it is more focused on a specific goal of career advising.

Quantitative measures result in data in the form of numbers or statistical measures in response to inquiries about the career advising process.

Quantitative measurement is descriptive and structured; the resulting data are interpreted objectively and deductively. Quantitative methods are used when students (or other target cohorts) are not available for extensive interactions or observations, when time and funds are limited, or when "hard numbers" are required. Quantitative methods may include surveys and questionnaires, with the key being that the responses to the items are forced-choice (e.g., multiple choice, rating scale, true-false) rather than open-ended (or qualitative). Examples include the use of Likert scales, which require students to make a single rating relative to an item (e.g., "On a scale of 1 to 7, with one being 'strongly agree' and 7 being 'strongly disagree,' please rate the item 'the advisor was helpful in providing appropriate course information in line with my career goals.'"). Note that such items are typically communicated as a positive statement with the respondent being "forced" to select a single numerical value as a rating, and the scale utilized is an odd-numbered scale with a true middle point which is typically identified as "no opinion."

Both direct and indirect measures may be qualitative or quantitative, with direct measures involving empirical or "first-hand" observation of or access to the process and resulting data and indirect measures reporting data that have already been gathered or recalling events that have already occurred. Examples of the former include direct observation of advising interaction, pre-test/post-test of variables leading to a desired outcome, standardized tests or inventories measuring student learning, tracking of student data (e.g., enrollment rates, retention rates, GPAs, transcript analysis), simple counts of use of services, and advisor:student ratios. Examples of indirect measures include focus groups, surveys, questionnaires, interviews, reports, tracking of student perceptions (e.g., satisfaction, ratings of advisors, ratings of service), and tracking of advisor perceptions (e.g., student preparedness, estimation of student learning). Whether direct and indirect measures are qualitative or quantitative depends upon the types of questions posed (open-ended or forced-choice); whether qualitative and quantitative measures are direct or indirect depends upon how the data are collected.

Once the multiple measures have been determined, the minimum criteria for success for each measurement must be identified. Whether process/delivery outcomes, student learning outcomes, or advisor learning outcomes, what the data must demonstrate in order to state that a given desired outcome has been met must clearly be identified. For example, when involving the process and delivery of career advising, the minimum percentage or raw number of students rating the advising interaction as being positive needed for that specific outcome to have been met must clearly be defined. Regarding student learning outcomes, the minimum percentage or raw number of students exhibiting a specific behavior (e.g., attending an informational session on internship opportunities as the result of being advised to do so during the career advising interaction) required to meet the student learning outcome goal for that behavior must be delineated. What minimum percentage or raw number of advisors would need to report, for example, that students were prepared for their advising meetings in order to report that students have achieved that learning outcome? What minimum percentage or raw number of advisors would need to say that they were prepared for the advising meeting in order to meet that advisor learning outcome? If there exists baseline information of some kind, the minimum criteria for a given outcome may be determined based on that data. If evaluation or assessment of career advising is being conducted for the first time, it may be beneficial to identify the initial process as gathering baseline or benchmarking data, and to not set minimum criteria this first time. In any event, the minimum acceptable criteria must be identified and achieved across multiple measures for a given desired outcome in order to consider that outcome as being met.

As implied above, there probably exist institutional data such as retention rates, grade point averages, and other student tracking data that may be utilized as part of the multiple measures for any given desired outcome. Similarly, there may be institutional benchmarking data, national benchmarking data, or peer institutional data that may be used as baseline or comparison data, or to inform minimum criteria for success. It may be that significant data are already being gathered relevant to the career advising outcomes being evaluated and assessed, which will not only add information but will save time as well.

Multiple measurement thus means using several qualitative, quantitative, direct, or indirect measures, or a combination thereof, for each individual identified desired outcome. Additional examples of multiple measures for evaluation of career advising and examples of multiple measures for assessment of career advising are described in subsequent sections.

EVALUATION OF CAREER ADVISING

There are distinct differences between the evaluation of career advising and the assessment of career advising. Before considering the overall assessment of career advising, evaluative processes of career advising at the individual advisor level will be considered.

Purposes

The purposes of evaluating advisors' career advising may include the following: (a) collect information with the goal of improving advisor effectiveness, (b) collect information as part of performance evaluation, and (c) collect information on individual advisors as part of an overall assessment process. These are not necessarily mutually exclusive purposes, nor is each individual purpose required. That is, advisor evaluation may focus on (a) and (c) above, but not be used as part of performance evaluation. Further, evaluation is typically part of a larger assessment process and an evaluation alone does not constitute assessment.

Evaluation of career advising further consists primarily of three foci: advisor knowledge (i.e., accuracy and timeliness of information provided), advisor helpfulness (i.e., perceived interest and concern, usefulness of information provided), and advisor accessibility (i.e., availability of advisor) (Creamer & Scott, 2000; Frost, 1991; Winston, Ender, & Miller, 1982; Winston, Miller, Ender, Grites, & Associates, 1984). This evaluation may be formative—focusing on how to improve advisor effectiveness for the future, or summative—summarizing advisor effectiveness over a period of time. The former tends to be regular but episodic whereas the latter is often compared against specific criteria such as previous performance or identified goals. Combined, formative and summative evaluation methods provide the best overall picture of career advisor effectiveness, but as periodic evaluation methods they do not constitute assessment in and of themselves. As Creamer and Scott (2000) suggest, "feedback from more than one constituency and using more than one method is a way to get the full picture of an advisor's performance in a number of settings" (p. 344). In other words, multiple methods of measurement are necessary to obtain valid and complete evaluative data for career advising.

Evaluative Processes

The most predominant form of evaluation in academic advising in general, and in most student services in higher education including career advising, is student evaluation of the advising interaction (Habley, 2004; Macaruso, 2007). The information resulting from student evaluation typically refers to students' perceptions of and satisfaction levels with various aspects of the career advising process. As such, student evaluation usually involves process/delivery outcomes only, and the data gathered are typically quantitative and indirect. Items on such instruments are usually forced-choice, and may be similar to "My advisor was courteous and friendly," "My advisor provided the appropriate information for my needs," "My advisor was on time for our appointment," and "I found the advising session to be helpful." Students may also participate in a self-evaluation as part of this process, responding to items such as "I was prepared for my advising meeting" or "I was on time for my advising appointment." Examples of items to evaluate student learning outcomes are "I know the eligibility criteria for an internship as the result of my advising meetings" (cognitive), "I participated in the mock interviews as suggested by my advisor" (behavioral), and "I understand the importance of advising in helping me achieve my career goals" (affective). Student self-evaluation is rarely performed, but may be of interest and can serve as one of multiple measures to evaluate the process/delivery and student learning outcomes for career advising.

When utilizing a satisfaction or student perception instrument, a qualitative measure can easily be added by including an open-needed item, such as "Please include any additional information you would like to add" at the end of the instrument. However, the development of a sound, valid satisfaction or perception instrument is not quick or simple. The process involves much more than simply putting together some items and asking students (or others) their thoughts or perceptions of advising experiences.

As with any evaluative measure, the desired process/delivery, student learning, and advisor learning outcomes need to be reflected in the items ultimately included on the evaluative instrument. In doing so, consideration must be given to outcomes determined to be immediately and locally important regarding career advising, as well as consideration of what information is important to any audience to whom the results are to be reported (e.g., University President, Board of Regents, Student Government, state and regional governing bodies, accreditation agencies). Once the specific desired outcomes for career advising to be incorporated into the satisfaction instrument are identified, those stated outcomes need to be translated into specific instrument items. For example, if the mission statement for career advising includes "to provide effective career advising to our students in order to promote their academic and career success," this statement can be translated into the specific measureable outcome goal of "the provision of accurate curricular information to assist students in achieving their desired career goals." An item for a student evaluation instrument could then be "my career advisor provided a list of relevant courses that will enhance my required courses to help me achieve my career goal." Such an item could be rated on a Likert-type scale, or possibly on a dichotomous scale of true-false. It is important to note that this would not be the *only* outcome goal resulting from that specific mission statement, however, as others such as "the provision of accurate internship information to assist students in achieving their desired career goals" and "the provision of accurate extracurricular information to assist students in achieving their desired career goals" also relate to that statement within the mission. While these latter goal statements may seem a bit tedious, it is important to be specific and as exhaustive as possible in developing evaluative items to ensure internal validity (that the item is asking exactly what it is intended to ask).

The previous example demonstrates why it is imperative to work with others who have experience in writing survey questions when developing a survey instrument for career advising, so as to avoid double-questions (e.g., "my advisor was pleasant and helpful . . . "), leading questions (e.g., "my internship, which I found as a result of my advising meetings, was a positive experience . . . "), and other relevant issues. Otherwise, valid information and data on which to base any changes or implementations may not be obtained. The ideal process for developing a student satisfaction or perception survey is to begin with qualitative questions provided to a small group of students (e.g., "What did you like best about . . . ?," or "What did you like least about . . . ?," or "If you could change one thing about . . . what would it be?"). Even more specific to the mission statement/outcome goal of "provision of accurate curricular information to assist students in achieving their desired career goals" would be an item such as "What is your opinion of the information you received regarding course selection relative to your career goals?" In all cases of the qualitative process, students would be allowed (and prompted as needed) to provide complete, detailed responses. Such a process could be via written items on an open-ended survey, or provided verbally or in writing during a focus group. In this phase of the process, there is no need to survey all students within the population or cohort of interest; rather, since getting a general idea of students' opinions and perceptions is the goal, a small, representative sample will suffice. However, it is important to collaborate with others experienced with writing qualitative items, prompting students for more information, transcribing and evaluating that information, or facilitating a focus group in order to obtain the most valid information.

Once the initial qualitative responses are recorded, they should be reviewed or "coded" by qualified coders who identify and clarify the specific responses to the questions offered. It is not as simple as asking different people to review qualitative responses to see what information emerges; coders trained by expert survey developers need to be utilized. Good places to find qualified coders on campus are institutional research units, social sciences and marketing academic departments, or a survey research unit. A minimum of three coders should be utilized, in order that a majority (if not a unanimity) can agree on what the responders stated. Further, the majority of the coders should agree at least 80% of the time (known as inter-rater reliability) in order for a given response to be considered valid and the information utilized.

As the responses are coded, specific patterns of response will emerge. In order to address the most relevant issues, coders should determine which responses or response patterns are occurring at least 50% of the time as those are the issues "floating to the top." Once the final qualitative response information is complete, quantitative items are then developed to reflect the issues resulting from the qualitative data. For example, if through the coding of qualitative responses it is agreed upon that respondents feel rushed during their career advising meetings, then the example desired outcome "career advisors will spend adequate time during individual meetings with students in order to meet students' needs" is likely not being met. The specific item "The time spent on the career advising session was adequate" can then be a scaled quantitative item for the final survey instrument. Any additional quantitative items specifically reflective of outcome goals that may not have emerged from the qualitative process can then be added to the instrument as well. Even after identifying emerging issues, quantifying these items, adding any additional quantitative items, and developing an evaluative instrument, the instrument should be piloted on a small group of students to determine whether the students understand the items, rating scales, and directions, and whether the questions asked are the appropriate ones to be asked.

After completion of this process and development of a final quantitative instrument, the instrument needs to be reviewed regularly and revised as needed. Any additional variables which might need future analysis should be available and added to the instrument when the timing is right. In addition, the process used to administer the survey (e.g., hard copy, Web-based, mail, immediately following the career advising interaction) should be thoughtfully based on programmatic needs and institutional capabilities. Attention should be paid to the number of items in the survey as well (Lynch, 2000) as students are more likely to complete a quick survey that takes no longer than a few minutes than an in-depth one taking several minutes or more. Space for open responses/additional comments should always be included, and responder anonymity and confidentiality must be assured in order to obtain the most valid information.

Resource information for Web-based examples of outcome statements and several existing standardized evaluation instruments that could be utilized for evaluation of career advising is listed in Appendix D. In the case of the instruments, they were originally developed to evaluate academic advising, but in some of these instruments specific additional items can be added by the user to evaluate career advising. The existing items could also be slightly revised to refer to career advising, based on the specific outcomes to be evaluated.

It is paramount to remember that a single survey is an evaluation, not assessment, and one survey may or may not provide valid data. Therefore, multiple measures are needed for any single evaluated phenomena. Further, there are dangers associated with student satisfaction surveys. One danger is the fact that there is often a difference between a student receiving good, effective career advising and being satisfied with the advising process. For example, receipt of negative information, which may be accurate and appropriate, may yield negative evaluations of the advisor or the career advising process. A student being informed that he or she does not possess the minimum grade point average to participate in an internship experience, for example, may rate the advisor as not being friendly or caring, or may rate the advising session as the worst ever experienced, even though the information was timely and accurate. Another possible example is a student meeting with an advisor desiring information only and the advisor being developmental and expecting more of the interaction than the student; or visa-versa with the student wanting a relational, developmental advising session and the advisor providing information only. The student may be expecting or desiring something different from what the advisor feels is appropriate given the specific needs and circumstances of the student. Here again, even though the advising interaction may be entirely appropriate, the student may rate the interaction or the advisor negatively. This danger of obtaining objectively invalid information based on a single survey is one of the main reasons for utilizing multiple measures.

It is also important to keep in mind that evaluation and assessment processes that are "hot" in the literature or reported at conferences, or such processes being used at other institutions, may not necessarily work best at a given institution with specific cohorts of students. The specific mission, goals, and needs of the career advising program for students on a specific campus in a specific campus climate must be kept in mind.

Another method used to evaluate career advising is peer evaluation, which involves a professional colleague (peer) observing or reviewing the advising interaction (process and delivery outcomes), the student learning outcomes of the advising process, or advisor learning outcomes—or a combination thereof. The exact outcomes observed depend upon the goals for career advising. For direct measurement, peer evaluation may be performed by a colleague actually sitting in on advising sessions, observing videos of advising sessions, or listening to audio recordings of advising sessions. In each case, the student's consent for a third-party observation should be provided, and the student should be provided explanation of how the observation will be completed, who will be observing, and the reason for the third-party observation. Such consent is best documented in a hard copy informed consent form. There are likely others on campus—members of social science faculty, marketing faculty, even legal counsel—who can assist in developing an informed consent form. It is best to check with the institutional research offices, and possibly legal counsel offices, to ensure that appropriate criteria for such a document are met. It is also important that an evaluation form or checklist (including a qualitative response opportunity) be developed for the observer to utilize, and such a form may be developed using the aforementioned process of developing a student evaluation survey. By utilizing a standard form, one can insure that all advising sessions are rated or evaluated in a uniform manner.

Multiple peer evaluators as coders may be utilized for a given advising session, in which case at least three such coders should be employed to obtain the inter-rater reliability and agreement as described for developing a student satisfaction survey. Alternatively, multiple coders reviewing the completed evaluations by the peer evaluators could be utilized, to again insure validity in the resulting data.

Self-evaluation by the advisor is a third evaluative method. Just as students' perceptions of the career advising process are evaluated, advisor perceptions may also be evaluated. This is an infrequently utilized evaluative method, which can include advisor perceptions of process and delivery outcomes, student learning outcomes, or advisor learning outcomes. Modifying the above examples regarding student evaluations of career advising, advisor perception or satisfaction items for process and delivery outcomes may include, for example, "the student found the advising session to be helpful" and "the time spent on the advising session was adequate." For student learning outcomes, items such as "the student knows the eligibility criteria for an internship as the result of our advising meetings" (cognitive), "the student participated in the mock interviews as advised by me as their advisor" (behavioral), and "the student understands the importance of advising in helping to achieve their career goals" (affective) could be included. Examples of advisor learning outcome statements could be "I know the required qualifications a student must possess to participate in an internship" (cognitive), "I provided the appropriate information for the student's needs" (behavioral), and "I appreciate the importance of career advising for students" (affective).

A 360-degree evaluation involves the combination of all of the above: student evaluation, peer evaluation, and self evaluation. To be a true 360-degree evaluation, however, supervisor evaluation should be included. In ideal situations, this would be different from the performance evaluation as required by an institution's human resources unit. Advisor evaluation by a supervisor should focus on the advisor meeting the goals and desired outcomes for career advising rather than an overall performance review. Methods would be similar to the peer evaluation processes, but with the supervisor performing the evaluation. If supervisor evaluations are to be utilized as part of the overall performance evaluation process, it is best to be informative and clear from the start that this is the case. Conversely, if career advisor evaluation data are not going to be included as part of performance evaluations, this needs to be communicated from the start to attain cooperation and trust in the process. In either case, inclusion is key as advisors who will be evaluated should be involved from the start and informed regarding the purpose of the evaluation. They should also be afforded the opportunity to provide input and feedback as part of the process. This will not only promote buy-in and cooperation, but can be a learning process in that advisors will be made aware of the mission, goals, desired outcomes, and expectations for career advising almost implicitly.

The discussions of the various methods for evaluating career advising demonstrate that the advisor evaluation is not simple or quick. It takes time to agree upon what and whom are to be evaluated, how to evaluate, how to measure, how to analyze the data, and what success criteria to follow. All of these decisions are based upon consideration of the specific mission, goals, and desired outcomes for career advising. Further, when observing or surveying students for any purpose, including evaluation of career advising, the appropriate institutional guidelines should be followed regarding using human subjects in evaluation, assessment, or research processes. Consultation with the human subjects review committee or institutional research review board (or whatever the entity's name on campus) to insure that such criteria are met is vital. This process alone can take significant time. Therefore, when planning for career advising evaluation, tell all stakeholders involved that the process need to remain informed throughout the entire process as it takes time for advisor evaluation to be conducted appropriately.

Use of Evaluative Data

The four primary uses of evaluative data are (a) setting goals for an individual advisor or all advisors, (b) identifying needs and developing professional development opportunities for advisors, (c) providing reward and recognition for advisors, and on a larger scale, (d) improving the overall advising program. The former three will be discussed in regard to an individual advisor, although strategies may also be implemented for multiple advisors as the evaluative data suggest.

Goal setting involves the identification of the advisor's current situation relative to the ideal situation for that advisor on some given performance outcome. For example, the evaluative data may suggest that the advisor is lacking interpersonal skills or knowledge of experiential opportunities for students while in college, and these discrepancies may be identified and steps delineated to develop the advisor to reach the goal state. Included in this process would be a formal timetable and identified benchmark measures toward the ideal goal state. Tied to the goal setting process is the development and offering of professional development opportunities for the advisor. Not only can the evaluative data be used to identify deficiencies in the advisor's skills and knowledge, the evaluative data can justify the need for development opportunities and determine the content of these development opportunities.

Most institutions do not reward or even recognize the value of effective academic or career advising. The linking of reward and recognition to effective advising sends a clear message about the importance of advising to the institution. Basing reward and recognition of advising on evaluative data, rather than simple caseload numbers or advisor:advisee ratios, allows specific, empirically gathered data on which to base reward and recognition. Further, by having evaluative data based on the advising program's mission, goals, desired outcomes, and expected career advising competencies, the reward and recognition process—when based on true evaluative data—can serve as a learning opportunity for all advisors by delineating expectations and providing reward and recognition for those attaining these expectancies.

When used as part of an overall assessment program, advisor evaluation can provide important data regarding the goals, needs, and shortcomings of advising services in general. Advisor evaluation, however, when used either individually or in the aggregate, is just one measurement or data point among multiple measures that should be utilized in the overall assessment process for career advising.

ASSESSMENT OF CAREER ADVISING

Although evaluation occurs at the level of the individual advisor, assessment occurs at the larger programmatic level. The purposes for both evaluation and assessment may be similar, but the processes differ. In this section, the assessment process for career advising is discussed.

Purposes

Although assessment is often viewed as a necessary and possibly even negative process of accountability, it is intended to be a positive, ongoing process focused on continuous feedback and improvement of services to students (Campbell et al., 2005). The assessment process for career advising, then, involves both descriptive and inferential analyses, both qualitative and quantitative methodologies, and individual evaluative methods to provide a formative measure of process and delivery outcomes, student learning outcomes, and advisor learning outcomes involved in career advising. The purposes for performing assessment of career advising are similar to those for evaluation of career advising, with the difference being that assessment is conducted at the programmatic level rather than the individual level. Such purposes include program effectiveness (e.g., is the program meeting its goals and the needs of the students?), program improvement (identification of programmatic shortcomings and strategies to improve the advising program), and as discussed earlier, program accountability and institutional curiosity (Maki, 2002). All too often, assessment is not performed unless the accountability purpose comes into play with some entity requesting or requiring assessment data. However, the other purposes are just as important, if not more important, reasons to perform assessment of career advising.

As with advisor evaluation, assessment of career advising cannot adequately be performed without delineated desired outcomes. Ideally, the desired career advising programmatic outcomes follow from the institutional values and vision, the institutional mission, the local mission of career advising, and the goals and objectives for the career advising as previously discussed. However, even if only the desired outcomes have been identified, the assessment process can begin.

Key Components

Assessment of career advising is not only a continuous process, but a collective process as well (Campbell et al., 2005). Therefore, two of the primary components of any assessment process are the identification and inclusion of stakeholders. Stakeholders should include representatives from cohorts affected by career advising, as well as those who can provide influence over the program. Colleagues, faculty, staff, administrators, institutional researchers, students, and others within the institutional community may be included. Stakeholders outside of the institution may include, for example, employers, internship site supervisors, alumni, parents, and members from governing agencies. The stakeholders identified depend on the specific programmatic mission, goals, and desired outcomes for career advising. Once identified and recruited as part of the assessment process, stakeholders should be involved at each and every step of the process—from pre-assessment through the reporting of results and facilitating change. Although not all stakeholders will be members of the working assessment team per se, by collaborating with stakeholders additional key components of the assessment process are promoted: shared trust, shared motivation, shared definition of terminology, shared agreement of goals, shared language, shared support, and shared ownership and belief in the assessment process (Campbell et al., 2005).

The assessment team, then, comprises stakeholders who actually implement and conduct the assessment process. It is important to note that assessment, when conducted correctly, is not quick or easy, nor is it an individual undertaking. The assessment team, therefore, works to identify those descriptive, inferential, qualitative, quantitative, and evaluative methods to be utilized; how these methods will be implemented and utilized relevant to the mission, goals, and desired outcomes for career advising; the timing of these measurements; the parties responsible for collecting and analyzing the data; and the reporting of results and actions taken based upon the resulting data. The assessment team also works with the identified stakeholders to promote the assessment process and build a culture for assessment of career advising. Building a culture for assessment may be challenging, which is why stakeholders need to be included from the start to share ownership and become proponents for the process. Once the assessment cycle is started for career advising, it should become a part of the daily responsibilities for all involved. In time, the tasks involved in assessment will become normalized and routine. In fact, many possible identified outcomes and measures for the assessment of career advising may already be in place, but not formally identified as part of the assessment process.

The Assessment Cycle

The initial assessment cycle actually begins with the identification of the institution's values, vision, and mission for career advising. The initial assessment cycle ends when the information gathered is acted upon and a new assessment cycle starts. In between, the assessment cycle involves the development and identification of programmatic goals related to the mission; the development and identification of measurable outcomes in the forms of process and delivery, student learning, and advisor learning outcomes; the identification of multiple measures for each outcome; the setting of satisfactory criteria for each measure employed for each desired outcome; the gathering of data; and the reporting and sharing of data—all leading to change based on the data and the start of another cycle of assessment. Maki (2002) illustrates the basic processes of the assessment cycle (Figure 12.1), and Darling (2005) elaborates on the assessment cycle with more detailed descriptions of each stage in the form of a flowchart (Figure 12.2).

While Maki's (2002) representation can be viewed as a basic and generic cycle of assessment to determine student learning, Darling's (2005) more thorough flowchart was developed to illustrate the process of assessment for academic advising in higher education. However, both provide a visual overview of the assessment cycle and are easily adaptable to the assessment of career

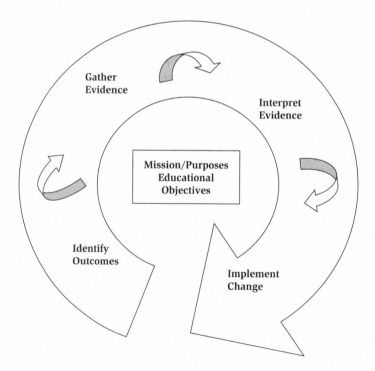

Figure 12.1 Maki's (2002) Assessment Cycle.

Reprinted from Maki, P. L. (2002). Developing an assessment plan to learn about student learning. *Journal of Academic Librarianship*, 28 (1–21), 8–13.

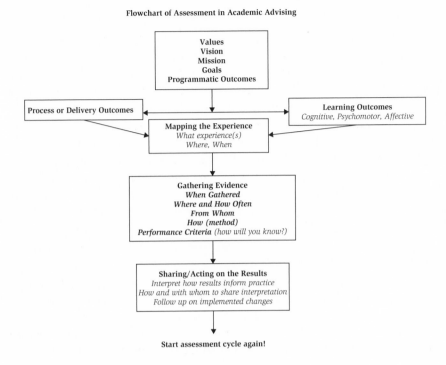

Flowchart of Assessment in Academic Advising

Figure 12.2 Darling's (2005) Assessment Flowchart.

advising. A third visual representation of the assessment cycle is the Assessment Matrix, which can be adapted to involve process and delivery outcomes, student learning outcomes, or advisor learning outcomes for career advising (Figure 12.3). Key to each of these depictions of the assessment process is the gathering evidence stage, which involves the mapping of student learning.

Mapping

Campbell et al. (2005) describe mapping as the process of determining when (or by when), where, and through what experiences the outcomes for advising will be accomplished over students' academic experiences. When mapping process and delivery outcomes for career advising, included are the identification of what should be involved in career advising (desired process and delivery outcome), what specific opportunities exist for the provision of career advising leading to this desired outcome, and delineation of when these opportunities occur during the student's academic career. An example is the desired process and delivery outcome of "Career advising will include a review of students' academic transcripts to ensure the appropriateness of courses taken relative to the students' academic and career goals," followed by identification of what opportunities occur (e.g., formal career advising sessions, career advising workshops, required as part of application for an internship) and when these opportunities occur (e.g., during the first year seminar, during every career advising meeting, at orientation to internships workshops).

Assessment of Delivery/Process Outcomes in Career Advising
How effectively was the information delivered? How did the career advisor perform?
What processes were involved in the career advising session?

Institutional Mission Statement	Local Mission Statement	Specific Goal or Objective	Specific Advising Delivery/ Process Outcome	Opportun-ities for Process to Occur	When or by When Process Occurs	Outcome Measures	Minimum Performance Criteria of Success	Measurement Instruments	Actions Based on Data

Assessment of Student Learning Outcomes in Career Advising
What has the student learned as a result of the career advising interaction?
(Cognitive, behavioral, affective learning)

Institutional Mission Statement	Local Mission Statement	Specific Goal or Objective	Specific Student Learning Outcome	Opportu-nities for Learning to Occur	When or by When Learning Occurs	Outcome Measures	Minimum Performance Criteria of Success	Measurement Instruments	Actions Based on Data

Assessment of Advisor Learning Outcomes in Career Advising
What has the career advisor learned (cognitive, behavioral, affective) as a result
of the career advising interaction?

Institutional Mission Statement	Local Mission Statement	Specific Goal or Objective	Specific Career Advisor Learning Outcome	Opportu-nities for Learning to Occur	When or by When Learning Occurs	Outcome Measures	Minimum Performance Criteria of Success	Measurement Instruments	Actions Based on Data

Figure 12.3. Assessment Matrices for Process and Delivery Outcomes, Student Learning Outcomes, and Career Advisor Learning Outcomes in Career Advising.

When mapping student learning outcomes, information that should be learned by students (cognitive student learning outcomes), behaviors students should perform (behavioral student learning outcomes), or values students should acquire (affective student learning outcomes) as a result of the career advising experience need to be identified, as well as the opportunities for students to obtain the information, skills, and values, and when or by when such opportunities occur. For example, if one of the desired student learning outcomes for career advising is "Students will participate in shadowing experiences during their sophomore year," the mapping of this specific outcome includes the identification of the specific opportunities for shadowing to occur (e.g., prerequisite for an internship, required assignment for a career course), including the timing of these opportunities (e.g., weekends during the semester, summer, mid-term break). Similar mapping is involved in career advisor learning outcomes. Given the advisor learning outcome "Advisors will be aware of current internship opportunities," opportunities for such learning to occur may include advisor professional development, electronic newsletters, or Web site information, with the timing of such learning opportunities being at the start of every semester, weekly, or daily. Mapping is, therefore, the "when" or "by when" component of assessment. Examples of the mapping of process and delivery, student learning, and advisor learning outcomes in career advising are presented in the examples of completed matrices (see Tables 12.1, 12.2, and 12.3, respectively).

The Career Advising Syllabus

The philosophy that academic advising is teaching has been promoted for decades (Appleby, 2008; Creamer, 2000; Crookston, 1972; Ender, Winston, & Miller, 1984; Frost, Habley, King, Vowell, & White, 1995; Grites, 1994; Hagen, 1994; Miller & Alberts, 1994; Ryan, 1992). Following from this premise, advisors are teachers and their discipline is academic advising (Thurmond, 2007). The same is true of career advising—career advising is a form of teaching with a true discipline. As such, there is a discipline, there is subject matter, and there is pedagogy to career advising. Actually, there are multiple pedagogies, each one contextually dependent upon the mission, goals, objectives, and desired outcomes of the respective institution and the individual career advising program, as well as upon the needs of the students utilizing that specific service. For example, McCalla-Wriggins (2000) suggests that students who are in the processes of making decisions about their academic majors and eventual careers need assistance with some basic issues; many skills involved in academic advising are the same skills used in career advising. The question then arises: What is taught in career advising? Taken further, what are the theories from which career advising operates? What are the core values of the discipline of career advising? What are students expected to learn as the result of career advising? What is expected of students in the career advising process? What is expected of career advisors in this process? The answers to these questions will vary from advising unit to advising unit and from institution to institution.

In an academic course, these questions are often answered via use of a course syllabus. A syllabus for career advising would likewise respond to such questions and further delineate how career advising focuses on student learning and how the course content involved connects student learning to the mission, vision, values, and goals for career advising. It also identifies how career advising contributes to student learning, who is expected to learn, what is expected to be learned, where the learning opportunities are available, when the learning opportunities are available, and how learning will take place. Finally, the syllabus communicates how student learning will be measured, including the set levels of expected performance and the minimum criteria for success. In essence, a syllabus for career advising reflects the basic aspects of those fundamental elements of the assessment process, yet in a format

Table 12.1. Mapping Example for Process and Delivery Outcomes in Career Advising (How effectively was the information delivered? How did the career advisor perform? What processes were involved in the career advising session?)

Institutional Mission Statement	Local Mission Statement	Specific Goal or Objective	Specific Delivery/Process Outcome (example)	Opportunities for Process to Occur	When or by When Process Occurs	Outcome Measures	Minimum Performance Criteria of Success	Measurement Instruments	Actions Based on Data
Specific to institution	Specific to career advising unit, office, department, etc.	Specific and developed based on desired outcome (e.g., local mission and goals, CAS Standards, NACE Standards)	Career advising will include a review of students' academic transcripts to ensure the appropriateness of courses taken relative to the students' academic and career goals	Individual career advising appointments; Group career advising interactions; Students' self-reviews of curricular choices; Web-based degree audits	Every semester; Every career advising meeting; Every time a student conducts a degree audit	Percentage or no. of career advisors initiating action during advising meetings; Students and career advisors rate "agree" or "strongly agree" to the corresponding instrument item	90% of all students surveyed report the career advisor did this; The advisor is rated as doing this 90% of the time by third observer(s); The advisor rates self as doing this 90% of the time	Student advisee survey; Peer observation of career advising session; Career advisor self-assessment; Student focus groups; Career advisor focus groups	What will you do based on the outcome data? Program development? Career advisor training? Request for resources? Other?

Table 12.2. Mapping Example for Student Learning Outcomes for Career Advising (What has the student learned [cognitive, behavioral, affective] as a result of the career advising interaction?)

Institutional Mission Statement	Local Mission Statement	Specific Goal or Objective	Specific Student Learning Outcome (Example)	Opportunities for Learning to Occur	When or by When Learning Occurs	Outcome Measures	Minimum Performance Criteria of Success	Measurement Instruments	Actions Based on Data
Specific to institution	Specific to career advising unit, office, department, etc.	Specific and developed based on desired outcome (e.g., local mission and goals, CAS Standards, NACE Standards)	Students will participate in shadowing experiences during their sophomore year (behavioral student learning outcome)	Career advising sessions (provision of relevant information) Information on opportunity placed on Web site, in brochures, etc. Actual shadowing placement	Information provided by end of freshman year Activity performed during sophomore year	Percentage or no. of students surveyed who report: a. knowing of opportunity b. that they learned of the opportunity from their career advisor Percentage or no. of students who participate in activity	90% of all students surveyed report the career advisor provided this information The career advisor rates self as providing information 90% of the time 90% of all eligible students do shadowing by end of soph year	Student advisee survey Career advisor self-assessment Student focus groups Career advisor focus groups Raw participation numbers	What will you do based on the outcome data? Program development? Career advisor training? Request for resources? Other?

Table 12.3. Mapping Example for Advisor Learning Outcomes for Career Advising (What has the career advisor learned [cognitive, behavioral, affective] as a result of the career advising interaction?)

Institutional Mission Statement	Local Mission Statement	Specific Goal or Objective	Specific Career Advisor Learning Outcome (example)	Opportunities for Learning to Occur	When or by When Learning Occurs	Outcome Measures	Minimum Performance Criteria of Success	Measurement Instruments	Actions Based on Data
Specific to institution	Specific to career advising unit, office, department, etc.	Specific and developed based on desired outcome (e.g., local mission and goals, CAS Standards, NACE Standards)	Career advisors will be aware of current internship opportunities (cognitive advisor learning outcome)	Career advisor training Review of relevant Web sites, literature Career advisor receipt of updated information	Career advisor training Prior to start of each semester Prior to start of each academic year	Career advisor discusses internship opportunities during advising meetings Students and career advisors rate "agree" or "strongly agree" to the corresponding instrument item	90% of all students surveyed say the career advisor provided this information The career advisor rates self as providing this information 90% of the time	Student advisee survey Peer observation of career advising session Career advisor self-assessment Student focus groups Career advisor focus groups	What will you do based on the outcome data? Program development? Career advisor training? Request for resources? Other?

that is typically familiar to those in higher education, including advisors and students (McKamey, 2007; Trabant, 2006). By describing the various components involved in the discipline of career advising via a syllabus, a shared and understood language is utilized to present a holistic picture to clarify what is often communicated in bits and pieces as needs arise. Developing a syllabus for career advising parallels the development of an assessment paradigm for career advising, but should not be considered an assessment plan per se. It is also important to keep in mind that a syllabus for career advising is a tool to foster student learning and not a substitute for an advisor, nor is it an evaluation instrument. A syllabus for career advising is analogous to a syllabus for an academic course and serves the same purposes. An example of a career advising syllabus is presented in Appendix E.

Use of Assessment Data

Once the evidence regarding achieving the identified and desired outcomes for the career advising program is gathered, the resulting data must be interpreted relative to how they inform career advising process and delivery, what student learning resulted from career advising, and what advisor learning resulted from career advising. Interpretation of specific data is dependent upon the measurements utilized, and will vary across individual evaluation and assessment processes. It is suggested that institutional research personnel be included in this analysis and interpretation, and since they should have been included as stakeholders from the beginning they will be familiar with the entire process.

The interpretation of the resulting data will then be followed by determination of with whom, how, and when the results are to be reported. For example, results will probably be reported to all stakeholders, but possibly to other constituents such as the institution's president, provost, faculty, various committees, students and student organizations, alumni, budgeting entities, and accrediting agencies. Depending on the recipient of the information, will all of the results or only selected pieces be provided? Will the results be communicated via an annual report, strategic plan, white paper, newsletter, budget request, self-study, accreditation report, Web site, or some other means? Will the results be in the form of text only for some audiences and charts and graphs for others? Who will get the full report, and who will get an executive summary? Therefore, the questions that need to be asked are: Why were the evaluations and assessment done? What is the story to be told? Who gets the information? How much information is shared? How should the information be presented? When should the information be presented? (Campbell et al., 2005). Consideration of institutional culture and political climate, as well as how the management of the reporting of the results will benefit the career advising program, are of paramount importance at this stage.

Exactly how the results of the evaluation and assessment will inform decision making and how changes will be implemented based on the results also need to be determined. Results may be used to revise the pedagogy or curriculum of career advising, to develop or revise advisor professional development programs focused on career advising, to design more effective programming for students, to justify the need for additional staff, or to help shape institutional decision making such as strategic planning and resource allocation—all relative to meeting the goals of career advising and the needs of students. Accordingly, a timetable to implement changes will also be required: Will all changes be implemented at once or will specific components be implemented on a schedule? Who will be involved at each implementation? Here again, the timetable chosen will depend upon specific programmatic goals, the results of the evaluation and assessment, and the campus culture specific to the institution. And, since assessment is continuous, assessment of the effectiveness of any implementations regarding process and delivery, student learning, and advisor learning outcomes relevant to programmatic goals will need to occur as part of the subsequent assessment cycle.

Bringing It All Together

As career advising is an integral part of academic advising, the above information and methodologies are relevant to evaluating and assessing career advising as an aspect of academic advising, to evaluating and assessing an integrated academic and career advising program, and to evaluating and assessing a solitary career advising program. In either case, neither evaluation nor assessment is quick or easy, nor is an individual undertaking. Further, there is indeed a difference between evaluation and assessment, and assessment is much more than a single evaluative survey. By involving stakeholders from the beginning, and by linking each phase of the evaluation and assessment processes for career advising back to the institutional mission and forward to desired programmatic outcomes, a culture for evaluation and assessment will begin to be built that will eventually become a regular and normal part of career advising. Communication and collaboration are the most important factors in the development of this culture and the garnering of support for evaluation and assessment efforts. But perhaps the most critical aspect to remember is to start small and have some successes. Identify one or two outcomes toward the programmatic goals, and start there. Do not attempt to do too much initially or the result is likely to be a lack of support and a perception of being overwhelmed by evaluation and assessment. After all, evaluation and assessment often have negative connotations, and part of this process is to demonstrate the utility for evaluation and assessment and the ways they can be part of the everyday activities involved in career advising.

References

Angelo, T. (1995, November). Reassessing and defining assessment. *AAHE Bulletin*.

Appleby, D. C. (2008). Advising as teaching and learning. In V. N. Gordon, W. R. Habley, & T. J. Grites, & Associates, *Academic advising: A comprehensive handbook* (2nd ed., pp. 85–102). San Francisco: Jossey-Bass.

Campbell, S. (2008). Vision, mission, goals, and programmatic objectives for academic advising programs. In V. N. Gordon, W. R. Habley, & T. J. Grites, & Associates,

Academic advising: A comprehensive handbook (2nd ed., pp. 229–241). San Francisco: Jossey-Bass.

Campbell, S., Nutt, C., Robbins, R., Kirk-Kuwaye, M., & Higa, L. (2005). *NACADA guide to assessment in academic advising*. Manhattan, KS: National Academic Advising Association.

Council for the Advancement of Standards in Higher Education. (2006). *CAS standards for higher education* (6th ed.). Washington, DC: Author.

Creamer, D. G. (2000). Use of theory in academic advising. In V. N. Gordon, W. R. Habley, & Associates, *Academic advising: A comprehensive handbook* (pp. 18–34). San Francisco: Jossey-Bass.

Creamer, E. G., & Scott, D. W. (2000). Assessing individual advisor effectiveness. In V. N. Gordon, W. R. Habley, & Associates, *Academic advising: A comprehensive handbook* (pp. 339–348). San Francisco: Jossey-Bass.

Crookston, B. B. (1972). A developmental view of academic advising as teaching. *Journal of College Student Personnel, 13,* 12–17.

Cuseo, J. (2008). Assessing advisor effectiveness. In V. N. Gordon, W. R. Habley, & T. J. Grites, *Academic advising: A comprehensive handbook* (2nd ed., pp. 369–385). San Francisco: Jossey-Bass.

Darling, R. (2005). Flowchart of assessment in academic advising. In S. Campbell, C. Nutt, R. Robbins, M. Kirk-Kuwaye, & L. Higa (Eds.), *NACADA guide to assessment in academic advising*. Manhattan, KS: National Academic Advising Association.

Ender, S. C., Winston, R. B., and Miller, T. K. (1984). Academic advising reconsidered. In R. B. Winston, Jr., T. K. Miller, S. C. Ender, T. J. Grites, & Associates (Eds.), *Developmental academic advising* (pp. 3–34). San Francisco: Jossey-Bass.

Ewell, P. (2000). *Assessment of learning*. Denver, CO: AAHE Assessment Forum.

Frost, S. H. (1991). *Academic advising for student success: A system of shared responsibility*. ASHE-ERIC Higher Education Report No. 3. Washington, DC: The George Washington School of Education and Human Development.

Frost, S. H., Habley, W. R., King, M. C., Vowell, F. N., & White, E. R. (1995). In G. Kramer (Ed.), *Reaffirming the role of faculty in academic advising*. NACADA Monograph Series Number 1. Manhattan, KS: National Academic Advising Association.

Gordon, V. N. (2006). *Career advising: An academic advisor's guide*. San Francisco: Jossey-Bass.

Grites, T. J. (1994). From principle to practice: Pain or gain? *NACADA Journal, 14*(2), 80–84.

Habley, W. R. (2004). *The status of academic advising: Findings from the ACT sixth national survey*. NACADA Monograph Series No. 10. Manhattan, KS: NACADA.

Hagen, P. L. (1994). Academic advising as dialectic. *NACADA Journal, 14*(2), 85–88.

Lynch, M. L. (2000). *Assessing the effectiveness of the advising program*. In V. N. Gordon, W. R. Habley, & Associates, *Academic advising: A comprehensive handbook* (pp. 324–338). San Francisco: Jossey-Bass.

Macaruso, V. (2007). From the co-editors: Brief report on the NACADA Commission on the assessment of advising 2004 survey results. *NACADA Journal, 27*(1), 3–8.

Maki, P. L. (2002). Developing an assessment plan to learn about student learning. *Journal of Academic Librarianship, 28*(1–2), 8–13.

Maki, P. L. (2004). *Assessing for learning: Building a sustainable commitment across the institution*. Sterling, VA: Stylus Publishing.

Marchese, T. (1993). *AAHE continuous quality improvement project: Profiles of campuses*. Braintree, MA: The Assessment Institute.

McCalla-Wriggins, B. (2000). Integrating academic advising and career and life planning. In V. N. Gordon, W. R. Habley, & Associates, *Academic advising: A comprehensive handbook* (pp. 162–179). San Francisco: Jossey-Bass.

McKamey, J. N. (2007). An advising syllabus: A tool to increase advising effectiveness. *The Mentor: An Academic Advising Journal, 9*(1). Retrieved from http://www.psu.edu/dus/mentor/070321jm.htm

Miller, M. A., & Alberts, B. (1994). Developmental advising: Where teaching and learning intersect. *NACADA Journal, 14*(2), 43–45.

National Association of Colleges and Employers. (2006). *NACE professional standards for college and university career services*. Bethlehem, PA: Author.

Palomba, C. A. (1999). *Assessment essentials: Planning, implementing, and improving assessment in higher education*. San Francisco: Jossey-Bass.

Pellegrino, J. W., Chudowsky, N., & Glaser, R. (2001). *Knowing what students know*. Washington, DC: National Academies Press.

Ryan, C. C. (1992). Advising as teaching. *NACADA Journal, 12*(1), 4–8.

Thurmond, K. (2007). *Academic advising syllabus: Advising as teaching in action* webinar and pocket guide. Manhattan, KS: National Academic Advising Association.

Trabant, T. M. (2006). *Advising syllabus 101*. NACADA Clearinghouse of Academic Advising Resources. Retrieved from http://www.nacada.ksu.edu/Clearninghouse/AdvisingIssues/syllabus101.htm

Troxel, W. G. (2008). Assessing the effectiveness of the advising program. In V. N. Gordon, W. R. Habley, T. J. Grites, & Associates, *Academic advising: A comprehensive handbook* (2nd ed., pp. 386–395). San Francisco: Jossey-Bass.

Upcraft, M. L., & Schuh, J. H. (1996). *Assessment in student affairs*. San Francisco: Jossey-Bass.

White, E. R. (2000). *Developing mission, goals, and objectives for the advising program*. In V. N. Gordon, W. R. Habley, & Associates, *Academic advising: A comprehensive handbook* (pp. 180–191). San Francisco: Jossey-Bass.

Wiggens, G., & McTighe, J. (2006). *Understanding by design*. Upper Saddle River, NJ: Pearson.

Winston, R. B., Ender, S. C., & Miller, T. K. (Eds.). (1982). *Developmental approaches to academic advising*. (New Directions for Student Services, No. 17). San Francisco: Jossey-Bass.

Winston, R. B., Miller, T. K., Ender, S. C., Grites, T. J., & Associates. (1984). *Developmental academic advising*. San Francisco: Jossey-Bass.

CHAPTER THIRTEEN

Career Advising

Challenges, Opportunities, and Recommendations for the Future

Betsy McCalla-Wriggins, Kenneth F. Hughey,
Joanne K. Damminger, Dorothy Burton Nelson

Harvard University was founded in 1620, and one mission of the university was to prepare young men for a profession, specifically the clergy (Frost, 2000). Since that time, there have been and continue to be many different philosophies about the role of higher education in preparing students for a career. However, today's students clearly express that several of the top reasons they attend college are related to preparing for a career. Therefore, it is incumbent upon the academy to pay attention to these students. This final chapter briefly describes the contributions a comprehensive career and academic advising program can have on transforming institutional challenges into opportunities and present a vision of career advising for the future. It also identifies some challenges to achieving the vision of integrating career advising in academic advising and offers recommendations to embrace this new future and work toward its creation.

TRANSFORMING INSTITUTIONAL CHALLENGES INTO OPPORTUNITIES

Each institution of higher education has its own unique challenges, but several cross the boundaries of institutional type, size, and location. Although academic and career advising is not the magic bullet that will solve all the issues, an institutional commitment to comprehensive academic and career advising can have a positive impact on these challenges. The specific challenges

293

addressed in this chapter include expectations of students and parents, reten-tion and graduation rates, financial concerns, and diversity. Although these challenges and opportunities are described with broad strokes, each institution must examine these within the context of their mission, student population, and environment to develop academic and career advising programs to meet the needs of their students.

Expectations of Students

Challenge. Students continue to indicate through national survey data (Astin, 2007) that several of the top reasons they attend college are related to gain-ing employment. They expect some payoff at graduation and that payoff, to which they often feel entitled, is directly related to a "good job." However, when asked to describe a "good job," students often cannot articulate what they want. Another component of this challenge is that even though students express this expectation, while in college they often do not take the steps nec-essary to prepare themselves to obtain any job, much less a "good job" con-sistent with their values, skills, and interests. This was clearly articulated by students in the Visions of the Future Learning Community for freshmen unde-clared students at Rowan University (Damminger, 2007). Students participated in a number of self-assessment and career exploration activities during this two-semester experience, and at the conclusion were asked about the value of these activities. They indicated that although the activities were extremely valuable, they acknowledged that they would not have engaged in any of them on their own.

Opportunity. A comprehensive academic and career advising program that begins at the freshman year and continues through sophomore, junior, and senior experiences can address both the expressed expectations of students and their acknowledged reluctance to seek this assistance and information on their own. Providing structured academic and career decision-making activ-ities both in and out of the classroom creates the opportunity for students to examine these important issues with the support of faculty and full-time advisors. Including specific learning outcomes for these activities is especially important so that students clearly understand the need to accept personal responsibility in this process. The more students are successful in meeting their expectations and in finding meaningful employment, the greater the probability they will be satisfied with their college experience and prepared for the future.

Expectations of Parents

Challenge. Parents today also have expectations of institutions of higher edu-cation. They expect that their sons or daughters will obtain a good educa-tion, and they also expect some ROI, return on investment. With college costs increasing each year, parents want some assurance that their tuition dollars will be well spent. They want to know the kind of employment opportunities that will be available upon graduation and the type of assistance that will be pro-vided so their son or daughter can obtain that "good job" he or she expects.

This expectation is often reflected in these questions: What types of internships are available? What assistance do you provide students in obtaining employment? What are the placement rates of graduates of this department, college, or university?

Many parents also have the expectation that they will continue to be involved with their children's life, much the way they have been in the past. In this age of technology, it is not uncommon for students and parents to continue to communicate daily and for students to continue to seek advice and counsel from their family (Keup & Kinzie, 2007). Some parents' expectations that they will continue to make decisions for their children is a significant challenge for institutions.

Opportunity. An institution with an integrated program of academic and career advising will be in a position to specifically address these concerns of parents. A comprehensive program will begin before the student enrolls and will be a major component of the freshmen orientation activity for both students and parents. Informing parents of the specific curricular and extracurricular activities that support informed academic and career decision making and how they can support their students in this process has a two-fold benefit. First, parents will see concrete examples of how students will be continually engaged in the academic and career advising process. This can ultimately lead to meaningful employment upon graduation which relates to their concern about a return on their investment. Second, it gives the institution the opportunity to articulate appropriate ways parents can communicate with and support their children. Including specific vignettes related to academic and career issues in orientation can clearly illustrate ways they can be connected and supportive. These same vignettes can also make clear the need for students to accept personal responsibility and to develop independent decision-making skills. Developing a partnership with parents in this process acknowledges the reality of this continuing need to connect. Many institutions provide parents with a copy of *A Family Guide to Academic Advising* (Smith & Gordon, 2008) as a resource for this partnership.

Retention and Graduation Rates

Challenge. Today there is increased competition among colleges for students. Many students are being courted by multiple institutions with various financial packages. Other students even wait until after the orientation experience to make the final decision as to which college or university they will attend. Once a student enrolls, it is highly desirable for the institution to retain that student. It is less expensive to retain that student than it is to recruit a new student. In general, the cost of recruiting one new student is close to the cost of retaining 3–5 currently enrolled students (Astin, 1993; Tinto, 1993). In addition, graduation rates are a key measure used to rate institutions and students must be retained in order to graduate.

Opportunity. Academic advising can be an effective retention strategy; adding the career advising component has the potential to create even more value. Students' experience during the first several weeks can be critical in determining their decision to stay or leave (Tinto, 1993). As a result, during that time faculty and full-time advisors need to be especially proactive in engaging students in the process of self discovery, a critical component in academic and career advising. Beginning that process during the first semester actively demonstrates that students are valued as unique individuals, have great potential, and have the opportunity to explore and investigate numerous options within a very supportive academic community. Consider the impact of asking the following questions in classes as well as advising sessions to support students in connecting academic experiences to future career options: What life skills are being developed in this experience? How can this content knowledge be used in a career or vocation? How do those both relate to your interests, skills, values, and passions? Another key question that has the potential to open many possibilities is, "What would you do if you knew you couldn't fail?" (Roberts, 2007, p. 97). Systematic and structured academic and career advising helps students to make choices that provide personal and professional meaning to their educational experiences that have the potential to contribute to increased retention and higher graduation rates.

Financial Concerns

Challenge. Across the nation, institutions are facing the reality of decreasing financial resources. More and more public institutions are seeking increased donations from alumni, other benefactors, foundations, and corporations. Students and their parents are also feeling the impact of these financial issues in the form of increasing tuition (Keup & Kinzie, 2007). In short, institutions as well as individuals are seeking ways to identify more financial resources.

Opportunity. A comprehensive academic and career advising program can assist in providing more financial resources in a variety of ways. For institutions, alumni are a major source of donations. It follows then that if students participate in meaningful career and academic advising activities throughout their time in college, it increases the probability that their expectations regarding meaningful employment after graduation will be met. This can have an extremely significant impact on their level of positive feelings for the institution.

For students, being able to gain experience and develop work-related skills are important components in academic and career decision making. Employers who are active partners with institutions can provide part-time work, off-campus work study positions, as well as internships and summer work for students. These positions provide much needed financial assistance to pay for ever-increasing college costs.

Another issue that relates to college costs for students is the issue of changing majors. There are many times that it is appropriate and wise for a student to change majors, especially when their decision to change is based on who they are and what they want to achieve. However, students often select and then change majors because they have not engaged in self-assessment and major and career exploration (Steele & McDonald, 2000). Their choices have been made in a vacuum and, as a result, they may have to spend an extra semester in college. If all students participate in structured academic and career advising beginning their first semester and continuing each semester, they could find the "right" fit earlier. Those that had made the "right" choice initially would have that decision validated. Students that made an inappropriate choice or who were uncertain about what to choose would have the opportunity to engage in activities to learn about themselves (e.g., values, skills, interests), as well as academic and career options congruent with themselves. Establishing a clear purpose and direction early in the collegiate experience not only will support student success and retention, but it can also save students' tuition dollars and possibly eliminate one semester of student loans.

Diversity

Challenge. Institutions of higher education, the communities, and the workplace are all becoming more culturally diverse. Through technological advances individuals are interfacing with people of different cultures both in person and through other means of communication. There is great value in learning from and appreciating the richness of multiple cultures, but there is also a significant challenge in helping people to value those cultural differences.

Opportunity. The foundation of comprehensive academic and career advising is students engaging in the process of learning about themselves. This is not a one-time event, but an ongoing process. Through individual advising sessions, group workshops, and classroom projects, students can participate in numerous activities that help them discover their values and passions. Working beside those of diverse backgrounds in a supportive environment where differences can be explained, explored, and examined can help individuals learn to value differences. Volunteering and participating in service learning projects with those from differing cultures can also provide opportunities to identify common threads. It is critical to help students understand and value their own gifts, and to learn to value and appreciate the differing gifts of others. Learning about oneself can no longer be left to chance. "If we do not teach our students to understand themselves, how can we expect them to understand and appreciate others?" (Astin, 2005).

A VISION FOR MAKING CAREER ADVISING INTEGRAL TO ACADEMIC ADVISING

Institutions that transform the challenges into opportunities will work toward creating a future that infuses career and academic advising into all phases of the academy. The goal of this vision is to support students' development, prepare them for the future, empower them to manage career and vocational options in a changing world, and become contributing members of society. The key components of this vision include making an institutional commitment to integrating academic and career advising, integrating career advising in academic advising by faculty and full-time advisors, incorporating activities and assignments that support academic and career exploration and decision making into course syllabi, developing co-curricular activities that provide students with the opportunity to explore and examine appropriate academic and career options, and valuing all individuals on campus and the unique contributions they can make toward student success.

The first component of this vision, the institutional commitment to integrating career advising in academic advising, is critical and needs to be explicitly stated by those in positions of leadership. All academic and student affairs' units will have career and academic advising as an integral part of their mission statement and assessment plan. Quality career and academic advising will be an important component in the promotion and tenure processes for faculty. Promotion and merit procedures for full-time advisors will also clearly state that integrating career and academic advising is an expectation. While there may still be designated career and academic advising units on campus, it will be clear that the responsibility for this process is not just within that specific functional unit. An institution that commits to this vision by providing this comprehensive assistance not only to students, but also to alumni, actively acknowledges the need for continuing support in this lifelong process.

Having faculty advisors and full-time advisors integrate career advising in academic advising is the second component of this vision. Although advisors do not have to develop all of the career advising competencies described in Chapter Three, they do need to be explicit about the support they can provide as their advisees make career and academic decisions. In 1972 O'Banion described the exploration of life goals and the exploration of vocational goals as the first two steps in academic advising. Self-knowledge is essential in these first two steps, and advisors have a unique opportunity to engage students in a dialogue that focuses on their values and skills, their reasons for attending college, and their hopes and dreams, as well as their uncertainties and fears for the future. Asking questions that explore these issues demonstrates that the advisor is concerned about the student as an individual and can support the student as the process of self-discovery begins or continues. Without the foundation of self-knowledge, students do not have parameters against which to evaluate and make informed decisions. Many students enter college without this foundation whereas others may have some self-knowledge but may not know how to apply it to academic and career decision making. Helping students examine and explore the connections between career and academic choices should be part of every conversation between students and advisors.

A third component of this vision is that all courses will have at least one activity and subsequent student learning outcome that incorporates information or skills that relate to academic and career decision making. Structured career and academic discussions, as well as exploration and decision-making activities, will become the norm in classrooms at all levels of the collegiate experience. These activities are limitless and could address any of the stages in the process of obtaining career goals: knowing oneself; gathering academic and career information and making a tentative decision; exploring and reality testing different options; determining which options to actively pursue; developing marketing strategies to obtain career goals; and then achieving those individual goals. Although any course could include activities related to any stage, courses in the first year might focus on self-knowledge and an initial identification of majors and careers of interest related to the specific subject matter. Junior level courses might begin to address the marketing strategies needed to gain meaningful employment in careers related to course-specific disciplines or to gain acceptance into graduate school. Including these structured and required activities in the curriculum actively demonstrates to students the value of this process and the institutions' commitment to helping them be successful after graduation.

Co-curricular activities will be designed to support students in making informed academic and career decisions. This is the fourth component of the vision to integrate career and academic advising. Volunteer and service learning experiences, major and student club-sponsored activities, resident hall and peer advisor positions, on- and off-campus student employment options, and learning communities are just a few examples where career and academic options can be presented, explored, and considered. Identifying the skills developed through these experiences and possible majors and careers connected to these activities can broaden students' perspectives and expand their horizons. Developing a database for every co-curricular activity on campus could provide students with very important information. Being intentional about the inclusion of this career and academic piece is the key.

The last component of the vision is to encourage and value the unique experiences that all on campus have in supporting students as they make academic and career decisions. Many faculty and staff come to the institution with various work experiences and can share what they learned and how that work was or was not a good match. Each person also has experience in the process of obtaining a job, and all of those activities require specific skills. Students who are seeking positions in a public school system can learn the specific hiring practices, procedures, and time lines from those who have worked in that environment. Students seeking employment in the field of budgeting and finance can speak with those employed at the college or university's budget department and financial aid, as well as faculty who have had that responsibility in the public or private sector. For the history major who also enjoys theater, career options connecting those two interests can be found by joining student clubs, speaking with faculty in both those departments, as well as interviewing individuals engaged in the many aspects of producing, directing, and staging plays on campus. Many people enjoy talking about themselves and their experiences and frequently feel honored that they are being asked for advice. As a result, students who seek these individuals will often find valuable resources to provide information and support as they make academic and career decisions.

Developing career advising as a part of academic advising will not only support students, but it also creates the opportunity to bring together people from various parts of the campus community to work toward a goal that transcends discipline, department, and college boundaries and interests. Breaking down those academic and departmental silos can create exciting new learning experiences for faculty and staff as well.

All student experiences can be enhanced when students see personal relevance. "Higher Education, and liberal education in particular, should be about providing learners of any age with the opportunity to reflect on the purpose and meaning they create with their lives and the contribution to the world they can make with their gifts. That, to me, is the highest calling of the academy" (Manning, 1999).

CHALLENGES TO INTEGRATING CAREER AND ACADEMIC ADVISING

Considering the vision of integrating career advising to academic advising can be energizing; however, transforming this vision into a reality can be challenging. Acknowledging these challenges is the first step in developing strategies to address and overcome them. Specific challenges addressed include institutional commitment, organizational structure, and resources. In addition, each institution may have other unique challenges based on their mission, student population, and environment.

One challenge to making career advising integral to academic advising is obtaining the needed institutional commitment. This commitment may begin at the unit, department, division, college, or institutional level; however, there must be an explicit statement that makes clear this is an expectation. Advisors can include career advising within their individual academic advising sessions and their students will benefit greatly from that experience; however, transforming a unit, department, division, college, or institution requires intentional and explicit behaviors. Having career advising as an integral part of academic advising must be clearly stated in mission statements, strategic plans, and assessment plans.

Another challenge is to create an organizational structure that supports the integration of career advising in academic advising. This can be achieved within many different organizational structures, and no one model is "best." The Exemplary Practices section of this handbook (Appendix D) illustrates that differing models can be very successful. To determine the most effective structure for any institution to meet this goal, key questions need to be considered. These include: What is the current structure? What can be done within the existing structure? Are modifications necessary and, if so, what are they? What are the consequences of making those modifications? What are the costs (e.g., financial) to make those changes? The answers to these questions will be different for each institution, but it is critical to discuss these questions with as many stakeholders as possible before making any significant changes.

A third challenge is resources that include appropriate staff, facilities and equipment, nonsalary budgets, and professional development opportunities.

People are the most important resource and, as indicated above, all potential stakeholders must participate in conversations about the goal of integrating career advising in academic advising. The attitudes of the staff involved in this process can either facilitate the initiative or create additional challenges that require significant time and energy to resolve. Issues that need to be addressed in the early stages of any type of major change for full-time advisors include changing job responsibilities, educational level required, and equity in pay. In addition, fear of the unknown needs to be addressed. Many full-time and faculty advisors will also be concerned about their "qualifications" and the time needed with students to provide career advising. Those on campus who currently have the responsibility of career advising also need to be involved in this process. Examples of questions that arise are: How will the integration of career advising in academic advising impact their work? Will there be new expectations for them?

New expectations relate directly to the need to be intentional in creating and providing professional development opportunities for advisors to obtain the skills and knowledge required for this task. If these professional development opportunities are not made available and there is no expectation that individuals will take advantage of and incorporate this new knowledge into their work with students, then it becomes clear to all involved that this is just another exercise and really has no value.

Advisors also need to have the space, equipment, materials, and other non-salary resources to meet these new expectations. A few of the questions that need to be asked as part of the planning process are: What resources currently exist? Are there duplicate resources that can be combined to become more effective and efficient? What are grant opportunities that support this new plan? Is the current location of the offices and staff involved positioned for easy access to students? There is no one model that institutions should try to emulate; however, having the basic tools and resources in place enhances opportunities for success for advisors and students.

RECOMMENDATIONS TO CREATE THE VISION

Transformational change is powerful but takes time and a commitment on the part of many people. To move a unit, department, division, college, or university toward making career advising an integral part of academic advising, the following recommendations are from an institutional perspective and intended for those in positions of leadership:

1. Seek support and commitment from key administrators. Obtaining support for the initiative is critical to its successful implementation.
2. Communicate to those in the designated area(s) that integrating career advising in academic advising is a priority and a goal to be achieved. Make clear the rationale for this initiative and the process to be used to implement it.

3. Develop a task force to further explore and to present specific recommendations about how to make the integration of career advising in academic advising an institutional, college, division, and unit or department strategic objective. Include on this task force individuals who are advocates and skeptics for the integration as well as stakeholders in the process.

4. Provide the task force with information and resources to make informed recommendations. Comparing practices at the institution to national data available from National Academic Advising Association (NACADA) as well as the National Resource Center for First Year Students and Students in Transition (FYE) can be very informative. Provide task force members with not only materials, but also the opportunity to attend regional and national meetings where programs on integrated models are discussed.

5. Inform individuals who are in similar positions at the institution about this initiative and explore ways that multiple units, departments, divisions, or colleges can collaborate to move toward an institutional goal of integrating career advising in academic advising.

6. Determine whether integrating career advising in academic advising is occurring in designated units and, if so, gather information about specific in and out of the classroom activities that support the integration of career advising in academic advising.

7. Share the information gathered with members in the specific areas where this integration will occur. Provide opportunities for those engaged in the integration of career advising in academic advising to meet informally, discuss how this is to be accomplished, and explore other ways students can be supported in making informed academic and career decisions. Encourage and provide resources for pilot program initiatives that further expand the integration of career advising in academic advising.

8. Publicly acknowledge the work of those providing this integration and actively support their efforts. An advisors' recognition event, support to attend national conferences, or even a plaque of appreciation are examples of how this can be accomplished.

9. Anticipate the real and perceived challenges to the integration of career advising in academic advising. Although there are general challenges described earlier in this chapter, each institution has its own unique challenges. Being able to anticipate and address these at the onset can provide guidance in developing a realistic plan of action and facilitate the process of making career advising integral to academic advising.

10. Determine how to implement the plan, create a time line, and provide appropriate resources for the successful implementation of the initiative. Work toward developing unit, department, division, college, or university mission statements that support the vision. Appoint a person or

persons to have overall accountability for implementation of the plan. All individuals involved in the process need to have specific tasks for which they also are accountable.

11. Make clear that a curriculum, pedagogy, and learning outcomes are required components of any integrated career and academic advising program. Provide advisors with resources to develop these essential components, which will vary depending on where students are in their academic and career decision making.

12. Provide resources to implement an ongoing assessment plan to determine how well this integration is being achieved. Engage stakeholders in this process so everyone is clear of the need for and rationale behind the assessment plan.

13. Support research on the impact of integrating career advising in academic advising. Provide resources and create incentives for faculty and full-time advisors to engage in this important research. In an environment of limited resources, research that supports the impact of integrating career advising in academic advising is critical.

In some situations, faculty and full-time advisors will find themselves in a place where their unit or department, division, college, or university is not ready to embrace integrating career advising in academic advising across the academy. However, advisors can begin integrating career advising in their academic advising interactions with students. The following recommendations are provided to move an individual advisor toward that goal:

1. Know oneself and assess how previous and current positions have been congruent with the values, skills, and interests espoused as important.

2. Identify areas for professional development and enhance the knowledge and competencies related to career advising. What additional skills and knowledge are needed to effectively incorporate career advising in academic advising? One's ability to assess and to develop new personal and professional competencies is critical in a world of change. Develop plans and strategies to obtain the required professional development and seek others on campus to be a resource. In addition, investigate the multiple options available through NACADA and FYE to support this need for lifelong learning.

3. Reach out to like-minded people on campus and brainstorm ways to collaboratively develop pilot programs that enhance career advising as a component of academic advising. These programs provide the opportunity to try different approaches, obtain feedback, refine the process, and formulate a program, process, or system that can be implemented on a larger scale.

4. Conduct action research on current practices and incorporate research components into new programs and practices that include career

advising as part of academic advising. Hard data are essential in persuading decision makers that career advising has the potential to increase the impact of academic advising.

5. Initiate conversations within your unit or department to develop and make explicit the curriculum, pedagogy, and outcomes that support students' academic and career decision making. Each academic and administrative department can have unique objectives that reflect their mission.

The final three recommendations apply to all professionals interested in making career advising integral to academic advising. The recommendations are as follows:

1. Share the impact of integrating career advising in academic advising with others. Through local, regional, and national conference presentations, journal articles, Web sites, listservs, and professional newsletters communicate with colleagues the integration process and the impact it has had on both students and advisors.

2. Communicate this integration of career advising in academic advising to the college or university community, as well as to current students and their parents. Make clear the responsibility of the institution as well as the specific responsibility of the student in this process.

3. Recognize the power of one and become intentional in efforts to integrate career advising in academic advising. Within one's area of influence, consider what can be completed differently today to help students make meaning of their academic and career experiences.

SUMMARY

The landscape of higher education is changing and will continue to change. There will be different challenges and opportunities, but one fact will not change. Regardless of what the future holds, people are this country's and the world's greatest resource. Consider a world where those who enter the workforce know themselves and are obtaining employment that is consistent with their values, skills, interests, talents, and passions. Individuals who feel good about themselves and the contribution they are making through their work can have an incredible positive impact on their environments at home, at work, and in the community.

Supporting students as they engage in the process of self-discovery, explore various academic and career options, and decide on their own unique path to a meaningful future is very important work. Reflect on all the opportunities available and select one place to begin. Participating in the process of integrating career advising in academic advising and into the fabric of the academy can be an exciting journey for all and one that benefits students and prepares them for the future.

References

Astin, A. W. (1993). *What matters in college?* San Francisco: Jossey-Bass.

Astin, A. W. (2005, February). *The first year experience and the whole student.* Keynote address presented at the meeting of the Annual Conference on the First-Year Experience, Phoenix, AZ.

Astin, A. W. (2007). *The American freshman: National norms for fall 2006.* Los Angeles: Higher Education Research Institute.

Damminger, J. K. (2007). Self-assessment: Relevance and value in first-year advising. In M. S. Hunter, B. McCalla-Wriggins, & E. R. White (Eds.), *Academic advising: New insights for teaching and learning in the first year* (Monograph No. 46 [National Resource Center]; Monograph No. 14 [National Academic Advising Association]; pp. 59–69). Columbia, SC: University of South Carolina, National Resource Center for the First-Year Experience and Students in Transition.

Frost, S. H. (2000). Historical and philosophical foundations for academic advising. In V. N. Gordon, W. R. Habley, & Associates, *Academic advising: A comprehensive handbook* (pp. 3–17). San Francisco: Jossey-Bass.

Keup, J. R., & Kinzie, J. (2007). A national portrait of first-year students. In M. S. Hunter, B. McCalla-Wriggins, & E. R. White (Eds.), *Academic advising: New insights for teaching and learning in the first year* (Monograph No. 46 [National Resource Center]; Monograph No. 14 [National Academic Advising Association]; pp. 19–38). Columbia, SC: University of South Carolina, National Resource Center for the First-Year Experience and Students in Transition.

Manning, M. (1999, October). *Quality and liberal education.* Keynote address presented at the meeting of the Association for General and Liberal Studies Conference, Richmond, VA.

O'Banion, T. (1972). An academic advising model. *Junior College Journal, 42*(6), 62–69.

Roberts, R. (2007). *From the heart: Seven rules to live by.* New York: Hyperion.

Smith, D. C., & Gordon, V. (2008). *A family guide to academic advising.* Columbia, SC and Manhattan, KS: National Resource Center for the First-Year Experience and Students in Transition and National Academic Advising Association.

Steele, G. E., & McDonald, M. L. (2000). Advising students in transition. In V. N. Gordon, W. R. Habley, & Associates, *Academic advising: A comprehensive handbook* (pp. 144–161). San Francisco: Jossey-Bass.

Tinto, V. (1993). *Leaving college: Rethinking the causes and cures for student attrition* (2nd ed.). Chicago: University of Chicago Press.

Exemplary Practices: Integrated Academic and Career Advising Centers

AIMS COMMUNITY COLLEGE

Center Name: Student Success Center: Academic Advising Office and Career Services Office
  Location: Greeley, CO

Institutional Information

- Two-year public, local-district community college
- Located in Northern Colorado with four campus locations, Greeley Main, Greeley Downtown, Fort Lupton, and Loveland
- Offers occupational certificates, associate of applied science and associate's degrees

Total Number of Students: 7,191 students attended the college in 2007–2008
  Center url: www.aims.edu/student/ssc; www.aims.edu/student/career; www.aims.edu/student/advising

Contact Information

  Rachel Davis

  Coordinator of Career Services

  rachel.davis@ aims.edu

  970–339–6251

John Batchelor

Coordinator of Advising

john.batchelor@aims.edu

970–339–6382

Mission and Objectives of the Center

The mission of the Student Success Center (SSC) is as follows: "a community of learner-focused professionals who advocate the empowerment and growth of individuals. As such, the center provides services in a confidential setting to assist students in achieving academic and career success" (*Aims Community College Catalog*, 2008–2009). Housed within the SSC are the following departments: assessment, academic advising, career services, and retention.

The academic advising program provides initial advising services to degree/certificate, undeclared, and undecided students. Advisors meet with students to assist them in their transition to college and develop an educational plan which serves as an academic road map for students to follow during their course of study at Aims.

The career services office is available to assist students and community members in discovering and moving towards their career goals. The mission of career services is to help students "Explore, Discover, Connect, [and] Succeed."

Center History

The SSC has always existed in some form since the inception of the college in 1967; however, in the early days, it was referred to as the Guidance and Counseling Center. In 1982, the Assessment Center was created and supported the implementation of the prescriptive model of advising. In the early 1990s, part-time, seasonal advisors were hired to provide more comprehensive advising, initial orientation, and screening to primarily new students based on a developmental model versus a schedule-building or prescriptive model of advising. Although a Career Resource Center and career courses were available to assist students at that time, limited, if any, career counseling existed. Based on the feedback from the advisors and students, the career services unit was added in 1999, which included a dedicated career counselor. Because of the expanding scope of the area and the desire to serve a growing academically disadvantaged and undecided student population, the area's name was changed to the Student Success Center. The retention services unit was added to the center in 2005 as a result of a Title III grant.

Based on institutional data and a concerted effort to improve the retention and persistence of students, especially academically underprepared and first generation students, the college moved to employ more advisors year round. Currently, all staff members flow between peak advising periods before terms, and retention, career, and allied health admissions services during academic terms. This enables the college to provide substantive advising even during busy periods while providing the other named services during the rest of the collegiate year.

Descriptions of Services and Programs Offered

In addition to individual, one-on-one advising the academic advising office also provides:

- Transfer Fairs featuring representatives from two local four-year universities and their academic programs
- Allied Health Orientations for nursing, nurse aide, surgical technology, and radiologic technology

The career services office provides:

- Career counseling in a series of three appointments for individual exploration and discovery
- Classroom and community presentations on job search skill development
- Job search skill development assistance including résumé building and reviews and mock interviews
- Career Advance, an online job board for students and alumni
- Career exploration programming on career pathways and an Aims-produced cable show called "Career Insider" to be launched Spring 2009
- Career exploration programming for local eighth-graders

Methods of Service Delivery

It is a priority to the staff of the SSC that new students receive one-on-one attention during their entrance or return to Aims. Through a state-mandated assessment process for college level placement, the first advising session is a requirement for new degree and certificate-seeking students. This initial appointment allows for relationship building and student screening regarding support needs for their transition. Due to the proximity of the departments and the current reporting structure, easy and direct referrals, based on students' needs, between academic advisors and career services are a natural and expected outcome.

Advisors start the initial advising session in such a way that students are able to express their expectations, needs, and questions regarding their enrollment. The advisor seeks to obtain information on their past educational history, their academic and career goals, and their sense of direction. Based on this conversation, advisors then assist students in selecting courses that reflect the current articulation of students' goals; college-level placement for reading, English, and math; and general or specific degree options. The result of the session is that students leave with an accurate schedule of classes, an initial understanding of college curriculum options and, if they are undecided or undeclared, a referral to career services.

Most students who are referred to career services through academic advising complete the career counseling process in order to provide clarification about how their personality and interests relate to the declaration of an academic program/career path. At the end of the counseling process, students are directed to explore specific career niches using online resources. They are then referred back to their original advisor to discuss their response to the process and to establish a more directed academic plan. In an effort to provide seamless and informed services, the results of the career counseling process are made available to the academic advisors for review.

In addition, the staff members of the SSC developed a service philosophy based on an understanding of the new students' perspective of the institution. Staff recognizes that the organization of offices and resources need to make sense to new students and that students expect assistance for their individual needs. Therefore, when students come to the advising and registration step in the admissions process, a concerted effort is made to teach the student about as many curricular, career and registration processes as possible.

Students Served

As the entry point for the college, new students are the largest group that the SSC serves. The SSC also provides continuing services to remedial/developmental, pre-allied health, and "very" undecided students. "Very undecided students" are those who could go either into career and technical programs or associate of arts or sciences transfer programs.

Center Staffing

Ten staff members work together from academic advising and career services to partner in serving students. The advising department includes a coordinator, one general advisor, three senior advisors (housed at outlying campus locations), two allied health advisors, and one pre-collegiate advisor. The career services office includes a coordinator and an employer relations specialist, both of whom provide comprehensive career counseling and job skill development appointments and resources. SSC staff also work collaboratively with the retention department coordinator and retention advisors who also provide general academic advising. The director of the SSC reports directly to the dean of student services.

Integration of Career Services and Academic Advising

The integration of career and advising services is accomplished in two fundamental ways. The first concerns the work assignments of personnel and the second is present in the typical way advising sessions progress. As mentioned in the Center History section, career service personnel provide advising during peak, pre-term periods and then return to career decision-making and employment preparation services. This provides continuity of service to undecided students who are advised, receive career counseling, and then could potentially receive continued advising from the same professional.

In addition, all advisors are very aware of how indecision can impact retention and progress toward educational goal completion. The state of Colorado now guarantees transfer of liberal arts community college degrees to the state universities. While easing transfer for students, this arrangement has specified the curriculum students need to follow. Undecided students run the risk of losing credits if they do not make career decisions early. Since advisors are aware of this situation, they urge students to take advantage of the resources provided through career services in order to progress through the decision-making process.

The second way integration is accomplished is by the manner in which advising is delivered. Advisors are trained to begin advising sessions with new students with very open-ended career questions. The students' responses help the advisor gauge the definitiveness of the student's career plans and knowledge of college processes. In nearly all instances, students need to refine their career plans. Therefore, when advisors review and define the next steps at the end of advising sessions, a referral to career services or at least an assignment to research or further define their career goals by using online career exploration resources is almost always suggested.

To accomplish this successfully, staff members commit to providing services designed from the students' viewpoint and willingly step out of traditionally defined, narrow roles. Through this student-centered approach to academic advising and career services, professionals establish a positive relationship thereby creating the opportunity for students to comfortably reconnect with staff when and if problems/issues are encountered.

Resources

Career Exploration Resources

- Career inventories: Myers-Briggs Type Indicator and Strong Interest Inventory
- Career exploration software: ECOSIS, Career Cruising, DISCOVER
- Hard copy library including many major-specific resources

Job Search Resources

- Career Advance, Career Services online job board
- Web site links and information updated yearly on job searching, career exploration, résumé, cover letter, and interviewing resources

Advising Resources

- Online degree program worksheets for most areas of study
- Ask an Advisor e-mail service for general questions
- Comprehensive Allied Health Advising Web site
- Online information and FAQs regarding selecting a degree program, academic resources, academic probation, transfer, and graduation information
- Hard copy information about transfer institutions including in-state and out-of-state schools

Data and Learning Outcomes

Both the academic advising and career services units collect quantitative and qualitative data. Quantitative data includes satisfaction surveys and tallies. In Spring semester 2006, the "Student Assessment of Academic Advising" survey was administered to 736 students to help inform advising practices and procedures. In Spring semester 2008, three focus groups were held to seek further feedback on those areas identified as student concerns.

From these surveys it was learned that students wanted their advisors to be able to provide better information on graduation requirements, financial aid information, and transfer and employment options following graduation. This led to increased cross training, especially in the financial aid area as well as the development of two college transfer fairs with the college's two main transfer institutions. In addition, Career Advance, a Web-based job board, was implemented to give students easy access to employment opportunities in the community and beyond. Finally, the students' request for more contact with advisors led to the practice of requiring students who are in the Emerging Scholars program to meet with their advisors three times during the semester. Continuous improvement is a consistent goal of the center. A major initiative of the Student Service Division is to develop more specific learning outcomes and assessment plans for each component unit.

Strengths of the Center

The strengths of the SSC: Academic Advising and Career Services include the following:

- Easy and direct referrals between Academic Advising and Career Services are facilitated by the physical proximity of departments.

- The conversational approach to advising helps advisors to identify students who need individualized career counseling and direction.

- Cross-training of staff aids advisors in making appropriate and early referrals to Career Services.

- The SSC houses the Emerging Scholars program designed to serve underprepared students. The program had a 76% fall-to-spring retention rate for the first semester cohort and is recognized internationally for retention outcomes.

- Partnerships with faculty produce opportunities to interact with students in the classroom often enabling reconnection with students missed through walk-in/rush advising.

- Proximity to Admissions & Records and Financial Aid offices allows for registration holds to be addressed and questions/issues to be resolved within Career Services and Advising appointments.

- Online career exploration resources on the Career Services Web site allow advisors to direct student to these resources thereby supporting the Career Services staff.

Challenges of the Center

The Student Success Center staff share two challenges common to many community colleges as well as specific regional employment issues related to emerging fields. The first challenge is that first-generation students comprise a high percentage of the new student population. While they bring the desire to achieve in college, they are often limited in their knowledge of higher education terms, processes, and college-related career opportunities. Although the staff are fully aware of these deficiencies and seek to address them, these students typically make late decisions to attend college, resulting in last-minute applications and late registration for enrollment. The pre-semester rush allows the staff little time to discuss academic goals and career options often resulting in self-registration and enrollment in classes that may or may not coincide with an eventual chosen career or college major.

Another challenge is the high number of academic probation and suspension students who need to be advised each semester. This advising is much more time intensive and often coincides with the general walk-in advising rush. This means that these students who are considered high risk are engaging with advisors and career counselors in a way that is not conducive to the lengthy and individualized conversations that often need to occur in to ensure their success and create accountability.

Thirdly, as a result of regional and national developments regarding new or emerging fields, SCC staff often need to react quickly to serve new, non-traditional students who are taking advantage of retraining opportunities. These fields require skill sets that are often ill-defined. This presents challenges concerning timely delivery of service, collaboration with partnering agencies, and consistent dissemination of information.

Professional Development Provided

Career Services staff members are cross-trained on advising processes and procedures to assist during the heavy registration periods. Conversely, academic advisors receive relevant training on career planning to effectively and appropriately lead the initial career planning conversation with students. Training on referral points is also provided so that advisors know when to redirect students to Career Services for individual counseling. Staff is provided cross-training both through SSC meetings as well as the division meetings with a strong emphasis placed on evaluation of services. Innovative tools, such as the StrengthsFinder, are being adopted by the division to enhance the development of student-centered advising relationships. The Career Services department seeks to stay on the cutting edge of employment trends, employer expectations, and service delivery through professional development and networking opportunities. Attendance at annual conferences for the purpose of networking, continuing education, and professional development is strongly encouraged by the SSC director and dean for student services.

Future Plans

Plans are already moving forward to relocate the student services division to Aims' College Center located in the heart of the main Greeley campus. The building will be redesigned so that students can truly have a "one-stop" experience for recruitment, admittance, assessment, financial aid, advising, career services, and retention. The more noticeable location will enable the division to enhance the seamless service delivery. The relocation is to be completed by 2010.

The college is currently marketing an online degree program that will create new challenges for SCC departments to overcome in serving that population. Software is already being piloted and considered so that both academic advising and career counseling can be offered through online means.

As Aims Community College moves forward in its efforts to provide affordable and quality education to the community, there is a need to continue to adjust based on student needs and expectations. However, no matter what the challenge, by focusing on the SSC mission of "advocating the empowerment and growth of individuals" staff will continue to innovatively deliver services and establish strong relationships with students.

This exemplary practice description was prepared by John Batchelor, coordinator of advising, and Rachel Davis, coordinator of career services.

BRIGHAM YOUNG UNIVERSITY

Program: University Advisement Center/Career Center (centers are separate but functions are integrated)
   Location: Provo, Utah

Contact Information

   Karen Evans, coordinator, University Advisement Center

   karen_evans@byu.edu

   801–422–3826

   Vaughn Worthen, director, Career Center

   vaughn_worthen@byu.edu

   Center url: http://ccc.byu.edu/

Institutional Information

Brigham Young University is a large, privately owned, church-sponsored university with 32,900 students. It is largely an undergraduate-oriented university, with 90% of the students registered as undergraduates. The highest degree awarded is a doctoral degree. In the Carnegie classifications it is listed as a Doctoral, STEM dominant institution (awards doctoral degrees in many fields with a focus on science, technology, engineering, and mathematics).

Mission and Objectives

The University Advisement Center and the Career Center work closely together to provide academic and career advising for students. The missions of the two units reflect both the need for assisting students in the exploration of careers, majors, and academic paths, as well as helping them in the preparation and process of conducting a job search. Although specific goals reflect a primary focus for each unit, both units see the need to participate in career exploration, job search, and career definition activities.

Center History

In the mid-1980s the Counseling and Development Center at BYU recognized the developmental needs that students have defining, designing, and planning their futures. In order to better address these developmental needs the Open Major Advisement Center was moved to the Counseling and Development Center. In the mid-1990s, as a result of a university accreditation review, the same rationale was discussed in terms of preparing students to enter the world of work and graduate from the university. Following this review, the Career Placement Services office was also moved into the newly named Counseling and Career Center. In 2007 it was decided that supervision for the University Advisement Center (previously Open Major Advisement) would be provided by the associate vice president for student life, but that the physical location would remain within the Counseling and Career Center in order to provide seamless service delivery of academic and career advisement to students.

Recent historical events include (a) positioning the University Advisement Center, the Career Center, and the Preprofessional Advisement Center (pre-law, pre-health, and pre-graduate management) in close proximity in a highly visible location in the student union; (b) creation of a career team made up of key players from these service units; (c) joint sponsorship of staff meetings to foster relationships, training, and information-sharing; (d) participation by staff of these centers in universitywide advisement councils and committees; and (e) collaborative support for universitywide new student orientation meetings, major fairs, career fairs, and other events.

Center Description and Services

Major services provided by the University Advisement Center and the Career Center include (a) advising students who are exploring majors and careers; (b) assisting students in developing job searching skills; (c) providing career interest inventories and test interpretations; (d) conducting workshops on résumé writing, interviewing, networking, and cover and thank you letters; (e) teaching career exploration/career strategies courses; (f) maintaining a career library with a full range of printed and online resources; and (g) reaching out to employers to cultivate good career and internship opportunities for students.

Methods of Service Delivery

Service delivery methods include one-on-one advising, classroom instruction, workshops, career fairs, major fairs, outreach presentations, online and electronic resources, events, and conferences.

Students Served by the Center

Both centers have a universitywide function in providing services to students. The University Advisement Center is responsible for advising undecided or undeclared students and special populations (e.g., international students, visiting students, and enriched environment students). Because of their visible location in the student union center, they often serve as the first point of contact for students, declared or undeclared, who have questions regarding choosing a major, choosing a career, or university policies and procedures. The Career Center serves all students who seek advisement on how to transition from their academic experience to the workplace. They work extensively with employers who hire BYU students, and prepare students to meet with these employers. Career advisors help students augment and position their academic, work, and internship experiences to meet the needs of employers. These services are also provided to alumni who may be redefining their career paths later in life.

Center Staffing

Staff in the University Advisement Center includes one coordinator who reports to the associate vice president for student life, six advisors, and one administrative employee. Employees in the Career Center include one director who reports to the director of the Counseling and Career Center, eight advisors, and five support staff.

How Career Services and Academic Advising Are Integrated

Two important factors help integrate academic and career advising functions traditionally found at the beginning and end of a student's academic experience. Both the commitment to development of career goals from freshmen through seniors and the physical location of academic and career centers strengthen the integration of advising and career development services.

Integration occurs as University Advisement Center academic advisors, who are typically viewed as service providers in the early phase of the education process, and Career Center advisors, who are typically thought of as helping students become employed at the end of the academic experience, work together to help students envision career development as intrinsically linked to careers and employment. Advisors work to suggest extracurricular activities and work experiences that will effectively prepare students to enter the work force. Advisors may use such activities to help students explore potential careers while strengthening academic and other credentials. It is not unusual for advisors to have students in the exploration phase visit with career specialists who can discuss the importance of a balanced development of skills, knowledge, and experience that lead to enhanced marketability. As career advisors work with freshmen and sophomores, they may seek consultation with academic advisors to help students define majors and other academic experiences to eventually increase employability.

Leaders from the University Advisement Center and the Career Center are also members of university councils that address career and advising issues and include administrators at the dean level and directors of advisement. Advisors from each unit also participate in universitywide advisor training meetings that include both advisement and career topics.

Both the advisement and career service units have the ability to directly communicate with the students they serve. Career advisors have the capacity to communicate to students registered in their on-campus recruiting database and the academic advisors in the University Advisement Center have an e-mail database for the approximately 3,700 undeclared students on campus over which they have jurisdiction.

The fact that these centers are co-located increases the likelihood that students will utilize both services in an integrated function. Advisors often walk students from one center to the other, not only to make appointments, but to introduce them to the advisors in that service area. This personal touch increases the probability that students will maximize the services offered in both units.

Staff from both units also hold joint training meetings; participate in each other's hiring committees, career fairs, and major fairs; and teach career classes for students. Both units are working toward developing and using a shared database so notes from advisement sessions conducted in either center can be viewed by other advisors in each area.

Resources

- Career Assessments: Strong Interest Inventory, Campbell Interest and Skills Survey, and Myers-Briggs Type Indicator
- Career Library: Printed resources such as *The Peterson's Guides, Occupational Outlook Handbook, US News and World Report College Rankings*, and *Salary and Outlook*. Sample résumés and cover letters are also available.
- Electronic Resources: *DISCOVER, Vault Online Career Library*, and *eRecruiting*.
- E-mail and phone advising and an "Ask-a-Counselor" Web feature for major exploration, career exploration, and for job search assistance.

Accountability and Data

Each center creates an annual report, where advisement appointments, career inventory interpretations, attendance at fairs, job recruiting appointments, classes taught, workshops offered, outreach presentations, and other information are reported. Both centers conduct satisfaction surveys and participate in institutional surveys that assess advising and career services including a Senior Survey, Alumni Survey, Employer Survey, and Career and Advisement Survey.

Initial assessments in the area of career services indicated that while the career fairs held once each semester were well attended and highly visible, most students were unaware and failed to take advantage of the many other services offered. Career advisors were largely underutilized, and the Career Center had no means of reaching out to students. This information led to several initiatives: (a) Efforts were made to increase visibility with college deans, faculty, and advisement leaders across campus. The director of the Career Center became a member of two important campuswide organizations, the Advisement Council and the Operational Advisement Committee. Career advisors joined academic advisors in their monthly campuswide informational and training meetings. Career advisors joined with other key leaders in visiting with college deans, department chairs, and faculty at their regular meetings. Several formal and informal presentations were given to many of these groups. (b) Efforts were made to increase visibility with students. The Career Center was remodeled to make its reception area more visible and appealing. A single entry door was replaced with double doors, the reception desk was enlarged, and new lighting and furniture were added. Career advisors were partially decentralized and given office space in several key colleges so they could advise students on site rather than expecting students to come to the student union center. A program was developed to automatically enroll students in e-recruiting, the online registration system used to connect students looking for jobs and internships to companies interested in hiring BYU students (previously, students had to request to be enrolled; now they are automatically enrolled). This allows the Career Center to send notices to students to inform them of their services, invite them to meet with advisors, or notify them about employment recruitment activities or other campus events. A monthly career services newsletter has also been developed by staff and is being sent electronically to interested students registered in the career services data base.

Strengths of the Center

Strengths of the center include (a) a diverse and highly trained staff with a minimum of a master's degree required of advisors; (b) co-location of resources to facilitate student information and referral; (c) a professional and experienced faculty of advisors who teach career courses firmly based in theoretical foundations and practical experience; (d) a collaborative and cooperative spirit fostered by jointly held staff meetings and activities; (e) participation in employer luncheons where advisors hear directly from recruiters; (f) shared support and mutual involvement in the sponsorship of fairs, conferences, and events; (g) a shared vision of how student-focused academic and career advising interface and are grounded in developmental thinking; and (h) development of student volunteer opportunities with major and career fairs to encourage trust and student use of the centers.

Challenges of the Center

Challenges of the center include (a) continued fostering of relationships between advisement and career services; (b) providing seamless service and appropriate referrals; and (c) finding resources to keep pace with the increasing demand for services.

Staff of both centers are continuing to find ways to build bridges between services by better understanding the unique purposes and shared purposes of the centers. Staff members are also working to enhance their knowledge of appropriate times to refer to each other by meeting as staff and communicating with each other. In addition, staff are working together to facilitate each other's programs (e.g., fairs), redefine roles (e.g., who can and should conduct interest inventory interpretations), and sharing in outreach and publicity efforts through joint brochures and outreach to colleges.

Future Plans

Future plans include (a) development of a combined database for use in advising and tracking students; (b) continued training of advisors of developmental and career theory and application; (c) periodic combined staff/training meetings; (d) collaborative development of resources; and (e) shared career conference planning.

A graduate-level Career Development and Assessment class is offered for the ongoing training of advisors on career theory, assessment, and intervention. It is anticipated this course will be continued and advisors from across campus will be invited to enroll. The staff is also trying to develop a shared intake point that is visible to students which is expected to increase student usage of our services. A career conference planning committee has been created with representatives from each area to continue in shared professional development. Each center's staff also participate in webinars and other training opportunities offered by either center.

Professional Development Opportunities

Professional development opportunities for staff include (a) participation in local, regional, and national advisement and career conferences; (b) involvement in universitywide advisement inservice meetings; (c) attendance in joint center staff meetings and training sessions; (d) sponsorship of a universitywide career conference; (e) participation in research supported by departmentally funded research grants; and (f) tuition benefits to include master's-level career development courses at BYU or Kansas State University.

This exemplary practice description was prepared by Karen Evans, coordinator, University Advisement Center; W. Kerry Hammock, academic and career advisor, University Advisement Center; Vaughn Worthen, director, career services; associate director, Counseling and Career Center.

JAMES MADISON UNIVERSITY

Integrated Academic and Career Advising Center: Career and Academic Planning
   Location: Harrisonburg, VA
   Institutional Type: Four-year, public
   Highest Degree Granted: Ph.D.
   Total Number of Students: 18,000 undergraduate; 1,000 graduate
   Center url: http://www.jmu.edu/cap
   Contact Information: Dr. Lee Ward, Director, wardwl@jmu.edu, 540–568–3788

History, Mission, and Objectives

The mission of Career and Academic Planning is to "provide opportunities and support that engages students in the process of exploring, evaluating, and choosing academic programs and careers." Integration began in 1997, and today professional staff members pursue all aspects of that mission.

The department conducts its business according to a vision, strategic plan, and annual objectives. In addition, it incorporates the following continuing goals:

- Students will experience seamless, intentionally inviting, meaningful transitions into, through, and out of the university.

- Students will understand academic responsibilities, expectations, and requirements related to General Education, their chosen major, and degree attainment.

- Students will become more aware of their individual values, abilities, interests, and personality characteristics, and will understand the relationship of these to decisions about major and careers.

- Students will be able to employ appropriate decision-making principles, practices, and resources in their choice of academic programs and careers.

- Students will know and be able to complete the steps in the job search process, including job research and location, networking, writing résumés and cover letters, and interviewing.

- Staff will work in a diverse and responsive organization characterized by understanding, compassion, respect, and appreciation for each other and those we serve.

- Staff will enjoy the time and space necessary to achieve personal and professional balance, engage in learning opportunities, and reflect on their practice and achievements.

- Staff will be able to share leadership responsibility, pursue innovation and change opportunities, participate in planning and decision-making activities, shape departmental values, and contribute to community and group cohesion.

Description of Services and Programs

Career and Academic Planning is the fully integrated office at James Madison University providing programs, services, and resources in the areas of academic advising, selecting or changing one's major, career counseling and development, and job search. The office offers a full range of programs and services, including academic advising, major decision-making support, academic and career resources, career assessment and counseling, instruction on job search techniques and strategies, résumé development, services for international students, peer educator programs, advisor training, internship location, externship placement, connections with alumni and parents, liaison services to all academic units, and employment tracking. The department also manages the university's centralized employer relations and on-campus interviewing functions.

Among these programs and services, those that are designed to instruct and assist students in effective decision-making practices have a visible and increasingly pivotal role in the department. In addition to the widely recognized transitions that college students make into and out of their institutions, a less talked about but perhaps more important transition is the one students make through the institution In this transition, students choose their major, change their major, experience most of their developmental growth, make sense of complex educational and personal situations, establish critical mentoring relationships, make the choice to engage in educationally purposeful activities that support their academic and career goals, and seek meaningful experiences through internships and service opportunities. Career and Academic Planning enhances this transition. A small group program focused on exploration of majors and careers allows students to make decisions in a self-paced environment. A credit course—Life and Career Planning—managed and taught by Career and Academic Planning staff each year provides hundreds of students, mostly freshmen, the opportunity to develop a high level of career decision-making self-efficacy. In addition, special advising programs designed to expose selected students to alternatives to the original major or career target proactively assists students who may not meet academic progression standards in their major department.

Program Delivery Methods

A variety of methods are employed, including one-on-one advising and counseling, small group interventions, large group presentations, formal academic courses, extensive written and published materials, self-paced Web-based programs, and a variety of digital technologies.

Students Served

The department provides academic advising to all freshmen and undeclared (exploratory) students, as well as most international students. First year students who enter undeclared are advised by a professional academic and career advisor in Career and Academic Planning; a student who enters with a declared major is advised by a full-time faculty freshmen advisor in his or her college. Career and Academic Planning provides career decision support, career assessment and counseling, job search preparation, and on-campus interviewing to students at all levels and in all colleges; none of the six colleges provides its own career counseling services or recruiting functions. Because of the nature of the university, services for graduate students and alumni exist but are less extensive.

Staffing

The staff of Career and Academic Planning are as follows:

- A director responsible for staffing, planning, financial management, facilities development, supervision, data management, and assessment. The director reports to an associate vice president for student affairs who, in an unusual but exceptionally productive relationship, reports to both the vice president for student affairs and the provost. The department is part of a unit known as Student Success (Career and Academic Planning, Orientation and First Year Programs, Community Service-Learning, and Learning Resource Centers).

- Three associate directors, each of whom is responsible for aspects of the day-to-day operations of the department, administration of major events and programs, and supervision of professional academic and career advisors.

- Eleven academic and career advisors, each of whom advises freshmen and other undeclared students, advises students at a variety of levels about selecting or changing their major, provides career assessment and counseling, offers job search instruction and guidance, teaches a course in life and career planning, serves as a liaison to several academic units, serves on internal and external committees, and manages major events and administrative operations (e.g., Web site, fairs, and other programs, staff training and development, graduate assistant coordination, marketing and publicity, technology development).

- A coordinator and assistant coordinator of employer relations and Recruiting who together manage all aspects of employer development, communication, on-campus recruiting services, career fairs, and employment tracking and reporting.

- A resource center coordinator who oversees acquisition, organization, and use of an extensive collection of print materials, digital data bases, and Web-based resources; supervises student staff; and trains professional staff.

- Seven support staff (clerical, technical, and financial).

- Four graduate assistants, each of whom has responsibilities that mirror those of the academic and career advisors, including a small freshmen advising load.

- Eight student assistants (resource center, on-campus interviewing, freshman advising services, marketing, Web) and 12 career education officers (peer educators).

- Fifty-six faculty freshman advisors, who are selected based on their ability to establish developmental relationships with first year students, their willingness to help students through difficult transitional situations, and their capacity to learn and adapt to changing institutional conditions.

How Integration Is Accomplished

Career and Academic Planning is fully integrated; that is, there are not two offices under one roof or under one executive director, nor is there one office providing two specialties; rather, one office provides one specialty—career and academic planning. Academic advising, choosing one's major, and career development are viewed as a seamless educational and experiential journey for students, and departmental programs and services are designed and coordinated with that in mind.

Accountability Information

The department is clear about how it wants students to grow. It produces innovative educational experiences to enhance that growth, it collaborates extensively with faculty to support student engagement, and it assesses learning outcomes. As industry pioneers and champions of integration, Career and Academic Planning sees integration not for its convenience or efficiency, but as a chosen educational practice that adds value to the student experience and best prepares students for their lives after college. Yet above all, the work is about student learning. Career and Academic Planning takes seriously its obligation to be accountable and to demonstrate the impact of its programs and services on student learning. The department assesses student outcomes, most notably career decision-making self-efficacy, to demonstrate how and where student growth occurs. Similarly, it uses an innovative and unique rubric for assessing changes in students' résumé writing skills. Finally, it regularly evaluates major programs and services to improve delivery, increase student engagement, and ensure that administrative goals for customer service fiscal responsibility are being met.

Key indicators of the effectiveness of the integrated department include assessment results related to career decision making and student engagement. Measurement efforts show that the impact of the Life and Career Planning course on career decision-making self-efficacy is very strong across all participant groups. Likewise, results from several administrations of the National Survey of Student Engagement have illustrated that James Madison University freshmen outpace national and peer group institutions in the degree to which first year students are engaged in advising and career development tasks.

Strengths

The greatest strength of Career and Academic Planning is its people. It hires the best people, develops them endlessly, expects them to achieve at high levels, and engages them in shared leadership. Although advising and career services have become complex, technologically advanced enterprises (factors which could be a barrier to integration), Career and Academic Planning steadfastly adheres to the principle that when the technology and complex structures are stripped away, the organization is left with people helping people. The integration of academic advising and career development is not about systems and all their accoutrements, but about really talented people whose passion in life is helping college students grow.

Challenges

Integration of academic advising and career development is a defining characteristic of the student experience at James Madison University, but it has not come without significant challenges, including finding the right people to do this work, balancing relationships with faculty and employers, and keeping the complexity of the work from becoming overwhelming. Throughout its integrated history, the largest challenge faced in Career and Academic Planning was the process of integration—the decision making, leadership, political maneuvering, negotiation, personnel decisions, resource acquisition, culture management, and communication that make or break such a significant departure from the norm. Without question, the most important lesson learned echoes the wisdom of professor Don Creamer of Virginia Tech ("Use of a planned change model to modify student affairs programs," in D. G. Creamer, Ed., *College Student Development for the 1990s* [Washington, DC: American College Personnel Association], pp. 181–191): Significant change efforts in higher education fail not because of deficient ideas, but because the people involved do not know how to do change. Integration of academic advising and career services is a perfectly reasonable idea, but its adoption and eventual success at James Madison University required a comprehensive understanding of change practices, exemplary leadership, exquisite communication, a thorough grasp of institutional culture, and transparent decision making at all levels, at all times.

Concerns about the ability to hire professionals who could be effective in an integrated position were managed by establishing a cultural expectation regarding the hiring process. Senior staff members in the department believe the most important decision they will ever make is who to hire; thus, the search processes used are painstakingly diligent and value-based. Likewise, complexity in the department has been made a front-burner issue; throughout the organization, simplicity is sought as staff attempt to "create time and space" to practice good developmental advising, collaborate across the campus, encourage creativity, and pursue professional development opportunities. In committee and staff meetings, planning activities, and individual supervisory discussions, staff seek ways to simplify, slow down, achieve balance, and narrow priorities—not because they are directed to do so, but because doing so is an agreed-upon cultural expectation.

Future Plans

The future holds additional challenges and rewards. The department developed a long-range plan to better serve minority students that received the President's Diversity Enhancement Award in 2008; the plan calls for increasing the presence of minority faculty among the ranks of freshmen advisors and taking steps to facilitate interaction between students and employers who are industry leaders in creating diverse work environments. It also recently engaged in a visioning process that resulted in commitments to more effectively use emerging technologies to communicate with and teach students, and to expand and improve outcomes assessment efforts. As a result, evaluation of advising will be expanded and introduced as a Web-based process, and the impact of programs and services aimed at assisting major-changers will be assessed. Likewise, the department is focusing a great deal of attention and resources on environmental stewardship—not only is it redesigning its business practices to reduce, reuse, and recycle resources, but it is concentrating efforts on preparing students to seek and enter environmentally focused majors and careers. Finally, Career and Academic Planning will reinvest the energy needed to ensure that it is a place characterized by trust, respect, effective communication, transparent decision making, compassion, shared leadership, balance, and good humor.

Professional Development

Staff members have extensive opportunities and support for professional development, including distinct orientation programs offered by the department, Student Success, and the Division of Student Affairs and University Planning. Every professional staff member receives an annual professional development allowance that includes full cost of attendance at a national conference or symposium of their choice, membership dues in up to two professional organizations, and the purchase of books and journals. In addition, numerous opportunities for training and continuing education are available. Aside from the various technical and administrative training programs offered by the university, Career and Academic Planning arranges its own training programs that target attitudes, skills, and knowledge suggested by its annual and long-range departmental goals. Finally, all staff members are eligible to take courses and pursue degree programs at the university at no cost.

Training for faculty freshmen advisors is extensive and focuses on principles of student learning and development, exemplary advising practices, helping strategies and resources, and institutional processes and policies. Faculty freshmen advisors receive constant support by advising administrators in Career and Academic Planning and are evaluated on their effectiveness with students and their support of university advising goals. Freshman advising is recognized at the university in the form of the Provost Award for Excellence in Advising, which annually honors one freshman advisor for exemplary practice. That honoree receives a cash award and is nominated for the NACADA Outstanding Advising Award.

This exemplary practice description was prepared by Dr. Lee Ward, director of career and academic planning.

KUTZTOWN UNIVERSITY

Integrated Academic and Career Advising Center Name: The Advising Center for Undeclared Students

Location: Located in the rural community of Kutztown, in southeastern Pennsylvania

Institutional Type: Four-year, public institution, one of the 14 state universities that comprise the Pennsylvania State System of Higher Education (PASSHE)

Highest Degree Granted: Master's Degree

Total Number of Students: Undergraduate Enrollment: 9,311 Graduate Enrollment: 834

Center url: www.kutztown.edu/academics/advisement

Contact Person: Linda Lantaff, instructor/advisor, lantaff@kutztown.edu, 610–683–4735

Mission and Objectives of Center and Program

Mission Statement. Serving as a connection between students and the campus community, the Advising Center for Undeclared Students advises and advocates for students to affect their decision-making skills, enabling them to explore and choose majors, transition to college, and pursue academic and personal goals. The objectives of the Advising Center are to

- Assist students in self-understanding and self-acceptance (understanding abilities, interests, and limitations)
- Assist students in clarifying their life goals by relating their vocational personality (interests, skills, and abilities) to careers, academic disciplines, and majors
- Assist students in developing an educational plan consistent with their life goals
- Assist students in developing decision-making skills
- Provide accurate information about institutional policies, procedures, resources, and programs
- Assist students in using university technology
- Assist students in evaluating or reevaluating progress toward established goals and educational plans
- Refer students to other campus services

Center History

At Kutztown University (KU), academic advisement is a formally assigned duty of the faculty and is performed exclusively by faculty members in accordance with the collective bargaining agreement. Accordingly, KU adopted a decentralized faculty-only model of academic advising. Undeclared students, historically, were assigned to faculty advisors from various departments in the College of Liberal Arts and Sciences, who had few declared advisees.

In 1998, in response to a growing awareness of the special needs of undeclared students, and in the face of increasing numbers of undeclared students, KU created the Advising Center for Undeclared Students. The Advising Center was established as a centralized office, under the direction of a tenured faculty member and staffed by volunteer faculty advisors from various academic departments. Reporting directly to the provost/vice president of academic affairs, the Advising Center operated in conjunction with the decentralized, faculty-based advisement model.

Over the course of the next 10 years, the enrollment of undeclared students grew 35%. Undeclared students currently represent over 22% of the entering freshmen class and 10% of Kutztown's undergraduate population. The staff of the Advising Center also grew to include several dedicated faculty advisors. In 2004, two academic planners (non-faculty, master's level, professional staff) were hired to complement the advising staff. With the hiring of the academic planners, the Advising Center was able to offer a full range of services to undeclared students and more fully integrate the concept of career advising.

Description of Center, Including Services and Programs Offered

The Advising Center for Undeclared Students serves as an academic home for undeclared students at KU. The center is staffed with both faculty advisors (advising specialists) and academic planners (career specialists) who, together, provide comprehensive, developmental career advising for undeclared students until the time they declare a major. The Advising Center assists students in selecting and scheduling courses, establishing and evaluating academic goals, understanding and navigating university policies and procedures, connecting with other university programs and resources, exploring majors and related careers, and declaring a major.

The Advising Center is located conveniently on campus and is in close proximity to other important campus offices, including the bursar's office, Career Development Center, the Counseling Center, the financial aid office, and the registrar's office. The layout of the Advising Center provides private offices for faculty advisors and academic planners, a comfortable waiting area, and a conference room with integrated technology for small group advising sessions and workshops.

Methods of Service or Program Delivery

The Advising Center offers one-on-one appointments for students throughout the academic year. Both faculty advisors and academic planners meet with students individually to help them establish and meet their educational goals and make informed decisions about their academic careers. Faculty advisors are responsible for course selection and course registration functions, helping students to evaluate their options in specific majors and selecting appropriate courses based on each student's individual goals. All students are required to meet with a faculty advisor at least once each semester for course selection purposes. Academic planners are responsible for the broader career development functions, including the administration and interpretation of the Career Key; helping students to connect their interests, abilities, and values to careers and academic majors; and helping students to locate and use career/major information and evaluate their options.

As a student moves through the decision-making process, referrals back and forth between academic planners and faculty advisors are easily accommodated. A system of common student files and session notes allow for a seamless process, during which both faculty advisors and academic planners can stay abreast of the students' goals and progress toward achieving those goals.

In addition, the Advising Center offers a variety of workshops. A series of major and career exploration workshops, including workshops on choosing a major, occupational trends, decision making, and academic goal setting, are facilitated by the academic planners, while academic workshops that focus on the entrance requirements of specific majors and are more advising focused are facilitated by the faculty advisors.

The Advising Center has developed a one-credit college success course, UST 015 University Studies, and a three-credit Experiential Learning Portfolio Development Seminar designed to help students earn credit for life experience. Undeclared students have the opportunity to participate in a voluntary living and learning community that focuses on helping them discover their interests.

Students Served by Center

The Advising Center serves students who enter Kutztown University as undeclared students, declared students who change their major to undeclared in order to explore other options, and declared students who are administratively removed from their major due to poor academic performance or failure to meet other departmental requirements.

While most of the students served by the Advising Center report that they are undecided or uncertain about their choice of major, not all undeclared students are undecided students. In fact in 2008, 16% of first-year undeclared students and 66.4% of undeclared transfer students reported that they were certain about their choice of major at the time of application, but were denied admission to that major. These students entered KU undeclared with the hopes of subsequently declaring their first choice major.

Center Staffing

A tenured faculty member serves as both the director of the advising center and the chair of the department of academic advisement. The director is responsible for the overall administration of the advising program for unde-clared students. The director reports to the associate provost/vice president of academic affairs.

Two tenure track faculty advisors provide advising services to undeclared students. Another tenure track faculty member serves as the coordinator of academic jeopardy and advises undeclared students with a GPA less than 2.00, in addition to providing supplemental advising to all declared students with a GPA below a 2.00. All faculty members teach the university studies course, serve on campuswide committees, and engage in professional devel-opment activities.

Two master's level, professional staff members serve as academic planners. Academic planners provide career advising to undeclared students; develop resources that assist in the career advising process; communicate with unde-clared students through periodic newsletters, e-mails, and telephone contacts; and are instrumental in the implementation of the assessment plan. Academic planners also serve on campuswide committees and engage in professional development.

How Are Career and Academic Advising Integrated?

The Advising Center utilizes John Holland's theory of personality and work environments as a framework to engage students in discussion and reflec-tion about potential majors, career paths, and course selection. The staff also employs a simple decision-making model to help students conceptualize the decision-making process. Both academic planners and faculty advisors use session notes to document where students are in the process and the goals they are working toward. Together they help students take responsibility in making their own decisions.

The concept of career advising is first introduced to students at orienta-tion, during which, the academic planners discuss the advising program and administer and interpret the Career Key. Undeclared students identify their Holland code and learn how occupations, majors, and work environments are categorized. Results of the Career Key are then placed in students' files in the Advising Center. This enables faculty advisors and academic planners to be prepared to integrate the concepts of vocational personality and work envi-ronments into the advising process when the students arrive on campus in the fall. As students become more aware of their interests and options, they are encouraged to move ahead or return to parts of the decision-making process. Being keenly aware that personal barriers may impede the decision-making process, the staff is trained to identify these concerns and make appropriate referrals when necessary.

Resources

The Advising Center publishes the *Academic Advising Portfolio* each year which serves as a student advising handbook and includes information on the advising process, responsibilities of the advisor and student, general education require-ments, the process for choosing and declaring a major, and campus resources.

The On-Track newsletter, which is published several times a year, is aimed at addressing the needs and concerns of first-year undeclared students.

The Advising Center maintains a comprehensive interactive Web site. A special section on choosing a major leads students through a decision-making process where they can learn about themselves, gather information about careers and majors, evaluate their options, and learn how to declare a major.

The Advising Center also maintains a wide range of handouts, including an inventory of graduation checklists for KU majors and minors, copies of *What Can I Do with a Major In*, as well as a series of informational guides on various topics including declaring a major, setting up an e-mail account, and registering for courses online.

The Advising Center maintains a close working relationship with the Career Development Center (CDC). Students are encouraged to visit the CDC to use the career library, attend employer presentations, and, in some cases, take additional assessments, including the Myers-Briggs Type Indicator, Major/Minor Finder, and the Self-Directed Search. Likewise, the CDC may refer declared students to the Advising Center if they are interested in changing their majors, but need time to explore their options before declaring other majors.

Accountability

Evidence of the effectiveness of the Advising Center for Undeclared Students is gathered through various sources including retention statistics, rates of major declaration, and student surveys. The Advising Center is currently making revisions and expanding its assessment plan to include the use of rubrics and focus groups to more effectively assess learning outcomes.

The Fall-to-Fall retention rate of first-time, full-time undeclared students for 2006–2007 was 74.4%. These numbers compare favorably to the 77% for all first-time, full-time students at KU during the same time period. The percentage of undeclared students declaring a major ranged from 44.5% to 49% over the last three years. Not reflected in these numbers are the students who decide on a major not offered at KU and transfer out as a "decided" student. The Advising Center views these students as "successful" in meeting the goals of the center, but currently these students are counted in the attrition statistics.

Strengths of Advising Center

The strength of the Advising Center for Undeclared Students begins with the commitment and enthusiasm of each staff member. The synergy of this group provides the foundation on which this center thrives.

Also, the structure of the Advising Center itself is a strength, with academic planners and advisors sharing the same physical space, mission, goals, reporting structure, common student files, and session notes. A student has the benefit of working with both advising specialists and career specialists who, together, provide a comprehensive, seamless approach to academic decision making.

The location of the Advising Center is another key to the success of the advising program. The centralized location provides easy access to important administrative offices, and the office layout provides a professional space for students and staff.

Challenges of Center

The Advising Center serves a significant number of students at KU. The complexity of the needs and concerns of these students require a committed and well trained staff of faculty advisors and academic planners. The Advising Center struggles with meeting the needs of these students at the current staffing level. Appointments with faculty advisors are now limited to 30-minute sessions to ensure that all students have access to the advising staff for course selection at minimum. Academic planners currently meet with students for 50-minute sessions, but student demand may also dictate shorter sessions in the future.

Future Plans

Future plans for the Advising Center for Undeclared Students include implementing a comprehensive outcomes-based assessment plan. The development of the systematic plan is to be completed in spring 2009 and implemented in the 2009–2010 academic year. By instituting a comprehensive assessment plan, the center will be in better position to make decisions about the allocation of both human and financial resources.

Professional Development Provided Staff to Enhance Career and Academic Advising

The faculty and staff of the Advising Center actively participate in various conferences, including conferences of the National Academic Advising Association (NACADA), the First-Year Experience (FYE), and the Mid-Atlantic Career Counseling Association (MACCA). In addition, the faculty and staff stay current in the field by reading various publications including the *Chronicle of Higher Education*, the *NACADA Journal*, the *Journal of The First-Year Experience & Students In Transition*, and the *Occupational Outlook Quarterly*.

This exemplary practice description was prepared by Linda Lantaff, instructor/academic planner II.

NORTHERN ARIZONA UNIVERSITY

Integrated Academic and Career Advising Center Name: Gateway Student Success Center

Location: Flagstaff, Arizona

Institutional Type: Located in rural Arizona, near edge of the largest Native Nation in the United States, Northern Arizona University is the largest residential campus west of Mississippi. Four-year public.

Highest Degree Granted: Doctoral

Total Number of Students: 16,787 undergraduate and 5,720 graduate students (Flagstaff Mountain Campus)

Center url: www.nau.edu/gateway

Contact Person

Todd Firth

Assistant Director

Gateway Student Success Center

Todd.Firth@nau.edu

928–523–4772

Mission and Objectives of Center

The overarching mission of the Gateway Student Success Center (Gateway) is to empower individuals to follow passion, realize potential, and pursue lives of purpose, and to create a collaborative campus culture of career and academic advising that focuses on student success by encouraging student learning, supporting advising and the campus advising staff, and providing increased opportunity for meaningful student contact.

Goals for staff and students are to

- Integrate career and academic planning in a developmentally appropriate manner

- Build collaborative partnerships

- Foster and apply self-directed independent learning

- Create environments of inclusion and respect through honest, civil, and open communication

- Adopt an attitude of discovery by identifying interests, clarifying values, assessing skills, and following passion

- Develop resiliency by navigating unfamiliar environments and adapting to change

Center History

Historically, the University Advisement Center (UAC) provided centralized advising for undeclared students. The colleges and units provided advising for declared majors. In 2003, President John Haeger expanded the centralized advising to include all freshmen and moved the UAC personnel into the newly created Gateway Student Success Center. Within a year the career services office was merged into the Gateway. The integrated model for the Gateway developed beyond housing career counselors and academic advisors under one roof to intentionally creating and developing individuals as career *and* academic advisors.

Description of Center, Including Services and Programs Offered

- Priority enrollment for incoming students
  - Individualized course scheduling and enrollment prior to attendance

- One-on-one sessions to discuss career goals and appropriate course selection
    - Orientation career & academic advising
    - Early Enrollment career & academic advising for continuing students
    - Early Enrollment career & academic advising for transitioning students
- Career & employment
    - Combined career and graduate school fairs in fall and spring
    - Specialized recruitment events for specific majors, formal interview opportunities, and recruiter information sessions
    - Mock interviews, résumé critiques, and job search

University Programs Coordinated or Managed by the Gateway

- Finish in Four: a universitywide initiative designed to support graduation in four years
- Student Readiness Inventory (SRI): advising sessions focused on SRI results to evaluate student strengths and weaknesses and connect students to appropriate campus resources
- Grade Performance Status (GPS): automated academic early alert system
- Biomedical Professions: advising, exploratory course, committee letters of recommendation, and preparation for professional school application
- Graduate School Preparation: coaching, research, and application
- Academic Continuation: probation and suspension reinstatement processes
- Course Capacity Management: assessment of course availability needs
- Degree Progression Plans: maintenance of semester plans for all undergraduate degrees
- Orientation Advising: development and implementation of centralized career and academic advising and presentations for all incoming students

Methods of Service or Program Delivery

Services and programs are provided utilizing multiple methods: online, in-person, phone and e-mail, group presentations, and one-unit courses.

Students Served by Center

As the centralized advising center on campus, the assigned advising student population includes all first year students and undeclared students. Career services are for all students and alumni. In addition, the Gateway provides services to assist students in transition and a referral network for all undergraduate students.

Center Staffing

Administration consists of one director (reports to vice provost), one associate director, and two assistant directors. In addition, the center has 12 career and academic advisors, six senior career and academic advisors, and six team leaders. Other staff consists of one business manager, four IT support staff, four administrative support staff, five graduate assistants, two teaching assistants, and two student workers. The following chart identifies the categorical job responsibilities for each position:

Responsibilities	Career & Academic Advising	Project Management	Personnel Supervision	Program Management	Organizational Management
Career & academic advisors (12)	✓				
Career & academic advisors, sr. (6)	✓	✓	✓		
Team leaders (6)	✓	✓	✓	✓	
Administration (4)	✓	✓	✓	✓	✓

How Are Career and Academic Advising Integrated?

The organization's infrastructure, the culture, and the people evolved to successfully create a new expectation that advisors be career and academic advisors. The infrastructure and processes were modified to facilitate merged career and academic conversations. For example, the intake/advising form was amended to reflect career and academic information. Group advising was eliminated to foster the one-on-one conversation connecting academic program to career goals. Lastly, the staff created a set curriculum for the series of required advising sessions to address the evolution of the career and academic concerns through the students' first three terms. The mission/vision/goals and assessment plan were also rewritten to ensure staff were "walking the talk" of integration.

Career and academic advisors are equipped with the knowledge and tools necessary to conduct the merged conversation with all students through staff development and training. All conversations, programs, and curricula include career aspirations and academic preparation. The staff is trained to conduct conversations that include questions designed to determine the depth/breadth of student commitment and understanding of future aspirations. Advisors ask questions like: Do you know what you want to do after graduation? What does that aspiration look like for you? What skills/abilities/courses/ experiences do you need to accomplish that goal?

Resources

- Gateway Connects: online employment system for all students and alumni
- Career Resource Library
- Workshops: Résumé Writing, Interview Strategies, Major Exploration
- One-Credit Courses: Graduate School Preparation, Career Preparation, Back on Track (academic success), Introduction to Biomedical Professions, and The "Major" Decision
- Recruiter Relations: assisting employers in recruiting efforts

Accountability Data and Information

One of the immediate priorities is taking advantage of the rich data collection processes that evolved since Gateway's inception. The last two years were spent designing a comprehensive assessment plan. This past year has been spent on the analysis of existing data and the gathering of baseline measures that will inform program decisions beginning Fall 2009.

Strengths of Center

- Gateway provides an open and collaborative environment with solution-centered atmosphere. Two guiding philosophies are "we break it internally before it goes public" and "we are a boulder in a puddle creating huge ripples."
- Gateway is staffed by high-caliber personnel who demonstrate a commitment to students and organization. Gateway interview and evaluation processes emphasize and reward a commitment to students.
- Gateway fosters and encourages an environment of adaptability, creativity, and humor. Gateway's leadership team fosters and encourages the above values by adopting the attitude that there "are no fires" and whatever occurs can be handled; that anyone at any level in any position can propose improvements and ideas in any area; and that airplanes, Frisbees, and candy are frequent projectiles in the open-cubicle office.

Challenges of Center

- Increased student enrollment and program assignments without corresponding resources are challenges for Gateway. Trained temporary staff is used to supplement Gateway staff during high-peak student traffic times; the program elements are augmented through alternative delivery techniques; and staff continuously discusses how to do more with less.

- Another challenge is physical space constraints. The physical capacity of building space has been exceeded and with expanded programming and staffing non-traditional office spaces have been used to accommodate organizational needs. Currently, the option of a modular office to supplement physical space is being explored.

- Another challenge at Gateway is staff turnover (institutional stepping stone for advancement). Staff turnover is accepted as a given. To mitigate the impact on the Gateway organization, tremendous improvements in hiring processes and improvements to the infrastructure have been made. Gateway staff tries to put a positive spin on turnover and embrace it for the new ideas and energy it creates.

Future Plans

Future plans are to continue to improve and expand the relevance and impact of integrated career and academic advising for the optimization of students' college experience and beyond. Data for the first graduating class are now available to help guide Gateway's integrated model. Initial student feedback indicates high satisfaction with major choice and career path decisions.

The Gateway staff looks forward to participation in conferences and networking opportunities to further explore exemplary practices as a source of ideas, solutions, and program offerings that address ongoing institutional and organizational struggles. The Gateway staff recognizes the only constant in higher education is that change is inevitable. As new initiatives and university priorities are identified, the Gateway staff is energized about creating and refining practices that will meet the needs of Northern Arizona University's students.

Professional Development Opportunities

Staff members are supported in participating in organizational, institutional, regional, and national opportunities related to their role within the organization. Examples of organizational and institutional professional development include new hire training, weekly training sessions, campus webinars, and relevant campuswide training. Examples of regional and national professional development opportunities include attending conferences or other professional development opportunities such as the following: NACADA, Statewide Career Services, National Association of Colleges and Employers, Mountain Pacific Association of Colleges and Employers, Western Association of Prelaw Advisors, Prelaw Advisors National Council, National Association of Advisors for the Health Professions, and Meyers-Briggs/Strong Inventory.

This exemplary practice was developed by the Gateway Student Success Center Coordinators and Leadership Team: Coordinators Monica Bai, Melanie Bertram, Stephenie Jerome, Lela Montfort, and Julia Spining; Assistant Directors Todd Firth and Mikhael Star; Associate Director Tammy Harrison.

NORTHWEST VISTA COLLEGE

Program: Northwest Vista College's Advising, Career and Transfer (ACT) Services

Institutional Information

- Two-year public
- Located in San Antonio, Texas
- Offers associate's degrees and certificates
- 12,200 students

  Center url: http://www.accd.edu/nvc/students/act/

Contact Information

Debi Gaitan, Director of Advising, Career and Transfer Services

dgaitan@mail.accd.edu, 210–486–4454

Mission and Center Objectives

Northwest Vista College's (NVC) Advising, Career and Transfer (ACT) Center provides integrated academic and career services. The mission of NVC and ACT is *Creating Opportunities for Success* and the vision is *To become responsible members of our world community, we create exemplary models for: learning to be; learning to work; learning to serve; and learning to lead . . . together.* The ACT Team's top priorities are to guide students through the career exploration process so they can declare a major and develop an education plan, attain their degree or certificate, graduate, and transfer to a four-year university, or successfully enter the workforce.

Center History

Providing quality, student-centered service is the foundation of the ACT Team. There is a deep commitment to developing students so they successfully complete their education and career goals. Providing high-quality, right-on-target academic and career advising is one of NVC's top strategic priorities. When NVC began, the academic and career advising teams were not integrated. Data from the Student Assessment of College Engagement survey (SACE), the Community College Survey of Student Engagement (CCSSE), and student focus groups, informed the ACT Team of the need to improve the non-integrated model for academic and career advising. Though students rated academic and career services as highly important to them, they were not systematically utilizing or benefiting from existing services. It became a strategic priority of the college to integrate and enhance career and academic advising so students could better navigate, utilize, and benefit from advising services. Therefore, in summer 2005, a fully integrated academic, career, and transfer advising team was formed to provide a comprehensive student support system. The first step involved restructuring an existing organizational model to assemble one academic, career, and transfer advising team. The next step produced a wide-ranging professional development program to provide the team with the necessary skills development to fully support NVC students. Finally, strategic work group action plans and scorecards were developed to track progress toward desired outcomes and measure results.

Description of Center, Including Services or Programs Offered and Students Served

The ACT Center, located within the larger Student Success Center, provides an easily-accessible, centralized location for students to receive academic, career, and transfer (ACT) advisement. The ACT concept was designed with a centralized advising structure with a self-contained model. However, recently ACT staff partnered with faculty to enhance the advisement of select students. The ACT Team offers a variety of resources and services for students, including the following:

- Welcome services for all students. The Wildcat Welcome and Resource Center is staffed by ACT advisors and provides intake services to ensure student needs are fully assessed and provided appropriate direction.

- Academic advising to support students with their educational goal planning.

- Group advising for all First Time in College (FTIC) students to provide quality academic advising and assist them in selecting their program of study and education plan, and assisting with their first semester course registration.

- Career and major exploration to help students define their education and career goals.

- Career and major assessments to aid students in identifying interests, values, experiences, and abilities. Assessments include Focus 2: Career and Educational Goal Solutions, Choices Planner, DISCOVER, and the Career Game.

- Change of major advising to help keep student records current and to make certain students are following the appropriate education plan.

- Transfer planning to facilitate ease of transfer for students to four-year institutions.

- Graduation planning to educate students on the benefits of degree completion.

- Job planning to assist students in their job search efforts and earn gainful employment. Wildcat Classifieds provides students with an easy-to-use online system to help them find job matches. Optimal Résumé is an online tool that helps students develop quality résumés and prepare for interviews.

- Veterans' advising to make certain veterans' courses are certified to receive full education financial benefits.

- International student advising and adherence of local, state, and federal regulations.

- Drop course advising to inform students of college support resources and to determine if there is another course of action.
- Early alert advising within the first three weeks of the semester for underperforming students.
- Focused academic advising for students on probation to increase academic success.
- College Connections advising at 11 local high schools to increase college entry rates.

At NVC, ACT advising is an ongoing, intentional interaction with students. Students are required to meet with an ACT advisor at various strategic points along their educational journey. The strategic points include the following:

- All FTIC students are required to attend a group advising session prior to the first time they register. During the 2.5-hour group advising session students learn about various academic programs, the benefits of selecting and completing their certificate or degree, services available to support their career exploration and education goals, and how to register for classes.
- All FTIC students are required to take an 11-week student development course (SDEV) designed explicitly to aid FTIC students. SDEV classes are either taught by or assigned to an ACT advisor. In SDEV, students meet with ACT advisors to discuss their education and career goals.
- Through the new Route 66 campaign students meet with an ACT advisor for educational goal and graduation planning when they complete 30 and 45 hours.
- Students on academic probation must meet with an ACT advisor three times a semester to discuss their academic status.

Center Staffing, Reporting Structure of Academic and Career Advising

The ACT services are provided by a team of 14 ACT advisors, one ACT distance advisor, six student success team leaders, one student success career coordinator, one center office supervisor, and two student success specialists. The ACT advisors report to the team leaders. The team leaders report to the director of advising, career and transfer services (ACT). The director of ACT reports to the vice president of student success.

Career and Academic Advising Integration

The ACT team consists of professional advisors who are responsible for academic and career advisement. The ACT Team participates in a fully integrated and comprehensive professional development program to enhance their academic and career advising skills and professional knowledge. The ACT advisors deliver academic and career advising to all NVC students. In addition, the team is located in a one-stop center that provides students with integrated academic and career advising. As students meet with ACT advisors, they will receive academic, career, and transfer advising to meet their advising needs.

Methods of Service or Program Delivery and Resources

The ACT Team provides in-person, one-on-one, group, online, e-mail, and phone advising to support both on-campus and distance students. Through employee development, the ACT Team makes certain students receive the same quality advising whether they are on campus or at a distance. In addition, there are classroom presentations, workshops, and events such as:

- Major Mania—an event that provides students an awareness of specific majors, careers, and educational goals. Academic experts from various majors and careers meet with students to discuss their future plans.

- Counselor Showcase—local high school career counselors meet with the ACT team to discuss how to collectively and collaboratively support students in their career exploration and planning process.

- Career Expos—local businesses meet with students about career and job opportunities.

- Transfer Fairs—university representatives meet with students about their transfer plans.

- Don't Cancel that Class—faculty invites an ACT advisor to teach the class instead of canceling it. ACT advisors will discuss educational goal, career, financial, graduation, and/or transfer planning.

- Be Advised—ACT advisors set up "on-the-go" advising stations in various locations around the NVC campus. This provides ease of advising access.

Accountability

ACT Goal 1: Increase the number students with declared majors who are following a prescribed Education Plan (EdP). Outcome: a 15% increase in the number of students from fall 2005 to fall 2008.

ACT Goal 2: Increase the number of NVC graduates. Outcome: a 106% increase in NVC associate degrees attained from 2005–2007. Based on US Department of Education information, NVC is tenth in the nation among the Top 100 Associate Degree producers for 2008.

ACT Goal 3: Increase the number of NVC students that transfer to a four-year institution. Outcome: 44.1% of NVC students transfer to a state institution while 26.4% of Texas-wide community college students transfer to a state institution. NVC currently leads the state in students who transfer to a four-year state institution.

ACT Goal 4: Increase the number of students receiving academic, career, and transfer advising services. Outcome: Student visits to the ACT Center for academic and career advising increased from 20,239 in 2005 to 37,929 in 2007, an 87.4% increase.

ACT Goal 5: ACT student survey results at or above 90%. Outcome: 98.5% of students reported having their academic and career advising needs met; 100% indicated they would recommend academic and career advising to a friend; 91% reported learning something important during an academic and career advising session; and 91% reported being satisfied with their overall academic and career advising experiences.

Strengths of Center and Professional Development

One of the strengths of the ACT Team is its fully integrated, collaborative, and effective model of providing academic, career, and transfer advising services. Providing seamless, integrated academic, career, and transfer advising by ACT advisors is a key factor in the success experienced. Another strength is the commitment to the ACT Team's professional development. The full commitment to assembling a first-rate Advising, Career and Transfer Team is contingent upon ACT's strategic, systematic, and comprehensive employee development program that has proven to not only increase the quality of advisement students receive, but also the retention of employees. Due to the support of NVC's executive team, four hours of employee development for the ACT Team are provided every week. The Friday Advising, Career, and Transfer Training (FACTT) consists of wide-ranging professional development sessions customized to the needs of the ACT Team. FACTT promotes continuity in academic, career, and transfer advising; standardizes and streamlines services; fully develops the skills and knowledge of the team; supports NVC's commitment to cross-training and collaboration; promotes job empowerment for the ACT Team; and highly develops the ACT Team to provide student-centered services. The team also participates in collegewide development sessions such as Steven Covey's *Seven Habits of Highly Effective People and Focus: Achieving Your Highest Priority*, the *FISH Philosophy*, SeaWorld's Whale Done Leadership Training, and Customer Service development. The ACT Team also attends local, state, and national seminars and conferences. In addition, the Career, Advising and Transfer Services (CATS) Lab is a strength of ACT. As support services became increasingly Web-based, the need was realized to create a support lab where students could obtain the help they needed as they accessed these services. The ACT Team oversees the CATS Lab because the online services are advising in nature. The CATS Lab provides support to students who are utilizing the Web to register for classes, complete career assessments, pay online, complete their FASFA, complete transfer applications, research and apply for scholarships, research Wildcat Classifieds for a job, accept financial aid awards, request their transcript, print transfer course descriptions, and other online services.

Challenges of the Center

Large student-to-advisor ratios make developmental advising difficult to provide. A non-caseload model makes it complicated for students to bond with ACT advisors. Appointments are not used. ACT's walk-in practice makes it challenging to pre-schedule work on initiatives as the number of students walking in varies. In 2009 ACT will move into a newly constructed facility. At that time, an assessment of current processes will be completed and necessary changes associated with new facility will be made. In 2010 a new student data system will be initiated. Many challenges are anticipated associated with the new student data system.

Future Plans for the Center and Team

The ACT Team plans to initiate a support program for minority males that will include a specialized SDEV course, academic and career advising, and mentoring. In addition, the plan is to enhance the early alert program to include all SDEV and preparatory students. The ACT Team is working with the entire campus community to engage everyone in an educational goal/graduation completion plan. By creating a culture of completion for students, NVC can be a national leader in the number of associate degrees awarded. Entry-to-exit processes are being enhanced to allow students to follow a university partner's degree plan and simultaneously earn associate's and bachelor's degrees. Through collaborative efforts with SDEV leaders, work is being completed to make certain educational goal and career planning remains at the center of the course curriculum. Online resources are being expanded through the creation of the Hands-on-Line Advising program (HOLA). An employee development certificate is being created that will be awarded to ACT Team members who successfully complete a designated series of professional development sessions. In the future the ACT Team will continue to be, work, serve and learn . . . together. This exemplary practice is dedicated to NVC's ACT Team. They *"create opportunities for success"* by providing high-quality, student-centered service to students. A special thanks to NVC's Vice President of Student Success Dr. Diana Muniz; ACT Director Debi Gaitan; and the ACT Team Leaders Betty Cunningham, Margaret "Jo" Garcia, Tim Molina, James Searles, Deanna Villarreal, Gary Walderman, and Katrice Woods-Bender.

This exemplary practice description was prepared by Debi Gaitan.

QUINSIGAMOND COMMUNITY COLLEGE

Integrated Academic and Career Advising Center Name: Career and Academic Planning Services (CAPS)

Location: Worcester, Massachusetts

Institutional Type: Public Community College

Highest Degree Granted: Associate's degree

Total Number of Students Enrolled at the Institution: 6,700 undergraduate (for credit)

Center url: http://www.qcc.edu/Advising.html

Contact Person: Colleen R. Doherty, Assistant Dean of Career and Academic Advisement, cdoherty@qcc.mass.edu, 508–854–4309

Mission and Objectives of Center or Program

The mission and objectives are to further student success through the respectful delivery of comprehensive career and academic advising services by employing a developmental advising model that provides assistance to our students during all stages of their college experience at Quinsigamond Community College (QCC). The advising model used at Valencia Community College was modified for use by QCC CAPS. From the college catalog, QCC CAPS recognizes that students' advising needs vary as they progress through the college. In response to these well-established needs, the college has created a developmental advising model that (a) is organized in four stages defined by numbers of credits earned toward a degree; and (b) prepares students to assume larger responsibility for decision making as they progress through a program of study.

Stage One	Stage Two	Stage Three	Stage Four
Advisor assumes primary responsibility	Advisor & student share responsibility	Advisor & student share responsibility	Student assumes primary responsibility
0–15 credits	15–30 credits	30^+–45 credits	45–60 credits

Center History

Over the past three years the center has had significant changes in three areas: staffing, scope of services, and professional development. Three new permanent full-time staff positions were created to assist the existing 20 part-time advisors, allowing for career and academic planning services to be offered year-round to students. Services have expanded from scheduling of courses to include career planning, academic advising, and strategies for student success. A Web-based student portfolio entitled CAPS—Career, Academic, and Personal Success—has been implemented and serves as a guide for students to receive and advisors to provide comprehensive advising services. An ongoing innovative professional development program for all QCC advisors (center and faculty advisors) occurs throughout the fall and spring semesters, covering topics ranging from advising basics to ESL advising to current trends in advising (e.g., millennial students, usage of technology, and hot jobs in the state).

Description of Center, Including Services and Programs Offered

The Center offers the following services to students: placement testing and interpretation of test scores; CAPS advising; group career planning sessions; course and major selection; instruction in online course registration; referrals to student success services; classroom course registration and overview of college advisement terminology and procedures; and early alert outreach (retention initiative).

The Web-based CAPS (career, academic, and personal success) is used to create a student portfolio which serves to integrate career and academic planning services. The plan also serves as a guideline for advisors to ensure that consistent questions and topics of discussion are addressed at all CAPS sessions. Topics discussed in the plan include career, academic, and personal goals; a strengths assessment (used a basis for discussion on strengths and barriers to college success); selection of college program of study; suitability to college program of study; intent to transfer; results of career assessments and career research; individualized referrals to specific college resources; selection of courses for current and future semesters; and course registration.

The Strengths Assessment portion of the CAPS Plan includes a survey of 10 topic areas: support from others, study habits, test-taking skills, time management, note-taking skills, taking initiative, financial support, planning skills, motivation, and transportation. The assessment is used as a basis for discussion between the student and advisor where the unique strengths and skills a student brings to the college serves as the start of this conversation. Often students are not encouraged to reflect on positive attributes in the context of an advising session, and this also allows for a segue into a discussion on those areas students may need assistance and referrals.

Group career planning sessions are open to all current and prospective students and alumni. The sessions are free and participants attend one session and can follow up with questions to the facilitator via e-mail. Topics include the following: an overview of career and academic planning; career assessment tools and interpretation of results; career research sources on the Internet; the process and importance of informational interviewing; selection of college programs of study; and next steps. Individual computer work, group discussions, and working with the facilitator in establishing next steps in the career planning process, including referrals, are the main modes of delivery and content of the sessions.

Methods of Service or Program Delivery

The following methods are utilized in delivering services to students: individual sessions (in person, phone, and online), group sessions, workshops, and a credit course (First Year Experience).

Students Served by Center

All categories of students are served by the center, including a large percentage of first-generation and minority students. Four thousand students are assigned to the Career and Academic Planning Services. During summer and between semesters, the center also provides services to students assigned to faculty advisors, brining the total to over 7,000 students.

Center Staffing (Number, Type, Roles, Responsibilities)

Full-time positions include director of career and academic planning; coordinator of career and academic planning (Web-based Services); four CAPS/Early Alert advisors; assessment specialist; three clerks/office support. Part-time positions include 20 advisors; five testing proctors; four clerks/office support. The director reports to the assistant dean of career and academic advisement. The center is under the Division of Academic Affairs at the college.

How Are Career and Academic Advising Integrated?

The very title and functions of CAPS (career, academic, and personal success) clearly implies the merging of career planning and academic advising. Staff job titles are CAPS Advisors. The Web-based CAPS Plan is merged into the student information system used to register students for courses. The offering of ongoing career planning sessions by the Center, the use of career assessments and career information resources, and the strong presence of career and academic planning in the college's first-year experience course, are mechanisms used to fully integrate career and academic planning. The Early Alert system also addresses career and academic planning.

The college's first-year experience course entitled Strategies for College and Career was initially designed to integrate career and academic planning. The course, now in its sixth year, was and is part of a retention and student success initiative at the college. Recognizing that having an established career goal(s), as well as a plan(s) to implement the goal(s), can be critical to student motivation and success served as the impetus and rationale for the course content. Over one-third of the course is devoted to career and academic planning and can be viewed at http://www.qcc.mass.edu/t3/ORT110/index.html. The themes of career, connecting to the college, and CAPS contain over 50 lesson plans and Web links which all faculty cover in the delivery of the course. Student completion of the course, their grades, and engaging in a meaningful and timely course registration for the following semester, are all built in incentives for student success.

Resources

Resources include Web-based CAPS Plans, which includes a Students Strengths Assessment and extensive referral network and process; Advisor Notes System; FYE career resources http://www.qcc.mass.edu/t3/ort/sites.html#careerassess; Career Link http://www.qcc.mass.edu/t3/ort/careerlink.html; and strong link to the Career Placement Office.

Accountability

The one component of the CAPS project that has been researched over the past six years has been the College Orientation Course—ORT 110 Strategies for College and Career. As shown in the chart below, student persistence to the second semester ranges from 15–25% above the baseline. As discussed earlier, the course has significant content on career and academic planning.

Impact of ORT 110 Students in Developmental Courses: Persistence to Second Semester

Baseline Persistence Rate* =		
Cohort	*Actual*	*Change over Baseline*
Fall 2002 FTQCC ORT Cohort	87.6%	23.4%
Fall 2003 FTQCC ORT Cohort	86.3%	21.5%
Fall 2004 FTQCC ORT Cohort	82.0%	15.5%
Fall 2005 FTQCC ORT Cohort	82.1%	15.6%
MEAN FA02-FA05	84.5%	19.0%
REVISED DATA		
Fall 2005 FTQCC ORT Cohort	82.1%	15.7%
Fall 2006 FTQCC ORT Cohort	89.4%	25.9%
Fall 2007 FTQCC ORT Cohort	87.4%	23.1%

The new Web-based CAPS Plan is constructed to produce a wealth of data on student retention and will be analyzed after the add/drop period in Fall 2009.

Strengths of Center

A strength of the center includes the work area being housed under the academic affairs division which is strongly linked to academics and faculty. The offering of comprehensive services (career planning, academic advising, early alert, and retention) is not only helpful to students, but provides an increased level of visibility throughout the college. In addition, the availability of services year round, as opposed to a seasonal service (as advising once was at the college) allows advisors to meet with students during the less stressful time periods in the semester.

Challenges of Center

Two evident challenges at present include adequate staffing and resources to support mission and function, including technology-related resources and tools, as well as improving the status of at-risk students via comprehensive CAPS. Challenges are multifaceted, dependent on economic factors, and known to the college administration. Within the past year the college administration allowed the hiring of three full-time advisors for the CAPS initiative.

Future Plans

Future plans include to fully merge the health careers center with CAPS, to evaluate the CAPS/Early Alert program, and to improve and expand online career and academic advising.

Professional Development Provided Staff to Enhance Career and Academic Advising

Each semester advisors participate in a professional development series. Recent topics have included CAPS and Career Development, Orientation to the new CAPS Plan, High Wage Career Trends, NACADA Career Advising Webinar, and Career Resources. In addition, 70% of advising staff teach the FYE course which includes five weeks of career development. FYE training occurs each semester. Participation in NACADA conferences and webinars occurs regularly.

Additional Information

The technology-related needs for this project, particularly the Web-based CAPS Plan, have been extensive. The plan was created independently of the student information system through the work of John LeFave, Web-Based Services Manager.

This exemplary practice description was prepared by Colleen R. Doherty, assistant dean of career and academic advisement; Liza Smith, coordinator, Web-based services.

STATE UNIVERSITY OF NEW YORK AT OSWEGO (SUNY OSWEGO)

Center Name: The Compass

    Location: Oswego, NY

    Institutional Type: Four-year, public institution

    Highest Degree Granted: Master's Degree and Certificate of Advance Study (CAS)

    Total Number of Students: 8,660 students including 7,680 undergraduate and 980 graduate students.

    Center url: www.oswego.edu/compass

    Contacts: Kathleen Evans, Assistant Vice President for Student Affairs, evans@oswego.edu; Christy Huynh, Assistant Director of Student Advisement, chuynh@oswego.edu, 610–683–4735

Mission and Objectives

The mission of the Compass is to assist students in planning for and achieving success in and after college by providing resources and opportunities for students to purposefully plan their education and career goals.

Center History

The origins of the Compass date back to Fall 2000 when the opportunity arose to bring together multiple departments into a new center dedicated to educational planning. The next seven years were spent developing the space, programs, and offerings. It was a unique opportunity to design not only programs but also to construct the space from a student-centered perspective. Intensive planning and conceptualization of offerings and services were undertaken during 2006 and 2007. The Compass was given its name in Spring 2007 and opened in August 2007.

The Compass was created to provide students with a cohesive, accessible center that would provide a framework to understand and plan for their education in a seamless and intentional manner. It comprises eight departments/units, including career services, student advisement, orientation, experience-based education, service learning and community service, First Year Programs, transfer services, and civic engagement.

Description of Center, Including Services and Programs Offered

The goal of the Compass is to encourage students to participate fully in curricular, co-curricular, and community experiences. The Compass helps students explore a wide variety of possible majors/minors; participate in a range of campus and community-based experiences to advance their academic, career, and personal goals; build the core skills valued by employers; create a knowledge base to launch successful careers; and create an educational plan that guides them through college and prepares them for the transition to future work and graduate study.

The Compass coordinates undeclared advisement (325 first year students, 200 sophomores) and first year advisement; provides major and career exploration resources; assists students through the job and graduate school search; and provides a reference folder mailing service, volunteer service transcripts, FirstChoice (academic experience), Living and Learning Communities, The Laker (GoalQuest's Web-based social and educational networking community), articulation agreements for transfer students, MOST mentoring program for transfer students, community and service learning opportunities, internships both on and off campus, a resource room with 10 computers and an extensive library, and Web-based resources including videos, newsletters, podcasts, listservs, and Web sites.

The framework for providing services is based on a developmental model, namely the "4Ds"—Discover, Develop, Define, and Distinguish. The 4Ds are based on student identity and career development theories and follow the developmental stages of college students. The 4Ds are intended to help students map their educational plan in an intentional, purposeful manner and to develop an action plan to progress through each stage—DISCOVER who they are, DEVELOP their skills, DEFINE their goals, and DISTINGUISH themselves from others.

DISCOVER—From the moment students arrive on campus they are introduced to the importance of developing an academic plan. During the Summer Orientation programs there are multiple presentations to students and parents regarding academic and career planning.

The First Year Program is a comprehensive program that supports students during their transition to college. The program integrates First Year Advisement (faculty and peer advisement model), FirstChoice courses (content courses, limited to 19 students and designed to help the transition into college), residential programs, assessment (College Student Inventory-measures academic motivation, career closure, and receptivity to support services), and social networking to build community. The Compass coordinates undeclared advisement for over 450 undeclared students and trains first year advisors on developmental advising and provides training for undeclared advisors.

Exploratory students are expected to actively explore their interests, values, skills, and strengths during their first year. A variety of options are available to support students during this process including two exploratory courses, GST 103 and GST 110, and Exploring Majors workshops. Self-assessments, strategies for researching majors, and career exploration are topics embedded in these exploratory courses. The workshops provide students with an overview of the resources available and the opportunity to create an action plan. A variety of self-assessments are available for students to complete and discuss with a professional including the Myers-Briggs Type Indicator® (MBTI®), DISCOVER (ACT's comprehensive career planning program), and Clifton StrengthsFinder (StrengthsQuest™, Gallup's strengths development program).

DEVELOP—The sophomore year can be very difficult and undefined for many students. The Compass encourages students to stay engaged by continuing to develop their interests, skills, abilities, and strengths. Students are encouraged to explore experientially through volunteering, Service Learning (GST 302), and Career Awareness (GST 303). The Compass provides multiple Internship Orientation Workshops each week (both in the Compass and Web-based) to introduce students to the relevance of experiential education during the major and career exploration and confirmation process. Self-assessments, as noted above, and additional assessments such as the Strong Interest Inventory® are available.

The Compass provides résumé and cover letter development and assists students in finding internship and networking opportunities to explore and confirm their major interests. Site visits to companies and agencies are co-sponsored with academic departments. Pizza with Professionals programs are hosted on campus as a way to bridge students with professionals in various career fields.

DEFINE—Students are encouraged to continue to define who they are through leadership experiences during their junior year. Students are informed about internships, service learning group leader positions, and leadership positions within the Compass and throughout campus. Career fairs, networking events, and workshops provide students with opportunities to engage in the career exploration process.

DISTINGUISH—As students prepare to transition out of college, many resources are provided to assist them in finding meaningful career and graduate school opportunities. Résumé, cover letter, and graduate school essay critiques are available. Mock interviews, career planning, and job search assistance are provided. Numerous workshops are offered to assist students throughout the job and graduate school search including Interviewing—The Good, the Bad, and the Ugly; Internet Job Search Workshop; and December

Graduate Job Search. Career, internship, volunteer, and graduate school fairs connect employers and graduate schools with students (e.g., Human Services and Volunteer Fair, Fall Career & Internship Fair, NYC Career Connections, Teacher Recruitment Days). Long-term volunteer opportunities panels inform students about the array of service opportunities. Employers partner with campus to interview and select students for jobs via the on-campus recruiting process.

The Compass offers nine credit-based courses, including five experiential courses that assist students through the academic, major, and career exploration process:

GST 100, College Orientation & Success, one credit hour: This course is designed to help freshmen become productive and successful members of the Oswego college community utilizing a Web-based networking community. Students are introduced to information about Oswego's history, strategies for being a successful student, campus resources, academic/career planning, and personal development.

GST 103 Exploring Your Strengths, one credit hour: This course is designed to assist undeclared/exploratory students through the major exploration and confirmation process utilizing a strengths-based perspective. The course utilizes assessments and inventories (Myers-Briggs Type Indicator®, DISCOVER, and Clifton StrengthsFinder).

GST 110 Life Planning and Major Exploration, two credit hours: This course helps undeclared/exploratory students to explore their interests, strengths, and values and to apply those to the process of choosing and/or confirming a major. During the course students build self-confidence and competency, and develop an educational plan.

MGT 494 Seminar in Career Planning, one credit hour: This course is designed to assist students in the career planning and job search process.

GST 302 Service Learning, one credit hour: This course provides students with the opportunity to volunteer with local agencies to provide direct service to those in need.

GST 302 Service Learning Group Leader, two credit hours: This course involves hands-on training at a community service site. Group leaders act as a liaison between the community partner and other service learning students.

GST 303 Career Awareness II, two to three credit hours: This course provides students whose career goals are uncertain with introductory work experience and the basic tools to begin the job search process.

GST 304 First Year Peer Advisement Program, three credit hours: This course is designed to provide first year peer advisors with the opportunity to work collaboratively with faculty and administration while gaining skills to assist first year students effectively.

GST 498 Internship, 2–12 credit hours: This course is designed for upper division students to provide a semester-long experiential learning experience related to their academic major or minor.

Methods of Service

The Compass programs and services are delivered utilizing multiple modalities including over 15 distinct workshops (both face-to-face and Web-based), nine credit-based courses, one-on-one academic and career advisement and counseling sessions, self-assessments, peer advisement, class presentations, residence hall presentations, drop-in advisement, drop-in resource room hours staffed by student interns, online searchable databases, newsletters, listservs, and Web-based resources and tutorials. The Compass offers dozens of special events each year (e.g., networking events, etiquette dinners, on campus recruitment).

The Compass strives to make information, services, and programs accessible to all students. The resource room is staffed throughout the day by trained peer assistants (Navigators) and staff is also available during designated drop-in hours to meet individually with students.

The Compass utilizes technology to disseminate information to students, as well as to track student progress. The Compass Web site includes a wiki, developmental Web-pathways for students to identify opportunities and resources, and podcast videos featuring alumni and employers.

Students Served by Center

The Compass programs and services are provided for students from the time they pay their deposit until after they graduate. Once students pay their deposit, The Compass begins connecting with them about transition services and programs.

The Compass continues to serve all students throughout their academic careers and also supports alumni who are facing career changes or need job search assistance. Specialized programs and services are offered for first year, transfer, exploratory, academic warning, international, and graduating students.

Center Staffing

There are 11 full-time professional staff, five full-time support staff, five part-time graduate assistants, two part-time graduate interns, 15 student interns, and 15 part-time paid student staff. The Compass has three directors, five assistant directors, and three coordinators. Two directors report to the dean of students in the Division of Student Affairs and Enrollment and one director reports to the provost in the Division of Academic Affairs.

The Compass has a sizeable staff reporting to different divisions. Decision making is completed through consensus during weekly planning meetings. Every quarter a half-day work retreat is scheduled with the entire full-time staff to vision, plan and implement initiatives, inform one another of new program ideas, and provide staff development activities.

Integration of Career and Academic Advisement

The staff work collaboratively to offer students in-depth, substantial, integrated, and comprehensive programs, courses, and advisement. The Compass integrates academic and career advising at every level and provides direction as students navigate the major and career exploration process. As students progress through the major exploration and confirmation process, they are supported by career counselors, undeclared/exploratory advisors, assigned faculty advisors, peer advisors, and Compass interns.

SUNY Oswego has a de-centralized advising model in which full-time faculty in academic departments provide academic advising to students. The Compass provides advisor training to first year faculty advisors and specialized training and resources for undeclared/exploratory advisors.

Resources

The Compass has a resource room dedicated to providing students access to information and resources to assist them in the major and career exploration and job and graduate school search processes. The Compass Resource Room is staffed by peer assistants, Navigators. The Navigators provide résumé critiquing, and assistance with the Web-based programs including DISCOVER. The resource room has 10 computers and an extensive library of publications and handouts regarding the major exploration and job and graduate school search process. The Compass Web site has three databases for internships, volunteer/service learning opportunities, and job vacancies.

All undeclared/exploratory advisors are provided a manual of resources, tools, and strategies for assisting students through the major exploration and confirmation process. This manual includes strategies and activities developed by the Compass staff (e.g., Major/Minor Elimination, Dissect a Major, Self-Exploration, My Academic Plan).

Accountability

Staff is assessing its impact on student learning in three ways—by tracking student usage of programs and services, by assessing student satisfaction, and by measuring the impact on student learning outcomes. Using new software that tracks student activity and participation, 4,426 unique student contacts with the Compass were noted in 2007–08. The ongoing Compass User Satisfaction Survey indicates that approximately 85% of student visitors to the Compass indicated that they receive the information they were seeking, 80% felt the staff responded quickly and appropriately to their needs, 89% felt comfortable during their visit to the Compass, 84% reported being satisfied with the Compass center overall, and 84% would recommend the Compass services to other students. In addition, staff members are committed to assessing efforts on learning outcomes in the following categories: commitment to learning, personal choice and responsibility, and civic responsibility. Departments have reviewed their programmatic efforts and developed intended outcomes for programs as well as assessment methods and timelines for all activities in 2008–09.

Strengths

The hallmark of the Compass is that it is a comprehensive, welcoming center that utilizes technology, teamwork, and collaboration to provide students with excellent programs and services. The Compass is founded on the principles of assisting students throughout the educational planning process. Each of the eight units in the Compass provides students with purposeful opportunities to plan for and achieve success throughout college by developing an intentional, comprehensive plan. The spaciousness of the center includes a resource room, two high-tech classrooms, four interview rooms, 13 individual staff offices, and 10 office stations. The multifaceted spaces of the Compass allow for confidential meeting spaces as well as smart classrooms for high-tech group meetings and classes. The Compass utilizes software that keeps record of each student's interface with the center and allows for seamless communication and services. It tracks students' progress and records this information that is accessible to staff working with students. Referrals are personal and immediate; students can be walked to the next office and introduced to the appropriate person. The Compass provides evening hours two days a week to accommodate students and provides extensive programs throughout campus. The Compass welcomes student referrals from faculty advisors and staff. Services and programs are offered in a synergistic, cohesive manner that exemplifies to students that educational planning is seamless and connected.

Challenges

The challenges of the Compass include working collaboratively across divisional lines, oversight, sharing expenses, and continuing to vision and redesign program offerings in a cohesive and collaborative way. It is challenging to maintain each department's identify while striving to be one comprehensive center. The complexities range from sharing resources, equipment, and space to making collective decisions aligned with each department's goals and vision. There is no centralized reporting structure for the center and working across divisional lines is difficult as resources are allocated differently and divisions are structured differently. Each director reports to his or her respective supervisor and it is sometimes challenging to gain comparable support from both divisions.

Future Plans

In the future, the Compass plans to launch CDPs (Compass Development Plans) to explicitly outline the process of developing and executing a multidimensional educational plan and to assist students in marketing themselves. Students will enroll in a CDP that matches their developmental stage, and their progress will be reported and documented utilizing the student tracking system. The Compass is also committed to developing additional major and career exploration courses and programs that support students in the sophomore and junior years.

Professional Development

The Compass staff is dedicated to continual professional development to stay abreast of the most innovative ways to provide career and academic advising. The Compass staff hold leadership positions on regional and national governing bodies, and attend and/or present at NACADA, Eastern ACE/NACE, SUNY CDO (Career Development Organization), First-Year Experience, NODA, and Campus Compact conferences and webinars each year.

The Compass provides professional development workshops throughout the year to advisors, faculty, and staff focused on developmental advising, strengths-based advising and teaching, and effectively working with exploratory students.

This exemplary practice description was prepared by Kathy Evans, assistant vice president for student affairs; Christy Huynh, assistant director of student advisement; and Robert Casper, director of career services.

THIEL COLLEGE

Program: Center for Learning and Advising

Location: Greenville, PA

Institutional Information: A four-year private liberal arts college, Thiel is located in rural northwestern Pennsylvania near the Ohio border. Offers the Bachelor of Arts and Bachelor of Science degrees. Serves 1,130 undergraduates (enrollment in Fall 2008).

Center url: www.thiel.edu/cla

Contact Information

Patricia Kelvin, CLA Coordinator of Teaching and Learning, pkelvin@thiel.edu

Kateri Linn, CLA Advisor, klinn@thiel.edu

Melissa Philson, CLA Advisor, mphilson@thiel.edu

724–589–2290

Mission and Objectives of Center or Program

The Center for Learning and Advising (CLA) provides an integrated academic and career advising program for all Thiel students. Its mission statement calls for the Center to "focus on creating a comprehensive learning experience by strengthening the advising process to be more responsive to the developmental, discernment and career needs of students through an integrated, supportive and challenging learning community." Within that mission, the center's objectives are to

- Integrate academic advising and career advising to support all students.
- Provide professional development for faculty and staff to help provide an integrated, supportive, and challenging learning community related to student advising.
- Strengthen the faculty advising process to be more responsive to the developmental, discernment and career needs of students and to help them identify their life objectives.

- Refer students to other campus resources for additional assistance.

- Draw on the latest research on student success to assist students in attaining their goals.

- Support meeting the goals of faculty advisors and advisors from the Academic Success Center (a campus unit with responsibilities for under-prepared students and those need extra academic assistance).

- Increase student satisfaction with advising and student retention/graduation rates.

Center History

Before 2007, career and advising services for Thiel students existed, but with little coordination. Students struggling with decisions about academic majors and minors, career choices, and life goals also struggled to find the right offices or individuals who could help them. Every Thiel student does have an academic advisor, but for some faculty members, advising focused on enrolling students in the right classes. Although for many years Thiel has had a career services center and an internship-arranging experiential educa-tion office as well as an academic success center that provided assistance in math, reading, writing, and study skills, differences in organizational structure and reporting authority made working together challenging. Consequently, students did not wrestle early enough with the hard questions of what they wanted to do with their lives and which programs and courses would allow them to reach their goals, resulting in their wasting time, energy, and money.

Faced with concerns about student retention that were seen as resulting from these (among other) problems, a study conducted during the 2005–06 academic year by faculty and staff determined that Thiel students needed additional, directed support in coping with academic demands and in choos-ing their majors and careers. The study concluded that the ideal way to address these concerns would integrate academic advising and career advis-ing while providing professional development for faculty and staff to enhance their roles in engaging students in and outside the classroom.

Those recommendations led to the application for and subsequent award of a $1.5 million, five-year Title III grant establishing the Center for Learning and Advising at Thiel College. The construction of new offices within the college library and the hiring of additional personnel permitted the center to open its doors to students in August 2007.

CLA Services and Programs

The CLA provides an entry point for students seeking to discern and deter-mine life choices; helps students at any point in their college careers when academic challenges necessitate intervention by a CLA advisor; coordinates job shadowing, internship, and career services; and offers professional devel-opment and consultation to faculty and staff in support of student-engaging pedagogies and developmental advising.

Methods of Service and Program Delivery

In addition to the many students who come to the center voluntarily to avail themselves of its services, at the beginning of each semester, the college's academic standing committee (one of whose members is a CLA advisor) requires students on academic probation and deemed to need assistance in clarifying life goals and/or choosing a major/career to see a CLA advisor. Typically, probationary students meet weekly with a CLA advisor for the support they need to regain their academic footing on the appropriate path to the future they have discerned with the CLA advisor's help.

During the academic year the CLA is open from 8 A.M.—5 P.M. Monday, Tuesday, Thursday, and Friday and until 8 P.M. on Wednesday, with additional hours by appointment. The center is also open during the summer and academic recesses when the college is open.

Whether students learn about the CLA in their first-semester freshman seminars or they seek career advice only months before graduation, whether they know exactly what they want from a career discernment program or they are not even sure they want to be in college, all students can gain needed direction from CLA staff.

As the semester progresses, the CLA is also advised of students in difficulty (e.g., attendance, class performance, emotional and other stresses) through an automated system with alerts submitted by faculty or staff. CLA advisors then coordinate the efforts to determine the problems or needs the student has and how best to resolve those issues. CLA advisors then report outcomes to the faculty or staff member initiating the alert. As part of that effort, CLA advisors may involve the student's faculty advisor, other professors, residence hall staff, athletic coaches, the academic success center, or the college counselor. As appropriate, students may also be invited to meet with a CLA advisor to discuss academic and career goals.

The CLA's career group works with students individually and in small groups to prepare them for internships and for post-college careers—from helping build résumés and conducting mock interviews, to seminars in workplace etiquette, to internship placement and job referral and coordination of career fairs.

Significantly, the CLA's ongoing collaboration and interaction with academic, administrative, and other student-support departments allow it to serve as the one place on campus students can come if they have questions or need help but do not know whom to contact, and either be assisted or referred to the appropriate office or person.

Finally, the CLA coordinator of teaching and learning assists students indirectly by providing individual and small-group consultation and professional development programs for faculty. Included over the last year were the following programs: a student learning workshop, an assessment workshop, three webinars on advising, two technology seminars, and six seminars on learning. In addition, the coordinator led a technology workshop for new faculty, funded attendance of 14 faculty/staff to attend national advising/teaching/

learning conferences. Three advising groups totaling 18 faculty members met monthly during the 2008–09 academic year to discuss faculty advising.

Students Served

All Thiel students can avail themselves of CLA services at any point in their college career.

Center Staffing

The CLA's staff includes a director who oversees the entire center, coordinates the activities under the grant, and represents CLA to the college. The CLA director reports jointly to the vice president for academic affairs and the vice president for student life. Two CLA advisors work directly with students—individually and in small groups. They make presentations about CLA's student-focused services to classes, to faculty groups, and to prospective students and their parents. They also coordinate discernment events where students develop self-knowledge and are helped to determine the most appropriate major, minor, and career. A coordinator for teaching and learning works with faculty, providing individual consulting and conducting workshops and seminars for professional development in student-engaging pedagogies.

Under the CLA umbrella, but funded directly through the college rather than the grant, are the CLA Career Group, comprising the director of career services and the director of experiential education, and the college's director of institutional research. The institutional research director provides assessment of CLA programs and chairs the CLA Project Advisory Committee for Evaluation, which was created to conduct the project evaluation and work with an external evaluator to ensure the objectivity and focus of evaluation efforts.

Integrating Career and Academic Advising

Basing its programs on the literature of personality and development theory as well as the extensive research on student engagement and learning, which together facilitate a holistic vantage of student and faculty needs, the CLA enjoys wide latitude in meeting its mission and objectives. The works of the following influenced development of the CLA: Pascarella and Terenzini; Tinto; Bean; Kuh; Astin; Lenning and Ebbers; Holland; and Super.

A CLA advisor can meet individually with students having difficulty deciding on a major, uncertain about the classes they need and the grade point averages required for potential majors; those experiencing academic difficulty in or a lack of enthusiasm about courses they are taking, particularly in their majors; and those unsure where to take their lives or wondering if a declared major is the best for them. Through such interaction, students begin to understand how career fields are related to their curricular and co-curricular educational decisions. Once a student has determined a major, a faculty advisor assumes the responsibilities for academic advising, often working with a CLA advisor or the CLA Career Group for career and co-curricular advice.

Students may choose to come to the CLA to explore the majors that might be appropriate and interesting to them and then work with CLA's Career Group to obtain a job shadow or short-term internship that could confirm a career choice. As they focus their studies in future semesters, students can return to the career group to seek an in-depth internship placement or help obtaining a first post-college job. While the CLA advisors tend to focus on the needs of lower division students and the career services director on the needs of students closer to graduation, each staff member has the professional credentials and theoretical background to help students at any point in their college careers. A CLA advisor might work with a college freshman to help her decide on the best major for her and to learn how to achieve necessary academic success. When that student becomes a sophomore, her consultations with her CLA advisor might be geared toward choosing co-curricular activities that would enhance her academic work for future employment opportunities. In her junior and senior years, she might meet with the career services director for the advice she will need to obtain a job in the career she has chosen.

Other CLA Resources

Since it is located in the college library, the center has resource shelves with books, CD-ROMs, and additional helpful resources for students and faculty that can be checked out through the library. In addition, the DISCOVER computerized guidance system is available through the CLA Web site, and students meet with a CLA advisor to receive and go over the results. Also, the online *Occupational Outlook Handbook* is available through the CLA Web site and used as a resource by students and CLA advisors working with students. The entire college has Web and Internet access, and all students are provided with laptop computers upon enrollment.

Program Evaluation and Accountability

The CLA evaluation plan calls for the collection of reliable, timely data that will provide formative information to guide the project and help identify problems for which alternative solutions can be explored with members of the college community. At the end of each grant year and the conclusion of the Title III project a comprehensive report documents outcomes; successful strategies and lessons learned regarding student learning; and the progress in the use of engaging teaching methodologies and technology. The data so far demonstrate substantive increases in the numbers and satisfaction of students using the CLA and the number of faculty taking advantage of professional development opportunities. Qualitative data describing student success support the quantitative data.

After the CLA has been in operation several years, year-to-year graduation and retention rates will be examined. The following standardized inventories were administered during Spring 2008 to provide baseline data for the purpose of CLA evaluation: Beginning College Survey of Student Engagement (BCSSE), Faculty Survey of Student Engagement (FSSE), National Survey of Student Engagement (NSSE), and Noel-Levitz Student Satisfaction Inventory (SSI). Beginning in 2009, year-to-year trends will be ascertained.

Strengths of the Center

- Boasts a dedicated and highly qualified staff
- Integrates academic and career advising
- Provides services for all students at all stages of their college careers
- Initiates support activities for students, faculty, and staff
- Works in conjunction with both academic affairs and student life
- Serves as a student "alert sounder," gatekeeper, and coordinating and referring agent
- Focuses on collaboration throughout the college regarding student discernment of vocation/career/major, student engagement, active learning, and student success
- Views advising as teaching

Challenges of the Center

Because Thiel had not had a center like the CLA before, its most difficult challenges were confusion among students and faculty about CLA functions and roles, gaining faculty support, and improving technological resources. In response to these challenges, the CLA staff worked with the faculty members of its advisory committee to differentiate faculty advising roles from CLA advisor roles and developed and begun implementation of a marketing plan for communicating with students, faculty, and staff. Technological difficulties, both with educational philosophy and resources, remain a major concern.

Future Plans for the Center

The CLA expects in the coming years to

- Expand programming to include group academic and career advising for students
- Transform the CLA Web site into a virtual career advising center through which students can develop knowledge about themselves and be linked to appropriate information about majors/careers and relevant academic courses
- Create a program for CLA advisors to interact with incoming students electronically and by phone about career goals, majors, and academic courses before they first arrive on campus (piloted in summer 2008)
- Provide special ongoing support programs for new full-time and adjunct faculty on academic/career advising and teaching/learning functions (the program for new full-time faculty was begun in late August, 2008 and is continuing monthly throughout the academic year plus providing consultation with individuals as needed)
- Institute evening academic/career advising for groups and individuals in residence halls

Professional Development

Title III funding provides opportunities for CLA staff to attend appropriate conferences and also for faculty to attend conferences that will help them develop an orientation toward developmental advising and student-engaging pedagogy. Mini-grants are also available through CLA for faculty wanting to redesign or develop courses that use more student-centered methods of teaching.

This exemplary practice description was prepared by Patricia Kelvin, Oscar T. Lenning, Kateri Linn, and Melissa Philson.

Diversity and Career Advising: Case Studies

A ppendix B presents two case studies, one about selecting an academic major and one about the job search process, and accompanying questions for use in applying the content of Chapter Six. The case studies are presented without information about the students' race/ethnicity, disability status, sexual orientation, or gender. It is suggested that demographic characteristics be assigned to the student before considering the questions for reflection. This format will allow the development of multiple profiles for each case study and provide multiple opportunities to reflect on the application of diversity issues in career advising.

CASE 1: SELECTING AN ACADEMIC MAJOR

An advisor meets with a 20-year-old sophomore who is seeking assistance with choosing an academic major. The student reports that her or his interests are generally best described as investigative and artistic. While in high school the student was very interested in math and economics and originally planned to major in economics and math, then pursue graduate studies in economics. However, at the time of the advising meeting with the student, her or his plans had changed, and she or he is contemplating pursuing a major in secondary education and math to become a math teacher but seems ambiguous about this choice. The student says that the possibility of pursuing teaching instead of graduate studies pleases both her or his family and girlfriend or boyfriend, because it will provide the opportunity to stay close to home and better balance family and work.

CASE 2: JOB SEARCH

An advisor meets with a 23-year-old senior who plans to graduate at the end of the semester with a double major in English literature and political science, and who is seeking assistance with starting his or her job search. The student looks forward to the possibility of obtaining a job in a medium to large size city, compared to the small, rural town in which the college is located. However, the student has mixed feelings about moving to a larger city because it will mean moving even farther from family than college. Further, he or she feels some anxiety about this decision because people are asking, "What can you do with those majors?" and this contributes to some doubts about the appropriateness of the program of study he or she pursued.

Questions for Reflection

1. What plans might an advisor make for establishing a culturally appropriate advising relationship?
2. What career development and planning needs does the student present?
3. What traditional career advising goals and activities could meet the student's needs?
4. What diversity issues might have affected the student's career development and planning prior to college? During college? After college?
5. How might an advisor plan to explore and learn the extent to which diversity issues affected the student's career goals and plans?
6. In what ways could traditional career advising goals and activities be modified to respond to the student's cultural context?
7. Which modifications could an advisor adequately address in advising? What referrals to or collaborations with campus and community resources could be helpful?
8. How might these modifications help the student's career development and planning (e.g., connecting a female student with a female mentor in the STEM fields can build self-efficacy beliefs and outcome expectations for gender non-traditional occupations)?
9. What might be your reactions to the possibility of making these modifications?
10. What might you need to learn about career development and planning associated with the student's race/ethnicity, disability status, sexual orientation, and gender? How might you learn what is needed to help the student?
11. How are you and the student culturally similar and dissimilar? How will this affect the way you address these issues with the student? How might your level of comfort with these similarities and differences influence the advising relationship? See Comas-Diaz and Jacobsen

(1991) for a discussion of reactions to cultural differences and similarities in helping relationships.

12. Consider your personal experiences and values, and compare and contrast these with the five underlying assumptions of traditional career development theories and activities? How might that influence the advising process with the student?

13. Reflect on the questions associated with the processes of building the skill of metacognitive awareness.

Reference

Comas-Diaz, L., & Jacobsen, F. M. (1991). Ethnocultural transference and countertransference in the therapeutic dyad. *American Journal of Orthopsychiatry, 61*, 392–402.

Advising Undecided Students: Case Studies

CASE OF LENA

Lena is a first-generation college student who is very excited about attending college. Her first meeting with an academic advisor is at New Student Orientation. At orientation, she exhibits a lot of enthusiasm about enrolling; she is looking forward to living away from her family and is confident that because she was a good student in high school she will be successful in college. At the orientation advising session, the advisor notes that Lena indicated a major in business on her application for admission. Her admission record also shows that she had a 3.1 cumulative grade point average in high school and a composite ACT score of 27. She was involved in high school activities, including serving as class treasurer.

The academic advisor starts the orientation advising session by inquiring about Lena's choice of a business major. Lena indicates that she liked being class treasurer, is good with money, and wants a major that will ensure she can get a good job after graduation. She is not aware that she needs to choose a field of study within business (e.g., marketing, accounting, management). The advisor recommends that Lena take 15 credits with 9 credits of general education courses (freshman writing, college algebra, and psychology) and 6 credits of introductory business courses. The advisor also recommends Lena get involved in the undergraduate business student association during her first semester on campus as a way to connect with other students who are interested in the same field of study.

When Lena comes in to be advised for spring enrollment, she tells the advisor that she is doing well in her general education courses and is currently earning a grade of D in the introductory course in business. In discussing the low grade in the business course, Lena indicates that she finds the financial concepts confusing. She does, however, talk a lot about her psychology course and how interesting she finds the material. She has volunteered to participate in a research study being conducted by a psychology faculty member and wants to take another psychology course in the spring to meet her requirements in the social sciences.

The advisor suggests that Lena explore other majors besides business. Lena is offended by the suggestion, thinking that the advisor is telling her that she cannot succeed in business. Lena is most concerned about getting a job after graduation and implies that she feels great pressure from her parents to major in business, since it is a "practical" degree that will allow her to earn a good salary. The more the advisor talks about exploring options, the more Lena insists that is just one part of the business course that is dragging her grade down and that business is indeed the major for her. After much discussion, Lena agrees that she is much more excited about what she is learning in psychology than business but she is unsure that she likes it enough to become a psychology major. Besides, she cannot possibly tell her parents that she wants to be a psychology major because, "You just can't get a job with a major in psychology."

Consider the following questions:

1. Where on the continuum of decided to undecided is Lena? Would you characterize Lena as an undecided student? Why or why not? How does your assessment of Lena fit within the subtypes of undecided students presented in Chapter 2?

2. What information in the case study provides insight into how Lena made her career decision? What factors are influencing Lena's major and career decision?

3. What questions might an advisor ask Lena to help gather more information about Lena's career decision and facilitate further career advising?

4. Should the advisor be encouraging Lena to explore other options at this point? Why or why not?

5. What actions might the advisor recommend Lena take to help facilitate her career decision making?

CASE OF ALONZO

Alonzo is a sophomore who was referred to an advisor who specializes in working with undecided students. His first advisor tried to engage Alonzo in conversations about choosing a major and career but after working with him for his entire freshman year, Alonzo is no closer to making a decision than he was when he first entered college.

Upon entering the institution, Alonzo participated in a first-year seminar course designed for undecided students. The curriculum of the course included topics related to making a successful transition to college as well as career exploration and decision making. Each student was required to engage in activities related to self-assessment (e.g., interests, values, skills), exploration of academic majors, and exploration of careers. As a final project in the class, each student was required to submit a paper about a major and career of interest. The paper was to describe the information the student gathered about the major and career as well as why this major and career were a good fit for him or her. During the semester Alonzo completed all the required course activities but could not determine what he was interested in studying, much less choosing his life's work. An uncle he respects works as a Web developer and is very happy in his job, so he chose to write his paper on computer science and the career of Web developer.

When Alonzo met with his advisor to plan for spring registration, he acknowledged that he was not committed to a computer science major but for lack of anything better he wanted to take courses in that curriculum. Based on this, he was advised to enroll in the prerequisite courses for a computer science major. Alonzo finished the spring semester with a 2.2 GPA in his computer courses. He liked the classes but found them to be very difficult, given that he does not have a strong background in mathematics.

One of the first things he did upon returning to campus for the fall term was to visit his advisor to tell her that was no longer sure about computer science as a major. He stated that he was "as confused about a major now as he was when started as a freshman." He was angry that he spent a considerable amount of time in the first-year seminar course that was supposed to help him choose a major and he still did not have one. Time was ticking and he could not afford to pay for more than four years of college.

As part of the conversation, Alonzo shared that over the summer he worked at a camp for kids and loved it. He made great friends with the camp counselors and enjoyed working with middle-school-age children. At the camp, he was responsible for organizing the daily outdoor activities, which allowed the students to learn about nature and the environment. He was particularly fond of teaching the kids about how to care for the environment and used technology to support the lessons he taught the kids. He found it fun to organize the lessons and activities the children would complete.

Alonzo and his advisor decided that Alonzo should drop his computer science classes and enroll in the few remaining general education requirements he had left to give him some time to continue to explore majors and careers. The advisor referred Alonzo to faculty members in the education and recreation departments to learn about these degree programs. She also suggested that Alonzo go to the Career Center, where staff can help him look at related careers.

Alonzo returned a few weeks later and indicated that he did not want to major in either education or recreation. He was even more frustrated and talked about dropping out of school next term unless he finds a major. His family runs a restaurant and he decided it would just be easier to work for the family business than be in college, which was leading him nowhere. Out of desperation, his advisor decides she has provided Alonzo with as much assistance as she can and refers him to a colleague who specializes in working with undecided students.

Consider the following questions:

1. Why might Alonzo have struggled in the first-year seminar course designed to help him find a major and career?

2. What are Alonzo's career needs? Does he need more information about himself, the world of work, and academic majors? Or does he need assistance in decision making?

3. If you were the advisor to whom Alonzo was referred, what questions would you ask him to gather more information about his situation?

4. What resources would you use to assist Alonzo?

5. What actions would you recommend Alonzo take to help him move forward with major and career decision making?

Resource Information for Examples of Existing Standardized Evaluation Instruments

- ACT Survey of Academic Advising

    Four-year institutions, http://www.act.org/ess/fouryear.html

    Two-year institutions, http://www.act.org/ess/twoyear.html

- Council for the Advancement of Standards in Higher Education (CAS) *Standards and Guidelines for Academic Advising*

    www.nacada.ksu.edu/Clearinghouse/Research_Related/
    CASStandardsForAdvising.pdf

- National Association of Colleges and Employers (NACE) Professional Standards for College and University Career Services

    http://www.naceweb.org/standards/standards_10.htm

- Noel-Levitz Student Satisfaction Inventory (SSI)

    https://www.noellevitz.com/Our + Services/Retention/Tools/
    Student + Satisfaction + Inventory/Student + Satisfaction +
    Inventory + overview.htm

- Winston and Sandor's Academic Advising Inventory (AAI)

    http://www.nacada.ksu.edu/Clearinghouse/Links/assessment.htm

Example of a Syllabus for Career Advising

University X Career Advising Syllabus

Room 111, ABC Building

(555) 555-5555

Career_adv@universityx

Monday through Friday, 8:00 A.M. to 5:00 P.M.

Mission Statement

The mission of career advising at X University is to assist students in realizing their fullest potential and achieving their career goals by offering superior career guidance and preparation to our students.

Goals of Career Advising

Career advising at X University is based on developmental, career, and learning theories and is responsive to the developmental and demographic profiles of the student population.

Objective of Career Advising

Career advising at X University supports the role of the academic experience in students achieving their career goals.

Student Learning Outcomes

1. Students complete an interest inventory by the end of the fall semester of their first year.

2. Students know the curricular requirements to be eligible to participate in an internship during their sophomore year.

3. Students appreciate the value of networking in achieving their career goals as a result of career advising.

4. Students understand the relationship between classroom experiences, extracurricular experiences, educational goals, personal goals, and career goals.

Complete the following five items based on the specific content.

Required Materials

_____

_____

University X Catalog

_____

_____

University X Career Advising Web Site URL

_____

_____

Career Planning Portfolio

_____

_____

Major Program Checklist

_____

_____

Student Responsibilities

As a Student at University X, You Are Expected to . . .

1. Schedule regular appointments with your career advisor.

2. Come prepared for each meeting with your career advisor.

3. Ask questions if you do not understand an issue.

4. Use the above listed materials as needed.

5. Clarify your personal and career goals with your career advisor.

6. Follow through with tasks.

7. Take ownership of your educational experience.

8. Accept responsibility for your actions and decisions.

Career Advisor Responsibilities: You Can Expect Your Career Advisor to . . .

1. Be available for scheduled meetings with students.
2. Be prepared for meetings with students.
3. Provide students with information and strategies for using available resources.
4. Listen to students' concerns and respect their values and choices.
5. Assist students in clarifying their academic and career goals.
6. Understand and effectively communicate the relationship between the student's selected curriculum and their career goals.
7. Monitor students' progress toward their academic and career goals.
8. Maintain confidentiality.

Demonstration of Student Learning

All University X students will complete an interest inventory by the end of the fall semester of their first year. In addition, students will be asked to participate in an annual evaluation of their experiences with the Career Advising Office, and career advisors will likewise participate in an annual evaluation of students' use of career advising services and students' knowledge gained as a result. Students will also maintain a current career portfolio in the Career Advising Office. This portfolio will consist of students' academic plans, semester schedules, records of use of various resources, results of students' interest inventories, and an evolving résumé.

Equal Opportunity

University X is committed to providing equal opportunity and access for every student. If you feel you need accommodations for a learning or physical disability, it is your responsibility to make your career advisor aware of these needs. In some cases, your career advisor may refer you to the Disability Services Office for assistance. The Disability Services Office provides a broad range of supportive services in an effort to ensure that the individual needs of each student are met.

NAME INDEX

SUBJECT INDEX

A

Academic advising: beliefs about, 31–35; career advising vs., 4–6, 20–21, 201–202; developmental model of, 229–230; evolving to career advising, 2–3; explaining global economy, 25–27; helping students use existing skills, 35–37; planning integration with career advising, 210–211; principles and competencies in, 51–52; recommending job success attributes, 38–39, 40–41; role in career advising, 229; structures helping undecided students, 234–235. *See also* Integrating advising programs

Academic Advising Inventory (AAI), 368

Academic majors: assessing courses relating to, 186–187; choosing, 70–71, 98–101; declaring and changing, 226–228; exploring, 231–232; fairs to explore, 233–234; matching to careers, 157–158, 170–173, 187–188; selecting, 151, 361–363

Accessibility software, 154

Accountability. *See* Assessments; Evaluations

ACT Survey of Academic Advising, 368

Active listening, 62

Acute situational indecision, 224–225

"Administrative Approaches to Advising Undecided Students" (Habley), 230

Adult students, 252–255

Advisees. *See* Students

Advising centers. *See* Exemplary advising centers

Advising sessions: content of, 48, 240; student commitment to, 195–196; for undecided students, 100, 200, 228–235, 364–367

Advisor evaluations: designing self-evaluations, 278–279; developing surveys, 274–277; by peers, 277–278; purpose of, 273–274; using data from, 279–280

Advisor learning outcomes, 268–269

Advisors: academic vs. career, 201–202; applying career advising steps, 183–184; appreciating students, 61; appreciative advising by, 231–232; assessing student values and interests, 56–58; career counselors vs. academic, 9–10; choosing for integrated programs, 211–212; collaborating for student development, 108–109, 203–206, 208, 249–250; competencies for, 51, 61–62; developing metacognitive awareness, 130–131; development theories used by, 97–98; evaluating student's needs, 185–187; gathering and using information, 151; helping in career interventions, 89, 188–189; identifying attributes via interviews, 62; influencing student development, 4, 62–63, 107–108; informally integrating advice, 202–203, 208; knowledge required, 55, 229; learning to support diversity, 135; linking education to career choices, 28–29; mapping learning by, 288; outlining student's resources, 187–188; participating in formally integrated programs, 206–215; providing